BILLY BRAGG

STILL SUITABLE FOR MINERS

ANDREW COLLINS

Virgin BOOKS

1 3 5 7 9 10 8 6 4 2

Virgin Books, an imprint of Ebury Publishing,
20 Vauxhall Bridge Road,
London SW1V 2SA

Virgin Books is part of the Penguin Random House group
of companies whose addresses can be found at
global.penguinrandomhouse.com

Penguin
Random House
UK

First published in the United Kingdom by Virgin Books in 1998
This revised edition published by Virgin Books in 2018

www.penguin.co.uk

A CIP catalogue record for this book is available from the
British Library

ISBN 9780753552711

Typeset in 10/11 pt Sabon
by Integra Software Services Pvt. Ltd, Pondicherry

Printed and bound in Great Britain by Clays Ltd, St Ives PLC

Penguin Random House is committed to a sustainable future
for our business, our readers and our planet. This book is made
from Forest Stewardship Council® certified paper.

BILLY
BRAGG

*This book is dedicated to
Reg Ward, my grandfather,
for political inspiration.*

CONTENTS

BRINGING IT ALL BACK HOME

Acknowledgements

To co-opt the words of Simon & Garfunkel, who meant so much to Billy Bragg in his early teens, I was 32 years when I started this book, I'm 52 now but I won't be for long. When, in August 1997, I formally pitched the idea of an official biography to the enabling Ian Gittins at Virgin Books, I posed this hypothetical: why a book about Billy Bragg? At the top of my list of ten answers was: he's 40 in December. (The second was: there's never been a book about him.) From such neat milestones, grand designs are sometimes launched. In December 2017, Billy turned 60. There's another one. And here we are again.

Rather than indulgently reprint each previous set of acknowledgements from each of the four extended editions since first publication in 1998, I thought I'd combine them into one: leaner, shorter, more focused. I began the first without a clue that there'd be a second, never mind that we'd all be still doing it twenty years later, and with the same completist urgency. I quoted one of my favourite American observers, Raymond Carver, who wrote the poem 'Sunday Night' in the year before he died, 1988: 'Make use of the things around you . . . Put it all in, make use.' I've followed his advice ever since, and I hope this chronicle has remained definitive. To me, the Billy Bragg story is the story of post-war Britain, of punk rock and Thatcherism, the fall of international communism, the end of the Cold War, the rise of the centre-left and the dawning of the populist era of Brexit. Try putting all that in.

I could have poured Billy Bragg's life into a book without Billy Bragg, but I didn't have to. When I say the pair of us have been on a journey together, I mean it literally (Barking, Oundle, Dublin, Burton Bradstock, Manchester, Oxford), figuratively and historically. This story begins in Saxon times. Although I've long since counted him as a friend – and he's finally started to call me his Boswell – I remain grateful for the time he's granted me over the years, the hospitality he and his partner, Juliet, have offered me, and the tea they've made me.

I list all of my generous interviewees at the back, but special nods to Wiggy, Riff Raff, Pete and Tiny, and to Neil Kinnock (these days, Barron Kinnock of Bedwelty in the County of Gwent). A handful of writers consistently made trawling the archives a pleasure: Adam Sweeting, Colin Irwin, Steven Wells, Robin Denselow, Karen Swayne and Danny Kelly. I was delighted to be able to use *The King's England Northamptonshire* in my analogue research, first published in 1945 and given to my father as a prize by Northampton Grammar School in 1953, thus linking this story back to my own family. It's that sort of circular stuff that makes it all worthwhile.

In September 2001, for the second edition, I sat with Billy on the cliffs at Burton Bradstock, looking out to sea with smoothies from the Hive Café, while the world was gearing up for George W. Bush's War on Terrorism. Current affairs have never been far away from Billy's story as we pieced it together for posterity. We lost a lot of important participants along the way: John Peel, Joe Strummer, Juliet's mother Margaret Pountain, Jay Bennett, Steven Wells, Hugo Dixon (whose photograph adorned the cover of the first edition) and Buster the labradoodle, but the highest debt of gratitude goes to the unforgettable Marie Bragg, who kindly invited this nosy stranger into her warmest room in Barking twenty years ago, and who passed away in March 2011.

We remain, I think, all hankerers after the truth, and for a more humanitarian world.

Andrew Collins, January 2018

FOREWORD

by Billy Bragg, 1998

The first time that I ever got to sit alone with Paul Weller was at the Solid Bond Studios sometime in 1984. While we discussed life, the universe and everything, his hands were busily occupied with cutting articles about himself out of newspapers and magazines and filing them away for his scrapbook. It impressed me greatly that, although arguably one of Britain's premier pop stars, he still did his own chores. I also felt a sense of relief that someone whom I admired so much might feel the same way that I did about preserving material, to the extent that he felt it was not a job he could safely entrust to someone else.

When I began to get notices in the papers, I would buy two or three copies, not so much from self-obsession, more to check that they were actually saying something about me in *every* copy. That sense of disbelief wore off after a couple of years, but I still kept my cuttings and tour passes and itineraries. It would have been better to keep a diary you might think, but with a diary you need time for reflection and then even more time to get your thoughts down clearly. And I just didn't have that time, nor those clear thoughts. I was tearing round the world, returning to my flat in West London only to check my mail and empty my bags. The place filled up with what I can only characterise as *stuff*, junk that

I hung on to for the sake of posterity. And one day posterity knocked on my door in the shape of Andrew Collins.

I had been approached by a few would-be biographers in the past but they were mostly earnest young men who I feared would portray me as some working-class hero whose life had been one long hard struggle. These were the same kind of people who described my friends as being 'a bit lumpen'. Andrew at least knew enough about me to realise that the personal was at least as important as the political, and that my life was a mess of contradictions rather than a shining path of political correctness. A feature he wrote in Q magazine convinced me he was the right person for the job. He had astutely taken a number of minor events in my career and threaded them together as a series of epiphanies. It was informative and insightful but, better than that, it was entertaining.

With an impeccable sense of timing, he began this project just as I started the long process of emptying my flat and fifteen years' worth of *stuff* started raining down on him (the rest was at my mum's. He helped me load it in to the back of my car). A nice young couple are now ensconced in my old place and a considerable amount of junk has been divided up between my attic, the local charity shops, the town dump and a lock-up in Acton Vale. But not before Andrew had had a chance to pore over it, just for the sake of posterity.

This leaves me with a lot of empty shelf space to stare at, but, as I write, Pete Jenner is concocting another tour itinerary for me, with, hopefully, that precious day off after Plymouth, and I feel that it can only be a matter of time before my living space attains once more the fabulous clutter to which I am accustomed.

Thanks to all my dear friends who took the time to contribute their thoughts and memories to this book and to Andrew Collins for matching my sense of history with his sense of humour.

PREFACE: HOW DID I GET HERE?

This bloke, 1957–2018

As a cat who was wiser than he looked once sang, you won't fool the children of the revolution. Tragically, the sloppy workmanship of a garage in Sheen killed the cat in 1977. As a result, he never lived to see how the children of Britain's newest revolution would turn out. They turned out just fine.

Punk rock was, for those who lived through it and came out permanently scathed, far more than a musical movement or a collection of diminishing guitar bands. For certain art-schooled *agents provocateurs* in London it was a situationist joke, but a good one, and a long one. For kids in the provinces and faraway towns, it was a clarion call. For a group of journalists in the right place at the right time, it was day one of a job-for-life. For the huddled wannabe masses still in the dark after 'Shine On You Crazy Diamond', it was all the excuse they needed to stop miming with a racket and start making one.

For Stephen William Bragg, exiled in Essex, punk was the flame that lit his fireworks; it was all the excuse he needed to change his name to Billy Bonkers and take in those 'Lionels'. (Lionel Blairs: flares. An example of hand-me-down Cockney rhyming slang forged in those far-off days when the grinning Palladium hoofer was the first Blair who came to mind. Funny.) On 9 May 1977, the nineteen-year-old Billy and his gang, from the relative safety of the Finsbury Park Rainbow balcony, witnessed the sleeveless fury and airborne masonry of the White Riot tour. Realising that The Clash were just a tighter, younger, sexier Rolling Stones – using the same amps, throwing the same shapes – Billy never looked back.

The cleansing fires of punk. This poetic notion arises again and again when you talk to or read about Billy Bragg, almost as frequently as reference to Lionels. Entering his forties when the first edition of this book was published, just like Strummer and Weller and Rotten, Billy is a textbook child of the revolution, born just three years after rationing was finally phased out in Britain, a year after that business in Suez, and halfway through a thirteen-year Tory administration that would eventually end not with a landslide but a polite cough. Anything could happen, but not much did.

They'd never had it so good, in the immortal words of Harold Macmillan (Prime Minister as superhero, thanks to *Evening Standard* cartoonist Vicky). Sure, out there in the Arts, down at the newly concreted South Bank, the Young Men were a trifle Angry – but in the real world of the latter 1950s and early 1960s, Britain felt fine: three television channels, full employment, *Hancock's Half Hour* and a staggering range of soap powders that washed whiter than white.

The decade rapidly deemed 'swinging' was one of insular national pride, of Merseybeat, Twiggy and Bobby Moore. A knockback by de Gaulle when Britain first tried to join the Common Market in 1961 served only to heighten its island mentality. In 1964 Labour scraped in, under Harold Wilson, but little changed on the landscape.

This was Britain Rebuilt, where working-class people owned cars and Kenwood mixers and went on package holidays to the continent, where homegrown rock'n'roll shook and rattled Amer-ica, and where tower blocks were the very height of modern architecture. But no one really knew that Russians loved their children too. And it was to shape an entire generation born between the wars (Two and Vietnam); ten years too late for the idealism of the Baby Boom and just old enough to know that you must never trust a hippie. Here were the young men and women who would soon learn that they couldn't change the world, but would create a New England in the process.

Generation Bragg reached voting age in the mid-70s – not that the political parties took much notice. In 1974, Edward Heath's skin-of-its-teeth Tory government was undone by the miners, who refused to call off their industrial action during the brief run-up to a rushed February election. 'Who governs?' it asked the electorate. 'Not you,' the electorate replied. Labour seized only four more seats than the Conservatives (301 to 297), but the government stood down anyway, and Harold Wilson bumped it up to a narrow majority of 319 to 276 in the October rerun. Politically, the country was in the grip of don't-know.

Labour survived until 1979 only by backscratching the Liberals and the nationalist parties, but it couldn't go on, and, after nearly twenty years of self-defeating tug-of-war between left and right, budging an inch this way, then an inch that way, the first election in which Billy Bragg was actually eligible to vote, 1979, was to be a pre-packaged humdinger. He didn't vote.

Why? Partly because the parties had yet to realise the power of mobilising the evasive youth vote, and partly because he fancied himself as an anarchist. So did a lot of young folks, anarchy being a pretty stubborn punk hangover (a capital A with a circle round it looked as good on the back of a jacket as it had done on pencil cases). While punk was undoubtedly empowering, energising and truculent, its ethos was one of no-future nihilism. Those untrustworthy hippies had done a lot of proactive sitting down, and they started up some cool magazines. The punks, unimpressed, took over the magazines, and jumped up and down, but at no point in the countercultural handover did *party* politics really enter the equation. Punks were, for the best part, passionate enough souls watching with distrust as the 70s turned into the 80s: many disagreed with the British presence in Northern Ireland; most fancied that the police were fascists-in-waiting, and the smartest ones recognised that homosexuality wasn't a communicable disease. Although punk had been a rock'n'roll phenomenon and peculiarly white, it was shot through with black influence, especially reggae, the embrace of which by

Britain's musical youth reflected an unforced, widespread new belief in racial integration. The cool kids knew that Eric Clapton was a twat for agreeing with Enoch Powell. In short, this was not a generation of political regressives or inactivists, merely one disillusioned by and excluded from democratic two-party tennis.

However, they were about to enter the most political period of their lives: the Thatcher years. For the duration of the 1980s, the Tories turned every man into an island: they divided; they ruled. In their utopian free market, their nation of shopkeepers, the manager – rather than the customer – was always right. She was only a greengrocer's daughter, but Margaret Thatcher knew when she had the country's plums in the palm of her hand. This Iron Lady, this Tinpot Dictator, defied anyone to disagree with her, and who dared lost. The miners, the Argies, the print workers, the dissident Tory wets, the GLC, the old, the sick and the Scottish. 'Margaret Thatcher made me a socialist,' Billy will now firmly state. 'She was going to start changing all the things I'd grown up with and taken for granted.'

Thatcher was not all bad. Her seemingly unassailable reign gave us alternative comedy – which was, admittedly, not all good – but it also gave us *Spitting Image, Boys From The Black Stuff*, 'Shipbuilding' and Billy Bragg. In creating a climate of self-help and shove-thy-neighbour, she nurtured oppression's illegitimate son: defiance. Her benign form of dictatorship even allowed for a 'safety valve' of anti-establishment satire, comment and heckling. So, being left wing may not have been supercool in the 1980s, but there were some great gigs.

The Falklands, the miners, Cruise, Tripoli, Wapping, poll tax . . . the Thatcher government gave budding insurrectionists so much to get insurrectionary about; such a wide range of pricks to kick against and statues to upend. And Billy Bragg, who would turn 30 in the year of Thatcher's historic third election victory in 1987 ('A fantastic triumph,' she gloated), became arguably the most famous lefty in Britain – after perhaps Ben Elton and one or two of the shadow cabinet.

By the time of the Tories' fall from disgrace in May 1997, celebrity Labour supporters were ten a penny, although very few of them were as active, questioning or informed as Billy Bragg. By then, he was, significantly, a lapsed party member, but still a pragmatic Labour voter. On the night of 1 May, on the very stage of London's Mean Fiddler where he'd seen Red Wedge's hopes turn to ashes, it all began to swing the other way, and Billy announced 'the end of the 80s'. This triumphant declaration was, in an odd way, tinged with irony – as the 80s had been a great decade for being in opposition. And a great decade for being Billy Bragg.

But it's not about politics. It's about this bloke.

Ex-punk, ex-soldier, ex-member of the Labour Party; one or two people and institutions have been left behind in Billy's 60 years on earth, but it's the names and places that stayed with him that maketh the man. He failed his eleven-plus and never went to college. Punk failed him and he joined the army. He passed basic training with flying colours and left after 90 days with a two-fingered salute. In 1982, he chose his weapon – the guitar – travelled the world, met interesting people and knocked them dead.

It's about this bloke whose mum called him Stephen all her life, but who's known and loved as Braggy or Bill or the big-nosed bard from Barking in every corner of the globe (except maybe France). He's typical of his generation in that he entered the twenty-first century as a caring parent, a homeowner and a careful carnivore who voted New Labour in at the 1997 election.

He's unique in that he's a recording artiste who owns every last note of his own 30-year back catalogue, and has become the chosen torch-bearer for the legendary folk singer Woody Guthrie's memory on earth. While a true internationalist with a passport held together by inks of the world, he also represents that corner of some foreign field that will be forever England. He is a protester and a politico, but he doesn't half write a good love song.

Billy Bragg has been striking chords since 1974. Let's hope his story strikes one, too. Up in his old Chiswick office in 1997 during the research stages of this book, the Braggphone rings and switches automatically to the ansaphone. Beeep.

'Hi. It's Lis Roberts from Radio Four, and I'd very much like to talk to you about the possibility of Billy presenting a programme for us about the history of unemployment . . .'

That sounds like something for the book, I'm thinking.

Billy laughs, but not unkindly. 'If it's not fucking bad enough being unemployed, here's Braggy to give you his thoughts.'

1. LONDON A TO B

A bit of history

Onward we went, the sun appearing
Painted with faint light the meadows nigh
When Barking's fair Monastic archway
And grey old Church we can descry

> Louisa Fry, from a poem written about the joy
> of travelling east out of London in the early 1800s

If you ever have to go to Shoeburyness
Take the A road, the OK road that's the best
Go motorin' on the A13
If you're looking for a thrill that's new
Take in Ford's, Dartford Tunnel and the river too
Go motorin' on the A13

> Billy Bragg, from a song written about the joy of
> travelling east out of London in the late 1900s

A book about Billy Bragg is a book about London and about Essex and the world beyond. But not just the clichés, picture postcards and the tourist traps – rather, the story behind the signposts, the history beneath the cartography.

'History, as we know it, is a flyover over reality,' Billy says. 'You can find out the history of World War Two down our street if you ask the right people.'

Billy Bragg is a keen historian. His career as an urbane folk singer and mobile political animal has taken him all around the world, where, in contrast to the rock'n'roll norm, he hasn't spent most of his time sitting in hotel rooms and loitering around lobbies. A bit of that has been unavoidable, but, for him, a Billy Bragg tour is a free geography lesson, with a bit of local history, sociology and politics thrown in.

He didn't know much about history at school, but that's a reflection of how they taught it. He didn't go to university, but his job has been a continual source of higher education.

A natural raconteur, Billy also possesses that rare teacher's gift: the ability to make anything interesting. Even history and its pale little brother, local history.

With this in mind, it would be remiss to start the Billy Bragg story without some background.

In the Mike Leigh film *Career Girls*, two young women view a luxury apartment high up in Canary Wharf, for a laugh. The more cynical of the two, Hannah (Katrin Cartlidge), looks out of the window and says, 'On a clear day I suppose you can see the class struggle from here.'

There's London in a nutshell. A great view of a great mess. Just as you can pick out the Great Wall of China from the moon, if you're stuck in a holding pattern over London on the way into Heathrow you can see the Northern Outfall Sewer, built in the 1860s, cutting through the North Circular around Beckton and delivering all of North London's shit into the Thames at Barking Creek. 'It looks like a ley line,' observes Billy Bragg, ever the poet. Billy was born Stephen William Bragg on 20 December 1957 in Upney Hospital, Barking, at the time part of Essex, but swallowed up in 1965 by Greater London, although you try telling the locals they don't live in Essex (you can take the town out of the county, but you can't take the county out of the town).

His father, Dennis Bragg, was of proud Essex stock. In 1870, a huge gaslight and coke plant was opened at Beckton, west of Barking, which supplied almost all the electric light for East London; the plant even had its own docks on the Thames. As an employer, the gasworks drew many into the area, including Dennis's grandfather Frederick Bragg, who

came from the ancestral home between the rivers Stour and
Colne, east of Colchester, in Essex.

Billy's mother, Marie D'Urso, came from the East End in
London. Her grandfather was an Italian immigrant who'd
run a fruit and veg shop on Cable Street from the turn of
the century through two world wars. He never learnt to
speak English, and even sold ice cream from a bicycle in
front of the Tower of London. Billy once visited the Italian
church in Clerkenwell, where his mum's grandfather and
grandmother were married, and looked up the happy event
in the register. 'This church was *so* Italian,' he remembers.
'The Monsignor had a picture of the Italian football team
up in his office.'

The D'Ursos had fourteen kids, of whom Marie's father
was the eldest. Billy, however, never knew him, as the couple
were divorced in 1950; very unfashionable, especially for
Roman Catholics. 'I can't think what my grandpa must've
been doing to my grandma,' he ponders, holding her in the
sort of high esteem he routinely reserves for the women
in his life. 'A great woman, she held the family together
through the war.'

It is the potent combination of East End Cockney and the
Essex suburbs that shaped Billy Bragg.

The East End is far and away the most mythologised corner
of the capital, thanks to such crafty Cockneys as the Kray
twins in the 60s, Alf Garnett in the 70s and the ever-chang-
ing residents of Albert Square in the 80s and beyond. True
Cocknitude is traditionally reserved for those born within
the sound of Bow Bells, which means, given the hundreds of
second- and third-generation Asians, among others, who may
legitimately claim the Bow-earshot birthright, even the source
of the area's anachronistic Pearly pride has been dragged into
the multicultural present. The East End's truly cosmopolitan
populace is ever at odds with the old-fashioned fascism that
lives on there. It doesn't take a genius to spot why institu-
tional racists get themselves organised in multiracial areas,
but when the British National Party secured a council seat
in Tower Hamlets in 1993 the East End became once again
identified as some kind of tatty, Neanderthal outpost. The
spectre of Sir Oswald Mosley, whose blackshirts marched
there in the 1930s, reared its ugly head.

Not just a hotbed of racial and political imparity, all socio-economic life could also be seen in the East, post-Thatcher, as Jack the Ripper ancient met regenerative modern. The area saw Rotherhithe, Wapping, Limehouse and the Isle Of Dogs transformed into a London Docklands Development utopia. A yuppie overspill that was handy for both your job in the City and cheap body shops for getting your Golf GTi fixed up after some local urchin had scratched it with a 50p piece. As they say in the area, 'Sweet as'.

Wapping itself became a totem of Thatcherite progress (or betrayal, depending on which side of the security fence you were on). Rupert Murdoch's News International relocated there without print-union agreement over manning levels, and riot police were sent in to 'ask' 5,000 pickets to move on. On a clear day you could hear the dismantling of the trade-union movement.

The East End has it all: pride, joy, hope, glory, violence, class war and beardedly hip artisanal coffee shops. It is entirely feasible to live in London all your life and avoid the place – unless, that is, you want to get out to Essex or the nearest bit of seaside (Leigh-On-Sea, Southend, Shoeburyness). In which case, to quote that famous Cockney song, 'Take the A road, the OK road that's the best/Go motorin' on the A13'.

The song, 'A13 Trunk Road To The Sea', is by Billy Bragg, who, unable at the time to get his kicks on Route 66, immortalised his own rock'n'roll thoroughfare ('starts down in Wapping/There ain't no stopping'). Although, at first, the lyric sounds like a colloquial, narrow-screen novelty, it actually reveals the historian in Billy as early as 1978 when he wrote it. (The song was never recorded, except for his first Peel session, but it remains a live treat for diehards.) In 1991, for the expanded songbook *Victim Of Geography*, he wrote a beautiful piece of 'me-history' about the A13's significance.

'Travelling eastwards,' he wrote, 'it's possible to read London's development as a city like the rings on a tree.' He recalls boyhood family holidays at Shoeburyness, his dad letting him drive the green Morris Oxford across the car park field behind the beach, 'a primal driving lesson that ended abruptly when I nervously stamped the clutch and the brake pedal down to the floor and he bumped his head on the windscreen. I must have been about twelve years old, yet I can still feel the leather of the driver's seat warm on my bare back and hear the bonk as Father, sitting sideways and caught unawares, hit the Triplex very hard.

'What great days.'

Except for the first evacuation, the schools never closed. Every common requirement of everyday life continued – the dustman, the postman, the paper boy and the milkman never missed their customary rounds, although the night had been a holocaust of noise.

Danger Over Dagenham, May 1947

The gasworks, the sewage treatment works, the docks and the car plant – it's little wonder the area comprising East Ham, Barking and Dagenham grew up in the last century into a working-class heartland. And it's no surprise that they got stonked during the Second World War.

Although war was not declared between Britain and Germany until 1939, things had been looking dicey ever since Adolf Hitler was made Chancellor in 1933, and the Nazis had begun their reign of terror on 'imperfect Germans'. Without the benefit of CNN, it seemed a long way away to most Britons, as did the Spanish civil war. However, when the Nazis marched into Czechoslovakia and Poland in the name of '*Lebensraum*' (more 'living space'), there was nothing else for it, and five years of gas-mask training, increased defence spending and the theoretical construction of air-raid shelters came to horrifying fruition on 3 September. By this time, roughly 17,000 mothers and children had already been evacuated from Dagenham to Norfolk and Suffolk, Marie D'Urso and her sisters among them.

Main target was the Ford Motor Works at Dagenham, or, as it's known locally, 'Ford's'. Built between 1929 and 1930 on Hornchurch Marshes near (aptly enough) America Farm, the car manufacturing giant quickly became the area's number-one employer. 'If Ford's packed up the whole borough would fall into the Thames,' Billy says. 'It's the buckle on the belt that keeps Barking and Dagenham from sliding into the marshes.' (Vehicle assembly ceased in 2002, its stamping plant was shut in 2013, but it still makes engines and employs around 4,000 workers.)

This self-contained, production-line shanty town seems to stretch as far as the eye can see. It's like a *Doctor Who* set made of steel, or the ugliest university ever built. Its gigantic, Stalinist warehouse blocks are untroubled by windows. Wind turbines have churned here on Ford's land since 2004, changing the landscape. Like many Essex schoolboys before them, Billy and his friends, aged thirteen or fourteen, were sent to Ford's for careers lessons, to be seduced or otherwise by the opportunity of riveting Ford Cortina after Ford Cortina after Ford Cortina – or the 'Dagenham Dustbin' as it was known. ('We hated it,' he confirms.) For those who failed their eleven-plus when Billy did, it was just about the only higher education available and, as such, looms large over the story of anybody from the area.

But let us not overlook the glamour of the place – there is more to its Mecca-like magnetism than sheer necessity. As a boy Billy recalls being dazzled by his peers whose dads worked here not on the production line, but as engineers and skilled labourers. Their families would disappear for six months to fictional-sounding American places called Dearborn and Ypsilanti in Michigan on company-funded retraining courses. They'd come back with *Boys' Own* exotica like baseball cards, Marvel comics, Superman toys and home-movie footage of being driven around Detroit in big-finned cars. (As a general rule, the Irish kids in Billy's street, whose unskilled dads banged out doors for Zephyrs, never got to go.)

As part of the war effort, Ford's were turning out endless V8 engines and 'tracked vehicles' at the plant. Billy's Grandad D'Urso was a Ford's spot welder and was required to stick around while his contemporaries went to Europe and Africa – quite a social stigma, especially over the back fence among war wives. Grandpa Bragg, born in 1893 and old enough to fight in the First World War, failed his army medical because he had one leg longer than the other, and was too old to fight in the Second. So he 'did his bit' as an ARP warden, wielding a stirrup pump and bucket, and putting out incendiary bombs that landed on the roofs. Dennis Bragg left school aged fifteen in the summer of 1939, to work for McQueen's, a milliner's, but was transferred from there after just a month, to relay messages between Barking's ARP units during lulls in the bombing.

In September 1940, the borough's very first casualty, a Mr H. Onslow, was taken to a makeshift mortuary in a school at Beacontree Heath. He was a Ford worker killed by an oil bomb as he rode his bike along the factory approach road. As the nightly bombing rained on, Ford's provided emergency food vans and even cooked meals-on-wheels in the factory canteens. At the end of the war, it was calculated that the embattled car plant had produced over 260,000 engines and over 300,000 vehicles.

Henry Ford. So much to answer for. Dagenham may well be the Detroit of England, the Motown of Essex, but Billy Bragg was a rare son indeed to have found musical inspiration here among the metal.

Barking: from the original *Berecingum* ('Berica's people'). A 'Beacon for England' in Saxon times. A fisher port in the 1300s. A fresh-aired country retreat for Londoners in the early 1800s, and noted producer of potatoes and flour. A bustling, ever improving town by the 1900s. It was granted borough status in 1931, marked by a visit from HRH Prince George and an historical pageant. In 1965, thanks to widespread boundary-jiggling, Barking stopped being in Essex.

If Ford's has characterised and dominated the area throughout the twentieth century, Barking Abbey had a millennium before that. Built in the rather inappropriate year of Our Lord 666, it was one of the most powerful institutions in the country, from late Saxon times into Norman – hence the Christian tag, Beacon for England. In 1066, after his coronation at Westminster Abbey, William the Conqueror kipped over in Barking while he had the builders in at the Tower of London.

In 1540, the Abbey was dissolved and demolished and its 30 nuns were paid off. Today, only the Curfew Tower remains. However, in 1910 Barking Urban District Council bought the land and excavated it, leaving remains of some walls exposed to view, and turned the site into the well-tended Abbey Playing Field. As the late local historian James Howson optimistically noted at the end of his article on the Abbey, 'demolition of old and unsightly buildings in the vicinity is opening up a pleasant prospect in the centre of town'.

7

Modern-day Barking could be anywhere in red-brick Britain: with a one-way system, a shopping arcade, a food court and a pedestrianised precinct. It's pay-and-display, homogeneous, interchangeable with a Chester or a Corby or a Merthyr or a Taunton. Even its riverside development and proposed rail extensions render it just like any other town of today. It would be easy to come here for a cup of coffee and a spin round Vicarage Field Shopping Centre and not have your life changed by the experience. There's nothing about it that says 'London', Greater or otherwise, except the underground symbol at Barking Station.

Only about seventeen tube stops from Central London, Barking is *connected*. When London's calling to the faraway towns, Barking can be there in 40 minutes. This proximity, we shall see, was key to Billy Bragg's musical and cultural education, and convenient as he found his first professional footholds in the music biz of the West End. But Barking made the man. Its one-step-away satellite self-sufficiency. Its proud Essex history. Its everybody-went-to-the-same-school community spirit. And its telltale working-class heart: from market trader to fisherman to builder to gas-worker to Cortina-basher, Barking's always been good with its hands.

At the turn of the century, the railway revolution completely refocused the town and turned it on its arse. Barking Station was built as far back as 1854, but was rebuilt in 1889 and again in 1905, as the London–Tilbury–Southend Railway became a fast track to Southend; an apex for low-cost holiday-hungry Londoners. A large chunk of bricks-and-mortar Barking went up in the 1890s – the schools, the law courts, the swimming baths, Barking Park – and gradually the town's natural centre moved away from the quay to the station. As a result, the former municipal spine, Barking Broadway, is 'miles away from anywhere', down near the quayside and the Abbey. Trams arrived in 1905.

In 1932, you could hop on a number 67 tram at Barking Broadway and travel in to Aldgate for 5½d one way, 9d return, via Barking Road, East India Dock Road and Commercial Road East. The timetable promised a 48-minute journey time.

It's easy to forget that the A13 goes back the other way as well. Billy says he finds it easy to relate to London's heavily mythologised Westway, that section of the A40 that rises high above The Clash's West London and off towards Oxford. Why? Because 'it's like the A13 going in the opposite direction'. It's funny how you imagine familiar roads to be one-way.

For now, the A13 goes east from the City of London to the suburbs, from A to B, Aldgate East to Bragg. And just round that corner is Park Avenue, the street where freckle-faced Stephen William was raised and where his mother lived until her death. The street where 'you could find out the history of World War Two if you ask the right people'.

Well, it's December 1957. Happy Christmas; war is over. And Billy Bragg is preparing to enter the world. One-two, one-two . . .

2. ALICE IS BENT

Childhood, 1957–1973

Got 'I'd Like To Teach The World To Sing' by The New Seekers – good riddance to 'Ernie'! I have been banned from receiving any pocket money until I get a haircut!

Diary of Stephen Bragg, aged fourteen

Stephen Bragg was born in Upney Hospital (nowadays Barking Hospital). In the same year, Bill Haley and his Comets came to Britain; 'Supermac' became Prime Minister; Humphrey Bogart died of throat cancer and the Russians sent a dog into space.

Five years later, Stephen's brother David was born. They grew up in a very matriarchal family with 'an infinitesimal number of aunties' and, as a result, cousins galore. Though Dennis Bragg, from Protestant stock, was an only child, marrying Marie gained him five sisters-in-law and a brother-in-law. Dennis worked as a chargehand in a warehouse; Marie was a cookery technician at night classes at the polytechnic. She later delivered leaflets and samples around the East End for 'a bit of extra money', and then worked at the Nat West sorting house in Aldgate.

In the spirit of clarity, I will refer to Billy as Billy from day one, even though he was Stephen or Steve throughout his school years, and adopted Billy only for the purposes of punk. Bizarrely, he was known by some as 'Doog', short for Dougal, after he changed schools in 1969, a nickname he cleverly gave *himself* to prevent the old epithet of 'Big Nose' plaguing him there. His name was Stephen, and he shall be called Billy.

Despite the East End Catholic background on his mother's side, there was little religion in Billy's early life outside Cub Scout church parade (which was a strictly Methodist affair, i.e. very few laughs). Marie never went to mass, due to the stigma of having married a Protestant ('a bit like becoming a Satanist'), although when Dennis died of cancer in October 1976, she drew a lot of strength from her faith and it helped her through a supremely difficult patch.

Marie's sister Pat and her husband Don had a farm in Warwickshire, and this is where the Braggs would regularly spend their holidays. Dennis helped with the harvest, driving the tractor, while the kids pitched in by trailing the combine harvester, stacking hay bales. A ride on top of the bales aboard the cart was their reward, before hopping off and unstacking them again. As a real treat, they were given a can of petrol and allowed to 'burn off' the stubble. Brilliant! 'All my best holiday memories as a kid are from up there.'

Back home, in the stained glass above the front door of the Bragg house, it said 'Stanley'. (It still does, actually.) Next door it said 'Livingstone', and further down 'Park' – the houses were all named after great explorers. Mungo Park followed the River Niger and wrote *Travels In The Interior Of Africa* in 1799. Sir Henry Morton Stanley traced the Congo to the sea almost a century later, and was famously sent by the *New York Herald* to find missionary David Livingstone up the Nile in 1871. Exotic gentlemen indeed, but they all started somewhere like Park Avenue.

Billy had a happy, family-oriented childhood, with noisy, overpopulated Christmases (as well as his four 'farm cousins', there were a further eight on Marie's side), sing-songs and many a tale from Dad about his time in India at the end of the Second World War. Billy's first point of purchase as a young explorer was Barking Park, a 76-acre, tree-filled wonderland conveniently situated 'over the back'. The crowbar-shaped Park Avenue can be seen on local maps made as far back as 1807, when the park didn't even exist in name, just as a recreation ground with a lake. It opened its park gates officially in April 1898, and was a typically well-groomed municipal showcase throughout the early 1900s.

A river runs through it – or at least, a tributary of the Roding does, called Loxford Water – in which Billy and pals would fish with nets for tiddlers, and over which they would throw stones at the Ilford kids during border skirmishes. The boating lake was another pivotal landmark in the happy wanderers' world, four feet deep, and drained for two months every winter. It was, and presumably still is, traditional for every child to fall in – although the water these days is full of horrible green gunk. Billy managed to fall in twice as a boy: the first time, he was simply running and didn't stop in time; the second, he was 'doing something nefarious with bangers' (fireworks, not prostitutes or sausages) in the boathouse with his mate John Murphy, and fell off the fence into the lake. Big problem. It was drained at the time, and he split his head open, which required three stitches courtesy of King George's Hospital (and a couple in his elbow for luck). He paid the waters a sentimental third visit aged 21, when, out walking the family Labrador Lucky during a freeze, he stepped on to the ice and went straight through. You can take the boating lake out of the boy, but . . .

More adventurous childhood manoeuvres took Billy as far as the marshland around Barking Creek, the link between the Thames and the Roding, where it's said King Alfred once sailed in longboats. This tributary of the Thames was vital to early Saxon settlement in Barking when it became a busy fishing port, but today it is conspicuously free of traffic, aside from the odd car wreck dumped in the adjoining swamp. It was all marshland round here when Billy was a lad. (In fact, the area's still marshy enough to give the residents of new housing in Beckton a problem with subsidence and malaria.) This was as far as young Billy ever ventured: he remembers chancing upon 'a suitcase full of nudey books, all warped from the rain. You had to be careful round here, though, it wasn't your neck of the woods.'

At the mouth of Barking Creek stands Barking's own flood barrier, a blue guillotine that is designed to come down after the Thames Barrier at Woolwich has successfully diverted rising flood waters and sent an almighty splashback up towards Essex. In the 70s, flood-warning practice around here was common, as it's below sea level. The dread sound of the siren meant buses to Ilford, which is higher up, in more ways than one. Billy's nan reckoned that's why the good folk of Ilford always voted Tory. 'All kippers and curtains,' she would say.

Other less savoury aspects of the Barking wetlands in history include a nearby guano factory, which basically made explosives out of bird shit, and teething trouble with the Victorian-built Northern Outfall Sewer, whose macabre effluent was repeatedly delivered up Barking Creek by the tide. In the late 1800s, a pleasure boat sank in these waters and its occupants died not from drowning but from ingesting raw sewage.

Billy would wait for the Woolwich ferry here on a Sunday afternoon with his dad. Looking out over the Thames towards Shooters Hill in Kent, Dad used to tell him, 'That's where Julius Caesar stood and looked across, and didn't like what he saw. He saw us.'

Marshlands included, Billy's childhood stomping ground hasn't altered a great deal since the 1960s. Certainly, Park Avenue is frozen in time, and Barking Park is as it ever was. A local artist has written 'FUCK' on the side of the boathouse; the Ilford Lane end of Billy's street has been blocked off to form a cul-de-sac; and what used to be the newsagents from where he did his paper round is now a mosque.

To supplement his weekly paper money, the enterprising Billy fetched shopping for an old geezer called Will Vernon at 152, Park Avenue. A former scoutmaster, he was badly gassed at the Somme and couldn't get out of the house like he used to. (Number 152 is locally famous for copping a direct hit in the Second World War, when the poor lodger who lived in the attic was catapulted right across the street.) Helping out old Mr Vernon was worth a shilling a week. Subsequent local errands bumped it up to half a crown.

In 1971, aged thirteen, Billy enjoyed an early whiff of fame, plucked from the universal routine of conkers and V-necks and offered a brief glimpse of what it feels like to be special. He wrote a poem for school called 'This Child', about Jesus saving the world. Written by candlelight during a power cut, when he handed it in his teacher asked Billy where he'd copied it from. Nowhere, he assured him. The school got in touch with Mr and Mrs Bragg, who confirmed their son's authorship, and the next thing anybody knew young Stephen Bragg was reading it out on Radio Essex.

'That was the first thing that stood me out from everybody else in the class,' he says. 'I'd done something that was *different*. I can't tell you how impressive that was, in the sense that it suggested I might be able to do this job that I do now.' The freckly thirteen-year-old had been granted a glance at the future.

Back on terra firma, newspapers delivered, the young poet would get on with less Bohemian pleasures: ritualistically dribbling a football up and down Park Avenue while he waited for his dad to come home from work, using his left foot up and right foot back, systematically tapping it off the front wall of every house in the street ('I was useless'). A West Ham supporter since the crib, he was chuffed when the Seventh Barking Sea Scouts merged with the Eleventh Barking and the combined scarf came out claret and blue (West Ham's colours, if you're not *au fait* with such detail, and for many years accompanied by the name of sponsors – who else? – Dagenham Motors).

The borough is steeped in football heritage. Arguably *the* most famous English footballer, Bobby Moore, was born and raised in Barking. He joined West Ham in 1958, and made the England team in 1962. He captained them 90 times, heroically holding aloft the World Cup in 1966. England's legendary manager, Sir Alf Ramsey, was a Dagenham boy, as were Jimmy Greaves, Terry Venables and Trevor Brooking. 'When I was a kid the only thing to do in Dagenham was play football,' says Greaves in his autobiography.

Billy has a clear early memory of watching the 1966 World Cup on TV (along with 30 million other Britons), and the image of his mum doing the ironing and expressing an ill-placed sympathy for 'those poor Germans' when the crowd thought it was all over. His dad took him out into the street, to Ilford Lane, and told him to savour the fact that there wasn't a single soul in sight. 'You'll never see this again, short of there being a world war,' he said. 'It was very spooky,' Billy remembers.

Billy's lifelong love affair with West Ham FC is borne of a loyalty passed down through the Bragg generations. Somewhere along Barking Road lies the exact spot where his family traditionally stands whenever West Ham bring back the cup (not an especially worn bit of pavement then, we may assume). He cannot divulge the exact location to anyone outside the family ('It's one of those kind of things'). Billy's own participation in West Ham's fortunes reached its dizziest heights in his early teens. A glance at his schoolboy's diary from 1971 reveals a typical, soccercentric entry: 'Most people in school were looking sad, after West Ham's sad but very good performance at Old Trafford last night. Today, West Ham lost 2–1 to Stoke City.'

He often went to see 'East Ham' (as his mum called them) at their Upton Park ground, but would strategically choose European matches, because there would be less chance of trouble from away fans. Billy admits that he had 'started getting in with a crew' around this time, but any potential slide towards hooliganism was fortunately curtailed by his first Saturday job in 1972, 'and that put the mockers on it. Saved my life really. I could've got killed.' In 1975, after West Ham had won the FA Cup (2–0 against Fulham), Billy proved that he hadn't grown out of his obsession by managing to collect some hallowed Wembley turf – not at the match itself, but from under the tarpaulin at a sub-sequent Elton John gig in the Stadium that summer. The dehydrated remnants still exist in a little plastic pot in a trunk in the attic ('Sad, sad, sad,' he says smiling, shaking his head). The adult Billy hasn't been to a Hammers game for five seasons, but he can still bluff his way through a football conversation.

John Murphy's family (he was the boy with the bangers in the boathouse) also lived down Park Avenue, as did the O'Briens and the Browns and the Handleys (clan of Robert, later the drummer in Riff Raff) – but the most important residents of all, certainly to the Billy Bragg story, were the Wiggs. They lived next door, in 'Livingstone'. (Curiously enough, the Braggs and the Wiggs had actually swapped houses in the 1930s, when the two dads had been kids. Talk about in and out of each other's front doors.)

Philip Wigg, better known as Wiggy, was born in 1960, two school years behind Billy, but, naturally enough, the two knee-high neighbours quickly became running mates, united by the park and bike culture. Wiggy had a three-wheeler with a boot at the back, seasonally full of conkers, while Billy rode an RSW (Raleigh Small Wheel). Wiggy has vivid memories of his knees hitting the trike's handlebars. He and Billy, he recollects, were initially brought together by the back fence and 'a bit of Cowboys and Indians'. Both boys had younger brothers, as if to complete the symmetry. Wiggy's was Alan, or 'Little Wiggy'.

'It's standard issue in Barking,' says Wiggy, 'to have two brothers, two or three years apart.' He was a tallish lad, so being two years junior to the rest of the Park Avenue mob was never an issue. 'I was always this height even when I was ten, so I could hang with them a bit.'

Although working class from one end to the other, Park Avenue concealed a subtle, two-tiered hierarchy between skilled and unskilled workers. The dads who were builders, plasterers, engineers and decorators formed a working-class aristocracy, and it was they who first had colour televisions. Billy takes the divide further: 'Their kids had Johnny Sevens [enviable plastic rifles subtitled the One Man Army, which came apart to make seven subsidiary guns], and later Gibson SGs, while the rest of us were playing Japanese cheesecutters [now he's talking about guitars].' When the Braggs belatedly acquired their first colour telly in 1972, Billy's great-aunt Hannah, the only surviving relative on his dad's side, would walk round specifically to watch *The Black And White Minstrel Show* on it.

Beyond the symbolic ownership of mod cons, young Billy's idea of 'posh' was anyone who went to Manor Junior School or lived on the nearby Leftley estate. (The Leftleys were an old dairy-farming family in Barking whose name was later ubiquitous on the sides of assorted goods lorries in the area.) Billy and Wiggy went to Northbury Junior School, then on to the 1920s-built Park Modern Secondary, as their fathers had. In September 1970, after Billy had been at Park Modern a year, it went comprehensive, merging with Barking Abbey Grammar School. It was here that he received his one dose of corporal punishment: six of the best for the heinous crime of playing football in the playground with a tennis ball. (It's the only language they understand.)

At Northbury Juniors, Billy had been a reasonable scholar, regularly ranking in the top five of his class. In his pen-ultimate year, he managed to come second, behind Ricky Ogland, the swot who was also good at football, 'so it was hard not to like him'. Billy's last chance to be top of the form, in 1969, was snatched when his mum went into hospital for an operation that April. While she was conva-lescing at home and unable to clear up after her two boys, Billy and brother David were packed off to Auntie Pat and Uncle Don's farm. They spent the summer term at a tiny Warwickshire school (where, Billy recalls, they brought jam biscuits round at playtime), thus depriving him of finishing Northbury as number one.

This near-miss would haunt Billy throughout life, signifi-cantly in the army, and even in pop. 'I felt it deep in my heart,' he reveals. 'When I was second Most Wonderful Human Being in the *NME* polls of 1987 behind Morrissey it brought it all back.' (Although it's of little consolation to Billy, they later knocked Ricky Ogland's house down to build the North Circular to Beckton.)

Those months at the farm were 'like already being on holiday', since it was where the Braggs customarily spent the summer break. (Otherwise, it was out to the seaside at Shoeburyness or a modest chalet belonging to one of Marie's friends, at St Osyth near Clacton.) Billy remembers watching the moon landing while he was a farm evacuee in July, and Dennis writing him a letter on that historic day. There was also a memorable dead cat by the side of a country lane which the boys would monitor on a diversion from the walk home from school while it gradually decomposed – better than any science lesson.

Back in Barking for a new term and a new school at the end of that lazy, hazy summer, Billy's learning curve seemed to take a nose dive. After he failed his eleven-plus, and effectively preordained the direction in which his education would take him – not to grammar school, not to university, very probably to Ford's production line – his Barking Abbey school reports tell a sorry tale with an all too predictable ending. When he was in form 4G1 (or 'Fourgone', as he so

17

enjoyed putting it on the fronts of his books), the recurring adjective in his end-of-term assessments was 'lazy'. Some lowlights from his 1971 reports: 'His lazy attitude is affecting his work . . . Far too lazy. More effort needed . . . Could do so much better.' Things picked up a little in 1972, despite what his physics teacher deemed 'an unfortunate result', but there is one particular appraisal from Christmas of that year that manages to define both Stephen Bragg of the time, and Billy Bragg in general: 'Uses his obvious intelligence more as a disruptive influence.'

It was almost career advice. His headmaster was moved to add: 'Take heed of these remarks!' (*His* exclamation mark.)

Away from school, young Billy's lifestyle can be glimpsed in another entry in the 1971 diary: 'Beat the rest of the family in a game of "Campaign": I was Russia and, after crushing Austria (Dave), and Spain (Dad), I grappled with Mum to gain control of Europe.

'Didn't feel well today after a long lie in. Got a new parka, and I went out to give it an airing. My parka was given a wink of acceptance from the lads. Oatmeal and soap flakes.' (Even the author doesn't know what he meant by the last line, but there is something deeply evocative about it.)

Diplomatic board games notwithstanding, politics did not loom large in the Bragg house. Dad didn't tell Mum how he voted, so as not to influence her vote, but Billy suspects he may have been voting Communist. Although not a Red in a card-carrying or even an ideological sense, one of Dennis's old friends from school, George Wake, stood for the Communist Party in their Barking constituency. 'I have a sneaking suspicion my dad voted for him out of loyalty and respect to a schoolfriend.' The mantra over the tea table was, 'It doesn't matter how you vote in Barking, Labour always get in.' (When Billy first voted in 1983, he voted Labour and Labour got in.) The nearest thing to a political discussion in the house where Billy grew up was when Marie complained to Dennis that, logically, if he didn't tell her which way he was voting, she might end up voting for the opposite lot, and thereby cancel out his vote. Immigration was an emotive issue in London – and across Britain – and Billy today is grateful for the tolerant attitude of his parents towards race. Tolerance was by no means guaranteed in the 1960s. The size of the immigrant population in Britain quadrupled between 1951 and 1961 (from 100,000 to 400,000, as the expanding labour market 'sucked in' workers and their families from the New Commonwealth). In 1962, the government's Commonwealth Immigrants Act, opposed by Labour, put restrictions on the incoming flow, but roughly 50,000 a year still passed through the gates, and, particularly in the cities, white Britons were forced to deal with a much more colourful view (indeed, the term 'coloured' quickly became the net-curtain euphemism for Blacks and Asians).

Billy's parents were fortunate enough to be able to associate the New Commonwealth intake with positive experiences: an Afro-Caribbean doctor had delivered both of Marie's babies in 1957 and 1963, and there was an Indian family over the road, whose dad would pop over to fix the television if you asked. They thus avoided the convenient xenophobic view that the immigrant community miraculously combine being lazy with a burning ambition to take all our jobs. It is hard to stomach but historian Peter Clarke, in his fine book *Hope And Glory*, cites an electoral slogan used unofficially by Tories in Smethwick in 1964 and Haringey in 1968: 'If you want a nigger for a neighbour, vote Labour.'

Billy says that race politics were the first he learnt, gleaning much of his multi-culturalist conviction from listening to music. Further parental enlightenment arose from Dennis's wartime posting to India, which, Billy believes, 'opened his eyes to a different culture'. (Like so many of his peers, Dennis hadn't been out of the South of England before he joined the army.) Billy was lucky to grow up in such a fair-minded, white working-class household. In 1990, he would crystallise his own beliefs in a rewrite of the socialist anthem 'The Internationale': 'We'll live together or we'll die alone.'

Away from such weighty matters, the Bragg-Wigg friendship flourished; albeit in a pragmatic, football-card-swapping way ('We got on,' recalls Wiggy. 'Not incredibly close, but always there'), but 1971 was a crucial year for them. When the eleven-year-old Wiggy joined a thirteen-year-old Billy up at 'big school' and bought Rod Stewart's 'Maggie May', the two boys entered a new phase of shared passion. They became bonded – for ever – by pop music. Wiggy had a record player and no records; Billy had the software but no hardware, and thus a symbiotic union etched in extruded polyvinyl was inevitable. They were Jack Spratt and his wife: made for each other. 'It was a definite mutual interest,' Wiggy confirms. 'After bikes and falling in the lake.'

Some years before Wiggy's affinity for gadgets would influence actual career options (guitarist, guitar tech, audio-visuals, production), he became the master of the reel-to-reel tape machine. He'd first felt his way around one aged four. Said machine was a cumbersome *Mission: Impossible*-style beast upon which the ramshackle Wigg & Bragg Radio Shows were recorded in either's bedroom. Ah, the reel-to-reel! Anyone with domestic experience of this type of voluptuous, boxy contraption will recall with fondness its ton weight, its circulation-stopping carrying handle, the inevitably battered, flat cardboard boxes the tapes came in and the heave-ho one-button controller that required shoving into stop/start/record/wind position like a Morris Minor's gearshift.

The two armchair DJs recorded singles on to tape by propping the microphone next to the record player's speakers and keeping quiet. Woe betide any kid brother who might noisily wander in while Simon & Garfunkel's 'Scarborough Fair' was being 'broadcast'. (Good fortune on this front came in David Bragg's natural talent for swimming, which took him off to frequent tournaments, with Mum and Dad in tow, leaving the house empty.)

Musically, the 1960s had kind of passed the two friends by. (Wiggy claims that he wasn't automatically allowed to watch *Top Of The Pops* on a Thursday, if, say, his mum wanted to watch a film on the other side, and Billy doesn't recall *ever* being able to watch it – 'It must've clashed with something, or else it was just too soppy in our house. We didn't watch a lot of BBC. We were *Magpie* kids, not *Blue Peter* kids.') But they 'got' the 1970s from the word go, and found every ebb and trickle of the Top 30 utterly enthralling, excitedly nipping home from school every Tuesday lunchtime to tape the new rundown, and then memorise it.

This was the time of 'Chirpy Chirpy Cheep Cheep' by Middle Of The Road, 'My Sweet Lord' by George Harrison and 'Knock Three Times' by Dawn. It was Mungo Jerry, T-Rex, the England World Cup Squad and R. Dean Taylor. In those formative years of 1970 and 1971, the Number One spot was graced by a motley parade: Dave & Ansell Collins, Edison Lighthouse, Lee Marvin, Clive Dunn, Free, Tony Christie and Benny Hill's 'Ernie' ('The Fastest Milkman In The West'), which occupied the top slot for five weeks until a rock cake caught him underneath the heart. Billy and Wiggy got into the Faces, Slade, Elton John and Bob Dylan. They started compiling personal weekly Top Twenties in exercise books, based on their own limited stocks of vinyl and tapes: never mind Ernie's reign; 'Scarborough Fair' was top of Billy's charts for two years, from February 1971 to January 1973. At one stage, fourteen out of the twenty songs in his list were by Simon & Garfunkel.

Billy had taken his first Saturday job, aged fourteen, in a hardware store called Guy Norris on Station Parade in Barking, sorting shelves and humping massive wallpaper books. 'It was the size of a small supermarket, like a Spar,' he recalls. There was a second branch at Gants Hill. The owner had inherited the business, and introduced a wider range of goods that reflected his own interests, namely records and model trains. ('I don't think he was into hardware very much.')

The trains were at the back, the records downstairs, where Billy would while away his lunch hour in the listening booths with a bun from Barton's the bakers. This was where he first heard Bob Dylan (a fairly natural progression from the more saintly Simon & Garfunkel), and where he bought his very first chart single with his first ever wages, Rod Stewart's 'You Wear It Well'. He also remembers buying Bob Dylan's *Greatest Hits* and playing it incessantly, like you do – 'The one where he's carrying a book on the front. It did my head in.'

Although a little suspicious of David Bowie – he was, after all, to use the favoured vernacular of the time, 'bent' – the friends shared vinyl copies of *Hunky Dory, Ziggy Stardust* and *Aladdin Sane*, and were never above a garish, TV-advertised treasure-trove like K-Tel's *20 Golden Greats*

('Original artists! Original hits!'). 'I was more of a singles man,' Billy recalls, 'I thought 45s were called 45s because they were 45p.' Wiggy could be relied upon to shell out for Faces albums: *A Nod Is As Good As A Wink . . . To A Blind Horse* in 1971, *Ooh La La* in 1973. These were heady, voracious days.

Girls? Who had time for girls? The knotty appeal of the inscrutable opposite sex was but a distraction to our dedicated pop cadets. Granted, going comprehensive had led Barking Abbey to introduce a rowing club into its extra-curriculum, and, as Billy freely admits, 'Some of the tastiest women were in the rowing club. So we all joined.' They were similarly motivated to sign up for the Methodists Association Youth Club ('tasty girls from the Leftley estate'), even though they had to be confirmed to get in. And in many ways, they got over Bowie's bentness because the girls at school loved him, and would go home at lunchtimes to listen to his LPs. But these lads weren't going to allow unrequited kiss chase to rain on their hit parade.

'I wanted to make noises like these records that I loved,' recalls Wiggy. 'But with the Faces it was really difficult because you didn't know if you wanted to be the singer or the guitar player or the drummer or the keyboard player, every bit of it was so individual and so good.' He plumped for the guitar – although had his Woolworths organ more closely resembled a Hammond & Leslie in ambience, it might've come a close runner-up. In 1972, Wiggy bought a Rudy Classic acoustic guitar, with nylon strings, and the attendant tune-a-day book. He couldn't tune it, however, and had little interest in learning 'Go And Tell Aunt Nancy'. 'I was frustrated but turned on by the music.'

In 1973, Billy got his hands on a harmonica, and they joined forces (with reel-to-reel forever rolling), Wiggy smashing out G, E minor, C and D, and Billy starting to sing his own words. Soon, they discovered the Rod Stewart songbook ('It used a lot of really nice-sounding chords like F Sharp Minor seventh,' Wiggy enthuses) and the Dylan songbook, both of which they devoured. In 1974, Billy's dad bought him his first guitar, for sixteen pounds, a Spanish-style acoustic from Nathaniel Berry, a piano shop in Ripple Road. After much tuition from Wiggy, Billy could manage C, F and G on it, and so they 'wrote some C, F and G stuff' – approximately twenty original songs of their own in a two-year period.

Enthused by their first big brush with popular music, Billy and Wiggy bought the company. Having eagerly soaked up the words to hit songs in *Disco 45* magazine since 1971, they graduated to reading the *New Musical Express*, or the *NME*. More than just a 50-year-old weekly newspaper, this durable cultural touchstone tends to hit way-of-life status for whey-faced suburban and provincial boys (and it is mostly boys) who are too young to go out to the colourful-sounding gigs reviewed at the back and too broke to do much more than pore over the endless, magical singles and albums reviewed in the front. For young teens, it acts as a passport. For older teens, it's a football team. For students, it's a tool for meeting people in the bar. And even for some 30-somethings who should have known better it remains rock's parish magazine until this century. Its print edition, already a free sheet, closed in March 2018.

It is difficult to overstate the cyclical importance of the *NME* down the generations; and, to a lesser extent, *Melody Maker* and *Sounds* (although the former turned into a bouncy pop rag before being closed down in 2000 and the latter went way back in 1990). The weekly music press flourished in the 1970s, just when Generation Bragg needed it. Run by graduates of the hippie publishing underground, and staffed by a fair share of old jazzers sucking briar pipes, the 'inkies', as they became known during the glossy style-magazine boom of the 80s, acted as a lifeline to pop's non-casual consumer. Around 1973, Billy and Wiggy joined the musical masons.

In a book that is essentially about a musician, it is easy to see the world through pop-tinted, guitar-shaped spectacles. But for sheer unification at a difficult age, music has far-reaching social properties. Put into perspective, it is easy to see why Billy Bragg's spiritual subscription to the music papers galvanised his ambitions to be a rock star.

Music carries immeasurable commercial clout and export potential, but for a more objective overview it's clearer to treat it, as publishing houses do, as a special interest or hobby, no different from trout fishing, canary breeding or period homes. As such, the *NME* and its subsequent glossy spin-offs, *Smash Hits*, *Q*, *Mojo*, *Word*, *Uncut* et al., are – or were – specialist publications, there not to serve record *buyers*, but record *enthusiasts*.

The fact that pop music provides a culture that permeates every corner of our lives and lifestyles, defines generations and soundtracks revolutions, should not distract from the fact that reading about rock is a big step on from listening to it. You can like pop music; you can *love* pop music; and you can join the vast, paying and non-paying consensus who still send tracks up and down the charts and algorithmic playlists, without once being moved to read about the artists beyond a Tweet or an Instagram comment. But those who did, and did so for over half a century like addicts, were the anal retentives, the list-makers, the trainspotters, the chart-memorisers, the vinyl junkies, the fanclub-joiners, the catalogue completists, the record collectors, the indie saddoes . . . a publisher's dream. And there are still a few of them about. Some of them form bands or write tunes on their Macs. Some get jobs in record companies or go on the road as crew. Others grow out of it. But there is an elementary distinction that separates the Billys and Wiggys from the rest of the population: you either listen to music, or else you read about the music *while* you're listening to it.

Once bitten, and forever smitten, Billy and Wiggy soon knew their *NME* – and, in the process, their enemy. Having never connected with the overblown likes of Led Zeppelin, Yes, Emerson, Lake or Palmer, they drew a line in the sand between themselves and the other kids at school. On their side were the blues-, soul-, and folk-influenced; on the other, 'sixth-form music' (a phrase which Billy stills spits out) – Deep Purple, Queen and Pink Floyd, whose 1973 opus *The Dark Side Of The Moon* was 'huge' at Barking Abbey Comp.

This keen distinction, 80 per cent musical, 20 per cent class war (classroom war, at any rate), was not one that would leave Billy when he left school, grew up and broadened his mind. He retains an instinctive 'thing' about those in voluntary higher education, who clearly represent the dreaded middle classes somewhere deep and murky within Billy's unreconstructed psyche. 'That's partly why I've never been big on drugs,' he admits. 'Because that was something *sixth-formers* did.' He and his compatriots were 'generally against people who went on to further education'. (When Billy was fourteen, the school leaving age went up from fifteen to sixteen, thereby adding another year to his penance, and scarring his better judgement for life.)

Very loosely, the musical battle lines partitioned authenticity from artifice. As far as Billy was concerned, Dylan meant it, man, while, say, Alice Cooper was just a clown. A glance at the cover of one of his school exercise books of the period reveals some germane doodles: a representation in biro of Alice Cooper looking unwell, 'after an attack by Dylan' according to the caption, and a copy of *School's Out* smashed into pieces. These primitive drawings are the propaganda of an emblematic war between Billy and Mark Whittaker, the Alice Cooper fan who sat next to him. Here is the news: 'Alice is bent; Dylan is great.'

Ah, you knew where you were in them days.

As the song by The The goes, 'It ain't easy to be born in an unknown city.' For anybody brought up in a satellite town, the feeling of dislocation is intense; it crawls beneath your skin and grits your teeth; it's like there's a party going on every night and you're not invited. Teenagers feel disenfranchised enough – by their parents, the education system, society – without being geographically disabled on top. Rich local history is no use to a teenager teetering on the brink of self-discovery: he'd readily swap all the mediaeval remains on the map for a decent gig venue. Billy Bragg was luckier than most suburban outcasts: once past the age of locomotive consent, he could get into the city and – if he timed it right and left before the encore – back home again.

At sixteen, like so many natives of the suburbs, Billy began to get restless. He left school with one O Level to his name (a grade A in English, which he'd taken a year early), having spent his final six months at Barking Abbey Comp anywhere *but*. This spell of truancy was not to fulfil the prophecies of his school reports, but a direct reaction to bullying. 'There were some kids in our year who were very violent, and it was only a matter of time before they got around to you.' This unsavoury wannabe firm had a technique: they'd pick on a likely-looking victim and, while four or five of them lay in wait inside an empty classroom, the hardest one would throw the meat into them – 'Then they'd knock the shit out of you.' When Billy's number came up, and one of the tinpot racketeers punched him square in the face followed by the dreaded order 'Get in there', he legged it – 'and I didn't come back'.

With both his parents working, it was a pushover to stay away from school and bum around the house or the park. Billy admits he was feeling 'cocky' about his impending O Levels because he had English Language already under his belt. And then, in the week of his exams, he fell in love with a girl from another school and couldn't eat or speak, let alone remember in what year the Corn Laws were repealed.

The girl's name was Kim. This cursed experience of one-way romance later found its way into a song, 'The Saturday Boy' (on 1984's *Brewing Up* album), but at this confused stage, all Billy could do was spew out his love in an entire exercise book full of poems, which, naturally, he presented to Kim – with no discernible comeback whatsoever. (They'd met on a week-long drama course in North Wales, working with the Theatre Clwyd – 'I thought I'd made some sort of mystical connection.') As it says in the song, 'In the end it took me a dictionary/To find out the meaning of the word unrequited/While she was giving herself for free/At a party to which I was never invited.'

As a postscript, on 10 April 1985, when Billy was playing a Save The GLC gig at Barking Assembly Hall, Kim turned up with her mum clutching 'the damn book', and presented herself to the would-be suitor of yesteryear backstage. Acute embarrassment was the order of the day. 'No doubt the book will turn up at Sotheby's one day. And I'll buy it!'

So. O Levels. Thanks to 'a girl not old enough to shave her legs', he failed the lot. The warnings had been there in his school reports ('still not getting down to the sort of work needed for O Level . . . shows no interest in this subject whatsoever'), and in the results of his mocks (two and a half per cent for French, which wasn't actually the lowest – Jackie Ewing got one and a quarter per cent and *she* became a policewoman). Billy's teachers had him branded as 'amiable but lazy' and, even today, Billy doesn't argue with their evaluation. 'I was bored, but they don't like to write that do they? Homework wasn't a strong point. I still have dreams where I wake up thinking I've not done my homework, and I'm relieved when I realise that I'm actually an adult.' A self-professed unnatural in the exam situation, Billy would later take four goes before he passed his driving test.

Wiggy passed 'about seventeen' O Levels (Billy's exaggeration), Robert Handley 'had them coming out of his ears', but nobody ever asked to see them, which was a comfort to Billy No Levels, and years later formed the inspiration for another song, 'To Have And To Have Not', which would appear on his first album in 1983: 'Just because you're better than me, doesn't mean I'm lazy.'

'When I left school, you didn't really have to have O Levels, just a nice suit. It was literally, go out, buy a suit, go to the interview and start a week later.' Thus, unencumbered by pieces of paper, Billy put on the qualification suit and started work at Overseas Containers Ltd at the other end of the A13, who'd just opened a big container depot at Tilbury and a sub depot at Barking ('everybody was working for them round our way').

'To Have And To Have Not' sums up Billy's job-seeking experience: 'If you look the part you'll get the job/In last year's trousers and your old school shoes/The truth is, son, it's a buyer's market/They can afford to pick and choose.'

At OCL, Billy was stamping bits of paper, processing claims by firms whose goods had been damaged in the containers in transit. His immediate boss, though no tyrant, sat right opposite him ('it was worse than being at school'), and after just six months, the would-be white-collar wonder jacked it in – 'much to the chagrin of my parents'. He left the lights of London behind him and bummed around France for the summer.

On his return, he got work as a bank messenger at the British wing of an American bank, Manufacturers Hanover Limited, literally in the shadow of the Bank of England on Princes Street. It was a vast improvement on rubberstamping detail at OCL for the itchy-footed seventeen-year-old. Some days the job entailed 'doing in-trays and tea making', but a large chunk of it meant wandering around the City and the West End on foot in a suit, 'busy going nowhere'. It gave the non-deskbound young Billy 'a bit of latitude' – plus the chance to pay regular visits to Revolver Records on Cheapside in his lunch hour and soak up the sounds of the mid-70s. During his eighteen-month stretch at MHL, he also became a Rank Xerox Key Operator, which would serve him well during the cut-and-paste DIY design boom of punk.

Without actually knowing it, he was a punk rocker waiting to happen.

But in this story, you don't get to punk without passing the Rolling Stones.

3. EXILE ON MAGNET

Forming a band, 1974–1977

It's a revelation/The next generation will be/Hear me
                    Junior Murvin, 'Police & Thieves'

There was one rock'n'roll group in the pre-punk 1970s who defined Billy and Wiggy's musical stockade as vividly as The Clash would do *during* punk – the Rolling Stones (a bunch of grammar school/art college/London School of Economics drop-outs, but that wasn't the point). The two vinyl junkies discovered the Stones out of necessity after the Faces had packed up in late 1975. They switched their unconditional allegiance sideways and went back-catalogue mad. This proved an enviable epiphany. Imagine coming in on 'Fool To Cry' and the *Black And Blue* album, and being granted instant access to such vintage delights as 1972's rough-edged *Exile On Main Street* or the epoch-making *Let It Bleed*. Our boys tucked in, methodically purchasing albums one by one whenever funds would allow, and learning them. 'They were the bee's knees,' says Wiggy. 'They defined what being a band was all about.' Their archaeological enthusiasm also meant tracing back the Stones' influences: Chuck Berry, Sam Cooke, blues and soul – an acceptable kind of further education. Jagger and Richards opened it all up. Wiggy recalls the knock-on effect, excitedly, 'We wanted to have a band, we wanted to tour America and stay up all night like the Rolling Stones!'

There was a feature in the *NME* about Randy Newman and the woes of touring at the time, and it was headlined 'THE AGONY AND THE AGONY'. The blurb went: 'If you have any desire to become a rock star, don't read this feature.'

Needless to say, Billy and Wiggy didn't read it.

Free of the noose that was the Barking Abbey school tie (Wiggy left in 1976), they did form a band. And although America wouldn't come until very much later, boy did they stay up all night a lot.

They didn't become Riff Raff until 1977, but the seeds of the band were sown in 1975, when Billy and Wiggy's two-man project had outgrown its own manpower limitations. Their first saviour came in the unlikely guise of a *sixth-former*. From *grammar school*.

He was Robert Handley, from round the corner, number 106, Park Avenue. No stranger, he'd been to the same infants and junior schools as Wiggy and Billy, but in the year above Billy. He owned shitloads of Marvel comics, and had The Beatles' *Magical Mystery Tour* at the age of twelve. They remember him coming round with a Paul McCartney violin bass to jam with them. 'He was dreadful,' says Billy. Undeterred, Robert gave up the bass on the spot and became the drummer – which is what he'd wanted anyway. 'We weren't really aware of bass,' Wiggy confesses. 'You don't really hear it on records. We dealt with things in order of importance, and bass was optional.'

The next recruit to the band with no name was Steven 'Ricey' Rice from Rainham, who also went to Barking Abbey, and played keyboards. Spotting a good potential 'mad frontman', they co-opted Ricey and his equipment, and he was soon sharing what music papers then called 'the vocal chores' with Billy. Ricey was big on Monty Python humour – 'a real character,' confirms Wiggy. 'Lovely bloke.'

So Robert would come round for backroom sessions with a Boys Brigade snare drum under his arm (it was so loud they had to cover it with teatowels). By dint of his one year's seniority (or three in Wiggy's case), Robert cut an impressive figure. 'He was the first punk rocker I knew,' says Billy. 'He was always a bit strange, Robert.' He was ahead of the trends and went to see The Damned and Johnny Thunders & The Heartbreakers before the other three knew what punk was.

'There weren't many punk rockers in East London. We might as well have been living on the moon. Heavy metal was the only live music in the pubs round our way. I think you had to be in West London or Bromley to really understand it.'

Robert, who would've enjoyed living on the moon, played it weird. A trainee undertaker at the Co-Op, he would remove the little silver plastic Jesuses from crucifixes, pin them to his lapels and wear them to gigs, which usually earned him a wide berth from the others at bus stops.

'We thought he might as well have walked around with a big sign on his back saying please feel free to kick the shit out of me.'

In 1976, Billy was spending his lunch breaks at Revolver Records on Cheapside. He vividly recalls a rep coming into Revolver with 'So It Goes' by Nick Lowe, the very first release on Stiff records (historic catalogue number: BUY 1). It may not have been punk, but it was a link. Revolver was also the place where Billy later became exposed to Elvis Costello, who blew his mind:

'I thought, Wow! This is it! Jackson Browne with attitude, I'll have some of that!'

Every year, Robert's parents would go away for a couple of weeks and leave him to hold the fort, so the newly hatched four-piece would decamp there, 'stay up all night and eat horrible takeaway food'. By now, they boasted two amplifiers, one of them a Burns purchased second hand from a local lad called Paul Charman, who'd previously sold Wiggy his first electric guitar: 'a fifteen-pound Kay job' with really hard strings that rattled when you plugged it in (this very instrument ended up being used on a Billy Bragg record in 1991 – the bottleneck parts on 'North Sea Bubble' on *Don't Try This At Home*). The all-new electric outfit would plug in and play and play and play and tape all evening, and then listen back to it all when the neighbours started banging on the wall. ('That was half the fun,' says Wiggy of the playback. 'Still is.')

Most young boys form a band for the sole purpose of sitting around trying to come up with a name, but this was not the case with Barking's backroomsters, who just got on with it – if they were referred to at all it was as Ricey's Mates or 'that lot'. But with a twenty-number set to their no-name and all of the requisite jack plugs, they *were* a real rock'n'roll band. Billy was the natural leader, Robert was the band nutter, Ricey was the shirt-off sex symbol-in-waiting and Wiggy was both the keeper of the rock'n'roll flame and the one who knew about equipment ('If it's got knobs on, I usually know what it does and how it can change your life').

'We were a bunch of chancers with no future,' Billy triumphantly declares.

Regardless of ability or prospects, they were, in the classic rock'n'roll sense, a gang, and were soon venturing mob-handed outside Barking on gig expeditions. They saw their mentors, the Stones, on the Black And Blue tour. They (minus Wiggy) saw The Eagles at Wembley. They witnessed The Who at Charlton.

Although Wiggy had caught 'probably one of the greatest gigs of all time' inside the local catchment area – the Faces at East Ham Granada in 1973 (Billy didn't go, and desperately regrets it now) – as a rule, you had to put the miles in if you wanted to see anyone more thrilling than Alvin Lee at the Dagenham Roundhouse.

They were presently forced to travel if they wanted to play, too. Robert put the tin hat on backroom rehearsals when he bought a Premier drum kit in black, white and grey, so they graduated to practising in a room at Gascoigne School with egg boxes on the walls and ceiling. (In fact, the band used this Victorian workhouse-like building until it was demolished, the first but not the last time they would bring the house down.) But the real rock'n'roll adventures took place in a suitably padded room next to the Magnet joinery on the A13, part of a complex that offered 'parking, storage, refreshments' for £1.50 an hour and threw in the constant blitzkrieg of lorries barrelling past for free. Like the band, it had no name, but they knew it, simply, as Magnet, and it certainly had its attractions.

Magnet became the venue for jam sessions that went on from Saturday morning to Sunday night, 'fuelled by beer and being away from our parents'. These weren't rehearsals as such, because the boys weren't strictly rehearsing for anything, but they felt important. The combination of adrenaline, Party Sevens, Smirnoff vodka and 'Smarties' made these sessions an end rather than a means. As Billy says, 'We didn't have a name, we didn't do gigs, but we *existed*.'

Predictably, they recorded everything, originals, fifteen-minute explorations of 'Midnight Rambler' and endless cover versions: Chuck Berry, the Faces, the Stones, Motown standards and, later, The Clash.

They would emerge from Magnet deaf, sweaty and itchy, due to the Rockwool insulation. Life was sweet.

'Please don't put your life in the hands of a rock'n'roll band,' wrote Noel Gallagher, but he knew as well as anyone that it was a futile request. Billy and Wiggy had already invested theirs.

This was not an easy time for Billy to put his faith in anything else. Diagnosed in the middle of 1975, his dad was dying of lung cancer. It took him eighteen months to go. 'He'd smoked like a chimney for 40 years and never had a day's illness,' Billy remembers. 'And then one day he just began to wither away.'

'You knew it was happening but you didn't mention it,' says Wiggy, who was as close as anyone outside the family to the unmentionable tragedy unfolding within. 'I'd go in quite a lot, and on a Monday night, we'd sit and watch *The Sweeney*, me, him and his dad. Sometimes he'd be fine, the next time he'd not be as well, and you just didn't want to mention it. But we were aware it was going on.'

'It felt like everything stopped while he was ill,' Billy remembers. 'He was definitely going to die, you could see he was going to die, but until it happened, everyone was in slow motion.'

The band were Billy's salvation. For Dennis, barely over 50, it would be death. Wiggy sums up the paradox: 'There was this heavy emotional thing going on, but we were still banging away. Billy was very quiet about it. Glimpses of it came out in the songs he was writing. It was really sad, it dragged on for so long. It was really horrible. He coped really well with it. A lot of it went in very deep, and it's still very deep. For a long time, I think Billy thought he'd never end up being a father.'

Up in the box room at Billy's old house on Park Avenue was a box, but not just any old box. It'd been up there since Billy packed it in 1976.

When Dennis Bragg was finally released from his suffering in October of that year, aged just 52, one of Billy's twelve cousins, Mel, came to live with them at Park Avenue. She took the spare room, so Billy set about clearing out his accumulated junk, all eighteen years' worth. Some of it was wheat – enough to fill a trunk – most of it chaff, but the effect of sifting it was more than just a belated spring clean, it formed a symbolic pyre, upon which the first act of a teenager's life was burnt. The very fact that he was ordered and forward thinking enough to put a trunkful of memories and artefacts into domestic storage demonstrates what a fastidious archivist Billy Bragg turned out to be. An incurable hoarder, in other words.

Today, the box serves as a musty time capsule; the life's inventory of a boy who was about to turn nineteen, released from the slow torture of waiting for his father to die, who trusted that Dennis would understand if he used this point in his life to close one chapter and open a fresh one. He packed away the treasures of his life-so-far into the heavy, brown chest, and metaphorically buried it.

In the course of researching this book, Billy decided to finally relieve his mum of the bulky time capsule, and move it to his own attic, reclaiming the first eighteen years of his life, if you like. The day he took it away was one pricked with emotion for Marie. An indomitable, active, proud, humorous woman with what is now internationally recognised as the Bragg nose, Marie was one of those people whose life was characterised by coping, and who, if you met her as I did, would make you wonder how *you'd* have fared under the same circumstances (with a sneaking suspicion you might not be up to the job). Although it was over twenty years since her husband was taken from her, when we ceremonially opened the box, the bond between them was strong enough that time would never erode it.

Not everything mother and son unearthed from the trunk was manifestly significant, but the sum of its parts still paints a precious picture of Billy Bragg up to eighteen. Many of the dog-eared effects tell tales, not least a cuddly toy dog whose lustre has been lost down the years, but which almost brought tears to Marie Bragg's eyes. She recalled coveting it in the shop window as she saved up to buy it for her new-born son, knowing she couldn't really afford it (or at least that there were more important things to buy).

A selective inventory runs like this:

A reel-to-reel tape.

A fish made in a school woodwork class.

A whoopee cushion.

An oversized plastic nose with moustache attached. (Well, he needed the moustache.)

A cub scouts Leaping Wolf badge. A bruised *TV21* **annual.**

A school economics folder bearing culturally significant ballpoint graffiti (Elvis, Andy Capp, Steeleye Span).

A box that once contained the equivalent of My First After Shave (Woodhue For Men by Fabergé), now full of plastic soldiers and footballers, a Red Indian figure ('That used to really move me,' mentions Billy, as he handles it), an elephant with no ears from the very fine Britains range, a gorilla and a selection of jelly-like monsters for the end of your pencil.

A Dinky car containing superhero the Green Hornet.

A bucket handle. (What earthly significance can possibly lurk within a plastic bucket handle? A great deal if, in May 1976, it was attached to the pail thrown into a perspiring Earls Court crowd by Mick Jagger when the Barking boys ventured into town to see the Stones. Ricey managed to wrestle it from the scrum.)

Assorted stones and a snatch of sheep wool from Trewern in North Wales where Billy decamped on the drama field trip in O Level year and fell for the unobtainable Kim. The fleece was also a trophy: it said 'I've seen a sheep!'

Some issues of *Disco 45* (1971–1974).

An autograph book proudly containing the signatures of the Mayor of Lambeth, the Archbishop of Canterbury, Jimmy Greaves and the presenters of ITV's *Magpie*.

Instructions for various Airfix models.

A holiday brochure named, enticingly, *Your France*, which makes the place look like a Silvikrin-advert paradise, and which inspired Billy to take his summer sabbatical there after he'd packed in his insurance clerk's job in 1975, in an impulsive bid for Bohemia. With £100 in his pocket, he thumbed down the west coast of France and across to the Mediterranean, kipping at youth hostels, on the beach and 'in hedges'. He saw Marseilles and Nice, stayed at a commune for a week with one of his brother's teachers in Menton, and turned back at the Italian border, when he got the word that his dad was going into hospital for his first exploratory operation. He'd exorcised the gypsy in him. Except he hadn't, as we shall see.

Countless school exercise books, covered, as was required, in pages torn from the *NME*. In one, containing some early Bragg poetry, there is an eye-catching verse entitled 'Roll Over Mrs T'. Having been written circa 1973 – when Margaret Thatcher was Secretary of State for Education, and earning notoriety for scrapping free milk for schoolchildren over seven – it initially appears to be a nascent example of Billy Bragg's anti-Conservative invective, but transpires to have been directed at a hated French teacher with the same initial ('I reckon all French people are bent,' it rages).

On the subject of this period fondness for the term 'bent' – in retrospect, a somewhat off-colour insult – Billy is unruffled. 'I had no idea what bent was,' he says, in his own defence. 'I never saw or knew anybody who was bent. I went on a Rock Against Racism march in 1978, and inadvertently ended up standing under huge banners that said SING IF YOU'RE GLAD TO BE GAY, and we didn't realise we were standing under them until Tom Robinson came on and sang the song and the blokes around us started kissing each other.'

Billy and his mum were known to engage in a little repartee about euphemisms for homosexuality, he teasing her about her use of the adjective 'funny'. (When, in 1991, Billy released the single 'Sexuality', with its calling-card line, 'Just because you're gay, I won't turn you away', Marie expressed fears that 'people might think he was *funny*'. His reply: 'Funny, Mummy? I'm bloody hilarious!')

Like any mother and son, there was an element of one putting up with the other's cross-generational quirks but

Marie was incredibly proud of Stephen (as she always called him), but not for the Billy Bragg reasons that get him invited on to late-night TV discussion shows, more for the fact that he'd given her a beautiful, bouncing grandson.

'At least I didn't grow up funny,' Billy joshed to his mum.

'I wish you hadn't grown up at all,' was her reply. She wasn't joking.

A month after Billy's dad died, as if to mark the beginning of Act Two, the band played their very first gig. Tragically, they'd christened themselves The Flying Tigers.

The Grand Rock Contest For Amateur Groups was a talent contest held at the Queen's Theatre in Hornchurch, on Saturday, 13 November 1976. It cost £5 to enter, and Billy had filled in the form while his dad had been on his last legs – as a result, his mind was understandably not on the job and, without thinking, he entered the band's name as The Flying Tigers. 'There's no significance,' he says. 'Everyone hated it.' Wiggy remembers the name Captain Mombassa & His Smelly Boathouse Oars coming up as a possibility, but it was 'a bit too long'. Band Of Hope And Glory was another reject, as was Special Fried Rice. Not a lot in it really.

The Tigers were allocated an eight-minute slot. They selected three covers that they were dead sure about: 'Sweet Little Rock'n'Roller', 'It's Only Rock And Roll' and 'Twisting The Night Away'. 'I can't tell you what a buzz it was,' says Billy, who still has the photographs taken on the day. Although the band look a little lost on the vast stage, Ricey cuts a surreal dash dressed as a Viking (Rick Wakeman-influenced cloak, and braid around his trousers). Billy has on a shiny, wet-look leatherette T-shirt and a pair of 'Lionel Blairs', which somewhat undermines the punk look. Of all rock'n'roll coincidences, on the very same bill as The Flying Tigers were a Leytonstone metal band called Iron Maiden, who'd only formed that May, and who would, six years later, knock Barbra Streisand off the top of the album charts with *The Number Of The Beast*. *That* Iron Maiden.

But no matter how much the rags-to-riches story demands it, they didn't win the Grand Rock Contest For Amateur

Groups. And nor did the Tigers. It was won by a fourteen-year-old in a West Ham bobble hat called Dougie Boyle who played guitar like Carlos Santana. (Astonishingly, in 1988, Boyle was hired by Led Zeppelin's Robert Plant to play in his backing band: he played guitar on the *Manic Nirvana* and *Fate Of Nations* albums.) That's rock'n'roll for you. For Billy and gang, however, it really *was* the taking part that counted: 'We'd been blooded. We'd played in front of an audience, we'd got applause. My God, it was incredible!'

In December, Billy turned nineteen, and punk rock happened. Although 1976 is traditionally cited as The Year That Punk Broke, it took a while longer to trickle through to the outskirts of youth culture.

The major players in the movement by which all future movements will be measured were certainly chopping up the ingredients and bringing the pan to the boil in 1976: Joe Strummer was enticed away from The 101ers to front the newly formed Clash; Stiff records put out what is widely recognised as the first punk single, 'New Rose' by The Damned; London's 100 Club held its overstated Punk Festival with the Buzzcocks and The Vibrators; the *NME* put Johnny Rotten on the cover in October on the eve of their Anarchy In The UK Tour, and, on 1 December, the Sex Pistols sealed their folk-devil fate by calling Thames TV's *Today* presenter Bill Grundy a dirty bastard and a fucking rotter, live. The *Daily Mirror* reported that a 47-year-old lorry driver, James Holmes, literally kicked the TV in. ('It blew up and I was knocked backwards.')

However, a survey of the Top 40 for 1976 totally belies this punk upsurge. A brief appearance by Eddie & The Hot Rods' 'Teenage Depression' at the non-business end of the chart in November provides but a lone ripple. For punk's historical Year Zero, there was an awful lot of Chicago, Showaddywaddy, Demis Roussos and Brotherhood of Man cluttering up the nation's consciousness. If popular music's cheesy equilibrium was ripe for upset, it categorically did not happen in 1976, although the Pistols' 'Anarchy In The UK' did sort of bump against the edge of the table in the week before Christmas – in at 38 with a pellet.

This would all change in 1977, the year in which the youth of Barking truly started to become self-conscious about trouser width. It was the year that changed rock'n'roll's life.

Over 40 years later, it is easy to belittle the musical merits of the revolution, but the whole ethos was that anyone could play the guitar, and a decade-long smokescreen was lifted from an instrument that had previously empowered working people from the blues through to white America's diluted interpretation, rock'n'roll. The joy of three chords had been hijacked by the virtuosos during progressive rock and 'sixth-form music' (even its dirty-fingernailed cousin, heavy metal, was prone to exhibition twiddling). 'Punk was a reaction to the increasing pride in technical virtuosity that was overrunning rock on every level,' concludes Ken Tucker in *Rolling Stone*'s 1987 history *Rock Of Ages*. Billy and Wiggy had sided with the Faces and the Stones because their guitar-playing was, as they saw it, honest and visceral rather than showy and over-tutored. Little wonder that punk mobilised them.

Charles Shaar Murray, writing in the *NME* in 1986, looked back on punk with the benefit of hindsight, and observed that it 'embodied the tension between the anarchists and the rock fundamentalists: those who wanted to make rock'n'roll exciting and worthwhile again and those who simply wanted to destroy it. Both factions had fun, both factions made money, and in the long run both sides lost.' The piece was rather gloomily headlined 'I Fought The Biz And The Biz Won', but Murray's analysis was on the money: punk was all about conflict and compromise, not least the trade-off between so-called anarchist doctrine and signing to a record company for £15,000. It was only apt that Pistols Svengali Malcolm McLaren would later mix the terminology of the confidence trickster with the deadspeak of marketing (*The Great Rock'n'Roll Swindle, Flogging A Dead Horse, Some Product*).

If the desire to destroy Pink Floyd and put a safety pin through the Queen's nose lay in the loins of the urban disenfranchised, a first wave of heroes was now required to release it. Once McLaren and his managerial Clash counterpart, Bernie Rhodes, had taken their respective scruffs by the neck, and turned them into punk's first icons, the sluice gates were open.

In March 1977, and first off the blocks, Robert Handley procured The Damned's first album, *Damned Damned Damned*, albeit on reel-to-reel tape (he'd recorded it from little Kevin Beech, another grammar school boy who would, much later, become the band's bass player). Billy and Wiggy gave this revolutionary noise their best ear, but thought it sounded like it was at the wrong speed. Too fast. But given time, punk would eventually turn all their heads – they were, after all, living the DIY dream so brilliantly encapsulated by *Sniffin' Glue* fanzine in 1976: 'This is a chord (A). This is another (E). This is a third (G). NOW FORM A BAND.'

Dropping the name Flying Tigers as nonchalantly as they'd adopted it, Billy, Ricey, Wiggy and Robert moved, namelessly, into proper recording. They shelled out for a day's studio time at Alvic in Wimbledon, a four-track with a piano. The resulting six songs, according to Billy, 'weren't that great, but we learnt a lot'. They made a leap in the right direction at Black Hole studios, an eight-track, by which time they had their hands on a Fender Champ guitar amp that sounded noticeably better when cranked up (by now, Wiggy had become immersed in the technical side of things, including sound). The recording trail took them from South London to what is now Dockland – each time they would 'make a day of it, and get pissed out of our brains. It validated us as a band.'

There were no legitimate gigs on the horizon as yet, but they gamely sent demo tapes out to likely London pub venues, the Bridge House, the Red Lion, the Greyhound in Fulham. This limbo period did not last too long.

In 1977, all four members of the band were working: Robert at the Co-Op, Ricey at Ford's, Billy as a bank messenger and Wiggy at a Barking insurance office ('I was slowly becoming in charge, due to the high staff turnover,' he says. 'I was the only one who knew where everything was'). They had money in their pockets and fire in their bellies and, in May, they enjoyed their first unmistakable punk rock epiphany.

Rock'n'roll has always nurtured tribalism, be it mods versus rockers, teddy boys versus beatniks, bikers versus soulboys, and though the early punks hungrily adopted a defiant 'us against everybody' stance, unity was rapidly undermined by the emergence of smaller, often geographical, factions. For instance, in the Paddington area, you had anachronistic long-hairs very much in the New York Dolls mould – whence rose the proto-Clash collective London SS. In direct opposition, you had the cropheaded Sex Shop crew down Chelsea's King's Road. Equally, round Barking way, you were either into the Sex Pistols or you were into Eddie & The Hot Rods, one a media-friendly art-school project, the other a choice name from the pub-rock boom.

Billy, Wiggy, Ricey and Robert were strictly Hot Rods. Billy still believes them to be the great lost punk band, but concedes that their heads-down brand of 800-miles-an-hour R&B – 'Get Out Of Denver', '96 Tears', 'Woolly Bully', 'Gloria' – was left standing still when the Sex Pistols turned into a one-band cultural revolution and created what film-maker Julian Temple called 'absurd anarchist theatre'. (Incidentally, Riff Raff covered 'Get Out Of Denver' without ever knowing what the original words were. 'I still don't,' Billy states with pride.)

The Hot Rods distinction led our boys swiftly to The Jam – working class, mod roots, no evidence of higher education – whom they saw live at London's Nashville Room in Kensington. 'We didn't discover them or anything,' Billy says. 'But they packed the place out.' Having failed to connect with The Damned or the Pistols ('I couldn't see where they were coming from. What's my connection to it? What does it mean to me?'), Billy found himself plugging into something he really related to with Paul Weller's Woking-based mob.

The real pivotal moment in all this occurred on 9 May, at the Rainbow in Finsbury Park. In attendance for another dollop of Jam, when they'd bought their tickets Billy and co were unaware that this was an early date on The Clash's now-legendary White Riot tour. Their debutante live jaunt whose 27 dates had kicked off at the Roxy on 1 May would project the CBS-signed, former Pistols warm-up act to nationwide notoriety (friction with The Jam, violence in the stalls, a pillowcase nicked from the Newcastle Holiday Inn). 'We didn't go for The Clash,' Billy confirms. 'And we *certainly* didn't go for Subway Sect or the Buzzcocks!'

The Barking contingent were in the front row of the balcony ('Just as well,' recalls Wiggy), and were soon mired in disappointment when it became clear that The Jam 'didn't work' in such a cavernous venue, their sinewy rage failing to fill the space around them, despite Weller's best scissor-kicking efforts. (The Jam, who'd had to 'buy on' to the tour in the first place, suspected that The Clash were actually tampering with the support bands' PA in order to make themselves sound unnaturally good and, whether this is true or not, it led to the trio's decision to quit the tour after a handful of dates. Despite Weller's admiration for The Clash, it was not a marriage made in punk heaven.)

This heart-sinking letdown was more than compensated for by the main act. The Clash exploded on to the stage in red trousers and white shirts, and it wasn't long before Billy and Wiggy had experienced the full Road To Damascus. Billy takes up the story: 'Not only were The Clash playing with the same equipment as the Rolling Stones, not only did they have the energy that we'd found in the Rolling Stones, but they were throwing the same Rolling Stones shapes that we were imitating up at Magnet! We looked at each other and it clicked, and that was it! We realised that *we* were what *they* were, even though we weren't officially punks yet.'

The audience, in what Jon Savage recognised in *England's Dreaming* as 'the first outbreak of pure punk mania', tore out the first few rows of seats and basically chucked them onstage. Former *Sounds* writer Jonh Ingham remembered, 'Standing in the lobby of the Rainbow between sets, all you could hear was the sound of plastic glasses being ground under people's heels.' If Billy's 'cleansing fires of punk' were ignited anywhere, it was here.

The other contributing factor to the intoxicating magic of The Clash was their evident love of black music, which Billy and Wiggy shared (the White Riot set included their staccato version of Junior Murvin's 'Police & Thieves'). The boys' roundabout appreciation of black music through the blues-influenced Rolling Stones was compounded by a new-found relish for Bob Marley, who, in 1977, was about to break big with his chart-busting *Exodus* set. Billy first heard Marley on Capitol Radio, and recalls thinking, 'Desmond Dekker with guitar solos! Incredible!'

'Without even knowing it, we were already on a par with where The Jam and The Clash were coming from.'

Joe Strummer was a ripe old 24 at the time, but most of punk's *dramatis personae* were in the 19–20-21 ballpark. Billy Bragg felt as if he was alongside his new heroes, having naturally idolised remote thirtysomethings in his teenage years (Dylan, Rod, Mick, Keith). This was what made punk so vital, so accessible, so imitable and so do-able.

Barking's counterfeit Stones were transformed, overnight, into a wannabe Clash, and agreed, like the four Musketeers, that it was all for punk and punk for all, and high time they struck out for glory. 'We were bursting,' says Wiggy. So it was, in the summer of 1977, and in the spirit of 1976, that the four decided to go on holiday together . . .

As Billy will hypothesise to this day, the 1970s in this country officially began in 1977. It's a fetching theory, if one that leaves the decade just two years in length bearing in mind that the 1980s began in 1979, when Thatcher got in. (To follow through: the 1980s ended in 1997 when Blair got in, and ended on Millennium Eve, 1999, since which, I would argue, nobody really bothers about decades any more.)

The lead-up to 1977 was a rehearsal – it took that long to shake off the spectre of the 1960s – and in Barking, from backroom via Gascoigne School to Magnet, the band who would be Riff Raff had really got their shit together. The prototype had legs. It even had wheels.

Ricey, being a skilled Ford's mechanic, had the car. (Somebody always has to have 'the car'.) It was a second-hand automatic, but, flashily enough, it was American: a Ford Mercury Calienti convertible. The band used to drive around in it and try to pull women, using the electric soft-top. Ricey would pull up at traffic lights, and, spying a couple of likely-looking lasses, hit the switch and flip the top. This might have been a more alluring gesture had the rest of them not sung the *Thunderbirds* theme as the canopy went back. By all accounts, birds remained resolutely unpulled – indeed, Billy looks back on his zero strike-rate with a measure of non-macho pride.

What chance did they have, when chat-up conversations promised an evening of 'going round Barking'?

Ricey had what has since been identified as 'a life' (as we shall soon see), but the other three had nothing of the sort, unless sitting around repeatedly listening to the fadeout of Rod Stewart & The Faces' 'Los Paraguayos' counts. Down at the Co-Op undertakers, Robert would while away his afternoons getting pissed on beer which he would keep cool in the obvious – if slightly macabre – way. Being left to lock up at the end of a working day, he would record inappropriately giggly outgoing messages on the answering machine for any overnight deaths. 'These were not serious jobs,' Billy vouchsafes. 'Our lives revolved around the band.'

Just as TS Eliot's tragic J Alfred Prufrock measured out his life 'in coffee spoons', Riff Raff (as they were on the verge of being christened) measured theirs in strips of photos from a booth in Barking Station. Whatever the significant occasion, the boys would record it in front of the little grey curtain: the night they saw the Stones at Earls Court and bagged the bucket handle; the night they saw ex-Small Face Ronnie Lane with his new band Slim Chance supporting Eric Clapton at the Rainbow; the day they travelled all the way out to leafy Richmond to buy an historic Ampeg amp from Ronnie Lane's roadie after seeing it advertised in *Melody Maker*; even the day they bought *Exile On Main St*.

The big idea, in August 1977, was to go away on holiday as a band to Butlins, play all week and sing for their supper. Sadly, they don't really encourage that at holiday camps, so Billy had another look through the back of *Melody Maker*. Something might come up.

4. BIG IN CLOPTON

Riff Raff, 1977–1980

Truly is Northamptonshire a county that he must know who would know England and learn more of its imperishable story!
Arthur Mee, Northamptonshire, 1945

Never mind the wonderful sights and the crazy sounds, there are three distinct smells that sum up 1977 for Billy Bragg. One of them is marijuana. 'In 1977, I did a number of things I'd never done before, like hang around with people who smoked dope.' Another is new carpet. 'I went in a lot of recording studios, which all had new carpet, and sometimes the smell of new carpet is very evocative of that year.' But to complete the olfactory picture, add the unmistakable whiff of the countryside.

'Getting it together in the country' is a rock cliché that dates back to 1967, when Steve Winwood and his brother Muff left Birmingham's Spencer Davis Group at the height of their success, and the former hooked up with three mates (Jim Capaldi, Dave Mason and Chris Wood) and took off for a cottage in the Berkshire village of Aston Tirrold. Here, they chilled out and came up with the first Traffic album, *Mr Fantasy*, and used the place as a base for two years, attracting such noteworthy visitors as Eric Clapton, Pete Townshend and Ginger Baker. The effect for musicians zonked out on the London music scene was like a breath of fresh air.

On scanning *Melody Maker*'s superior classified-ads section (it remained the paper's major selling point for years), Billy happened across the key to the next stage in the band's development:

Get it right. Save money. Rehearse your music in acoustically excellent country farmhouse studio. Check out our album/stage set on TEAC 3340 and Revox A77. Bring a mobile/do masters. We have Steinway, Fender, Wurlitzer, Peavey, AKG, MM, PA and desk available. Eat good, sleep good, very reasonable charges. Phone now.

Bingo! Exactly ten years after Traffic, they decided to go wild in the country – for a week. The studio was called Bearshank Lodge (or just Bearshanks), and it was situated just outside Oundle in East Northamptonshire, which Billy knew was roughly one county along from Warwickshire, where he'd spent so many idyllic farm summers – and about as far away from Magnet, Cheapside, Ford's and the Co-Op as any of the band could imagine. They couldn't even pronounce Oundle, so they 'phoned now'.

By this stage, although the exact timing is indistinct, a local lad named Johnny Waugh had joined the band on bass (finally, they had a bass player!). Although not from Billy, Wiggy, Robert or Ricey's *alma mater*, Johnny could play at 'school-band level', and was a crucial addition. So, on 19 August 1977, the five-piece went to Oundle, on a trip that would knock the rock'n'roll world they were in love with off its axis.

Ricey was dispatched up the A1 in his bird-magnet with all the gear in the back and little idea just how muddy his journey was going to get before he reached the other end, while the rest of them took the train to Peterborough, and then the bus into snoozy Oundle.

Traffic's reasons for a rural retreat were remarkably similar to Riff Raff's. 'In London, the neighbours would be banging on the walls,' recalled Steve Winwood. 'We wanted somewhere we could play whenever we wanted.' Traffic's country cottage was 'a hovel' a gamekeeper's cottage on a sumptuous estate set against the rolling Berkshire Downs. 'It was very cut off with no road to it, just a track, and there were only about three weeks in the year when you could get a car up there.'

Bearshanks – or 'Bare Shanks' as *Zig Zag* magazine misspelt it in 1980 – was similarly off the beaten path, but rather than nestling within a country estate, it was on the way up to a farm belonging to a grumpy farmer. Owned by Ruan O'Lochlainn and his wife Jackie, they'd bought it in 1976 for £4,000, and subsequently spent £20,000 refurbishing it. It was 'just a pile of stones', they told the *Peterborough Evening Telegraph*, and they had to put in electricity, rebuild the roof, install windows and carry out 'hundreds of repairs'.

It was worth it. Riff Raff – named by Jackie, because they were just that – became Bearshanks's first live-in customers. The studio cost £25 a day, or £150 a week, and for that you got use of a mobile mixing desk, and the rehearsal room.

Ruan O'Lochlainn was a 34-year-old Dubliner and former advertising executive with a rock heritage that made Billy and Wiggy's jaws drop. Although they knew nothing of Ruan's CV when they phoned up, he would soon leapfrog the Ronnie Lane roadie from whom they'd bought the Ampeg as a genuine hook into rock'n'roll legitimacy. In Wiggy's words, 'an incredible musician, a wonderful saxophonist, and a great keyboard player', he'd formed Bees Make Honey and ridden the London/Essex pub-rock boom, and before that he'd been in no less than Ronnie Lane's Slim Chance.

There he was, on the left in the group photograph inside the *Slim Chance* album sleeve from 1975; he'd played piano, organ, soprano, alto and tenor saxophone, and had co-written two of the songs, 'Street Gang' and 'Ain't No Lady'. A renaissance sort of chap, he'd also photographed the back sleeve of pub overlords Brinsley Schwarz's *Don't Ever Change Your Mind* album. He'd played with Link Wray and Kevin Coyne, and the sax solo on Bryan Ferry's 'Smoke Gets In Your Eyes'.

'This was another incredible moment of us touching greatness,' Billy states. 'It was our first brush with anyone from the music industry.'

'He gave us a stamp of authority,' says Wiggy. 'Musically, he was sort of much better than us, but a bit too busy in some ways. I really liked the guy. There were points where we didn't get on later, but when he was on it, he was so good.'

The O'Lochlainns had two kids, Oscar, aged nine, and Fionn, eight, and they became the first of two families in Oundle to effectively adopt Barking's urban runaways. 'We went up for a week and never really came back,' says Billy.

That first week was a blast. The band stayed up every night, playing and recording under the experienced eye of Ruan, and Jackie took cool, NME-style photographs of them in peculiar rural settings (Billy looks conspicuous in these shots for his lone refusal to wear eye make-up). Better than that, the O'Lochlainns gave Riff Raff *encouragement*. 'They were the first people ever to say, "You can do this, can't you? You really are quite good,"' Billy recalls. 'Our parents didn't take us seriously, nobody took us seriously, we hardly did.'

In that highly charged first week at Bearshanks, Riff Raff spontaneously wrote eight new songs, including 'Apathy' ('I don't give a fuck about apathy'), 'Fantocide' (on which Ruan played saxophone), 'Talk's Cheap', 'Comprehensive', 'I Wanna Be A Cosmonaut', 'Serengeti Boogie' ('that was just us banging things'), and the definitive 'Romford Girls' ('Riff Raff's finest moment'), for which Robert, not Billy, wrote the lyrics. Wiggy remembers not the momentous night they wrote it, but the morning after, and the overwhelming sense of empowerment: at last, they could proudly announce 'and this is one of ours'. Riff Raff, in effect, were born. 'Now we were armed with the capability to put all that gusto which we put into those covers into our own material,' Wiggy says. They even tried a bit of reggae.

The white heat of creativity generated by the combination of Bearshanks, Ruan and the Traffic effect was immense. Billy says that this is where his songwriting started to sound like his own ('Not every song. I was still capable of writing utterly derivative songs. I still am'). Meanwhile, they did all the rock'n'roll things they'd read about, plus, at the end of the week, their first gig as Riff Raff at the Bull, a pub in nearby Irthlingborough. Supporting Ruan's band Wild Thing, they debuted 'Romford Girls' with Ricey stripped to the waist, to an audience of Hell's Angels – and lived. Riff Raff had arrived in Oundle without a name and feeling like cultural evacuees. They left with the best tape they'd ever made, 'Romford Girls' on the set-list and the determination to go back up to Oundle the very next weekend.

The King's England series of books, published just after the war, makes Northamptonshire sound like Shangri La: 'This thousand square miles in the middle of England is as completely representative of our green and pleasant land as Shakespeare's Warwickshire; but it is all too little known.'

Oundle gets an honourable mention in the Northants volume, but less as a town, and more as a school. Oundle School *is* the town. In many ways, Riff Raff made a name for themselves in Oundle *because* of the big, old public school that dominates the surrounding area physically, historically, financially and spiritually, and gave our strangers in paradise something to react against. 'Its name is renowned throughout the world,' says *The King's England*. 'It has pointed the way to the solution of many of our educational problems, and has set an example for other schools to follow.'

The school owns the land, which is one of the reasons why Oundle hasn't expanded over the years, but the locals like it that way. Its first Labour MP since the war was voted in at the May 1997 election but the Corby constituency has toggled between red and blue ever since, a textbook marginal. Oundle sits on the River Nene, has a population density of one person per two acres, boasts 30 churches in six miles, and full employment. It is well treed, unspoilt and these days even quieter than it was in 1977, as it's no longer a through route for lorries.

Dr Andrew Spurrell, now retired but active in the local arts, he was Oundle's local vet when he became an unlikely supporting player in the Riff Raff story. He'd lived here all his life and when we met, he eulogised his hometown thus: 'It is almost in the centre of England. It is very picturesque. Some of the surrounding villages are as picturesque as the Cotswolds, but somehow, by some quirk of nature or geography – the Romans missing us as they went up North – we've never been discovered. It's quiet, it's pretty and we have access to every road going everywhere.'

As for the public school: 'That *has* changed, and they're just as big a bunch of hooligans as everyone else now.'

49

Not in 1977 when Riff Raff hit town, and became the local *bêtes noires*. Imagine dropping five (later four) rock'n'roll ruffians from London into the middle of a sleepy rural idyll populated by everyday country folk and public schoolchildren. Sparks flew, heads rolled and the police arrived.

The surrounding Northamptonshire countryside, which became Riff Raff's adopted manor, is very flat and embossed with some spanking new roads, resurfaced and strengthened in the early 80s in order to get Cruise missiles in and out of the US Air Force base Molesworth; an unwanted focal point during the last decade of the Cold War and site of a peace camp when Cruise arrived in 1983. (Billy once asked Dr Spurrell what he'd do if it 'went off' between the Russians and the Americans and East Northamptonshire became a nuclear target, and he said, 'I'd pour myself a large gin and tonic, sit and wait.') Closer to Riff Raff's second home, directly behind Bearshanks in the woods, is a seventeenth-century monument known as the New Build. Built by Thomas Tresham, a Catholic at a time when being one was illegal, it's a weird, two-storey, cross-shaped folly with no roof and no floor. Less concerned with local history in 1977 than Billy is today, Riff Raff found it a brilliantly spooky place to walk on a moonlit night. They might have shattered the peace of Oundle, but at least it provided some in the first place.

It was the sort of town you could become *notorious* in without doing all that much.

Paradoxically, just as the band had made their countryside alliance, spending every available weekend up at Bearshanks for the rest of 1977 and into 1978, the O'Lochlainns unlocked the elusive London live circuit for them.

Ruan and Jackie had connections in London – including at the now legendary pub/new-wave label, Chiswick records (boss Roger Armstrong had lived at their house, and owed them a favour). Because for their sins they believed in Riff Raff, they wangled them a string of support gigs at such hallowed venues as the Nashville in Cromwell Road where they'd seen The Jam, the Rock Garden, the Pegasus, the Red Cow and Stoke Newington's Rochester Castle, every one a dues-paying punk stepping stone.

They'd warm up for such Chiswick-signed bands as The Radiators From Space ('nice enough lads, but they thought they were the Irish Clash') and the Radio Stars ('a bunch of hippies with short hair'). Although Wiggy and Johnny Waugh never cut their hair (Wiggy's visual debt to Keith Richards never really got paid), the rest of Riff Raff rose to the occasion and became ever more punkish, with cut-off Clash shirts, harsh crops and slim ties.

In the historic week of 8–13 September 1977, Riff Raff made their 'advertising debut', that is, their name appeared in two live adverts in the back of the *NME* (it isn't hard to understand the significance of *that*). In that week's run of gigs at Hammersmith's Red Cow, between XTC, The Jolt and The Lurkers, was Riff Raff on Saturday, 10 September ('free'). Directly underneath, in the box ad for the Nashville, Siouxsie & the Banshees, Little Acre, The Jam, John Otway and Shakin' Stevens were listed; modestly enough, Riff Raff were opening for Little Acre on the Friday, but it was the night *before* The Jam (they would tread the same boards), and it did cost the full 75p to get in.

Anyone who ever read a music paper before the digital revolution that effectively killed music papers will recall that it was irresistible to fill in the end-of-year readers' poll form, but nominating your Best Band and Best Album and Most Wonderful Human Being was one thing, and actually cutting it out and sending it in was another (this is why the poll results are really only a reflection of the most committed end of the paper's readership). At the start of 1978, Billy filled out the *Sounds* readers' poll form. This we know, because he never sent it in either. He has cheekily nominated Riff Raff in almost every category (although for moderation's sake, Best Drummer is Ringo, and Best Keyboard Player, Mantovani). Even though he didn't vote, you can bet, like the rest of us, he complained about the results.

Though Riff Raff hadn't reached readers' poll stage yet, they had made the press: a small write-up in *International Musician* in October saying, 'The band have been together for some months now and expect to start recording soon.' They misspelt Ruan as 'Rowan' and Johnny as 'Johnny Waw', but it was a start, and the recording bit was true.

In December, Riff Raff recorded their first tracks for the EP that Chiswick would put out six months later, not at Bearshanks, but at Riverside Studios in West London, which then became Sonnet, then JD's, and is now flats, coincidentally just down the road from where Wiggy lives. The band walked out of Chiswick Park tube station, more *au fait* with Northamptonshire than West London, and got lost on Acton Lane, which is ironic only when you realise just how central this area would become to the Billy Bragg story after Riff Raff.

In March 1978, the *Barking & Dagenham Advertiser* finally discovered that it had some local heroes in its midst, and devoted the centre spread of its 10 March edition to Riff Raff, headlined 'School Chums Who Found A Way To Stardom'. 'They have already played in London's top pubs and a record deal is in the offing,' it ran, carrying two live line-up shots, a disproportionately large portrait of a goateed Robert ('showing the latest fashion in tearaway shirt sleeves') and a strip of school photos. Ricey had decided he was now called S.D.R. Gol'fish, and Wiggy declined to give his full name, true to form.

It was a generous splash, written by a local journalist called Martin Burr, who later notoriously wrote for soft-porn magazine *Mayfair*, where he would knavishly insert 'Billy Bragg' in the nude models' list of likes. (All publicity is good publicity.) The rival *Barking & Dagenham Post* followed in April, a smaller piece by Dave Morley inexplicably entitled 'Happy Days Are Here Again', by which time Johnny Waugh had left (replaced by Ruan O'Lochlainn on bass) – and S.D.R. Gol'fish was also but a memory.

Ricey/S.D.R.'s departure was the bigger wrench, and it occurred when Riff Raff had finally decided it was time to give up their day jobs. The Co-Op's loss was rock'n'roll's gain (likewise Manufacturers Hanover and Wiggy's insurance office), but, alas, Henry Ford would not be losing a mechanic. When it came to the crunch decision, Ricey opted out.

In the spirit of melodrama, he vowed that he would jump in Barking Park lake if the others agreed to move up to Oundle full time. They did, and he kept his word. After the fateful band meeting, Ricey drove home soaking wet (back to his career and his life).

By April 1978, Riff Raff were residents of Bearshanks and citizens of Oundle. And in May they were on telly, thanks to farmer Mr Knight, who owned the land around Bearshanks. No fan of the O'Lochlainns and the devil's music they'd brought to Oundle, he continued to dump silage opposite their house in the same way he had done when it was just a pile of unoccupied bricks. Ruan and Jackie got in touch with BBC1's *That's Life*, who were evidently tickled by their plight.

A film crew arrived, and shot Riff Raff playing a specially written song on top of the offending shitheap. It was broadcast on the same night as the band were playing a pub in Northampton; they duly stopped the show mid-set in order to watch themselves on a little portable. The customary gag went: 'Did you see Riff Raff on telly? I've never seen a bigger pile of shit in my life.'

Sounds mentioned it in their gossip column on 27 May: 'They were filmed playing on top of a pile of manure and their wives haven't spoken to them since.'

Billy Bragg had well and truly swapped town for country, grey for green. Journalist Neil Spencer, with whom Billy had yet to cross paths, believes that his rural sabbatical had far-reaching effects: 'He comes from a very drab, urban environment, and I think that living out there in a pretty posh bit of a shire changed him. I sense that that was where he discovered a delight in the countryside, nature and history. I think it changed his way of looking at reality.'

The reality of the Riff Raff situation was that, by now, they were a tight, if largely unmarried, working unit, with Ruan taking a player-manager role and Wiggy doubling as in-house roadie/soundman. (Says Billy, 'He knew how to put the PA together. We knew how to carry it. It was an awful amount of responsibility he didn't want.')

In June, they hopped up another rung on the legitimacy ladder, when Chiswick put out their first single. In fact, they put out three separate singles on the same day as a conceptual set called *Suburban Rock'n'Roll*: Riff Raff's *Cosmonaut* EP (containing 'I Wanna Be A Cosmonaut', 'Romford Girls', 'What's The Latest' and 'Sweet As Pie'), *The Jook* EP by The Jook (they were fancifully tipped as the new Slade) and the *Make A Record* EP by The Drug Addix (notable for being

Kirsty MacColl's first release, and for the provocative title of its lead track 'Gay Boys In Bondage'). Each single was a 4,000-copy limited edition.

As an indicator of Billy Bragg's later genius, the EP is largely inessential, but as a snapshot of what punk sounded like in 1978, it's fine. 'I Wanna Be A Cosmonaut' certainly reveals Riff Raff to be tight, and Robert's drumming is adventurous, but it's little more than a shoutalong ('I wanna be a star in the USSR'). 'Romford Girls' is more considered, but if the lyrics seem to have the scent of Bragg about them – 'Romford girls make love with their hair in curlers . . . Underneath their clothes from C&A's/ Romford girls have bodies that amaze' – it's wishful thinking, since Robert wrote them anyway. 'What's The Latest' is very like early Members, with what can only be described as a by-numbers yob vocal from Billy, but the 50s-style rock'n'roll guitar is grown-up and the shout of 'Sticky fingers!' is a nice nod to their beloved Stones. Last track 'Sweet As Pie' is pure Jilted John. As the song says, 'Shoulda known bettah!'

Billy recalls the EP's release with great pleasure: 'I can't tell you what we felt like when we first got our hands on this record. It's like seeing your first article in print. You actually exist.'

The reviews trickled in. In *Record Mirror* on 24 June, Kelly Pike said of 'I Wanna Be A Cosmonaut', 'I wish he was – he may take his record with him.' David Brown in *Sounds* on 17 June described the songs as 'fairly average '77 new wave bashes winning few prizes for originality or surprises'. *NME*'s Roy Carr dismissed Riff Raff along with Eater and The Cybermen as purveyors of 'predictable faster-than-the-speed-of-sound bouts of Neanderthal rock'n'rant'.

Any new band will tell you it's better to be slagged off than ignored, and for Riff Raff, being judged 'fairly average' in *Sounds* was a great leap forward. The gigs, local and London, continued. In July, a friend of Ruan's, soulboy Pete Watkins, joined on bass, and Ruan moved across to guitar for a while before leaving the line-up completely.

In September, The Stranglers played Peterborough's 1,100-capacity Wirrina ice rink, supported by The Skids and Riff Raff. (This would turn out to be Riff Raff's biggest audience, but they didn't know it.) The *Peterborough Advertiser* gave the show a big review, noting that the 'Oundle-based Riff Raff gave an energetic performance which soon got the live entertainment-starved audience aroused and ready for more.' With some relief, it was reported as a 'trouble-free' gig (this, perhaps because of the fact that only non-alcoholic drinks were on sale).

In November, when Riff Raff supported Coil at The Paddock in Harpole just outside Northampton, one local newspaper ad billed them as 'London's top pub band', the other specified 'From London and the John Peel show' (Peel had played 'Cosmonaut' when it came out).

By dint of being the only punks Oundle had ever seen (never mind the only Londoners), Riff Raff had genuinely become locally famous – infamous, at any rate. Regardless of Billy's assurance that they 'didn't mix with the posh kids', the pupils at Oundle School obviously found Riff Raff titillating, as evidenced by a breathless page article in the Xeroxed school magazine, *The Spire*, in December, which announced the arrival of a new bass player, Kevin Beech, otherwise known as 'Little Kevin'; he was a contemporary of Robert at Barking Abbey Grammar School, but he couldn't even play the bass. 'He would play all the wrong songs,' remembers Billy. 'But he would still play all the way through.'

Kevin – severe crop, slightly effete, rapier wit – arrived in Northants just in time for the end of one adventure and the beginning of a new one. At the end of 1978, The Stranglers moved in to Bearshanks, and Riff Raff were homeless.

Worse than that, it put paid to their wheeze of telling the locals that *they* were The Stranglers.

'The Stranglers were proper pop stars,' Billy says. 'Such twats.' Drummer Jet Black, by then the first punk to have turned 30, was like their mum – he'd send the other Stranglers into town with £30 for the week's shopping and bassist Jean Jacques Burnel would come back with £30's worth of Wagon Wheels.

In December, *Sounds* wrote that The Stranglers were 'the first new wave outfit to get it together in a cottage in the country', which was so very nearly true. When they moved in to Bearshanks, the O'Lochlainns' marriage was evidently falling apart, and all things considered, it seemed like a very good time for Riff Raff to move out. But where to?

The answer came in the form of local girl Katy Spurrell, who the band met in February at a gig at the Bridge Hotel. Billy and Katy hadn't yet but would later form a romantic attachment, and it was through her that all four members of Riff Raff moved into her parents' home – 'a lovely detached house on the edge of Oundle' – for six months. This noble act of charity towards a bunch of Barking oiks was a clear indication that veterinary surgeon Andrew Spurrell and his wife Carol were anything but stuffy, green-welly Oundle locals. In fact, they turned out to be liberal-minded groovers beyond the call of duty. As Billy sees it, the strange new lodgers provided 'a wonderful distraction from nice, straight, middle-class family life. They were lovely, but they were a bit out of kilter, and we became their badge of honour.'

The Spurrells, of Welsh ancestry, had three children, Matthew, Katy and Fenella, none of whom, reassuringly, went to Oundle School. Andrew, whose father was Oundle's local doctor before him, was an amateur dramatics nut and a keen member of the local Gilbert & Sullivan Society and the Stamford Shakespeare Company – who put on plays in the grounds of a sixteenth-century manor house, the largest open-air theatre after Regents Park – and worth a mention because he once talked Wiggy and Ruan into playing a gala night there. At the time, Carol Spurrell bred Chihuahuas. Between them, they increased Riff Raff's local approval rating by association.

And not only did the Spurrells put a very pleasant, middle-class roof over Riff Raff's heads in 1978, but, like the O'Lochlainns, they encouraged them in their quest for rock'n'roll supremacy, to the unlikely extent of Andrew driving them to gigs in his Ford Cortina.

An instantly likeable James Herriot figure, he jokes that he'd like Richard Briers to play him if they ever make a film of Billy Bragg's life.

'They hadn't got any money,' is his reasoning for taking Riff Raff in. Though Billy suggests that it was Andrew's theatrical bent that drew the band to him ('I always thought that made it easier for us to connect with him'), Andrew cannily believes it was more likely his daughter.

He also dismisses the description of the lads as punk rockers. 'They weren't punk rockers. They were just normal. They slept when I was at work.' (Mind you, he suspects that Kevin kept a bottle of gin under his bed.) Billy describes those six months as 'a regular sort of life'. It was a much-needed oasis of ordered calm after the weirdness of the previous stint at Bearshanks; it wasn't just rock'n'roll, there were also goats to look after, and a lamb they named Pretty Vacant. One particularly oversized goat among the herd became Desmond The Mutant. It accidentally hanged itself one night trying to reach some leaves on a tree while tethered to another one, and Billy had the job of burying it, which involved breaking its legs to get it in the hole.

He extended his animal husbandry skills at the Spurrells' by helping out in the vet's surgery, but was put off by the experience of carrying a huge greyhound out the back in a black bin liner after it had been put to sleep.

In return for any help, the Spurrells allowed Riff Raff to rehearse in their garage and play at their garden parties. Andrew would offer them gin and tonics when he got in from work (Robert was always a taker). In Billy's words, they 'really put up with a lot of teenage behaviour'. It was a crucial break for the boys, or else they'd have had to go back to their mums, and the band would have suffered a premature demise. In the true spirit of over-accommodation, Andrew even found himself transporting Riff Raff and all their gear right the way down to London (his Cortina had a trailer on the back). The gig was at semi-legendary punk hostelry the Hope & Anchor in Islington, and Billy remembers hurtling down the A1 at 90 mph.

Andrew has a clear memory of the night: 'We picked up the PA system in Peterborough, put it on the roof rack, they sat in the back with the backline on their knees. There were eight of us. I even set the equipment up! *And* packed it away afterwards while they talked to their fans. You could say I was their *de facto* manager.'

On the way home, the touring party stopped on Islington Road and picked up a Chinese takeaway, guaranteeing the Cortina stank of sweet and sour pork balls for days afterwards. It shouldn't happen to a vet.

Although Billy, Wiggy, Robert and Little Kevin had left home, they'd effectively been living with surrogate parents ever since, in proper little home-from-homes to boot. They'd had it easy, in other words, and it was time for them to suffer. Like artists.

It wasn't that the Spurrells evicted Riff Raff, nor that the boys broke the house rules or outstayed their welcome, but six months *is* six months, and Andrew helped them find a new place to live. (He continued to drive them to gigs after they'd moved out, and thanks to the continuing Katy connection, Billy has never lost touch. 'He always comes back to see us,' says Andrew. 'And when he does, William is still the same as he was, there are no frills.')

In 1979, Riff Raff began a fifteen-month stint in Studentland. The four of them moved into a rented house at 15, North Street, owned by a taxidermist. (From real animals to stuffed ones – there was a mounted badger in the attic.) North Street is a narrow terrace of mostly eighteenth-century houses with no front gardens: the pavement is your doorstep and the front door opens straight into the living room. These days, it is relatively shy of traffic. In the 70s, it was a main artery for articulated lorries hammering, usually during the hours of darkness, from the Midlands to Harwich. As they flew past, Riff Raff's new home would literally shake.

Within no time, it was named Wobbling Heights (or 'Wobbling Ice' as, again, *Zig Zag* magazine misheard it). 'It was our university,' says Billy. 'Meeting weird people, taking weird substances, staying up all night. It was somewhere between *The Young Ones* and the Manson family.'

A slender, three-storey house, number 15 was one-up, one-down, one-in-the-middle. It had no shower and no central heating. The top room (where nobody ventured much, but Robert called it his own) was full of dead butterflies. A single Calor Gas heater meant that the downstairs lounge was the only habitable room in cold weather, and that's where everybody would sleep, huddled up in sleeping bags. The odd outbreak of crabs was not uncommon. A Clash poster was soon erected in the toilet, a shot of them posing in some toilet cubicle, to which a poet later added the legend: 'REBEL ROCKERS WHO SHIT STANDING UP'.

Wobbling Heights had a black cat with no name, who used to sleep atop the stuffed badger, once it was brought down to the lounge and placed in the front window. Though no one liked the cat, the cat worshipped Kevin, and it would express its undying love by presenting him with bits of mouse. (Still, at least one resident of the house was eating properly – when a potato lorry collided with another lorry on North Street and spilled its load, Riff Raff could be seen scrabbling around in the road, collecting spuds for their tea.)

They rarely cooked, as the electric stove had a habit of giving shocks. The toilet came away from the wall if you sat too heavily on it, and the bathroom sink leant precariously if you were ever foolhardy enough to fill it up with water. People talk of the University of Life (formerly Life Polytechnic) – well, the tenants of number 15, North Street had just enrolled on a one-year course.

That winter, during a particularly cold snap (Oundle was virtually cut off from the world by heavy snow), Riff Raff had assumed the massed-sleeping-bags position for shared body warmth downstairs, when, in the middle of the night, the street lights went out, the house started shuddering, and the deafening noise outside convinced them all that the end of the world was nigh. It turned out to be no more than a larger-than-normal juggernaut, blocking out the lamps as it rumbled past, and it was soon gone into the night – but they truly felt as if they'd come close. This was the Cold War, after all, and the foursome were already living like the dead.

'Initially it was fun,' says Billy. 'But it was pretty horrible as well. It got too squalid really.'

Wobbling Heights, for all its architectural faults and no mod cons, became an ideal HQ for Riff Raff; Bomber Command for a bunch of supposed anarchists, a safehouse for the detritus of Oundle, and a parent-free drop-in centre for the local schoolgirls, who would pop by for a cigarette and occasionally bring sandwiches. Riff Raff signed on, did gigs, drank pinched Black Tower wine, lived like the students they categorically were not, and frankly courted notoriety with the attitude, 'Well, if they think we're a blot on the landscape, let's give them something to twitch their net curtains about.'

Robert Handley proved himself adept at planting ideas among the neighbours. For instance, they never took their empty milk bottles back to the Co-Op, or indeed rinsed them out. As a consequence, the table in the kitchen – for which there wasn't a great deal of culinary demand – became a kind of art installation made of unwashed milk bottles in 'various states of decomposition'. In fine *Withnail And I* style, nobody went in there.

Eventually, as word got around of the North Street Dairy Mountain, Riff Raff were accused of artificially putting up the price of milk in the area. Next thing anyone knew, thanks to some expert Handley rumour-mongering, they were actually saving the bottles to use for Molotov cocktails come the revolution. Within 24 hours of this one getting out, a Co-Op van arrived and kindly took the whole lot away. Notoriety travels fast.

As does the scent of sexual availability. Riff Raff never really experienced the inconvenience of steady girlfriends until they got to Oundle. 'There were women around,' Billy admits. 'Before that, there weren't any around. How were we gonna find women? If they weren't gonna come and knock on the door and say, "Shag me", we didn't have a clue. Not that they ever did that in Oundle, but at least they showed interest. They knew we were in a band, they knew we were up late, and everyone knew you could come round our house and have a smoke. We became a centre for all that sort of stuff.'

Smoking and canoodling are, as anyone who's ever lived in sub-zero housing knows, both surefire methods of keeping warm. Riff Raff also ensured that one of their number was always romantically entangled with a girl who worked directly over the road, in the Oundle School refectory – this meant left-overs. If push came to shove, and the life of the Cratchitts became unbearable, Billy had an army-style greatcoat with 'poacher's pockets', an excellent way of liberating pork pies from Safeway ('a regular occurrence', he admits, but he is not proud of the fact). If solids were in short supply, there was always a flagon of Ruddle's County from the Angel pub. They called it Jekyll & Hyde, for obvious reasons, and Billy recalls plenty of 'Ruddles-induced oblivion. We'd wake up the next morning and say, "Oh my God, did I really say that? I don't even know the woman!" Dreadful.' Ricey would frequently drive up on a Friday for some r'n'r from Ford's, 'and the whole weekend would be lost'. He was often accompanied by his semi-legendary mate

Steamy – a big-hearted, larger-than-life nutter who worked the high-powered steam-wash at the factory, and whose party trick was to hold his breath until he went blue if you wouldn't do what he wanted.

Crazy scenes. But it wasn't all sexually-transmitted disease leaflets, shoplifting and debauchery. The band were still very much 'go', and rock'n'roll paid their rent. An Oundle lad called Pete Goodman became essential to Riff Raff's movements: he had a van, and routinely drove them out to hotspots like Clopton, five miles south of Oundle, for gigs (he would also occasionally dep for Kevin on bass). The local bands, it seems, didn't much care for Riff Raff, even if the punters did. 'Not only were we punks,' explains Billy. 'But because we had a record out, we were a real, proper band, and they were just playing at it. To be honest, there wasn't much of a scene.'

Peterborough's one punk band, called The Now, had split up by 1978, although, to their credit, like Riff Raff, they *did* get a single out, 'Development Corporation'. Their drummer, Joe MacColl, and his partner, Brenda Woods, became great friends of the Wobbling Heights lot, eventually moving from Peterborough, where Joe worked at Andy's Records, to Stoke Doyle, which is little more than a row of houses between Oundle and Pilton. It's about one horse short of a one-horse town. The sign claims it is 'twinned with Barcelona'. I wonder if Barcelona knows about this.

They still live here, in a lovely, low-ceilinged place (beams, roaring fire, cat) that was, when they first squatted here, not lovely at all – there was grass growing through the floor, and no toilet connection. Along with the Spurrells, Brenda and Joe are another point of contact with Oundle that Billy has been careful to keep through the years. In fact, the couple have an impressive collection of postcards Billy has sent them from whichever corner of the globe he's in since going professional. It's unusual enough for the rest of us to stay in touch with old friends or college room-mates, but a rock musician?! There's plenty about Billy Bragg to mark him out as different from the music biz herd, but the more you find out about the importance he invests in old pals and family, the more convincing his political focus on the power of the community.

In 1978, the odds on Billy and Joe becoming friends at all were slim, as Brenda explains: 'The Oundle bands didn't like the Peterborough bands, because they thought they were coming after their girls.'

But Joe had a sneaking respect for Riff Raff, as he'd enjoyed 'I Wanna Be A Cosmonaut' in the shop, unaware that they were 'an Oundle band'. He and Brenda even saw them at the Wirrina. Stout Labourites (the old, left-wing kind) and hardened peace campaigners, the couple had no time for the Peterborough–Oundle wars, and had allies in both camps. They were soon part of the Wobbling Heights universe, and beyond. As Billy says, 'Brenda and Joe became family.'

Put the three of them in a room together today, and the Riff Raff years come flooding back (these were truly college days without the college, just as rich with stories of squalor and bad behaviour). After The Now, Joe joined The Name, also from Peterborough, a mod five-piece who later (in 1980) also pulled off the trick of getting a single out, on the Din Disc label during the UK's first mod revival. They even toured with fleeting New Mod luminaries The Lambrettas, The Purple Hearts and The Chords ('The Ocean Colour Scene of their day,' spots Billy). During The Name's two-year lifespan, they took Riff Raff down to London as their support band at a Hope and Anchor gig. The proprietor apparently said, 'Fuckin' 'ell! If I'd known you were gonna bring Riff Raff, neither of you would be playing.'

Of Billy at that time, Joe remarks, 'He certainly lived up to his nickname' (i.e. Billy Bonkers, a punk pseudonym inspired by Willy Wonka of Chocolate Factory fame). The endless local gig circuit meant that Riff Raff were *everywhere*, they were well and truly in Northamptonshire's face: the Focus Club, Dogsthorpe; Victoria Hall, Oundle; Oundle Rugby Club ('Bar applied for'); Warmington Football Club Dance ('Pancake race. £1. Supersound disco'); even the US Air Force base at Alconbury. Of these bread-and-butter dates, Billy recalls, 'There'd always be a break in the middle for a fight.' Riff Raff even pulled off a residency. Out at Clopton lay The Red Lion. Built in 1650, it still stands but is no longer a pub. In those days, inside what looks like a barn next door, was a club called The Lion's Den, appropriately enough, for it attracted a very specific clientele 'Dare we say it?' smiles Andrew Spurrell. It was a gay pub. In rural middle England. Visitors came from as far afield as Scandinavia to see it. And Riff Raff made it their home.

The Lion's Den ran on Thursday, Friday, Saturday and Sunday, entrance 50p, capacity 120 people, late bar. A write-up in *Gay News* on 3 May 1979 declared it 'totally gay' on Thursday and Saturday. Riff Raff would play on Sunday lunchtimes, in return for the door takings. 'It was hit and miss,' Billy says. 'But none of the locals would go, because obviously homosexuality was a communicable disease.' The boys in the band had a rare old time. Robert Handley developed a habit of forcibly dancing with the other members of Riff Raff in a suggestive way ('He was a provocative fucker'), but there was no friction between the Essex heterosexuals and Northamptonshire's gatepost queens. That said, an atmosphere of heightened tension, sexual or otherwise, was always guaranteed at the gigs. Brenda, Joe and Billy all cherish the memory of Robert's bid to deflect some potential grief from a heckling biker: he faced up to the disruptive element, raised his own straight beer glass, and took a huge bite out of it. The biker fled. 'After that, everybody left Robert alone.'

The summer of '79 gave Riff Raff the closest thing to their glory days, even though, in retrospect, it was to be their last big push, and one that only really ran as far as the county line. Having fallen in with some silk screen printers, at least their odyssey was immortalised by a string of creditable posters, tickets and stickers (and Billy was still 'a keen photocopier'). As he says, 'Between Oundle and the A1, we were *it*. Every single football dance, they wanted us.'

But local fame is a flirtatious mistress. Riff Raff's non-contract with Chiswick Records never stretched to a second single, which was a shame, as it put a glass ceiling on the band's ascent to superstardom (or even the expansion into Leicestershire and Bedfordshire). At the beginning of that year, they'd appeared on a single through the Albion label, but it was really Ruan O'Lochlainn's – they backed him on his composition 'Sweet Sweet Narcissus', and in return provided the B-side, 'Barking Park Lake', written by Robert and Wiggy, based on a Billy Bonkers riff (Billy owns one copy of this rare item). Without a product, you're strictly small time.

In August Riff Raff sent a new demo to John Peel, who kindly returned it with a slip saying, 'Thanks for your tape – trouble is, I can't play demos on wunnerful Radio One. Any chance that you'll make another handy record? Glad you enjoyed me on Blankety Blank. Isn't there only one "t" in "vomiting"? And not a single song about tower-blocks! For shame! John Peel.'

In an unsuccessful small ad for a manager they'd placed in the *NME* in May, Riff Raff described themselves as 'talented but disorganised. Track record includes plenty of London gigs + one EP. Current activities mainly gigging in Midlands. More London gigs urgently required, so if you have plenty of drive, ambition, audacity, organisational ability etc. APPLY TODAY. Seriously tho'.'

The occasional London show came up – at the Rock Garden supporting The Merton Parkas (just after they'd done their one Top 40 hit 'You Need Wheels' on *Top Of The Pops*), The Head Boys or Vic & The Vagues; Sore Throat at the Nashville – but it was now a full year since *Cosmonaut*.

Riff Raff's next record was a criminal one.

Riff Raff were not villains. They'd been caught in the crossfire of the occasional Oundle-Peterborough skirmish in a pub car park. Billy took a bloke outside at a party in Clopton for dancing with Katy, but so pickled were they in Drambuie and vodka, they ended up not fighting but laughing at each other ('Although the bloke's brothers threw me round the car park a few times'). There was the odd Safeway's pork pie with no receipt. But Wobbling Heights was a den only of hygienic iniquity. ('They weren't into cleanliness,' recounts Brenda.)

This didn't count for much, for Riff Raff's reputation preceded them, and in many cases made up stories about them before they even got there. For example, Wobbling Heights' garden backed on to an old, disused yard, and during the winter, a tramp sleeping there died of hypothermia. It was six months before anyone found his body, but when they did, North Street was instantly full of police cars and ambulances, and cordoned off. Word went round behind the do-not-cross line that Riff Raff had blown their brains out in a suicide pact.

'Anything that happened was attached to us,' Billy says. While not exactly under police surveillance, 15, North Street was certainly top of the house-call list if anything unconstitutional went on.

Some sixth-formers at Prince William Comprehensive in Oundle were found in possession of marijuana, which brought the drug squad sniffing round. There was a rumour that cocaine was being refined somewhere in the town (Billy has a good idea where, but it would be improper to reveal) – needless to say, the tenants of Wobbling Heights became prime suspects. Next thing, just like one of those episodes of *The Sweeney* that Wiggy used to come round to watch with Billy and his dad, the police kicked down Riff Raff's front door.

It wasn't just the local drug squad. It was the big guns from Rushden, near Wellingborough – and they had dogs. Before any of Wobbling Heights' dozing inmates had time to flush the kaolin and morphine down the toilet, the front room was full of uniformed coppers, eight of them. Little Kevin had just been round to the post office, and now he realised why there had been such a large police presence halfway up the driveway of the Anglian Water Board. He, Billy and Robert assumed the position up against the wall – (Wiggy was luckily in London) while all three floors were searched for illicit substances and chaz-manufacturing paraphernalia – and yes, rubber gloves were used on the hapless quartet ('The same hands that were then used to sift through the tea!' Billy recalls with horror). A single moment of comic relief came when one officer picked up a tin on the mantelpiece, willing it to be a stashbox but finding instead a mummified mouse's head (one of the cat's offerings to Kevin, which they'd morbidly opted to preserve). The officer carefully put the tin back where he'd found it. Ironically enough, the tin itself *was* stolen property, nicked by a mate from a local curio (i.e. junk) shop. At a later stage, for a wheeze, the lads stealthily and successfully returned the item to the shop – rather sweetly, with the rank mouse head still inside ('That's how bored we'd got!' says Billy).

Although the police didn't find anything incriminating ('It was as much as we could do to get enough money together to get *drunk*,' Billy says in their drug-free defence), the three lads were, rather dramatically, led away in handcuffs. Because there wasn't room down the narrow North Street for the squad cars to park, the young offenders were forced to suffer the shame of being paraded up the road, shackled, in front of village onlookers, many of whom already had the punk rock seditionaries tried, convicted and hanged. (Perhaps it wasn't shame at all, but outlaw pride.) They were questioned and held for four hours, and then bailed by, who else but the kindly Spurrells, who needed no convincing of their innocence.

Riff Raff arrived home to find the front door being screwed back on – although it was never the same again. In fact, they left such a pronounced gap at the bottom, Wobbling Heights' mail would frequently be sucked out under it in the slipstream of passing lorries, and it was not an uncommon occurrence for letters from the DHSS to be found up the road in a puddle three days later.

'They thought we were some kind of Satanic cult,' Billy says of the locals. 'We did the most outrageous things: we cut our own hair! We didn't seem to have any visible means of support. There were no blacks in Oundle, no Jewish – we were the "white wogs".'

That said, after the fruitless drugs swoop, there was a growing feeling around Oundle that Riff Raff had been scapegoats, unfairly victimised, and their new reputation as victims of police zeal gave them what Billy describes as 'social cachet'.

The *Guardian* ran a famous TV ad in the 80s in which a skinhead seemingly mugs a commuter type, but it turns out, when shown from a different camera angle, that he's actually shoving him out of the way of a pallet of falling housebricks. It was about not making up your mind until you'd seen the whole picture, and it illustrates Riff Raff's dilemma in Oundle (where *Guardian* readers are outnumbered by *Telegraph* readers, one would imagine). They wore leather jackets, army surplus and badges. Robert and Wiggy's hair was too long, Billy and Kevin's was too short. In August 1979, Billy went under the hairclippers and had his one and only skinhead crop, a fashion decision he soon regretted: three weeks later he fell off a push-bike and split his lip, requiring stitches, and as a result looked so intimidating, one of the Indian kids in Park Avenue actually ran away from him during a home visit (not the required effect).

There *was* one other incident with the law and this time Billy pleaded guilty, even if society was to blame. He broke into the public school.

Even though Joe jokes that 'breaking into the school is a local tradition', Billy's misadventure led to him being charged by the police – though it never went to court. He likes to think that it was a blow struck for Class War, retaliation for the fact that Oundle School pupils would stir it up by throwing pennies out of the windows for 'the peasants', and other such provocative nonsense. One Ruddled evening, Billy's ill-will towards the poshos turned into direct action, thanks to a self-styled local Hell's Angel calling himself Killer. He was one of the ever-increasing circle of locals who would kip on the floor at Wobbling Heights, usually without official invitation. Obsessed with Otis Redding and Northern Soul (not exactly typical biker fuel), he wore leathers, rode a bike and carried a knife. 'He was intent on murder that night!' remembers Joe.

In an act whose political motivation was soon mislaid, Billy and Killer broke into the school refectory and lifted a sack of potatoes and some cups. Unsurprisingly, and before the two Robin Hoods could redistribute their spoils to the poor, they were stopped by the police in the centre of Oundle. It's difficult to imagine how Billy and Killer lugging their bag of spuds could've looked *more* conspicuous. Collars were felt, and it was recorded not as a misguided attempt to redress the vegetable balance between the haves and the have-nots, but simply as a 'misdemeanour'.

During the discontented winter of 1979 and after the End Of The World (mistaken but prophetic), Wobbling Heights, they decided, was no longer fit for living. Wiggy, who was getting a relationship together with Jackie O'Lochlainn (she'd split up from Ruan), had had enough of East Northants.

'We have to go to London! That's where it's all happening!' was his rallying cry, but the others were too far down in their sleeping bags to listen. Taking the ailing bull by its horns, Wiggy tried to rustle up some more exciting gigs in the Smoke, hawking a Riff Raff tape around, and spending way too much time travelling up and down to London on a coach. 'I was really crap at self-promotion,' he says. 'But somebody had to do it.'

Kevin, meanwhile, was getting seriously ill. He had a recurring heart condition, and was forced to return to his parents' home in Barking. Two years later, on Billy's 25th birthday, Kevin died of a heart attack, but he is remembered with true affection by those who were around him during Riff Raff. 'Not very musical but a really great guy,' says Billy. 'A proto-Morrissey.'

With Wiggy and Kevin gone, Robert took a day job running an industrial Hoover over the concrete foundations of a supermarket that hadn't been built, and Billy found a night job washing up in a restaurant in Oundle, which at least meant the two of them ate well. He remembers bringing home a pint of caramel custard which they drank like beer.

In December, they gave up Wobbling Heights and the stuffed badger and the dodgy cooker and the over-ventilated front door, and Billy went home to London, leaving only the resolute Robert, who moved out to Stoke Doyle – the house where Brenda and Joe now live – and opted to extend his Northamptonshire visa. But what Billy describes as 'the retreat from Moscow' – bedraggled, beaten, undernourished – was an inevitability.

'It wasn't going anywhere. We were just existing,' he says. 'No laughs. So we said, "OK, we've done this, we'll have to do something else or we'll just disintegrate." '

Things seemed mighty quiet around Oundle after three-quarters of Riff Raff had left, and Robert had withdrawn into the upstairs half of the house at Stoke Doyle. Jackie O'Lochlainn divorced Ruan, reverted to her maiden name of Mackay, and went to London with Wiggy. Ruan died in 1988 of lung cancer. Their two children, Fionn and Oscar formed a rock band in London called Headspace, extending Ruan's legacy. (In March 1998, Riff Raff reunited without instruments to attend a Headspace gig at Kensington's Orange club. It was a confirmed hoot.)

Brenda and Joe came to Oundle in 1981, attempted to shake up the moribund local Labour Party, and got thrown out after twelve months. ('They had about forty members, eight of whom turned up to meetings,' says Joe. 'They'd have a raffle, make six pounds and send it off to one of the mining villages.') In 1983, when the Air Force base at Molesworth became a launchpad for American Cruise missiles, Billy would come up to visit. Like-minded CND types would gather at Brenda and Joe's, play Clash records to vibe themselves up, and then tramp off to the peace camp at Molesworth to shout at the police, get covered in mud and have 'a whale of a time'. (To get an idea of how popular the protesters were in the area, Clopton Church turned the standpipe off in their graveyard so that those living at the peace camp couldn't get fresh water.)

Andrew Spurrell, no longer with Carol, moved into a bigger surgery. Katy Spurrell moved to London to be with Billy. Robert eventually enrolled at Manchester University, becoming the only one of Billy's Barking contemporaries to join the traffic-cone-collecting classes. Ricey left Ford's and joined an insurance company for which he wrote off cars; he lives on Mersea Island, near Clacton.

For old time's sake, he joined Billy onstage at the Hackney Empire one New Year's Eve, and sang 'A13 Trunk Road To The Sea' (Billy introduced him as the winner of some competition). 'He just took the mic off me. It was like going back to The Flying Tigers,' says Billy. 'Ricey had the spirit of rock'n'roll in him but he never managed to channel it in a way that would make professional sense. He would've made a great front man for a real rock band.'

There is a prevailing sense of 'would've' about Riff Raff: would've and could've and should've. But in Oundle at least, they *did*. Although they lived on after quitting East Northamptonshire, it was here that they made most sense, and where they gave rock'n'roll the best years of their life.

5. I VOW TO THEE MY COUNTRY

The army, 1980–1981

This is my rifle. There are many like it, but this one is mine. My rifle is my best friend. It is my life. I must master it, as I must master my life. Without me my rifle is useless. Without my rifle I am useless.
Marine Corps prayer, Full Metal Jacket (1987)

Elvis was called up to join the army on the day that Billy Bragg was born. Many say the king of rock'n'roll was never the same again.

In 1980, a change was precisely what the retiring Riff Raffer needed. First though, he had a rest, playing the prodigal son back at his mum's house in Park Avenue, where he hungrily caught up on telly, warmth, toast, Marmite and all those other pleasures denied him at the University of Life. 'He actually got quite tubby for a while,' recalls Joe. But despite the checklist of comforts exclusive to home, Billy was a broken reed:

'I felt that it had all come to naught, everything I'd achieved, all my status. I *meant* something in Oundle.'

There was no irony in this. He and the band *had* made a mark in Oundle as the first gang in town, but it's like changing schools or leaving college to start work – you lose your Big Fish credentials when you change ponds. It is, as Pulp would later sing, funny how it all falls away. Big in East Northamptonshire, nobody in Barking.

'And I was 22. All the dynamic and energy had disappeared from punk, all the political energy had dissipated, changing the world didn't mean anything. Really depressing.'

Riff Raff soldiered on into 1980 from their new base in Barking, and briefly recruited another drummer to replace Robert. His name was Eddie, and he was straight out of the back of the *Melody Maker*: 'Drummer, handsome, modest, seeks rock band with gigs, future. Own drums, feet, hands etc. No dabblers, druggies or skankers please. Into new music, Ultravox, Tubes, Hot Rods.'

As evinced by Eddie's musical likes, around this time the synthesiser had really started to rear its ugly head ('We were playing the wrong kind of music in the wrong kind of places,' Billy reckons). 1980 was the year of the new romantics, a movement sometimes provincially known as futurism – pop's reflex reaction to the spit and sawdust of punk's wild years. Though on the face of it, this preening, synthetic trend seemed violently different from punk, it took a similar cue from King's Road fashion and was correspondingly London based, but eschewed ripped cotton and stencilled slogans for tartan wraps and pirate frills. It was a chance for those who dressed down for the Jubilee to dress up for the new decade.

Gigs turned back into 'events'. (Who can honestly say they weren't *at* Spandau Ballet, HMS *Belfast*, 26 July?) Guitars turned into Roland synths. Drummers turned into machines. And boys turned into girls. (Even in Essex! Basildon natives Depeche Mode were making their name around Southend and Rayleigh in 1980, looking not as other men.)

'I felt completely becalmed,' says Billy. 'I'd lost my edge. I started getting obsessed with my youth, sitting around mournfully listening to my old Jackson Browne records. I needed a kick up the arse.'

There was always the so-called black economy. Those run-ins with the law in Oundle had marked Billy's card, but the step from pinching pies to a life of crime is very like the leap from marijuana to Class A drugs – natural enough but inherently avoidable.

'I didn't really want to go down that route,' he claims. 'There's a grey area between duckin' and divin' and being a real villain, and I was never a real villain.'

Billy's mum made him sign on, chiefly to generate some housekeeping money, but also to prevent the returning hero from developing sofa sores. There was pressure on him to do *something*, especially with younger brother David now building a dependable trade in bricklaying. 'David had his own life, and his own mates,' says Billy, who didn't even claim a functioning social life in Barking.

He started working the late shift in an all-night garage, first in Earls Court, then in Ilford. For Billy, it was the proverbial Worst Job I Ever Had, due to the unsociable hours and the fact that he seemed to spend all of his waking hours either working or travelling to and from work ('I was working so I could work – going nowhere fast'). Second division West Ham won the FA Cup that year, which offered some respite (1–0 against Arsenal). Billy started signing on again.

Since the retreat, Wiggy and Jackie had set up AVM, Audio Visual Movies, combining his affinity for gadgets ('He'd always have the back off and have a twiddle about,' says Billy) with hers for the photographic arts. Between them they started producing slide and video presentations, eventually for firms such as British Rail, Barratt Homes and the *Financial Times*.

Wiggy, ever the humble servant to understatement, says they 'made a bit of a living for a couple of years. It gave me the chance to muck about with lots of toys'; but it was AVM who endowed Riff Raff with what was to be their last stand.

'There are people out there with video cameras and, good grief, they're using them to make films,' gasped *Music & Video* magazine in September 1980. It's hard to credit the fuss now, but at the time, video was a relatively new tool in the music business.

America's 24-hour-a-day music video channel, MTV, wasn't even launched until August 1981 (at which point the pop promo turned marketing crowbar, and record company accountants never looked back) and although films were often purpose-shot to accompany singles, they were far from the money-shredding phenomena they became in the ensuing decade. Egghead synth-duo Buggles seemed to be predicting the end of the world in their 1979 hit 'Video Killed The Radio Star' (men with great faces for radio, ironically enough). So when Riff Raff announced that they were releasing four singles and a long-form video simultaneously, the media almost sat up and took notice – after a cry of 'Are they still *going*?'

Jackie Mackay was the mastermind behind the venture – or, as Billy calls it, 'the last piece of madness'. Eight Riff Raff songs were recorded at Pathway Studios in North London (where Elvis Costello had recorded his first ever demos), featuring Billy on guitar and vocals, Wiggy on guitar and bass, a chap called Mark Earwood on 'electrical piano', and twelve-year-old Oscar O'Lochlainn on drums. Robert Handley came down from Stoke Doyle to guest on backing vocals and get his hirsute features in the sleeve photo session – taken by Jackie – in which the lads hold up cut-out pictures of famous women (Virginia Wade, Margaret Thatcher, Hayley Mills, Sue Barker and Dame Barbara Cartland).

The A-sides were 'Every Girl', 'Kitten', 'New Home Town' and 'Little Girls Know', backed, respectively, by 'You Shaped House', 'Fantocide', 'Richard' and 'She Don't Matter' (all Bragg compositions except Handley's 'You Shaped House' and Wigg/Handley's 'Fantocide'). These were pressed – in Paris for cheapness – as four seven-inch singles, 1,000 of each. They were released on the newly minted Geezer Records label, which, in the spirit of Stiff, at least had some catchy mottoes ('Sending confusion to the world . . . Where eggs is eggs . . . Taking the Mickey or what? . . . At last the sound of the MCMLXXX's). The unified sleeve artwork, courtesy of an old Oundle acquaintance calling himself Jarvis Pamphlet (John Parfitt), was notable for its stylised line drawings of nude ladies. To Riff Raff's credit, the singles form an attractive if slightly saucy-looking set, and the eight songs are a fitting legacy ('Welcome to the legend of Riff Raff,' wrote Billy on one of the sleeves).

The same songs comprise the 30-minute video entitled *Every Girl An English Rose*, visualised with stills and slides and the odd bit of moving footage taken on a leased Sony video camera. It went on sale 'in selected shops' for £15 a throw, or by mail order from Wiggy and Jackie's Bayham Road house in Acton for £18. 'We were too stupid to think of an album,' says Billy – but that, in a radical format, is what it was.

Music & Video magazine gave the release a reasonable punt, saying that Jackie had 'put together a programme which almost certainly will win no awards, but which, in terms of interest and creative energy, certainly challenges the currently accepted form of music videos'. They described Riff Raff as 'a rough and ready outfit with a nifty line in hard-headed pop; three years ago, they'd have been called punk, two years ago New Wave. Now they're just another band who'll sink or swim on the strength of their material and their determination to succeed.'

Disappointingly, the singles slipped through the net, re-view-wise. *Zig Zag* gave 'Little Girls Know' a generous appraisal as late as January 1981 ('Exuberant finish. Good one') and the video was plugged in *Melody Maker* and *Musicians Only* – but all in all, it was clear that Riff Raff had breathed their last. They came, they saw, they conked out. 'A bunch of chancers with no future' they may have been ultimately, but what a catalyst they turned out to be.

Though not just yet.

Wiggy sorted Billy out with a cash-in-hand job at the beginning of 1981: artexing a ceiling (he was doing up a room in his house as a flat for one of his mates). It was not punk rock, and Billy came home with spots of plaster all over his face, but this odd-job for Wiggy led directly to an even odder job for Queen and country.

The trek to Wiggy's place took him past the Army Careers Information Office in Acton High Road every day. Eventually, and quite against the wishes of his hero Elvis Costello – whose 1979 *Armed Forces* album actually advised punters not to join the army – Billy strode in there and signed up. 'There was nothing else I could think of,' he says. 'My whole identity had been based on being in a band.' He'd artexed himself into a corner.

Although Billy says he wasn't aware of it at the time, by joining the army, and more specifically the Royal Armoured Corps, he was following in his father's footsteps: 'I was actually trying to escape sitting round at my mum's all the time, but subconsciously, because my old man wasn't around, I was looking for something he'd done to measure myself against. You're quite welcome to assume that me joining the Royal Armoured Corps had something to do with that.'

Dennis Bragg was called up in 1942 and joined the 43rd Battalion of the Royal Tank Regiment. His squadron spent most of the Second World War stationed in Suffolk, testing tanks, amphibious landing craft and other hardware like flame throwers, and then training other tank crews how to use them ('He sat out the European war while everybody they trained went off to Normandy and Anzio'). Dennis never saw combat.

Then, on 15 May 1945, just two days after VE Day, he learnt that his battalion was going to be posted to India to back up the British 14th Army in Burma, where they were pushing out the Japanese after three years' occupation. Billy bitterly regrets never having had the chance to talk to his dad about this cruel twist of fate – victory in Europe, London's safe, 115,000 servicemen a month are getting demobbed and you're off to fight the Japs, notoriously committed warriors who take no prisoners. How must he have felt?

On 6 August, when Dennis was halfway there on a slow boat to India, American President Truman did him a favour. He dropped the big one. Hiroshima was destroyed by the world's first atomic bomb, dropped by a US Navy Super-Fortress aircraft nicknamed 'Enola Gay' (after the pilot's mum). Three days later, the same fate befell Nagasaki, and five days after that Japan surrendered unconditionally to the Allies after what Truman *had* promised would be 'a rain of ruin from the air'. There would be no more fighting in Rangoon.

'In some ways, the atomic bomb saved my dad's life,' Billy says, all too aware of the irony. (If only he could've had a conversation with his father about *that* at the height of CND.)

Dennis stayed in India until 1947 and moved about between Hyderabad and Calcutta during the run-up to partition. Unrest was rife, as demonstrators demanded freedom from British rule, and the cities erupted with Hindu–Muslim rioting. After the war, Lord Mountbatten was appointed Viceroy of India and charged with presiding over the hand-over. He kept the troops back with all their equipment to keep the peace between the Hindus and the Muslims. 'The tanks weren't any good for battles any more,' Billy recounts. 'But if one comes down your street it certainly gives you pause for thought.'

The job of Dennis's regiment was principally to turn up. One bit of kit patented for the war came in particularly useful: the Canal Defence Light, which was a powerful searchlight mounted on a tank that was designed for crossing the Rhine into Germany and never used. It was great for crowd control.

Billy knew that his dad had never killed anyone, and was always quite envious that he'd driven a tank, so a benign military role model was indirectly already in place. He also knew that, broadly, he didn't agree with the presence of British troops in Northern Ireland and that nuclear weapons had made conventional warfare obsolete. You might say that Billy Bragg, peacenik, was not the textbook soldier, but he had read *The Third World War* by General Sir John Hackett, which made it pretty plain that we were more than just living in the *shadow* of the neutron bomb. So he was more than ready to don the khaki.

At that delicate time, Billy felt that 'it' was about to happen: 'We'd had Thatcher in 1979, Reagan in 1980, Tito had died, Solidarity went off, Brezhnev was on his last legs, and the Tories were winding up the Cold War. It all seemed very, very likely – and part of my decision to join the army was based on the fact that I'd rather be on the German Plain in a tank when it goes off, and *know* what's going to happen, than be sitting at home watching *Match Of The Day* or panicking. I'd rather be *there*. It wasn't the army or the empire or the country I was looking to believe in; I was looking for something to prove my own worth.' He had a couple of stipulations for the Army Careers Information Service when he dropped in to join: 'I wanted to drive a tank, and I didn't want to go to Northern Ireland.'

Well, the tank was a possibility in one of the mechanised cavalry regiments and as for the other seemingly unmanageable proviso he was also in luck. West London, due to the high Irish population, is a favoured recruiting ground for the Irish Hussars, who were almost 100 per cent Protestant. Somebody at the MOD had sussed out that it wasn't too clever an idea to take Johnny Protestant off the streets of Belfast, take him to England for six months, train him how to kill, give him a gun and put him back on his own street. As a result, the Irish regiments didn't 'do' Northern Ireland. So, you were unlikely to be posted there in a mechanised cavalry regiment, and *double*-unlikely to go if you were in an Irish regiment. 'So that hurdle I'd hopefully put in the way of my progress didn't really work out.'

He was in. Joe and Brenda bought him a single as a present: 'The Call-Up' by The Clash.

May 1981 was precisely the right time for Billy to join the army, and precisely the wrong time. Six weeks before he took the train to Catterick for basic training, his brother David was involved in a nasty traffic accident: he hit a tree and, worryingly, was unconscious for a whole month ('It was dreadful,' recalls Billy. 'If he'd died it would've destroyed my mum'). Thankfully, David came round and was discharged from hospital by the time Billy went away, but he wasn't well and was largely immobile – 'in a dream', as Billy puts it. Part of him felt he ought to stay in Barking with his family, and it clawed at him inside when he did go.

First, he failed his medical: 'It was no surprise to me to find that I wasn't very fit.' Never a muscular lad, nor a subscriber to chin-ups, sit-ups or press-ups, he wasn't dreadfully overweight, but nor was he a lean, mean fighting machine. 'At the time,' he remembers, 'they'd take you into the British Army if you couldn't read or write, and they'd teach you. And they'd still take you if you weren't quite fit.'

He was dispatched to Solihull in the West Midlands on a special army fitness programme that lasted a month and concentrated on running and what Billy calls 'knees-up Mother Brown'. Frankly, it was fun. There were no uniforms, just a form of PE kit, and it was all reassuringly not like being in the army at all, more like 'having a games lesson for four weeks non-stop. There was very little proper army shit.'

Billy was 23, which gave him the advantage (many boys join the army straight from school at sixteen). Plus, he was surrounded by 'some of the most pathetic human specimens I've ever seen in my life'. The holiday camp atmosphere was shattered on 11 May, when Bob Marley died of cancer in Miami, aged 36.

It wasn't just the premature death of a musical hero that took the wind out of Billy's shorts, it was the sudden, suffocating feeling that he was in the wrong place: no one else there gave a hoot about Marley. 'It was the first time

I realised how totally, utterly different I was from these people, completely and utterly out of place and alone in what I was doing. I had a different value system.'

He found a single kindred spirit in the shape of a lad from the Midlands, and he clearly remembers volunteering for extra bog-cleaning duty in order to earn the privilege of sitting in a little room with a TV in it, and the two of them, still stunned, watching Granada's Marley tribute presented by Tony Wilson.

Billy felt marooned.

Four weeks of physical jerk-ups, and he was off to join the basic training programme at Catterick Garrison in North Yorkshire.

This was where, before anyone would set foot inside the Royal Armoured Corps itself, they'd be licked into shape by a cavalry regiment based in Leeds ('Nutty Yorkshiremen'). On the fitness course the environment was chummy, with very little pressure; here, the army's gloves were off, and Billy was tossed into the machine ('This was the proper army, a real shock to the system. I really did feel very much alone'). The very night he got to Catterick, he remembers phoning home and making himself feel even worse: 'Another really low moment. I thought to myself, I've fucked up here.'

The image of raw recruits being put through their gruelling, dehumanising paces is one that's proved an evergreen at the cinema – and cinematic images are the closest most people will ever get to basic training now that National Service is no more. There's comedy (*Carry On Sergeant, Stripes*) and brutal drama (*An Officer And A Gentleman, GI Jane*), but no film has drawn quite so much power from army training as Stanley Kubrick's 1987 Vietnam tale, *Full Metal Jacket*, which devotes almost half of its screen time to US Marine instruction at Parris Island in South Carolina.

This becomes a weirdly emblematic film in the Billy Bragg story when you know that its Vietnam sequences were shot at Beckton, south of Barking, around the old disused gasworks where great grandfather Bragg worked. The area became known locally as Kubricktown, although there was very little evidence left of the time the maverick director came to town and literally dynamited the buildings to recreate Hué City. It was surprisingly effective; the scenes where Matthew

Modine's platoon are ambushed by a lone sniper lack only a South-East Asian sky for total authenticity. (The area was more recently utilised by Oasis in the video for their anthemic 1997 single 'D'You Know What I Mean?')

It's tempting to see 24600765 Trooper S. W. Bragg and the 35 other recruits that made up Intake 81/09 transplanted into the first act of *Full Metal Jacket*, being told to 'Sound off like you got a pair!' by some sadistic drill instructor. Tempting, and not far from the truth.

The army, be it the British Army or the US Marines, operates a brutal, effective and time-honoured form of psychology. Unlike the music press, it doesn't build 'em up and knock 'em down, but the exact opposite. If you're looking for 'a kick up the arse' you've come to the right place.

Billy hit his lowest ebb in that first week at Catterick, which is all part of the army's plan. 'I lost all confidence, I was scrambling to get up to running speed, to get a grip on it, make a go of it.' At the end of the first week, some of his number buckled and went home (you could go at any time, but the peer pressure and dumb male pride are chest high). At this juncture, the surviving recruits were gathered together by their boss, Sergeant Lee, a tanned, fit, intelligent Yorkshire tank commander who Billy describes with total respect as 'a working-class Superman' (he was the highest-ranking NCO or non-commissioned officer; there were also three lance corporals). 'What you've seen this first week is *not* the British Army,' he assured them, meaning: it's about to get really nasty. He urged them to stick it out for the remaining nine weeks, to complete the full basic training. He gave them his word that if, after the full nine weeks, any of them *still* wanted out, they could come to him on the last week and he'd sign their paper 'without question'.

'Fair enough,' thought Billy. He took the Sarge at his word, and trusted him. 'I would even go so far as to say I hero-worshipped him, but that's what we were encouraged to do. He was God.'

In return for the intake's nine-week commitment ('a fucking long nine weeks', says Billy), Sarge gave them encouragement. This is how the mind-science works – nice Sergeant, nasty 2nd Lieutenant. Both men would shout in your face, but, unlike the 2nd Lieutenant, Sarge would shout in your face and then tell you how to do it. They were woken in the mornings by the hymn 'I Vow To Thee My Country' to get them out of bed, accompanied by the insistent percussion of boots marching down the parquet flooring. An officer says 'Jump!', you ask 'How high?'

The psychology continues: for the first six weeks out of the nine, you don't get your uniform, you don't have access to a radio, your privileges are precisely nil, and you're not permitted to go home. They've got you. The army is your world, and, in the words of *Full Metal Jacket*'s Sergeant Hartman, it is 'a world of shit'. 'Everything you do is shit,' says Billy. 'You never get a let-up. Shit, shit, shit, shit, shit, shit . . . Then they let you go home for a weekend!'

This pivotal weekend's leave marks the beginning of the second phase of headfuck. On your return, you are given a uniform and a hat. You're in. Suddenly, you are allowed to listen to the radio and visit the NAAFI (Navy, Army & Air Force Institutes, the organisation that provides canteen and shop facilities for the services). Better than all that, you start getting recognition.

'It's blunt psychology,' says Billy. 'But it don't half work. You are so desperate for them to like you! You can't understand why they hate you so much!'

Lance Corporal Wood, known as 'Stumpy', who'd come to pick Billy up from Darlington station when he'd first arrived from Solihull, was a short, yes, stumpy fellow, and he told him that he was going to be the best recruit – 'And I near as dammit was. I was very good at it.'

After that shaky first week, and having worked the knot of homesickness out of his guts, Trooper Bragg proved himself quite a natural at this soldiering caper. Being older than the others was a start, but he was also frankly a little cleverer and funnier, too. 'There was not a high literacy rate,' he says. 'And not a high communication level. Plus, there wasn't much wit.' It goes without saying that nobody believed he'd made a record, and he had to get Wiggy to send one up for proof.

His unit came from all over the country, but it soon became clear that they were lacking a decent minority to make sport with. The barracks were arranged not as *Full Metal Jacket* (one dorm, two rows of beds), but in four-person rooms. The four soldiers were known as a crew. In with Billy was

a Polish guy called Marshalek, the spelling of which had the
lance corporals bursting in on day one, shouting, 'Where is
he? Where's the Paki?' (It was no surprise to Billy to discover,
after he'd left, that one of his lance corporals was in the
British Movement.) In the event, of the 36 grunts, there were
no Pakistanis and no Afro-Caribbeans. Most disappointing
for the racists. Any Catholics? No. What's next? Southerners!
There were two Southerners, and Billy was one of them.
This was the first time he'd been a minority.

'The inherent racism is pretty heavy,' he says. 'And the
anti-Catholic songs we used to sing on the way to the firing
range . . . It's the worst aspects of rugby clubs all together,
the British Army. Too many blokes, all swearing allegiance to
the flag.' As if to prove the rugby allusion, Billy remembers
one private boasting that, if everyone gave him a pound,
he'd drink a pint of his own piss. He managed it – although
he was dry heaving for the whole of that night – and next
morning, the corporal made them own up to it, with the
line, 'For £25 I'd eat a shit sandwich!'

So, there may not have been much wit within the recruits,
but the corporals made up for it with their Wildean repartee. On parade, they would talk about shagging their wives
to taunt the recruits. 'I got my hole last night,' they would
brag. 'My finger went through the toilet paper.' Boom, boom.

There were no women around except the ones working in
the NAAFI canteen. ('They were great cooks,' recalls Billy.
'But they weren't chosen for their looks.') In the circumstances, the cover of a Nolans album took on an unnaturally
erotic significance in those early weeks of basic – 'it became
a real object of desire.' As the course went on, Sunday
became the day on which the NCOs sold the recruits copies
of *Mayfair* and *Penthouse*, encouraging them to 'clear the
custard'. This necessary release meant fewer fights and better
concentration.

After all the other kind, a spot of *self*-abuse was essential.

Billy learnt a great deal in the army. He learnt about military tactics, about the army's role in the British constitution,
about why we were in Northern Ireland. He also discovered
macabre things about nuclear, chemical and germ warfare.
Don't look at a nuclear explosion, and, in the event, dig

a small, shallow trench, lie in it and put fifteen inches of earth over the top of yourself (ready for the Pioneer Corps to come round and stick a gravestone in). Billy learnt about nerve gas: the Russians have a particularly effective one that makes the walls of your lungs weep so you literally drown in your own juices – and it smells like new-mown hay. Every time Billy smells new-mown hay . . .

Half-way up the stairs of the blockhouse was a huge map of the Soviet Union, so Billy quickly learnt what they were all doing there ('There was never any doubt'). He learnt that it is just fifteen miles from the Soviet Union to the United States of America (a short hop from Chukotsky Khrebet to Alaska across the Bering Strait). He understood what a red alert felt like, as the IRA hunger-striker Bobby Sands died on 5 May, and the barracks was put on one for three days. He learnt what real boredom felt like on guard duty, an eight-hour shift with a pick-axe handle. (He'd heard that even the real guards who had guns didn't have bullets in them. It's called a deterrent.)

Billy also trained with a Sterling sub-machine gun and knows how to dismantle one. Like all recruits, he was forced to take his gas mask off in a roomful of CS gas, recite his name, rank and number thereby forcing him to swallow, and then run out choking and crying. It's a man's life. Billy believes he is one of the only people who's ever appeared on *Top Of The Pops* who's both experienced the effects of CS gas and knows why it's called that. (It was invented by Ben Carson and Roger Staughton.)

But more importantly than all of this practical knowledge, the British Army taught Billy Bragg about class.

This was the first time he'd tangibly seen class. There had been plenty of race politics in Barking, but not class politics. You never really met any middle-class people in Barking. The Leftley estate had a bit more money – carpenters, sparks, more working-class aristocracy – but those people weren't genuinely middle class. Only middle-class people who'd fallen on hard times lived in Barking. They were social not geographical immigrants, with the pretensions to prove it, like violin lessons, but the very act of living there meant 'they were prey to the same vices as all of us and worked in the same set of values.' And the public schoolkids of Oundle operated in a surreal, countrified bubble.

In the army, meanwhile, class is an important, clearly defined issue. You can see it in operation, in living colour, within the ranks. Sergeants are the last working-class people in the officer hierarchy; after that it's 2nd Lieutenants, the COs (commissioned officers), who leapfrog the system from Sandringham, polo-playing, horsey types who are pissed off that they're not in the Household Cavalry. Billy had a nightmare 2nd Lieutenant, named Page, whose father was a general – 'a stuck-up twat with no idea of our value system, or why certain things were important to us, and no man-management skills whatsoever'. He recalls being out on exercise, digging trenches on the Yorkshire Moors, and the NAAFI van turned up. The recruits ran at it to get tea and biscuits, while 2nd Lieutenant Page stood and laughed at them. Billy remembers thinking, 'You bastard. You really don't understand. You've driven up here in your fucking sports car, you're going home tonight, you're not going to sleep in a trench like the rest of us, and you think it's funny that we're desperate for a cup of tea! Such a prat.' Another time, after his unit had run up a notorious hill called The Snake, Page turned up at the top – in his sports car, with not a shred of respect for the proles – and ran back down with them, an act that symbolised the class barrier for Billy, who was moved to make a snidey remark. As a consequence, as if to reinforce the injustice, he was thrown in the guardhouse for two hours, his bootlaces and belt taken off him, as is the standard procedure. This happened to Billy twice during his army days – both times for being lippy. His only consolation was knowing that this privileged CO hated being in the army more than he did.

When Billy decided to leave after basic training was over, 2nd Lieutenant Page said, 'Well done, Bragg, you're the only one in this entire unit with any sense.' This incensed him further: 'For a long time after, I felt that if I ever saw him in Civvy Street, I'd chin him. Whether or not I still feel that way I don't know.'

There was a climactic, weekend-long exercise at the end of basic training, a glorified game of Cowboys and Indians (Blue Army versus Red Army) out in the pine woods at which, again, Billy proved adept. His crew was the only one to negotiate successfully their way back to base on the exercise. When faced with the task of map-reading in the pitch black, Billy's brainwave was to trace their way around the perimeters of fields until they found a gate. The rest of the recruits got lost, and had to be picked up afterwards. Billy and co won the Best Crew shield. 'I can't tell you what the joy is like taking your helmet off after three days!' he says.

He managed to write a letter to Brenda and Joe in Peterborough while on exercise, and his slightly embroidered words sum up the loaded, rarefied nature of military life:

'There is something mystic about lying in semi-darkness at the edge of a pine forest waiting for a barrage to start, dressed in full combats with an SMG (sub-machine gun) lying under your chin, safety catch on. There are about 30 other blokes in this forest but you can't hear them or see them. It's twilight and no light penetrates. We come out into the open and move towards where we think the enemy will be. Rolling and crawling in the half-darkness we discover four Royal Signallers. Sure enough they're wearing Red Army armlets, but they're brewing a cup of tea! "What the fuck are you doing?" they ask. "Creeping up on you," we say. "Would you like some tea?" they ask.'

The battle report continues, and he concludes that this exercise 'has been the most interesting thing that's happened to me since joining the army. The rest has been polishing floors, ironing kit, making beds and being humiliated by various NCOs. The only spare time I get is spent thinking and shitting simultaneously, so I shit often and think about anything but ARMY.'

The only other opportunity for privacy a soldier gets is having a bath ('your own little world'). Billy was in the bath when his corporal came in and told him that it was he or Trooper Harding who would be named Best Recruit at the end of training: 'My immediate thought was – they're not going to let the Best Recruit leave are they?' So he dried off and went to see the sergeant immediately, cap in hand, informing him that he wanted out. 'He was very pissed off, but he stayed true to his word.'

That was it. After three months of army life at what *Full Metal Jacket*'s Private Joker called 'a college for the phony-tough and the crazy-brave', 24600765 Trooper Bragg had decided to become Billy Bragg again. He bought himself out for £175.

That wasn't quite it. So many had left or fallen back a squad during basic training, there were only sixteen of the original 36 left. If Billy left, they'd have an odd number – you can't have a pass-out parade with fifteen men, because you can't make a square. So they asked him to stay for the parade, and, as a favour to Queen and country, he did.

Soon-to-be-ex-Trooper Bragg ceremonially passed out, which was, as he says, 'a nice ending'. (He'd promised Brenda and Joe in a letter that he was 'not coming out till Adam & The Ants drop from Number One', in reference to the four-week reign of 'Stand And Deliver'. He'd kept his promise.) Katy came up to Catterick to collect him and take him home – he'd been the only one in his unit who had a girlfriend who wrote – and she sat between proud parents to watch him make up the square in the march-past. Unlike the other fifteen, he carried on marching, straight out of the gates, saluting as he went.

'I felt so lucky to be back on the street again. And not *there*.'

One piece of advice given to Billy by Sergeant Lee when he quit has always stayed with him: 'Whatever you do out in Civvy Street, don't ever become anti-squaddie. Remember these guys, they're ordinary guys.'

This hit home. He'd liked the blokes in his intake, particularly his three room-mates, and it had given him a more informed view of the world as it continued to teeter on the brink of mutually assured destruction (or so we thought). Soldiers, Billy had discovered, were just plasterers and car mechanics in another line of work, working-class pegs trying to squeeze themselves into a hole (in this case, a foxhole). It *is* possible, he realised, to be pro-disarmament without being anti-squaddie – and to spare a thought for the little boy soldiers who give the warmongers a chance. The sergeant's sound advice still stops Billy from being completely damning of those who find themselves fighting other people's battles. It was, he admits, weird during CND, but the songs he went on to write about the Falklands and other conflicts were richer for his own experiences on the North Yorkshire front. It may be good for absolutely nothing, but war is what the army's there for. Without his rifle, the Marine is nothing; without war, the soldier is redundant. Having been on the inside, Billy understands precisely why British soldiers were gung-ho for the Falklands when it went off in 1982: 'Wars are like the World Cup, there's only so many of them.'

As such, when HMS *Sheffield* was sunk on 4 May by Argentine aircraft (the first British warship to be lost in 37 years), Billy found it all too easy to imagine what those young sailors who lost their lives were like – they were just like him and the rest of Intake 81/09. An Exocet missile hit the ship's galley, and Billy couldn't shake off the image of trainee chefs who'd joined the Navy to get away, 'and there they are in the water'. A soldier is not a number, even if he is far from being a free man.

Billy's three-month sabbatical had changed him, broadened his mind, flattened his stomach and galvanised him for what he wanted to do next: play some gigs again. Perhaps you truly have to wear a tin hat to know how good it feels not to wear one.

6. LICENSEE: JACK RUBY

Birth of Billy, 1981–1983

What will you do when the war is over, tender comrade
When we lay down our weary guns
When we return home to our wives and families
And look into the eyes of our sons

'Tender Comrade' Workers Playtime, 1988

Truly demob-happy, ex-Trooper Bragg marched on to Civvy Street in the summer of '81, returning if not to wife, family and son, certainly to girlfriend, family and Wiggs. The British Army had, like it said in the posters, made a man of him. Broken, no; strengthened, yes.

'I felt very positive, as if I'd done EST or something. I felt that in some way I was stronger than the British Army. It had been a real sabbatical. I was really determined to do what I wanted to do. But it's not something I'd recommend to anyone else.'

He was as fit as he'd ever been in his life. The reduced Spurrell family (no Carol) treated him to a holiday in southern Italy, Andrew Spurrell in the long-distance driving seat. From there they drove to Switzerland, to Venice, right down to the boot of Italy, and then into France, clocking up 960 miles in twelve hours and arriving just in time to catch a quaint village festival where they served French lager that was coloured red and green. Each evening, Billy and Andrew ran a mile and a half, not something they imagined they'd ever be doing together during Riff Raff, which already seemed a lifetime ago. (Andrew would go on to compete in three London marathons, while Billy contented himself with globe-trotting.)

Late in 1981, Andrew moved to an impressive new vet's surgery, and Billy went up and helped with the stock-taking.

'Did we actually pay you?' asks Andrew. 'I probably owed you it,' replies Billy.

Britain's unemployment total tipped three million for the first time since the 1930s. Back in Barking, Billy had continued working for AV Movies over at Wiggy and Jackie's, running messages and helping out, but, in Wiggy's words, 'the company was starting to fall apart a bit' (money troubles). So Billy found a regular job, determined this time that nine-to-five work was going to be a stop-gap while he found his creative feet. He started work in a record shop, Low Price Records on East Ham High Road (a modest chain with two other branches in Stratford and Barking). It was close to a dream job. He wrote it off as research and development.

Low Price specialised in 'cut outs', that is, unsold, written off, deleted or overpressed stock: boxes of vinyl records with the corners of the covers snapped off, sold on at 5p a unit. To the 24-year-old Billy, these were chests of buried treasure, and fed his insatiable appetite for plastic, stretching as far as Indian classical music, film scores and jazz. Todd Rundgren, he recalls, was on heavy rotation, thanks to shop manager Steve Goldstein, a practitioner of Britfunk bass who lived with his mum in a block of flats on Commercial Road.

Against this background of vinyl intoxication, the re-energised Billy began working out how he was going to do gigs. It was the buzz of the live experience that he craved after those three months of pointless manoeuvres and standing in line ('I wanted the rawest, scariest possible adrenaline rush'). He felt even *more* like an individual, having survived the army's dogged attempts to pat him into an identical shape on their conveyor belt. Perhaps this is why he never even considered joining or forming a band. He'd *been* a team player, now it was time to strike out on his own. No compromise.

Billy calls 1982 'the year I stopped fucking around'. It was a long year. He went through the later songs he'd written for Riff Raff and filtered out just the one: 'Richard', a wounded love song that he considered worthy of his new-found voice ('Do you think I only love you because you sleep with other boys?'). This and 'A New England', which he also wrote in Oundle, but which the disintegrating Riff Raff never played, were the only pre-army songs that would later make it on to his first album, but he'd been very prolific since getting out, and a new set was taking shape.

Fortunately for Billy, always in need of something to fly in the face of, the new romantics hadn't completely gone away and the march of electronic and digital technology had, for him, sucked most of the soul out of chart music. When he'd come out of the army, Spandau Ballet had greeted him doing 'Chant No. 1 (I Don't Need This Pressure On)' on *Top Of The Pops*, and it was all the proof he needed that punk had died with its boots on.

The Top 40 was full of it. Adam & The Ants, a panto-mime Glitter Band led by a former punk, were everywhere ('Marco, Merrick, Terry Lee, Gary Tibbs and yours tru-lee'), and ridicule, for them, was nothing to be scared of. The surgical, all-synthetic Kraftwerk from Düsseldorf were enjoying a commercial renaissance – the pop equivalent of that early 80s Fiat Strada advert set to the operatic strains of *Figaro* in which not a single human worker is seen on the shop floor of a car factory ('Handbuilt by robots' it proudly proclaimed). Soft Cell, Duran Duran, Modern Romance, Ultravox, Orchestral Manoeuvres In The Dark – the Casio fops and the art students seemed to be taking over the asylum. Even *Top Of The Pops* had a new electro theme tune, 'Yellow Pearl'. It was, as the Gary Numan hit of the day had it, 'Music For Chameleons'.

'It was those fucking Bowie fans,' Billy says. 'They never went away. It was *Station To Station* and *Low* that did it [Bowie's gloomy late-70s albums that coincided with him moving to Germany and upsetting Russian/Polish border guards with the Nazi memorabilia in his suitcase] – good enough records, but they spawned Tubeway Army, Visage and Bauhaus, all those fucking bands, and they were the *cutting edge!*'

It wasn't just music that had forgotten how to rock. The whole world seemed to Billy to be on target for a rendezvous with George Orwell's soul-free futurevision. Day-to-day technology that we take for granted seemed like *Logan's Run* in 1982 – the Sinclair ZX computer, the Phillips 2000 VCR, fibre optic cables, watches you didn't have to wind up, microchips with everything – and it brought out the Luddite in Billy Bragg, as he plotted his one-man revolt.

He bought himself a drum machine.

The summer of 1982 was the summer of *Fame*. The American TV series spun off from Alan Parker's film about the New York School Of Performing Arts was attracting eight million viewers on BBC; the nation was transfixed by a bunch of starry-eyed stage school brats in legwarmers. Perhaps it was the self-motivated ambition of Leroy, Bruno and co that caught the on-your-bike Thatcherite mood – 'Here's where you start paying,' ran teacher Debbie Allen's introductory pep-talk, 'with sweat.'

Although Billy was anything but a Lycra-clad chorus boy, the message of *Fame* was for him. That summer, Katy went away for six months to Australia and Thailand during her year out before starting University College London. This was, on the face of it, a bummer, but having her on the other side of the world gave Billy the space and time he needed to reinvent himself.

It also gave him the freedom to go up to Oundle and get Brenda to peroxide his hair without the boyfriend–girlfriend discussion. 'I wanted to be another person,' he says. 'I didn't want to be Stephen Bragg anymore, I wanted to be Billy Bragg.'

In actual fact, he became Spy Vs Spy, his first stage name. It was taken from a long-running comic strip of the same name by Antonio Prohias in the American humour magazine *Mad*, a hotbed for anti-establishment, hippy satire in the 70s and a valuable cross-section of the US counterculture, but robbed of its bite in the 80s when the UK-licensed edition was hamfistedly 'adapted' for the British audience. *Spy Vs Spy* was a black-and-white, wordless cartoon that followed the incessant, violent feud between two bird-like secret agents, one in black, the other in white (although neither was obviously good or bad).

Billy admits that, on paper, the name Spy Vs Spy was 'a bit new romantic-sounding', but relished the notion that 'people wouldn't know what they were getting'. Plus, it sounded like a band's name, and he knew that he wasn't going to get gigs as a solo performer, as solo performer meant folk music – hardly an alluring concept in the post-punk circles Billy intended to move in. The British folk circuit had quietly boomed ever since Dylan.

As Patrick Humphries notes in his Richard Thompson biography, plenty of singer-songwriters 'slipped under the door named "folk" simply because they played the acoustic guitar' – but it would be some time before Billy Bragg ventured into that arcane world, despite the audible tinge of folkiness in his style. It took Bob Dylan three years to 'go electric' (he was booed by purists at the Newport Folk Festival in 1965); Billy intended to be plugged in from the start.

This conceit of bastardising the stand-up folkie tradition by swapping the acoustic guitar for an electric one was fairly radical at the time. During punk, John Otway and Wild Willy Barrett had defied their folk-club roots and brought electric minimalism to *Top Of The Pops* in 1977 with 'Really Free', but this was very much a one-off, and hardly a statement of intent. The so-called 'punk poet', Patrick Fitzgerald, used an acoustic, and Billy had seen him bottled off for this crime at a Rock Against Racism gig in 1978. (Billy ended up on the same bill as Fitzgerald in Switzerland some years later.)

So plugging folk into an amplifier was Billy's inadvertent gimmick, if you like. Not much of one at a time when bands were as famous for what they wore as what they played – Dexys Midnight Runners (gypsy chic), ABC (gold lamé suits), Bow Wow Wow (pirate costumes, and, in singer Annabella Lwin's case, nothing) – but it would certainly mark him out from the endless stream of keyboard-prodders and raincoat-rockers.

Billy's songs were more punk than folk (he has often described his earliest incarnation as 'a one-man Clash'), and the chugging ghost of Riff Raff still stalked songs like 'The Busy Girl Buys Beauty' and 'To Have And To Have Not', but there was more to Spy Vs Spy than choppy guitar and uncosmeticised cockney vowels. For one thing, there was humour in the words or, if not belly laughs, certainly an easy, lyrical dexterity in couplets such as 'Just because I dress like this/Doesn't mean I'm a Communist' and 'I am the milkman of human kindness/I will leave an extra pint'.

Although in 1982 Billy had yet to hone his performing style and between-song banter, the raw materials with which he was about to step out into the spotlight were impressive indeed. The capital's spit'n'sawdust pub circuit had never heard the like – and that was precisely where Billy Bragg intended to go public. Billed as a band and dressed as himself, the sound of two musical traditions colliding.

Back in October, Billy had written to the *Melody Maker*, not a letter for publication but a heartfelt plea to writer Adam Sweeting, nowadays a respected journalist, author and obituarist for the *Guardian*, then very possibly an angel sent from heaven as far as Billy was concerned. He'd identified with a piece Sweeting had written called 'The Clash And The Cocktail Culture': 'It is the story of my life,' Billy wrote. 'The music industry is wallpapering over the cracks in our society . . . For the first time in two years I've found someone writing what I am feeling 24 hours a day. You are the voice in my darkness.'

Having pinpointed a sympathetic soul, Billy asked Sweeting to come and see him play live, as his debut was approaching. Proving himself a bit of a maverick in rock journalist terms, Sweeting did just that, on the strength of one hand-written letter from a self-confessed 'whining bastard'. After an aborted first shot at the City Of London Poly in November – and an agonising five-month gestation – Spy Vs Spy finally supported The Sensible Jerseys at a North London Poly sociology disco in Highbury Grove in March 1982, and Sweeting came along. (Jerseys bassist Steve Ives had played in the very last incarnation of Riff Raff, a sixth-former at Oundle's Prince William Comprehensive.) With a real, live music hack in attendance, Billy's nerves were in ribbons, and, unusually for him, he downed three pints before he went on.

He was using the drum machine for one song, 'The Cloth'. It was operated by a foot pedal, but when the song was over he couldn't get it to switch off, and was forced to turn the volume down to prevent it from tip-tap-tip-tapping throughout the rest of the set – an early omen that technology and

Billy Bragg were not natural bedfellows. Mercifully, there was no review, but Billy had planted a seed.

He met Sweeting for a chat at the Hospital Tavern in the East End, just by London Hospital. On the way in, Billy noticed that the licensee's name was Jack Ruby, which he took as a good omen though he's not sure exactly why. (Jack Ruby had not brought much luck to Lee Harvey Oswald, but he did run a nightclub, which was pretty showbiz, and he was famous. Who says an omen has to bear up to cross-examination?) Without fully realising it, Billy was laying important foundations for the near future.

Notwithstanding a further support with the Jerseys at legendary Soho jazz club Ronnie Scott's (in the small upstairs room, mind) in May, what Billy describes as Spy Vs Spy's very first 'proper' gig took place at the Rock Garden (where Riff Raff had played so many times) on 6 June 1982. With not a single dark root showing, and wearing a home-made T-shirt with Spy Vs Spy painted on the chest in fabric dye, Billy officially presented himself to the world: one man and his guitar. And his drum machine.

A fortnight earlier he'd won the first heat of a live talent contest at the Bridge House in Canning Town, a landmark boozer venue in the East London area that had initially defied the punk rock boom by booking heavy metal acts and Rory Gallagher. (It was sadly bulldozed in the mid-80s.) In its day it was just beside the flyover as the beloved A13 segues from East India Dock Road into Newham Way. Billy also came first in the second heat on 10 July and reached the final on 24 July, up against such hopefuls as Hiss The Villain, The Boobies, Raw Recruit and On His Own. With roots starting to appear in his banana-blond crop, this time Billy wore a T-shirt bearing the logo of 2000AD comic and its rozzer figurehead Judge Dredd ('He brings law to the cursed Earth'). He wore it again at the final, and came second. The prize was £50.

Billy Bragg was suddenly in the game.

Steve Goldstein, who was the manager at Low Price Records and lived with his mum, owned a Portastudio. In non-professional rock terms, this is even better than knowing someone who owns a van.

The chance was too good to pass up. It was time for Billy Bragg to commit himself to tape. Over one weekend, Billy recorded six songs from his live set at Mrs Goldstein's, with Steve at the controls. (The block of flats was called Gilmour House, off Commercial Road, on the left as you travel east on the A13, now redeveloped, but a crucial site on the Billy Bragg Rock Tour of London, and a marker flag on the road from obscurity to ubiquity.)

Played 'as live' – not such a surprise bearing in mind the economical nature of Billy's act – he satisfactorily entrusted the following numbers to tape: 'A New England' (written after seeing two satellites flying alongside each other in the clear Northants sky), 'The Milkman Of Human Kindness', 'The Man In The Iron Mask', 'Strange Things Happen', 'The Cloth' and 'To Have And To Have Not'. Only one ('The Cloth') failed to make it into Billy Bragg's professionally recorded canon. The others defined what he was all about. Some might say that 'A New England' still most succinctly demonstrates what makes Billy Bragg such a durable, widely loved performer. It's essentially a love song, but one that packs a subtle political punch, and joins the dots between personal, ideological and lyrical.

I was 21 years when I wrote this song
I'm 22 now, but I won't be for long
People ask me when will you grow up to be a man
But all the girls I loved at school
Are already pushing prams

I don't want to change the world
I'm not looking for a new England
'm just looking for another girl

The central conceit of the song lies in the claim that the singer doesn't want to change the world, merely get a shag. It is not hard to hear the irony. Billy is desperate for some romantic inspiration, but the two shooting stars in his song turn out to be satellites. 'Is it wrong to wish on space hardware?' he asks. No, seems to be the adaptable answer. Here is a poet trapped in the modern world, so besotted with a girl he does not yet know, he is prepared to cast all broader ideals aside in favour of a domestic utopia. When Kirsty MacColl recorded 'A New England' in 1985 and took it into the Top Ten, the paradox of the chorus was rinsed out by a pop arrangement and a sweet voice, but the way Billy plays it, with the lone Duane Eddy guitar and that plaintive quality to the vocal, says it all.

Many of Billy's early songs disclose a failure in love, a sense of having been left behind. In 'Richard', a song written in Riff Raff days, the rhapsody 'There will be parties/There will be fun/There will be prizes for everyone' implicitly counts Billy out. There is more of Morrissey in Billy Bragg than many critics give him credit for – the difference between the two men as lyricists (there are plenty of differences between them as men) lies in the desire to fit in. Morrissey revels in his outsider status; Billy's banging on the door of acceptance.

Of the Gilmour House set, it is 'To Have And To Have Not' that ploughs the most purely political furrow. There is punk rhetoric in blunt graffiti-like observations such as 'The factories are closing and the army is full', but it is the repeated mantra 'Just because you're better than me, doesn't mean I'm lazy' that unlocks the song's power. Here is a young man who has been failed by the education system, defeated on the day, but isn't griping *at* the system, he's pleading at society not to judge him on his one O Level. Punk was a howl of disapproval, but it sought no answers from the state. Billy Bragg is frustrated but not crushed. He shall overcome.

Although rough and ready, this first Spy Vs Spy demo had plenty going on behind the punk rock electric guitar and the Essex delivery. He became famous for his non-singsong voice, and yet 'The Man In The Iron Mask' finds him delivering a disarmingly tender lament to an unfaithful partner, give or take 'the fings you've done'. The tape was duly mailed to anyone in the record industry who might cock a sympathetic ear, from Rough Trade to EMI. All was quiet.

Until, that is, the *Melody Maker* dated 16 October 1982.

In line with the paper's sympathies with musicians, they actually reviewed demo tapes. (The featurette survived umpteen makeovers.) Billy remembers the column being called 'Shit Demos'. It was, as he well knows, called Playback, and it provided the post-Riff Raff Billy with his very first words of endorsement. Having spent years worshipping the

95

NME, and the equivalent time treating *Melody Maker* as a classified ad-sheet and *Sounds* as the last resort in an ill-stocked newsagent, it would prove educational for Billy that the 'other two' picked up on him first.

Playback was written by – who else? – Adam Sweeting. Referring to the man behind Spy Vs Spy as Bill Bragg, he raved thus: 'His demo tape is a small goldmine of strong, simple tunes which he uses as scaffolding for some of the sharpest and funniest lyrics I've heard in years. Bragg, with his rough, hoarse voice, sings about working girls, the dole and how to cope with frustration. Meanwhile, he's able to view love with a child's sense of wonder. 'Already, Bill Bragg possesses a view of the world which is simultaneously knowing and naked, appallingly vulnerable, but strong enough to look at the fact without flinching. Consequently his songs are both uncomfortably perceptive and reassuring, small rubber dinghies on a stormy sea. The wit and wisdom of Bragg's songs puts to shame most of the people who go around calling themselves songwriters, and regardless of whether or not there is any justice in the world, you'll hear more from him soon.'

Quite a review, and one that Bill Bragg would soon be able to recite from memory. The music papers, traditionally in the shops on Wednesday, but were available a day early in Central London, which, in 1982, was where Billy's girl-friend Katy worked. She picked up the papers, discovered the heaven-sent Playback column and immediately rang Billy up at the record shop to read the 'fucking brilliant review' down the phone to him. 'Are you sitting down?' she asked. He was.

Fortunately, the shop was empty, as Billy was overcome with emotion, and would've been in no fit state to work out anybody's change. 'It was such a relief,' he recalls. 'Here was a possibility that I might be able to do this. Here was someone, a music writer in a music paper, saying the songs I'd written were really good. That filled me with real confidence.'

On the same page in the *Maker* was a review of a demo by some jokers calling themselves Nux Vomica, which, in contrast to Spy Vs Spy, Sweeting trashed: 'facetious ditties with horrible singing and a truly repulsive guitar sound'. Nux Vomica was Billy Bragg and the brothers Wigg posing as

Ian Moody, Graham Moody and Andy Anonymous, playing 'naff pop songs' that they'd taped a year earlier, and sent in as a control experiment – a very scientific coup indeed, and one that worked. Sweeting was no fool. He knew a good demo from a rotten demo. (Nux Vomica were named after a medicinal compound in a bell-jar Billy remembers seeing in Andrew Spurrell's surgery – but few people were ever going to ask them where they got their crazy name.)

Billy never did tell Sweeting who Nux Vomica actually were.

Around this time began Billy's solo apprenticeship. There are baptisms by fire, and there are baptisms by beer. The Tunnel club specialised in the latter, and provided Billy with his first residency, playing Tuesday nights, opening for anybody, £5 a night (he was later granted 60 per cent of the door takings). The Tunnel, later a venue that was synonymous with alternative comedians and the appalling treatment thereof, was housed at a pub called the Mitre on the Greenwich side of London's notorious Blackwall Tunnel. Driven down there either by Wiggy's brother Alan, Katy, or even his mum, Billy set about paying his dues. Up north, you do the working men's clubs; this was worse, a talking men's club. Despite the cavalcade of live entertainment on offer, they were only here for the beer.

Warming up may be too showbiz a term for it, but Billy attempted to *distract* the Tunnel's pathologically ungrateful punters before the main act came on, be it a heavy metal band like Blood & Roses, former-Groundhog Tony McPhee, The Gymslips, Doll By Doll, Doctor & The Medics or crowd-pleasing striptease outfit True Life Confessions. If anyone broke a string at a Riff Raff gig, Billy would keep the audience amused by singing 'I'm Forever Blowing Bubbles', and it was this blitz spirit that saw him through the Tunnel. He would play his songs, obviously – thrashing away at his customised 'Route 66', 'A13 Trunk Road To The Sea', for five minutes 'until someone took a blind bit of notice' – but he would also talk to the audience, and wind them up ('this really sharpened up my patter'). The dreaded video juke box, fast becoming a pub fixture in this age of 'fun', was rarely turned off during Billy's act, and spying opportunity under every hurdle, he turned it to his advantage.

Tears For Fears, then very much a raincoat band, were having their fist hit with 'Mad World' in October '82, and if the video came on, Billy would make a facetious comment about their silly student dance. The audience would laugh, and, having snared their sympathy, he'd riff off it for a while. (This trick has remained in his arsenal: on his first trip to New York in 1984, in order to find some valuable common ground with the Americans, he sparred with them about what was on MTV.)

Also noteworthy in the Billy Bragg set at this time was a brave cover of Cliff Richard's 'A Voice In The Wilderness' (a ballad from the 1959 beat movie *Expresso Bongo*), which, for attention-grabbing purposes, he reworked as 'The Voice Of The Wildebeest' ('My wife and the wildebeest left hoof marks on me'). It's fitting that the Tunnel later became semi-legendary for its high body count of dying comedians. It was here that Billy Bragg became a stand-up.

He'd turned out funny.

Meanwhile, over in Marble Arch, a man called Jeff Chegwin at the music publishers Chappell (yes, he *is* the late Keith Chegwin's brother), was about to make Billy's day. He'd phoned him in October after the Playback review had caught his eye in *Melody Maker* and requested a copy of the tape. 'This was equally astounding,' Billy recalls. 'The first *industry* person who'd shown interest.' It turned out to be more than interest.

Chegwin loved the tape, but didn't have the available money or in-house support to sign him to a concrete publishing deal. But the enthusiasm was there, so he gave Billy a list of contacts to send the tape on to, and touted it around himself, in the hope that a record company might provide the cash for Billy and Chappell to do something.

'I got absolutely no response,' says Billy. 'Every now and again I bump into one of the music business people who I sent it to and I remind them of the fact. I've got their names.' (In a follow-up letter to Adam Sweeting, Billy mentioned 'a flat refusal from CBS and a "not sure" from Polydor'.)

The Catch 22 goes, if you haven't got a record out, you can't get in the music press, and if you haven't been in the music press, you don't exist. As priceless as Adam Sweeting's rave review was, it hadn't opened any record company doors, so Billy set about opening them for himself. First, he reasoned, he needed a manager. As luck would have it, he'd been chatting to an artist he knew called Jim Davidson, who'd painted backdrops for The Clash back in 1980, and had been impressed by one of their co-managers, Peter Jenner. Billy had calculated that he specifically needed a manager who was a socialist and a father figure. A tall order, perhaps, but that was precisely what Peter Jenner turned out to be.

Jenner taught at the London School Of Economics in 1967, then moved into managing Pink Floyd when they were still an underground concern. He put on the Rolling Stones at Hyde Park, and, with his partner in Blackhill management Andrew King, had handled T Rex, Roy Harper, Edgar Broughton and – most impressively to Billy – The Clash, between the time they sacked journalist Caroline Coon and reinstated original Svengali Bernie Rhodes (just over twelve months, during which time they toured the epic *London Calling* and recorded the triple-album folly *Sandinista!*). Blackhill also looked after Ian Dury & The Block heads until 1980, when they were just over their commercial peak.

Billy spoke to Sumi Jenner, Peter's wife, and was dismayed to find that he was no longer in management, and Blackhill had shut up shop. He was now Head of Marketing & A&R (Artists & Repertoire) at the Charisma label and had been for nine months.

'I don't know what I was,' Jenner recalls. 'Charisma was in a real mess.' Charisma had been set up as a stable for innovative artists in the late 60s by Tony Stratton-Smith, or 'Strat' as he was known. Building on a nascent roster that included The Nice and Van Der Graaf Generator, Stratton-Smith had had the foresight to sign public school progressive rockers Genesis, then two albums away from commercial success (their *Foxtrot* album went Top Ten in 1972), but they were the sort of band upon whom a label's reputation is forged. Stratton-Smith also managed them until 1973. When singer Peter Gabriel left the group in 1975, he stayed with Charisma, and recorded all four of his confusingly eponymous solo albums for the label, every one a Top Ten hit.

Charisma's ornate Mad Hatter logo will be equally well known to Monty Python fans, as Stratton-Smith released seven Python albums between 1971 and 1980, giving them total artistic control and risking the wrath of many a nervous retailer. (Charisma triumphantly pushed the Pythons into the album Top Ten in 1980, with the *Contractual Obligation Album*, which was banned from TV or radio advertising for being 'crude in the extreme' and ran into legal trouble for its unauthorised and defamatory use of John Denver's 'Annie's Song' – subsequently removed.)

A rum label, to be sure, but not really Peter Jenner's cup of tea although he admits it's unlikely he would've been happy as Head of Marketing & A&R at any label, and was quite a fan of Strat. In 1980, Charisma had placed a toe in the waters of movie-making, with the wilfully eccentric *Sir Henry At Rawlinson's End*, produced by Stratton-Smith and showing disappointing financial returns. Jenner recalls 'constant cashflow problems – we were haemorrhaging money'. He reasons that 'Charisma's golden era was pre-punk, they'd never really got hold of post-punk.'

By 1982, the last studio album Peter Gabriel would record for the label was in the charts, and a deal with Dutch giant PolyGram meant that Charisma's pressings were paid for, but Jenner describes his job thus: 'I was there to fire everybody' – by which he means artists who were past their sell-by date. His task was to 'thin out' the roster; unfortunately he was not much cop at the high-powered corporate game: 'I was a real fucking softy. I just let bands make another record. I was really unsuccessful at that job.'

As cash-flow slowed down to a trickle, the pressure from PolyGram mounted: they were saying, if you want more money, we'll have to take over. Stratton-Smith's response to the crisis was admirable, as Jenner relates: 'He would come into work at twelve, go to lunch at one, come back at four, and then go out all night. Great geezer. Old School. Very sharp.' (Strat died aged 53 in 1987.)

These qualities were also true of Jenner, who'd been round the music biz block himself. 'I realised that if I was going to sign anything, I was going to have to be very economical.'

Because Charisma was part-independent, part major label, as an A&R, Jenner simply couldn't get involved in bidding wars for hot, unsigned artists: 'The nightmare of being an A&R man is trying to work out whether somebody's worth spending £100,000 on as a business investment. It's a crap shoot, it's madness.'

But this turned out to be a blessing.

Billy had by then left Low Price Records ('the last proper job I ever had'), and had more time on his hands to go wandering in central London, hawking his wares around. On 2 November 1982, Channel 4 went on the air, as, in the same week, did the first ever edition of Tyne Tees' live Friday evening music show *The Tube*. And here's where divine intervention takes over.

Peter Gabriel was on that first *Tube* the same day that Billy Bragg turned up in reception at Charisma, hoping to get to see Peter Jenner and give him his tape (he liked what he'd heard about Jenner, and the Clash connection said 'kindred spirit'). He sat, like Rupert Pupkin in Martin Scorsese's *The King Of Comedy* ('I'll wait. I'm happy to wait'), when someone came out looking for the TV repairman. Because Gabriel was on *The Tube*, they were keen to video it, but didn't know how to tune the VCR into the new channel. Now, Billy was more than *au fait* with video equipment, thanks to his time working for Wiggy, and saw his way in.

'And I did look a bit like a TV repairman!'

Yes, he said, he *was* there to fix the video, and he was duly taken into the room where the telly was to perform his alchemy. Job done, he wandered down the corridor and found Peter Jenner's office. Putting a tape or record into someone's influential hand is a hundred times better than putting it in the post, or leaving it at reception, as any plugger will tell you, and Billy made the drop. Not only that, he made an impression.

'He was a laugh,' says Jenner. 'Instantly likeable.'

That weekend, Jenner was off to see his parents at their place in the country, and he took the opportunity to listen to a clutch of demos. He liked Billy's, picking up on 'the enthusiasm and the vibe. I especially liked "The Busy Girl Buys Beauty". Having been involved with Roy Harper and The Clash, I'd been aware of singer-songwriters, and I guess I had become a lyric man rather than a music man.'

Jenner vowed to himself he'd get back in touch with the bogus TV repairman.

Better, he ventured down to the Tunnel Club to catch Billy play. There's no venue too obscure or too far away for a good A&R, even if Jenner wasn't a particularly good one – he committed the cardinal A&R sin and turned up just as the artist he was there to see had reached his last two numbers. However, the atmosphere inside the pub was tangibly electric, and Jenner's radar sensed that something was in the air. He took in Billy's last couple of songs, made a mental note of the buzz, and took care on his way out to ask somebody at the bar if Billy had been any good (evergreen A&R stand-by). The answer was an unequivocal yes, so Jenner left the Tunnel satisfied that his hunch was correct. The bloke on the tape had something.

More spooky coincidence: the reason the Tunnel's audience were so wired was that someone had just knocked a pint glass off a table and, following the sound of breaking glass, everyone was waiting for the fight to start, including Billy. This air of tension did not dissipate for the remainder of his set. And the punter who Jenner consulted at the bar? Katy Spurrell. The space hardware was evidently lined up in Billy Bragg's favour that night.

As he left, Jenner made his pledge to Billy: 'We must do something, however trivial.'

By the end of 1982, Billy had moved out of his mum's to a new base in Southfields, near Wimbledon (Katy was house-sitting there for some friends of hers who'd gone to Africa). On the map, it's not much closer to the action than Barking, but it *felt* more central.

Even though it was a large house, Billy and Katy never had the heating on full, and as a result the warmest room was the bathroom, where the hot water tank was. There was a small vanity table in there, which meant that Billy could use the room as his study and write songs. He remembers Katy banging on the door wanting to use the bathroom while he was in the throes of writing 'Between The Wars'. 'She just doesn't understand,' moaned the tortured artist, forced to write the last verse out on Wimbledon Common ('I'm surprised it didn't turn out like the Wombles').

Wiggy remembers taking food parcels round to the refugees in Southfields: 'They were going through their starvation days.'

Because there was simply no Charisma money forthcoming, Billy was caught between a rock and hard place. 'He wasn't doing what was "happening",' Jenner explains. He knew that they would have to find a more wily way of getting a Billy Bragg record out than simply finding the funds and paying for it: 'If you can get a tape done,' he told Billy, 'I'll put it out.' He was out on a limb with his belief in Billy, and needed a co-visionary. Jeff Chegwin turned out to be that soldier. Bearing in mind Charisma's interest, Chappell stumped up a special one-off publishing deal, which basically meant three days in their demo studio at Park Street – and no money. To Billy it was like winning the pools, and it solved Peter Jenner's financial niggles. Between Chappell and Charisma, he could make a record.

'The principle that you had to spend an enormous amount of money was wrong,' reasons Jenner. 'So we came up with the mini-album for £2.99. If you can put out a twelve-inch for £2.99, why not put out an album with seven tracks on it? Same piece of vinyl.' He made Billy an offer.

There would be no contract. PolyGram would pay for the pressing. Chappell would look after the recording costs. Jenner passed the artwork through as petty cash. He aimed to cover his arse with £500 he had left over from what has since passed into Bragg folklore as a Gregory Isaacs record, but may have been something else entirely.

Jenner drafted Billy a letter, dated 21 January 1983, on Charisma headed notepaper:

'Dear Billy, this is to confirm our intention to release some tracks of yours which you will be doing at Chappell's expense. We expect to release, unless it is indescribably ghastly, a record of some sort between four and twelve tracks long depending on what you come back with. We would own the record for the world and would pay a royalty of eight per cent, rising to nine per cent after 10,000 sales and ten per cent after 50,000 sales. Hope this reflects our discussion and I look forward to hearing the tapes.'

Booked to go into Chappell on 2 February for those three days, Billy performed his last gig at the Tunnel the night before. He was supporting a band called Shark Taboo. He played his songs to a total of eight people in the bar ('not uncommon'). He finished up, collected his money, and he and

Wiggy, who'd driven him down, were preparing to leave – at which point the entire audience got onstage. Shark Taboo *were* the audience. Too embarrassed to go, Billy and Wiggy sat down to offer their moral support to these fellow travellers round the U-bend of rock'n'roll. Mercifully, after just two songs, the barman told them to get off, as they were bothering the customers in the other bar.

Billy Bragg had, he felt, done his time.

On 2, 3 and 4 February, between 1 p.m. and 6 p.m. at Park Street Studio, Billy recorded what would be his debut album. As with the Gilmour House dry run, he just played his proven live set over and over again, this time in a soundproof booth with in-house producer Oliver Hitch pressing record and stop. There was no mixing, they just ran it straight on to quarter-inch tape.

Billy recalls doing thirteen versions of 'A New England'.

He takes his hat off to Jeff Chegwin, who was 'enthusiastic and encouraging' throughout, if unable to express his appreciation at the end of the three days, having just had his wisdom teeth out.

'Really good!' he mumbled through a broken mouth.

'Nobody else there gave a shit,' Billy reckons. 'They didn't know what the fuck I was on about.'

Not a problem. He'd found two men at two separate companies who knew exactly what the fuck he was on about, and were willing to sidestep corporate consensus and chuck Billy Bragg a few scraps. Without Chegwin and Jenner, Billy would be wandering around Wimbledon Common telling passers-by that he'd had his tape reviewed in *Melody Maker* and coulda been a contender.

On the subject of which, uplifted by the stirrings in the record industry, Billy continued to push his nose up against the media's window. Not about to let his first print admirer off the hook, Billy pestered Adam Sweeting for a follow-up review or an article to legitimise his quest.

This has been a recurring theme: all the way through the Flying Tigers and Riff Raff, Billy has striven for conventional legitimacy, be it the band's 'advertising debut', or the first gig in Hornchurch, or the keenly clutched copies of *Cosmonaut*. For a hardened music press reader, these are the given points of reference, and it would take Billy a few years before he realised that achievement on his own terms was more important to him than the orthodox requirements of the music biz.

Adam Sweeting arranged to meet Billy and interview him for possible publication at a later, unspecified date (after all, Billy had no product out to tie in with a feature, and that's the way the supposedly alternative press worked). On the bus there, Billy was bursting with excitement and nerves at the prospect of talking into a tape recorder, and wrote down all the things he wanted to say, so as not to waste this first crack at bending the world's ear. The singer and the writer met at a pub near the British Museum. The interview went well. Billy even ran through his checklist in the toilet midway through, and was, of course, duly outraged that *Melody Maker* didn't print it all when the piece ran in April.

Before that though, during the interminable limbo period between the recording of the album and the day it came out (five and a half months), Billy went back to Peterborough to play The Glasshouse at the Key Theatre. It was a modest lunchtime gig ('A bar and food are available and accompanied children are welcome'), but the local press treated him as a returning local hero. 'Well known locally,' said the *Classified Standard*, 'Riff Raff became a regular feature on the Peterborough music scene.'

Billy played on after the bar closed, and was invited back in June. 'A selection of his songs have already been recorded for release in the near future,' noted Cheryl Przybyl in her Pop Scene column in the *Peterborough Evening Telegraph*. (In June, she was still talking about it in the future tense, saying the album was 'due for release any time now'.)

Back in London, Billy played three nights at the Latchmere pub in Battersea, performing two sets a night. One night, between the two sets, an A&R from CBS records made himself known and said, 'Very entertaining, Bill, but do I hear a hit single?' He might as well have tweaked Billy's nose. Jenner had never asked him about hit singles.

In *Melody Maker* dated 26 March, Mick Mercer reviewed a Spy Vs Spy gig at the Moonlight Club in West Hampstead supporting two-piece Re-Set, in front of what Mercer calculated was 'a motley two dozen' people. It was a

PA-stacked-on-beer-crates sort of place with posters advertising gigs by Blurt, Play Dead and The Impossible Dreamers. 'Billy The Kid could enjoy himself playing to one person, let alone 30,' ran the review. 'What a cool nerve! What a voice! The night belonged to Old Bill. Dull he wasn't.' (Mercer, later willingly pigeon-holed as the country's leading expert on goth music, had written the only ever national feature on Riff Raff in *Zig Zag*. Sympathetic souls continually hove in and out of view.)

A week later, Sweeting's interview appeared, under the headline 'The Climate Of Reason', and accompanied by a three-column photograph by Tom Sheehan confirming that he was still Billy Bleach. Overenthusiastically announcing that the album was coming out in May, Sweeting expertly described Billy as 'part stand-up comedian, part musical flying picket'. Among the quotes Billy did manage to get into print were a confession to buying *Smash Hits* religiously, some well-expressed fears for the welfare state and details of his Spandau Ballet epiphany (seeing them perform 'Chant No. 1' on *Top Of The Pops* and feeling that punk was truly dead).

It was the last time he'd use the name Spy Vs Spy.

He may have been in a music paper at last, but his album was trapped in the ether somewhere between Chappell in Marble Arch and Charisma in Wardour Street (above the old Marquee club); a pleasant little stroll apart down London's busy Oxford Street, or three short stops on the tube. Billy found himself bouncing between the two a great deal during April, May and June. 'It seemed to take for ever,' he says, recalling a knot of dread every time he stepped out of Marble Arch tube, for fear that this was the time they'd tell him, Sorry, the record's not actually coming out. 'I was so close to getting my hands on that record and going and doing it,' he says. 'But I didn't have any kudos at either company, they had much more important things to do.'

In April and May, Billy Bragg did his first gigs up North: at The Gallery in Manchester, and at a twenty-fifth birthday party for a bloke he knew called Dave C in Liverpool at the Warehouse. His initiation to Liverpool was beset with stereotypical trouble. Katy drove him up there and duly had her car broken into during the soundcheck. Billy remembers two coppers taking down all the details out in the street, with Katy in tears, when the party's host came out and said 'You're on.' There's nothing like centring yourself before a show, and that was nothing like it. (Dave C's now a sheep farmer.)

In June, having acquired a booking agent, 'the fabulous' Nigel Morton, Billy went out on his first support tour with Incantation; as he describes them, 'musos pretending to be from the Andes', they were still cashing in on their one hit from December '82, 'Cacharpaya'. Though they were ill matched, Billy's piggyback with the 'Cantation took him to such civic meccas as the Towngate Centre in Basildon, the Hatfield Forum and the Theatre Royal, Plymouth.

Being a solo performer was already proving useful. Letting the train take the strain, Billy Bragg was infinitely more mobile than any other support band in the country, requiring no parking space at the venue, just the one microphone and no roadies. This would become more of a marketing angle in time, but for now, it was sheer economics. Guitar on his back, Roland Cube amplifier in one hand, train ticket in the other, he was the rock'n'roll equivalent of a certain Italian vermouth: anytime, anyplace, anywhere. 'Woe betide if I broke a string.'

Peter Jenner describes Billy as 'quite a solitary person', which is what he believes made that first flurry of gigs so achievable. 'He's very happy to be on his own, sitting in a car, in a hotel room, reading the paper, going for a walk, going shopping – he doesn't feel the need to have people all around him.'

He had, incidentally, parted company with the drum machine due to technical differences. There was no love lost between man and box, but Peter Jenner is happy to take credit for splitting them up: 'That was the one thing I suggested. It was very Spandau Ballet – if you're going to do a drum machine, do it properly. It was a Mickey Mouse drum machine.'

But where is it now? (Wiggy's got it, actually.)

On 1 July 1983, the wait was over. *Life's A Riot With Spy Vs Spy*, the debut long-player by Billy Bragg, was released on Utility/Charisma, with 'Pay no more than £2.99' emblazoned on the sleeve. 1,500 copies had been pressed. Jeff Chegwin would handle the plugging (i.e. getting the record into the right hands in radioland), Charisma's in-house PR

Lee Ellen Newman would scare up some press and Billy himself mucked in with a bit of both. Jenner gave him 25 copies of the album and sent him out to do his own promo.

The trade magazine *Music And Video Week* announced the formation of the Utility label, the first act of political union between Billy and the man called PJ. Utility was described as 'a label for the new age of austerity'. In interview, Jenner made an unusually ideological case for what was just a record company label imprint: 'It seems obvious that the record industry has to come to terms with the colossal scale of unemployment, especially for young people, and the consequent shortage of readies. The reaction, up to now, has been to brutalise and decimate sales and releases by non-chart artists. At Charisma, we want to fight this. Our philosophy at Utility is that it is the idea, the song, the personality, the talent that matters, not the technology, the hype or the styling.' One can easily imagine 'Land Of Hope And Glory' playing in the background to this rousing speech. He finished by saying that the Billy Bragg album, 'in both price and quality, is a foretaste of lots more to come'.

It was, as Lou Reed later sang, the beginning of a great adventure.

Andy Kershaw at Radio Aire in Leeds was the first DJ to write to Charisma and express his interest. The Rochdale-born headmaster's son was formerly Leeds University's upstart ents sec (he booked Iron Maiden, Duran Duran, The Clash and UB40 – and failed his degree) and was now hosting a late-night alternative show in John Peel mould called *Uneasy Listening*, spinning a very similar musical mix to the one he became famous for on Radio 1, the World Service and ultimately Radio 3. He also put together his own blues show. 'I suppose for that station it was pretty radical,' he says.

Kershaw actually rescued *Life's A Riot* from the station's reject bin. He was paid so little he couldn't even afford to go to the pub at lunchtimes, so instead he would sit in the record library and sift through a huge box (the kind washing machines come in). 'If it wasn't Elton John or Lionel Ritchie they threw it in there and gave it to charities,' he recalls. 'I used to do half my programme from that box.' The sleeve of *Life's A Riot* caught Kershaw's eye: 'When I dug around, there were about four copies of this bugger in there. So I picked up the lot and took them home. That night I put the needle on the record and "A New England" came on, and I know it's a cliché, but I can genuinely say that it changed my life. I would not be sitting here doing what I'm doing now, I wouldn't even be living in London, if I'd not pulled that record out of the box that afternoon. I just loved the simplicity and directness of it, the attack and the percussive quality of the guitar.'

Kershaw had run into Pete Jenner when he booked The Clash and Ian Dury at Leeds University, and found him 'a gentleman in a business of rogues and ill-mannered loud-mouths'. He wrote to Charisma not realising that Jenner was involved and declared *Life's A Riot* 'the best record I've heard in years', signing off, 'more power to your plectrum'. Kershaw and Billy met in London at a café called Sandwich Scene, along with Kershaw's mate Dave Woodhead who would later play brass on Billy's records. They clicked. Soon, Kershaw had Billy playing live on his show, and secured him some gigs through promoter John Keenan in Leeds, always offering him floorspace for the night. The bond was immediate.

Getting airplay on the Peel show was the Holy Grail. And it happened through a delicious mixture of chance and in-genuity. Jeff Chegwin played in the Chappell football team, once a week after work in Hyde Park, and Billy occasionally lent them his good right foot. One Wednesday evening, they were all standing around post-match having cans of beer and listening to Radio 1 on somebody's car radio with the doors open when John Peel dropped in during David 'Kid' Jensen's show, saying he'd do anything for a mushroom biryani. Chegwin spotted a gold-plated plugging moment. He and Billy drove over to where Radio 1 broadcast from – Egton House in the shadow of Broadcasting House – and took a mushroom biryani they'd just bought on Oxford Street into reception. Peel was an old hand, well aware of plugger's bullshit, and accustomed to a steady stream of nutters in the lobby, but to his credit he came down in person and gratefully accepted the vegetable biryani. Billy and Chegwin asked him to listen to their record in return. It's what's known as currying favour.

All concerned tuned in later that night, and were rewarded for their quick-thinking: Peel thanked Billy for the biryani, said he would've played the record *anyway*, and proceeded to spin 'The Milkman Of Human Kindness' at the wrong speed (it was cut at 45 rpm for better sound quality, and sounds a bit like a scary monster at 33). It was clearly time for some bright spark to invent CD.

This was Billy Bragg's first ever play on national radio. The biryani scam was even reported in the gossip column of pop magazine *No. 1*.

The first reviews came in dribs and drabs. On 21 July, *City Limits*, the lefty London listings magazine, paired *Life's A Riot* with the new album by rockin' anarcho-syndicalists Crass, *Yes Sir, I Will*, also underpriced at £2.75 (hence the connection – for a comparison, Paul Young's *No Parlez* album came out in the same week and cost £3.99, while Big Country's *The Crossing* was £4.79). The review by Dave Hill said that Billy's album contained 'simple, poignant, even delightful paeans to various unobtainables', and that it ought to 'touch anyone whose blood is warm'.

Robin Denselow, in the *Guardian* on the same day, was more cautious: 'Nothing extraordinary, but this could be an interesting label to watch.'

A week later, and *Sounds* became the first of the three music inkies to get a review out, written by Garry Bushell – these days a self-styled tabloid attack-columnist and 'political correctness'-baiter, then a music hack and reformed SWP member with a stiffy for so-called 'Oi!' bands (Cockney-esque skinheads of sometimes questionable politics). He gave the album three and a half stars out of five: 'Bill's no maudlin seer; he's closer to a busking Paul Weller. He ain't gonna make *Top Of The Pops* but at three notes for seven songs, his album's well worth your attention.' (Bushell would interview Billy for *Sounds* in October, in which he compared him to an aforementioned punk poet: 'Patwick Fitzgewaldkins he ain't, mate.')

Billy was invited to record his first session for John Peel – an important stepping stone for new faces, up there with first *NME* feature and, if things really took off, first *Top Of The Pops*. The news came as Billy returned from a gig up North: Katy met him at the train station and told him that Peel personally had been on the phone. 'This was the Crown Jewels!' Billy says. He went into the BBC's Maida Vale studios on 27 July, and taped seven songs. It was such a special occasion, Billy went wild and took a taxi up there. Like any wet-behind-the-ears musician, he was disappointed that John Peel wasn't actually *at* the recording session (Maida Vale is miles away from Egton House, miles away from anywhere) and flabbergasted that he also got paid – £150, thank you very much. He wrote Peel a thank-you note, and the session was broadcast on 3 August. He was still signing on at this stage, but not for much longer.

On 6 August, better late than never, *Melody Maker* joined the Billy Bragg cuttings file, with a review by Adam Sweeting (now a long-standing fan, he lamented the omission of both 'The Cloth' and the drum machine). *Record Mirror* followed (four stars out of five), then the *Sunday Times* ('Paul Weller meets Jilted John!'), and that was it. For now.

Peter Jenner went on holiday in August. When he returned to work, he 'got the pink slip'. Charisma were letting him go.

This was a blessing in disguise – the disguise being a beard and some oversized teeth, for the man behind his career change was the neo-hippy entrepreneur Richard Branson. These days, he runs trains, planes and private health and social care providers (when he isn't suing an underfunded NHS for failing to let Virgin have an £82m contract); in the early eighties, it was just his little corner of the record business: mail order, shops, label. The first Virgin record store was opened in 1970, and the label was launched in 1973 off the back of then-nineteen-year-old Mike Oldfield's magnum opus *Tubular Bells* (which went on to sell over ten million). Despite the label's bell-bottomed beginnings it astutely managed to keep its cool during and after punk, signing the Sex Pistols from 'God Save The Queen' until the bitter end, then The Skids, The Members and XTC. It is difficult to imagine now, but when Branson paid £15,000 for the Pistols, his was a truly independent label, with no shareholders and no US money. As Jon Savage says in *England's Dreaming*, '[Malcolm] McLaren now had to deal with a company head younger than him and equally ruthless. Branson's appearance belied his character. Despite the long hair and the air of woolliness, Branson had never really lived the hippie lifestyle.'

In 1983, in a puff of cheap incense, Virgin swallowed Charisma, thereby inheriting the bankable Peter Gabriel, the bankable Genesis and the not-yet-bankable Billy Bragg (they'd shifted only a modest one thousand copies of *Life's A Riot*). The Charisma name was dissolved and the Mad Hatter logo laid off. Peter Jenner wasn't chuffed with the takeover – he was no fan of Branson. 'I'd never liked him. Flash bugger, he didn't understand music – but you don't need to understand music, you need to understand marketing, which he does. He's good at that. He has an instinct for what the people want, which I *don't* have.'

Jenner was seen as a hangover from the label's PolyGram-linked past ('I was a PolyGram person, I was the enemy'), and the inevitable 'restructuring' saw him out of a job. Billy remembers going in and helping him clear out his office, at which point Jenner made him a logical offer: 'I can't be your record company any more, I'd better be your manager.'

Management was what PJ knew best. He was a fixer, not a desk jockey. So, in September 1983, with his wife Sumi and Ian Richards, he founded Sincere, a management umbrella that would handle Billy Bragg, Hank Wangford the country and western gynaecologist, and The Opposition, a rare band Jenner had signed to Charisma; they were, to borrow a rock biz cliché, big in France ('They could have been up there with the U2s and Simply Reds, filling up the stadiums,' Jenner reckons. 'But their lead guitarist had a problem playing live').

Sensing that Utility wasn't going to last long under the Virgin regime, Jenner started scouting round for another record company to put out Billy's records. Not a sniff. But his belief in Billy's music – and in the sound logic of Utility – was rock steady: 'This was still the early days of Thatcherism. I felt it was becoming clear that there was going to be a fucking huge recession, and while everyone else was doing glamour and glitz, the new romantic bit, I thought that someone going round being a bit Dylanish, doing social-realism would go down well. Cheap, go-anywhere, do-anything. He did it. But I suppose *my* claim to fame is that I knew there'd be a market for it. I've often had these thoughts and I'm usually wrong. On this one I happened to be right.'

While Jenner hunted around for some new sponsors, Billy continued to put himself about. On 30 August, he trekked down to Penzance to join a frankly bizarre all-star bill containing Meat Loaf, Chuck Berry, Aswad and a kind of almost-10cc (they were minus founders Kevin Godley and Lol Creme, and in fact two months away from splitting completely). The day was called Penwith '83, 'Cornwall's largest ever open-air concert', and Billy was playing for train fare only – which was £90, as he'd travelled all the way from Edinburgh, where he was scatter-gunning the Fringe Festival. (Scotland–Cornwall–Scotland was a typically impractical itinerary for the furiously available Billy Bragg, and peanuts compared to some of the zigzags he would later pull off in Europe.)

Sadly, Cornwall's largest ever open-air gig hadn't pulled Cornwall's largest ever crowd: it failed to break even at the gates. After playing his set (and securing Chuck Berry's autograph), Billy discovered that nobody was getting paid. He begged the deflated organisers to reimburse at least his £90, which they eventually did, cash in hand. He hopped back on the train to Edinburgh and put it all behind him; at least now secure in the knowledge that he and Wiggy could play Chuck Berry better than Chuck Berry.

Billy's relationship with Katy 'had gone pear-shaped', and as a result of the ensuing romantic and domestic uproot, it felt as if he never really came back from the Edinburgh Festival. He stayed in 'a lovely big house' with a friend called Rose, and from this agreeable base he played virtually anywhere with a bar and a play on, sometimes twice a day, sometimes twice a night ('I made sure I was in everybody's face'). On a typical evening, you could see *The Accidental Death Of An Anarchist* at the Little Lyceum, then catch a Canadian folk outfit called Stringband and Billy Bragg at the Theatre Workshop (bar open till 2 a.m.). There really is no place like it for three weeks.

Edinburgh '83 was good to Billy. The Peel Session was coincidentally repeated while he was up there and improved his profile on the spot ('the power of Peel cannot be overestimated'), he made an awful lot of useful contacts and broke an awful lot of guitar strings. As far as Billy is concerned, from there on, he was a professional musician.

Billy Bragg was go.

7. GO!

Signing off, signing up, 1983

nipple n. the small conical projection in the centre of each breast
nirvana n. final release from the cycle of reincarnation attained by
extinction of all desires and individual existence
Nissen hut n. a military shelter of semicircular cross section made of
corrugated steel

Collins English Dictionary

The Billy Bragg story-so-far was told, in précis, many times over at the business end of 1983, from *Melody Maker, NME* and *Sounds* to *Zig Zag, Record Mirror, No. 1* and *Time Out*. In December he told it to *Melody Maker* for the second time. This was the way it was going to be, as Billy graduated from nuisance sitting in reception to centre of attention.

A pop career is like a damp pile of twigs – it sits there for ages, unloved and pathetic, and then suddenly it catches light, turning into a blazing, acrid-smelling bonfire within seconds, spreading warmth and orange light all around. It takes only one bright spark to set it off.

At the beginning of the year, Billy hadn't even recorded his debut album. At the end of it, *Life's A Riot* was Number One in the indie charts, Number 44 in the real charts and rising, and Number Three in *NME*'s esteemed Vinyl Finals, the writers' albums of the year. How did *that* happen?

It goes without saying that the record itself was a contributing factor, but this is pop music, whose roadside is littered with good records; even good records handbuilt by robots. In its favour, regardless of whether it was your cup of tea or not, *Life's A Riot* was pure honesty on vinyl; its sheer, unabashed humanity crystallised down for all to hear. As music became ever more technical and ready polished, here was a big lump of wood. The combination of Billy's original brainwave and Jenner's marketing foresight put *Life's A Riot* in a unique rack. There had been punk rock, there had been folk, there had been folk-rock and folk-pop, and there had been visionary singer-songwriters. There had been delta blues and urban blues, one-man bands and buskers. There had been politically charged music, and there had been love songs, but there had never been anything or anyone like Billy Bragg. Brutal yet tender, old-fashioned yet bang up to date, punky yet poetic – in the fine tradition of all the best innovative art, it was the precise cocktail of existing elements that made it new.

As such, the record stood apart. But again, plenty of music that has been different has wound up in the same bargain bin. So what was it that catapulted Billy Bragg to the front of the queue?

Partly, it was the man himself. In the same way that he'd made an instant impression on Peter Jenner, on Andrew Spurrell, on Adam Sweeting and on Lance Corporal Wood, he was not going to pass through the music biz and the media unnoticed. When he was interviewed by the press, he threw himself into the job. When an audience talked among themselves he heckled *them*. When he met music's foot soldiers – engineers, promoters, receptionists, PAs, photographer's assistants, radio producers, even students' union ents secs – he impressed them with his down-to-earth manner. He was self-effacing and helpful, humorous and talkative. He refused to recognise any hierarchy and treated everyone equally. Calling it a charm offensive makes it sound more planned than it actually was, but it meant that wherever Billy Bragg went, people remembered him.

Billy's affable personality, vital PR tool that it undeniably is, is no more manufactured than his Essex accent, but it has served him well down the years, especially in an industry where historically artists feel obliged to maintain a mask of cool.

It would be unkind to tar all rock musicians with the same brush, but, for the most part, when they are pushed into situations that involve contact with anyone outside their own cabal, protection of image becomes paramount. Up goes the shield of aloofness, ignorance or disdain. As a rule, the rocking'n'rolling classes are only erudite and forthcoming in song, if at all. Like star footballers who can talk only in handed-down television clichés, or politicians who are incapable of answering a yes-no question, it's a prerequisite of the job. If you're a rock star, you need only have opinions about yourself and other bands. If the generalisation sounds harsh, you have to work in the music press for a short time only to understand why Morrissey, the late, irate Mark E Smith and Happy Monday Shaun Ryder were always such evergreen favourites during the music papers' golden years – they could string a sentence together.

Billy Bragg falls into the same category. He's what's known in the trade as 'good for a quote', and if that sounds trivial, it usually is. You might say that Katie Hopkins and Nigel Farage are good for a quote (they don't even have to wait to be asked any more). But if you can cultivate a reputation in the media for being quoteworthy, they'll ask you back. And visibility is everything.

So Billy's fairly rapid ascent was down to a fine product and a friendly face. These were the raw materials, but, as the link with Peter Jenner had already proved, the perfect pop package needs delivering, and that's where the record company comes in.

Be it a monolithic, multinational conglomerate, a cottage outfit based in a bedroom, or the latter bankrolled by the former, the record company ensures that The Product is available in The Shops (or these days, that The MP3 is available on iTunes). Otherwise you're whistling in the dark.

Back in July, Billy had been photographed for *Sounds*, by snapper Virginia Turbett. It took place at Turbett's house, against a white wall for studio-style effect, and Billy was coerced into wearing some daft wraparound shades. At the shoot, Billy was doing his usual bit, vibing everyone up, giving it some patter while the photographer changed films; the equivalent of singing 'I'm Forever Blowing Bubbles' to fill in the gaps. One of Turbett's friends was there, Alison Macdonald, who came away with a copy of *Life's A Riot* on cassette, touched by the hand of gawd-blimey.

It so happened that Alison's brother Andy, aged 25 and two years her junior, had started his own independent record label in January, Go! Discs, based in one room in his Shepherd's Bush flat. She requested a copy of Billy's album for Go!, and sure enough, it arrived on the mat the next day. Macdonald remembers his sister enthusing about Billy: 'She was quite lit up by him, saying, You *have* to meet this character, there's an aura about him. She was obviously very affected by him.'

Macdonald played Side 1 of *Life's A Riot* six times in a row and was knocked out by it: 'My mind was made up. I definitely wanted to work with him.'

An Arsenal fan with a law degree, Macdonald hails from Redruth in Cornwall. He worked as an English teacher in Southampton, lived in Sheffield for a while where he compiled crosswords, then came to London to work for Stiff records as a press officer. Stiff, founded in 1976 by two pub-rock managers Jake Riviera (who handled Nick Lowe) and Dave Robinson (Graham Parker), had risen from new wave curiosity shop to home-of-the-hits status thanks to Ian Dury & The Blockheads, Madness, Jona Lewie and Lene Lovich, but it had peaked commercially in 1981, when turnover exceeded £3 million. Macdonald was in the PR seat in 1982, by which time it was all Tracey Ullman and The Belle Stars. The age-old company slogan 'If it ain't Stiff, it ain't worth a fuck' was losing credibility.

At the end of 1982, after eleven months at Stiff, a couple of Macdonald's mates from Sheffield who'd been in unsuccessful gloom-rock band Clock DVA, formed a new group called The Box, and they wanted somebody to put their first single out. Macdonald, in his own words, 'took a flyer', and used his £750 savings to set up Go! Discs. He knew about press and marketing, and setting up your own label is a very speedy way of finding out about distribution and manufacturing. He soon signed another band, a duo from West London called The Bic (in fact, he signed only acts beginning with

B in the first year). Neither act had Number One hits, but they brushed past the indie charts, nabbed a bit of press (perhaps unsurprisingly, given the boss's previous job) and an early label history, written by Macdonald, declared that The Box's first three releases 'showed a healthy profit, which was immediately ploughed back into developing other acts', and The Bic's 'Musica Pop' single made 'a few bob thanks to good export sales on the twelve-inch'. Macdonald's pioneer spirit was not about to desert him.

In August 1983, he'd heard the artist he wanted, and set about procuring him. Pete Jenner's first memory of Andy Macdonald is of 'a mouthy geezer who kept knocking on my door'. This is not as damning as it sounds, for Macdonald was nothing if not persistent. When he wants something, people say, he gets it. He even travelled up to the Edinburgh Festival and continued his pestering campaign.

'Edinburgh was the first time we realised he was a fucking nuisance and wasn't going to go away,' Jenner recalls, in the nicest possible way. This coincided with rejection for Billy Bragg from just about every major record company, and some minor ones, so he went to see Macdonald in his tiny 'office'. Macdonald got friends to phone in while Jenner was there, to simulate the busy hum of commerce.

'Pete had a lot more experience in the music biz than I had,' Macdonald admits, but nevertheless the puppy dog and the wise old owl entered into a 'mutual understanding' that they would do something together, however trivial.

After Edinburgh, unable to go back to Katy and the warmest room in Wimbledon, Billy went to stay with Wiggy in his new Barratt home in Beardsley Way, Acton. He was never much of an imposition as, by now, touring had become Billy Bragg's middle name.

Life's A Riot was very much at the bottom of Charisma's priority list (Charisma would cease to exist by November), so Andy Macdonald set about trying to relieve them of it. Meanwhile, Billy continued to gig, and in doing so, finally caught the desired attention of the *NME*. They hadn't reviewed the LP even in August, but in September, they compensated. Billy's first notice was for a gig at a club called New Merlin's Cave in London's seedy King's Cross.

The writer, who went by the *nom de punk* of X Moore, but was called Chris Dean, admitted in his piece that he'd 'stumbled across Billy Bragg'. This was no PR coup, but an *NME* enthusiast getting blown away by a new artist. Dean marvelled that Billy played for 105 minutes (the main act hadn't turned up and he did every song he knew to fill the time). He called him 'a man worth having infringe pop's sacred airspace'.

They do say that if you can't *do*, teach, and if you can't teach, teach gym. It's the same in music. If you can't do, form a band. If you can't make it in a band, write about those who can. As a rule, rock journalists are failed musicians. (This is such a truism that *not* having been in a crap band carries quite a cachet among hacks.) X Moore was different, in that his band hadn't failed. They were The Redskins, quite a talking point in the mid-80s for their fierce mod-rock-soul and immovable Socialist Worker Party views. They signed to PolyGram's Decca label in 1984, and had a Number 33 hit with 'Bring It Down (This Insane Thing)', which, compared with the SWP's mainstream political impact, was akin to storming Whitehall. Although Billy Bragg's pure socialism would never tally with The Redskins' hardline hard-left stance, they formed a vague alliance in the benefit years to follow.

It was another SWP tub-thumper who picked up the Billy baton at the *NME* – Steven Wells, better known as 'Swells', also writing under a pseudonym (Susan Williams), and a performer by night (Seething Wells, a stand-up poet). This was a boom time for the so-called 'ranting poets', an inevitable by-product of punk's get-up-and-do-it ethic. They were angry youngish men playing at being Doctor Marten's own town criers and – like Billy – proving a cheap-and-cheerful booking for pub and student promoters. Swells, a hot-headed Swindon intellectual who'd cultivated a spotless prole accent in Leeds, was Billy's next supporter.

Swells recalls his first meeting: 'I was on a Right To Work march. This stiff-spined young chap came up to me and said, "Er, this is a tape of my music, I thought you might want to listen to it." He gave me this tape *of Life's A Riot With Spy Vs Spy*. I took it home to Leeds, and, like you do when you get loads of tapes from people, I stuck it in the machine, listened to two seconds and thought, Fuck this! It's some Cockney whining over an acoustic guitar! I taped over it almost immediately with something good off the radio, probably John Peel.'

Swells had only just started writing for the *NME* in August, but has no idea how Billy knew this, as his girly pseudonym had been designed to put detractors off his scent while he/she wrote positive reviews of Seething Wells. 'So they commissioned me as the *NME*'s first secret transvestite writer to review the Leeds Futurama.'

Futurama was an annual two-day alternative music festival in Swells' adopted Leeds. The 1983 line-up, held at the Queens Hall on 17–18 September, included such rising art-rockers as The Comsat Angels, The Armoury Show and The Chameleons, plus the unknown Smiths, gothic monstrosities like Death Cult and Killing Joke, and, as an ironic flourish, The Bay City Rollers. Billy Bragg was very low down on Saturday's bill under 'special guests', next to another whining poet John Cooper Clarke. It was, as Swells noted, 'hairdressers' hell'. He arrived, not in the best frame of mind:

'I'd just had the shit kicked out of me by the NF who stormed out of the Scarborough pub and beat the crap out of me and Little Brother, another poet.

'There were lots of Scottish bands and it was just dreadful – the early 1980s equivalent of Ned's Atomic Dustbin. And then, onstage, is this git, this Cockney geezer with a huge nose. He moved like a Thunderbirds puppet and talked in short, clipped, army-like sentences, and he just thrashed the shit out of his guitar and sang his fucking heart out. It was totally punk rock! The stark minimalism gave me an immediate stiffy, I just fell in love with the bloke. I scrawled all these words of sycophantic lust in my notebook.'

These words were honed into a review in the next week's *NME*: 'Salvation! Solo electronic guitarist Billy Bragg tears asunder the guffy, grey clouds of doom and despondency with low slung, highly strung screaming riff backed tales of lost love, manic wimp whinery and political mistrust. A marbles-intact urban surfboy, a blistering volcano of passion, wit and style, he packed more light, shade and aggression into his twenty-minute set than all of tonight's posing Jack Dullards combined.'

Faithful Adam Sweeting was also at the Queens Hall, and concurred in *Melody Maker*, remarking that only Billy Bragg and The Armoury Show's Richard Jobson, formerly of The Skids, later a TV presenter and filmmaker, were 'big enough to wrench the perspective of the day out of the dead hand of passive acceptance and to mould it in his own image'.

It seems that the greyer his surroundings, the more Billy Bragg shone out like a beacon of England.

Meanwhile, over at the restructured Charisma, they'd installed a replacement for Peter Jenner, who was making it difficult for Andy Macdonald to extricate Billy's album from a label that couldn't care less about him. On the contrary, said the new A&R, 'He's a Charisma artist, we've got a lot of faith in him. We think he's got a great future.'

Macdonald offered them £1,500. 'That'll do nicely.'

And with that, Billy Bragg was transferred like a footballer from the cash-rich Premier League club to the up-and-coming Beazer Homes League side. (Football fans may wish to adjust the analogy to fit.)

It was Armistice Day, and the peace was about to be shattered. *Life's A Riot With Spy Vs Spy* was re-released but this time through Utility/Go! Discs on 11 November 1983, again for £2.99. The initial pressing was 5,000 copies.

At Charisma, it had almost been an unofficial release. At Go!, it was what they'd all been waiting for ('all' being Macdonald and his very first member of staff, Lesley Symons). Go! Discs had considerably less muscle than the major record companies – and indeed, less than most of the better-established indies – but it had a lot more heart and, as Woody Allen said, 'the heart is a resilient little muscle.' What happened next was a success story that would put Go! Discs on the map, and Billy Bragg all over it.

'Billy worked his nuts off,' recalls Macdonald. '*He* made the record a hit. He was grafting like crazy, all over the country. The ultimate mobile musician.'

The label may have been short staffed, but they had a roster of just three acts, and could throw every drop of their support behind one record, while bigger outfits have to prioritise. An extensive 21-date tour was announced (Billy's first properly organised nationwide live assault), and press coverage was generous. There were more album reviews – 'Buy it' said Johnny Waller in *No. 1*; 'It's a classic!' said *Zig Zag*; 'Will sell well' predicted trade mag *Music Week* – the *Sounds* feature ran, and Billy was booked to appear on the first edition of *The Tube*'s second, 25-week series.

Wearing a Clash-style cut-off shirt, he played surrounded by Newcastle's young dispossessed on 28 October. On the same show were The Eurythmics, Public Image Limited (giving Billy the chance to rub shoulders in the green room with John Lydon, former Sex Pistol), Paul Young and metal-bashers SPK. From there, he went off on tour, supporting either The Icicle Works, New Model Army or Richard Thompson, depending on what day of the week it was.

At that time Andy Kershaw lost his job at Radio Aire after a 'rethink' of the station's format. 'It was the same with all those commercial stations,' he says. 'When they were set up they all made grand promises to the IBA about the breadth of music they would cover, and when the financial reality hit them, they suddenly realised that me playing Television Personalities' EPs wasn't going to get them a huge audience, nor was me and a pile of old Muddy Waters records. So I was radically downsized.'

Ever resourceful, Kershaw duplicated a letter asking for a job, and sent out about 250 to everybody he could think of in the music business. At the bottom of the letter was a tear-off coupon bearing a passport photo of Kershaw's face ('like they have on the side of buses when somebody's won the pools') and two boxes to tick: one saying 'Yes! I would like to learn more about this exciting youth', the other saying 'No! We have no employment opportunities at the moment.' He got one reply, from Sincere management.

Having identified Kershaw as a kindred spirit, Jenner phoned him ('Can you drive, dear boy?') and he was duly hired to come down to London and help out in the Sincere office, and, when needed, act as road manager, driver and pal for Billy. They couldn't afford to pay him, but Pete and Sumi offered to put him up in their box room and feed him, which Kershaw saw as a generous offer. He would start in January.

Meanwhile, in a year bulging with firsts, the two-pronged support tour gave Billy his first ride in an aeroplane, not something he'd been looking forward to. It is one of the overriding ironies of the Billy Bragg Travels The World story: he's afraid of flying. This is God playing his joker.

It's like a heroin addict being afraid of needles. Here is a man whose very career is founded on gigging, yet one who imagines he is going to die in a hot metal tube every time he leaves the ground. It's not a rare affliction among musicians – apparently Robert Smith of stadium goths The Cure takes the QE2 to America now that he's famous enough to call the shots, and Paul Heaton of The Beautiful South adheres to a rigorous regime of lucky charm stroking whenever he taxis down a runway – but it does seem a cruel twist. On 3 November, Billy didn't even know how scared he was of flying as he boarded a short flight to Glasgow to play the Henry Africas club with The Icicle Works: 'I thought, I'd better find out if I can do this.'

Looking back, he wishes he'd gone *with* someone, who might've reassured him that the plane wasn't about to drop out of the sky when it got bumpy, and that was what it was *supposed* to sound like when the landing gear came down. On his own, Billy allowed his fertile artist's imagination to spill over, and looked on in terror as his coffee acted as a spirit level. He locked himself in the toilet, and read the Swells interview with him in that week's *NME* over and over again. Whatever gets you through the flight is all right.

Billy had supported a parade of almost-rans in his short career, but the October–November tour pitched him up against 'names' (Icicle Works were weeks away from the first Top Twenty hit, New Model Army were developing a loyal live following with their hob-nailed anthems and Thompson had been a British folk legend since the 60s, heyday of Fairport Convention).

'I never really clicked with New Model Army,' Billy recalls. 'At the time, they were very much a clique. It was like touring with a coven. And they did goth it a bit.' At the Tiffany's club in Leeds, he shared a dressing room with the trio, and the vintage vampire film *Nosferatu* was on the television – NMA insisted that all the lights go out while they watched it. Billy kept his neck covered up.

There was a typically Braggian mix-up in Manchester, when, booked to play the University with another ubiquitous shouty poet Attila The Stockbroker, he mistakenly turned up at the Polytechnic. Never one to miss an opportunity to plug in, he blagged a gig at the Poly, dashed over to the Uni to honour his original booking, then dashed back to the Poly to support Death Cult. All in a night's work. (Bottom of the bill at the Poly were a local band called The Frantic Elevators – lead singer: Mick Hucknall, later of Simply Red and the international jet set.)

Macdonald was present at many of these gigs, as if to prove how unlike a record company boss he was.

On the apparent dichotomy of supporting goth bands and old folkies, Billy told Swells in the *NME*, 'I want both those audiences and everyone in between.' On 10 November, Billy played with Thompson at the New Cross Venue in grotty south-east London, where he met his old economics teacher at the bar. The exchange went like this:

'Was that you up there, Bragg?'

'Yes, sir. That's what I do for a living.' 'Stop calling me sir and buy me a drink.'

On the final night of The Icicle Works leg in their home-town of Liverpool, Billy appeared with them on stage dressed in a gorilla costume for the conceptual finale. Possibly in response to The Smiths, who were making a name for them-selves by chucking fresh flowers around at gigs, The Icicle Works had collected a dozen bin bags full of leaves to have scattered around the stage by the gorilla. Unfortunately, Billy remembers with horror, the bags also contained 'old, hard bits of dog shit'. Not that he cared, he was inside a monkey suit.

While he was out there peddling, his wares got their biggest push to date. In the issue dated 19 November, the *NME* finally ran a review of *Life's A Riot* – the sort you couldn't buy. Billy had previously been up to the *NME*'s Carnaby Street office with an album under his arm, relying on Swells as his point of contact. He'd met X Moore, who subsequently listened to the record, picked up on the clenched fist of 'To Have And To Have Not' and decided to pen the review. It was the biggest of the lot, a five-column 'page lead', as they're known, headed 'BRAGG ART'.

'DOWN WITH MISERABLISM!' wrote X Moore (*his* capitals). 'When pop's operative word is WALLOW, when all around is flat INDULGENCE and the Gallup machines on high click gamely to the grim beat of the dollar, a man like Billy Bragg is a sparkling tonic. Be lifted by his AMBITION, laugh at his EXUBERANCE, trust him to make a fool of himself – Billy Bragg is some kind of wonderful.'

It is pertinent that the writer picked up on Billy as an alternative to the increasingly commercialised, wipe-clean pop status quo. By side-stepping both the available technology and the fast-track corporate infrastructure, Billy Bragg became an instant cause, a pocket revolutionary – music to the ears of the *NME*'s ardently politicised writing staff. As pop became more remote and its practitioners more unreal, Billy arrived on the doorstep and demanded they put the kettle on.

Neil Spencer, the *NME*'s editor at the time, reckons Billy's appearances at Carnaby Street were 'a complete managerial masterstroke, because nobody came round the office; musicians kept their distance. I remember Bananarama and Wham! came up in their earliest days, but in general you just didn't do it. Peter Jenner saw very astutely that if you met the musician, you were less likely to dis him. If you've met musicians, providing they're not awful people, then you realise that at the end of your cutting, witty prose there is another human being, and you may not feel quite so casual about putting him down. It wouldn't have worked if Billy hadn't been such a personable bloke, but of course he was.' Spencer became evangelistic about Billy. He even sent his PA Karen Walter home for the weekend with a copy of *Life's A Riot*, saying it was 'the most important record she'd hear all year'. Walter remembers taking it home to her mum's, and on first listen thinking, 'What on earth is this? Then I put it on at the right speed and realised what all the fuss was about.'

The fuss was snowballing.

'He was in the office all the time,' Walter recalls. 'It wasn't just his music, but his music reflected how most of the office felt about politics. He had a lot in common with the staff.'

'*Life's A Riot* was fantastically refreshing at that time,' says Spencer, summing up precisely the malaise that Billy had set out to detonate. 'By 1983, punk ideals had got pretty much lost, the idea of do-it-yourself, back-to-basics, take-no-crap was fast disappearing under a welter of double-breasted suits, cocktail hours and absurd and shallow glamour bands like Duran Duran and Spandau Ballet. And at the other extreme was a dreadful, Oxfam dreariness and fatalism summed up by people like New Order. You had bogus glamour on one side and bogus industrialism on the other.'

He recalls a pervasive sense of gloom at the paper. At the end of 1983, the writers were asked to pick Next Year's Big Thing, and one of them, Biba Kopf, wrote: 'The end of the world (please).'

'There was a feeling of defeat. Billy's record went right against all those ideas. It was true to the spirit of punk inasmuch as it was DIY and coming up fighting. It immediately stood out. And Barney Bubbles' design on the sleeve was very important, because record sleeves are a statement of intent.'

Bubbles was dear to the *NME*'s heart, as he'd designed their enduring, blocky logo. He was famous for his graphic record sleeve designs for Elvis Costello, Ian Dury and others (the Dury connection was how Jenner had drafted him in to work on *Life's A Riot*). Spencer goes as far as saying Bubbles 'was undoubtedly the most gifted designer of his generation'. The *Life's A Riot* artwork – utilitarian, simple, two-colour, based on the old Penguin book covers for 'classic' allusions – without a doubt played its part in Billy's early success. It was the kind of record you wanted to *have*. (When Billy revived the Utility imprint in 1988, the Bubbles template was used as a unifying label identity.)

'The early songs are as good as Bill's ever written,' maintains Spencer. '"St Swithin's Day", "A New England", these are evergreen songs.'

Things were looking up for Billy Bragg. Fame was on the counter and he was paying for it in sweat. While the press file grew, he was usually in transit – without the aid of a Transit van. In 1982, he'd done 28 gigs; in 1983, he clocked up 96. After that, he pulled his finger out.

Billy may have been getting pretty practised at the art of gigging, but this, coupled with an unforgiving itinerary, did not have the effect of blending one town into the next. There was always something to mark each gig date from the next – although perhaps none so vivid and unsavoury as what happened in Newcastle. It was during the November campaign, fireworks night, an unscheduled stopover to play at a rowdy, pissed student-only ball in the University.

The dressing room was a huge student common room with a telly (just the ticket for the football results), and Billy was buoyant enough not to care about the fact that he was sharing with three strippers: two women and a bloke. Thinking nothing of it, he went out and did the gig. Not having anywhere to go in Newcastle but back to his digs, he decided to stay for the main act. If only. The college rector got up onstage and announced to the pickled audience that the strippers would not be performing. A near-riot ensued, so Billy nipped back to the dressing room for his gear. It was locked. He banged on the door, demanding to be let into *his* dressing room. The door opened a crack, and he saw that the common room was full of students. The banned strippers were going to do the show right here.

It's worth stressing again that Billy knew no one in Newcastle, and had nowhere better to go. He sat down to enjoy the show (bit of harmless fun) and was forced by lack of available seats to sit in the front row.

'There are two things I remember,' he now recalls. 'The sound of the geezer's member thwacking against his belly and knees, which was much too close, and then this woman takes one of the bananas off the rider and puts it up her. I thought, if this is what college is all about, I should've gone! Anyway, she takes the banana out of herself and offers it to the front row. All these students go, Eeeeuurgh! I think, fuck it, and when it comes to me, I nearly bite her fingers off!'

Cue: a roar of approval from the undergraduate crowd. Billy cites beer intake in mitigation, and society is obviously to blame, but this unfortunate display was not allowed to fade from his memory. Months later, on 10 March 1984, Billy found himself doing a National Union of Students gig in Battersea Park. All of a sudden, mid-set, a banana was thrown onstage with a shout of 'Newcastle!' – the reference was lost to the majority of the audience, but Billy knew that somewhere out there in the sea of faces was a student from the North East with a good memory.

'There was a period when I could not play a student gig in the North East without a banana coming onstage, or someone shouting, "Banana!" They were still doing it during Red Wedge at Newcastle City Hall!'

A regrettable incident maybe, but it proved that Billy Bragg's audience were starting to follow him about. He was an attraction, and the significance was not lost on him: 'My people were out there. They were coming to see me, writing to me.'

Billy had played many a London date with Sincere's other white hopes The Opposition, but by December, rather embarrassingly, he started accidentally blowing them offstage. A gig at the Half Moon pub in South London's Herne Hill on 12 December was reviewed in both *Sounds* and *Melody Maker* ('Pity [Billy Bragg's] doting followers, who arrived in their buzzing droves, didn't have the decency to stay for the main act. Most of them left before the Oppos played a note').

It was like the scene in the film *Jaws* when Police Chief Brody sees the shark for the first time, and says, quietly, 'We're gonna need a bigger boat.' Billy Bragg was getting too big for support slots.

On 17 December, *Life's A Riot* topped *Melody Maker*'s indie charts, although at the time, indie charts were a bit hit-and-miss, relying on a random selection of specialist shops for their sales information (*Melody Maker*'s that week were supplied by Jumbo Records in Leeds). In the same week, Billy was Number Five in *NME*'s indie charts. But more importantly, the album had entered the real, national chart at 44. Here, he was competing with the big boys.

In the Christmas issue of *Sounds*, Billy was invited to write about life on the road, and his single O Level came in handy yet again: 'Oh, the joys of being a pop star. I think my amp-carrying arm is getting longer.' There were tips on following in his pioneering footsteps, and a look to the future that was either totally disingenuous or the talk of a man who had kept his head while all about him people were losing theirs:

'There's a possibility of going to America, but if that doesn't work out, well sod it, it's only a hobby.'

Thanks to the tireless commitment of Go! Discs, the unshakeable belief of Sincere, and all the hoopla over at the super-influential *NME*, Billy Bragg had a full-time job of work: seven-day week, unsociable hours, no company car, short-term contracts, no pension, no save-as-you-earn share scheme, and yet, the best job in the world.

Billy was invited to play the *NME*'s Christmas party ('Prance, Preen and Promenade' said the ticket) on 22 December. Karen Walter remembers that 'a few people were talking during his set and Neil was furious!'

Some kind of *NME* mascot (without the patronising tone that might go with such an honour), Billy found his album in the Vinyl Finals, beaten only by Tom Waits' oompah-epic *Swordfishtrombones* and at Number One, Elvis Costello's mighty *Punch The Clock* (which contained his heart-rending Falklands lament 'Ship-building'). 'Number Three was pretty good going,' says Billy. 'I was really proud of that.'

In the *Sunday Times*, academic Simon Frith named it as one of his Records Of The Year. On 31 December, none other than the *Daily Mirror* predicted fame for Billy Bragg in 1984: 'Excellent, if odd, solo performer from London.' Similar tips came from *Music Week* and the *Guardian*.

Only a hobby.

He was asked by one of the papers to sum up 1983: 'It was the year that I realised that the only place I could ever truly find nirvana was between nipples and Nissen Hut in a dictionary.'

8. A GREAT FRIEND OF DAVE GILMOUR'S

Take-off, 1984

I'm looking for a ride

David Bowie, '1984'

Beware the savage roar of 1984. This was the year that the future arrived in Britain: an overused graphic of Big Brother is watching you. George Orwell set his nightmare vision *Nineteen Eighty-Four* in that year because it was written in 1948, but what the heck, it was as good a reason as any for twelve months of designer paranoia. After all, scientists discovered the Aids virus, the Soviet Union boycotted the Los Angeles Olympics, the year-long miners' strike began and American nuclear warheads were strategically placed all over the English countryside.

'We shall abolish the orgasm,' promises torturer O'Brien in Orwell's book. 'Our neurologists are at work on it now.' No wonder Frankie Goes To Hollywood and their multi-sexual apocalypto-disco took off in 1984.

London's Institute of Contemporary Arts, rock's foremost ponceteria, got the bandwagon moving, staging a nine-day New Year Rock Week from 23 December 1983 to 7 January 1984. Orwell's Big Brother glared out of the tickets, posters, flyers and stage backdrop. The second Thursday night gig, 5 January, saw the first real example of what shall be dubbed Braggmania, when Billy performed on the same bill as The Redskins and the little-known Bronski Beat, featuring a falsetto-voiced Jimmy Somerville. (Also playing during that bonanza week of ICA gigs were Prefab Sprout, Gene Loves Jezebel and Modern English, plus Einsturzende Neubaten's Concerto For Voice And Machinery. It was not a week of comedy.)

Billy knew in his bones that this was his coming of age: 'None of this bollocking about playing the Half Moon and the Rock Garden, this was a proper gig that got proper reviews by everyone.'

'The audience was like putty in his hands,' observed Paul Bradshaw in the *NME* a week later, just one of the predicted umpteen reviews of the ICA shows. 'Braggmania is sweeping the nation,' spied Adam Sweeting at the *Melody Maker*.

Also in January, Andy Macdonald borrowed some money from his uncle in order to pay for another pressing of *Life's A Riot*. It was a small price to stump up. Go! Discs famously spent just £150 on the marketing of the album. Billy paid his own way. He'd signed to Go! for just the one album, and his dotted-line fee was a complete set of *Motown Chartbusters* albums and a 1965 tin of Beatles talcum powder that he coveted, belonging to Macdonald. Usually, a record company will lavish a new signing with a handsome advance in the comfortable thousands, but a) neither Macdonald nor his uncle could afford one, and b) Billy didn't want one. ('He doesn't like to feel he's in hock to someone,' Macdonald notes.) In fact, Billy would never take a whopping advance from Go! Discs, even when they could afford it, and he only ever signed for one album at a time. As the years went by, this irritated Macdonald no end, but it kept Billy and PJ happy, and they paid him back with eight years' worth of loyalty (and many thousand sales).

The sales of the second pressing of *Life's A Riot* pushed it into the national Top 40 (to 32 according to the *Music Week* chart of 4 February). It sold 50,000 copies, just shy of a silver disc (it would subsequently pass silver and go gold). 'A New England', though not even a single, had been voted Number Seven in John Peel's annual, listener-led Festive Fifty on Radio 1. As his Go! Discs biography, finely crafted by

Kershaw, declared: 'Billy Bragg has risen from obscurity to the status of semi-obscurity.'

Before all this, Billy had always carried with him a mental check-list of three distinct musical ambitions:

1. Make an album.
2. Tour America.
3. Be on the cover of the *NME*.

One down. The 14 January issue of *NME* made it two. 'GIRLS, GUNS, GUTS, GUITARS' ran the cover-line, subtitled 'Billy Bragg's New England by Gavin Martin.' He'd made it. Just as models move into a new orbit when they become 'cover girls', so a music press cover star carries a certain cachet – but it's not *quite* the equivalent passport to success. For a kick-off, the glory lasts only a week. Sure, it means *everything* for the seven days that your mug is on the news-stand, but next Wednesday, you're chip paper, potentially never to be heard of again. That said, such long-term realism rarely tarnished the kudos when you were on the cover of the *NME* – for that week, you were the most significant name in rock.

In these competitive times for the media, choice of cover star continues to matter for those music publications still arranged on racks in WHSmith in the traditional, bound manner. In 1984, before the music-'glossy' boom, the *NME* used its cover as a manifesto. Billy Bragg *was* the *NME*, and vice versa. Times have changed so much in the intervening years, it is inconceivable now even to imagine a newspaper without colour, but that was then. The *NME* wasn't about undignified jostling in Smith's, it was . . . the *NME*. Billy was photographed by that season's in-house image-maker Anton Corbijn in front of the Houses of Parliament: very dark, very oppressive, very end-of-the-world-(please). Martin, a Northern Irish firebrand who'd risen during punk, provided a comprehensive interrogation inside, and declared Billy 'a damn sight funnier than George Orwell'. Which, for all the studied, apocalyptic gloom in the air, was crucial.

It is worth noting the near-parallel rise of The Smiths, whose transformation from Manchester cult band to national pop phenomenon occurred at the same time as Billy went overground, and the two acts would frequently cross paths. In January 1984, by which time The Smiths had garnered some ecstatic early press, recorded their first Peel Session, topped the indie charts and scored a Top 30 hit with 'This Charming Man', Billy had his ears opened to the songwriting genius of Morrissey and Johnny Marr by Andy Kershaw, now ensconced at the Jenners'. (Kershaw recalls his sister Liz seeing him off to London on the coach from Leeds, and he told her, 'I'm going down for ten days, and if I don't like it I'll be back. And I'm still here.')

It was in the lull after a soundcheck at a Billy Bragg headline gig at Sheffield Poly: Kershaw had taped Billy the third Smiths single 'What Difference Does It Make?', and Billy gave the tape to the sound man, who duly played it over the PA. It was the tender B-side 'Back To The Old House' that did it for Billy. He recalls a divine moment of understanding and empathy: 'This marked a return to people writing songs about things. As far as I was concerned, the new romantic movement was dead.'

In a synthesised world, Billy seized on The Smiths' *old* romanticism, and was enthused by both Morrissey's arch lyricism and Marr's dynamic guitarwork. 'The Smiths coming along gave me a lot of encouragement, something to measure myself against although not as a competition.' Even media shorthand seemed to rope them off together: Morrissey and Marr were the new Lennon and McCartney, Billy Bragg was the new Bob Dylan. Both began 1984 with their first *NME* cover, and both would have a great year.

At the end of January, Billy and Jenner engineered another residency at a new venue called the Captain's Cabin, in London's Haymarket, on a night they specifically tailored for solo performers. It ran throughout February and March, and was more salubrious than the Tunnel (Billy was known to busk for the people in the Cabin queue before his own shows). On 10 February, having ticked off BBC1 (*That's Life*) and Channel 4 (*The Tube*), Billy made his BBC2 debut on *The Old Grey Whistle Test* – then in its last series before being spruced up for the 80s by dumping bearded presenter Bob Harris, dropping the Old and Grey – for obvious demographic reasons – and having it taken over by men who looked like groovy schoolteachers, Mark Ellen and David Hepworth (actually, they were music journalists, but Hepworth used to teach – nowadays they are like two retired generals of magazine publishing, still writing, talking and offering sage-like wisdom via the publications of others). It was, at the time, a prime TV slot, as bands played live, and there were no balloons.

Looking back on *Whistle Test* now (Old Grey version and New Paisley-print), it's charmingly amateurish, with much looking at scripts and many a bungled handover, but it did its bit for new talent. Perhaps more importantly than Billy's TV exposure, the booking brought Andy Kershaw to the attention of *OGWT* producer Trevor Dann, who, after bumping into him a couple more times, was so impressed with his vim and bluff Northern good humour that he later hired him for October's revamp as a co-presenter. (This, in turn, would lead to his own world music show on Radio 1, which remained on the air until 2000, when moved to Radio 3.)

Also in February, Go! Discs went upmarket and had a nice new logo designed by Barney Bubbles, which soon graced notepaper, comp slip and record sleeve alike – a dotted arrow pointing at the centre-hole of a record, forming the letters G and O, with the Stiff-influenced motto beneath: 'Giving the green light to the young lions.' Go! Mansions, christened so as a joke, was an upstairs room in Wendell Road, South Acton, but Macdonald had signed a licensing deal with Chrysalis records, which meant that, while Go! maintained artistic control of its output, the major would distribute the records. Macdonald claimed he sealed the deal with Chrysalis MD Doug D'Arcy at an Arsenal home game, but it had been touch-and-go, chiefly because Billy, the label's pivotal act, was signed for only one album. (Macdonald's relationship with his star name was based on trust, and 'trust' is a very difficult concept for major record company lawyers to grasp.) Chrysalis were also unsure if Billy's appeal would travel, internationally.

By now, Macdonald had signed The Boothill Foot Tappers, a seven-piece good-time country revival outfit, A Thousand Miles Of Sunshine, a pop six-piece with two seventeen-year-old girl singers, and Chakk, a Sheffield electro-funk group. As luck would have it, the Boothills got a *Sounds* front cover just when the Chrysalis deal looked like it might fall through, and a copy dropped on Doug D'Arcy's desk did the trick.

The sales and the profile of *Life's A Riot* had given Go! Discs life. Billy Bragg was taking off, but 'semi-obscurity' wasn't going to spoil him. Eschewing the unpredictable rail network, he was now occasionally driven to gigs. Macdonald would sometimes drive, at least until the office started to get too busy, and he is still effusive about what he sees as that 'golden period. Some of those gigs were probably the best gigs I had ever seen, and probably will see. The directness, the way he really charmed an audience, very thought provoking. Seeing those songs work with audiences, seeing them pick up on it for the first time, it was a really fresh experience.'

Necessity even saw Billy soften his view on students – after all, they did form a large slice of his growing audience. 'After a while, you have to stop thinking of people as students,' he reasons.

On 29 February, he played his first gig abroad, at the Paris Forum Des Halles with The Opposition (very much their patch, remember, and a country that never really took to Billy Bragg). Although an inauspicious start, this was the beginning of the world domination enterprise, in which Billy's outward mobility really came into its own.

'He was very cheap to run,' confirms Peter Jenner. 'We had this rule right from the start: we'll do any gig providing it doesn't cost him any money. Providing we had enough to pay his fares, and a meal, and to put him up – and in the early days he was very easy on what all that meant, he was very obliging, he'd sleep on someone's floor.

'And then when we started doing reasonably well, we'd be in a car, and that was it. We never even hired cars, we used mine.'

Jenner's car was a beaten-up black Volvo estate, registration PLF 343R, and it quickly became iconic to anyone involved in the Billy Bragg story. (It would even later appear on 1985's Billy Bragg *South Bank Show*.) It was a bit of a dad's car, and because Billy couldn't drive he always needed a dad to drive it, usually Kershaw, sometimes Ian Richards, often Jenner himself – not just hands-on, this was foot-down management.

Jenner was keen to muck in – after all, this was refreshingly unlike touring with a band and their road crew. 'With Billy, you weren't stuck with a fucking entourage,' he enthuses. 'It was always a very personal relationship he had with people. I'd spent a lot of time with Roy Harper. I learnt that if you're good at being a solo artist, be happy to be a good solo artist. Don't trade that in to become a second-rate rock star – that was always my advice to Billy.'

So Billy stayed small, as he got bigger. In terms of pop, he adhered to the Rudyard Kipling poem 'If': 'If you can keep your head when all about you are losing theirs . . .' He managed to keep his feet on the ground and his mind on the job, never allowing his improving status or new-found financial solvency to turn his head. Quite how he turned out so incorruptible is a mystery, although the loss of his father had placed health way ahead of wealth in his priority list early on in his life, and as such the traditional excesses enjoyed by working-class musicians with new money never held that much allure for him.

'He's always been incredibly low on normal rock star consumption,' Jenner confirms. 'He's not a big drinker and not a big drugger. He drinks a tiny bit, and drugs are very rare. He never collected expensive cars – nor expensive road accidents – he always travelled by tube, and we always made money at gigs.'

Life on the road was made far more bearable by the company, and by the compact nature of the non-stop operation. Kershaw describes his role as 'Jeeves to Billy's Wooster', and says, 'We had an absolute whale of a time.' They would swap specialist music – folk for country and western, The Watersons for Hank Williams or play a double Willie Nelson live album while driving south out of Calais, belting out the words to gypsy song 'Thirty Foot Trailer' on a Dutch motorway. ('It was a long way from what I imagine the *NME* thought we were listening to,' laughs Kershaw.)

If it was Billy and Jenner in the Bragg Battlebus, they would put the world to rights: 'You have to know about the political history of the world if Pete's driving,' says Billy. 'It's *Star Trek* or *Thunderbirds* if you want to have a conversation with Wiggy.' Jenner combined a love of driving with a short temper when lost and a temptation to become more interested in his passenger's newspaper than the road ahead. Billy would map-read (his speciality), and get flashbacks of being on military exercise.

Billy and Kershaw did a four-date tour of Holland, and the two of them fell in love with the place. Billy explains why: 'We liked the gigs, we liked the women, we liked the dope, we liked the beer, we liked the chips with mayonnaise.'

Kershaw concurs: 'We loved the whole free-wheeling, easy-going liberalism of Holland. Of course, the dope thing was especially attractive to me, even though Billy still had that strong East End, working-class suspicion of that type of thing. But in those days, if the British authorities saw you having fun they would introduce legislation to stop you! The Dutch were the complete opposite.'

In rock'n'roll, the road goes on for ever; services 15 m.

Please print this, the voice of the probably silent majority: as a social poet and as a songwriter, Roy Harper pisses all over Billy Bragg and his fashionable ilk
anonymous letter, *Sounds*

March put Billy Bragg into some of the largest venues he'd ever played, thanks to a full-tour support slot with The Style Council (Paul Weller's grand, funk solution to splitting up The Jam): Newcastle City Hall, Birmingham Odeon, Glasgow Apollo and *two* Dominion Theatre shows in London. This was the band's first UK tour, the gigs labelled 'Council Meetings'.

On a smaller scale, but equally educational, Billy played with The Redskins in places like Queen's University, Belfast and the Trade Union Hall in Watford. Both Weller and The Redskins were political animals – the latter more affiliated and active – and between them and Billy, they were inad-vertently spearheading a new awareness in music, of which more later.

On 31 March, Billy trod the boards at Dublin's National Stadium. An incongruous setting and an incongruous connec-tion: he was supporting Pink Floyd guitarist Dave Gilmour, touring his second solo album *About Face*. Jenner, whose handiwork this was, actually stopped managing the Floyd very soon after Gilmour joined in 68, but he wasn't one to leave an old contact unexploited, and it led to three gigs, including two nights at Hammersmith Odeon. As if to ease the middle-aged audience into Billy's rough-and-ready style, tour promoter Harvey Goldsmith personally went on to introduce him as 'a great friend of Dave Gilmour's'. Billy remembers seeing a strange, long-haired bloke in the wings at Hammersmith wearing a suit and tie. Gilmour's accountant? No. He introduced himself to Billy as Roy Harper, the eccentric folkie once managed by Jenner and famously referred to by Led Zeppelin as 'Harpic' because he was clean round the bend. (Jenner saw some fundamental parallels between Billy and Harper: they were both single-minded solo singer-songwriters, although only one of them was notorious for cancelling a tour after catching something off a sheep he'd tried to resuscitate, mouth to mouth.)

Since 1981, London had been governed by the conspicuously Labour-controlled Greater London Council. By 1985, PM Margaret Thatcher would set about shutting it down (in his book *Thatcher And Thatcherism*, Eric J Evans likens this to her grasping a 'significant nettle'). In 1984, the GLC, under leader Ken Livingstone, set about promoting itself in time-honoured GLC fashion: by putting on concerts and events. In April, Billy played a number of GLC shows as part of the London Against Racism campaign, at Ilford Town Hall, Camden's bijou Shaw Theatre and Acklam Hall in Notting Hill. He also played a NUPE gig at Watford Trade Union Hall, in aid of saving school dinners ('Don't let spam fritters become a thing of the past!' went the poster) and a GLC show at Bishop Douglas School in East Finchley (he would play many a GLC gig during 84, 85 and 86). The date was memorable for being in a gym. While Rastafarian poet Benjamin Zephaniah was on, Billy Bragg and the other support act John Hegley and the Popticians could be seen distractingly swinging on ropes. ('We took our shoes off,' Billy assures any Bishop Douglas staff who may be reading.)

Politically, Billy Bragg was hotting up. On 20 May 1984 he played his first show for the Labour Party at Manchester's Free Trade Hall. Eurofest, a Festival for a Socialist Europe, was intended to drum up support for 14 June's Euro-elections (Larry Adler, The Panorama Steel Band and *Dad's Army*'s Clive Dunn also appeared, and Billy recalls he and Kershaw 'blowing up balloons for socialism'). This was the first time Billy met Labour leader Neil Kinnock, who proved that his toast was buttered on the right side by picking up a guitar and singing, 'Take the ribbon from your hair . . .' ('Help Me Make It Through The Night' would prove a poignant plea for Kinnock before the decade was out).

At the end of the evening's entertainment, all concerned joined in a community singsong of 'The Red Flag'. As if to illustrate the tentative nature of Billy's first steps into partydom, he admits he didn't know the words ('I wasn't sufficiently Labour'), so he tore out the page from the programme with them printed on and surreptitiously stuck it on MP Gerald Kaufman's back. (Six years later, Billy would record 'The Red Flag' on his album *The Internationale*, to its original 1889 tune, not the 'funeral dirge' sung by the Labour Party.)

In June, Billy and Kershaw hit the Scottish Highlands, by way of gigs in Edinburgh, Dundee and Aberdeen. They drove the whole way in the Volvo from Leeds for a show at the Albert Hotel, Kirkwell, Orkney, often overlooked by myopic rock promoters. To get there from Aberdeen, they motored up the A96 all night, making the most of the bright light up there, listening to Radio 4, whose Shipping Forecast has long romanticised place names like Cromarty from that coast. The two day-trippers stopped off at Dornoch and ran around like fools on the beach; they drove up a hill and watched an early morning trawler coming in with seagulls around it like bees; they saw rabbits warming themselves on the deserted tarmac of the A9. It wasn't rock'n'roll but they liked it.

In order to get over the Pentland Firth to Kirkwall, there's a tiny ferry – too small for a Volvo at any rate, so Billy and Kershaw left it at John O'Groats and took the amps and equipment on board. En route, they were soaked by a big wave, much to the merriment of the local passengers, who knew precisely where to sit to avoid such a soaking. Billy describes Kirkwall as 'a one-tree town, pretty basic' (the *Rough Guide To Scotland* says 'a bustling metropolis, by Orkney standards'), but the gig was a cracker, playing punk songs and precipitating bursts of country dancing. Between songs, the punters would politely retreat to the walls.

They drove back the next day to Inverness for a less captivating show at Pharaohs Disco. ('Dreadful,' Billy recalls. 'The PA gave up, there was no stage and very few beers.')

The night was saved by a friend of theirs called Tam Kenny, who talked them into joining him for a moonlight yomp to Culloden Moor. Fuelled by Tartan bitter, the three of them scared themselves to death on the site of the 1746 massacre, spooked by the thought of the 1,200 Jacobites who perished at the hands of the better-equipped government troops ('The wind that day was so strong that the clansmen were blinded by their own gunsmoke, and when they finally charged they did so in ragged fashion,' notes Tom Steel in *Scotland's Story*). This was not the first time Billy would be touched by history.

Having already played a handful of GLC-organised gigs, on 10 June Billy joined The Smiths at a GLC one called Jobs For A Change, in Jubilee Gardens next to County Hall on the South Bank, with Hank Wangford, The Redskins, reggae stars Misty In Roots and bee-hived popstress Mari Wilson – a typical GLC line-up, you might say. It was not a perfect day, as a fascist element in the crowd physically attacked both The Redskins and Wangford's band. Rather less sensationally, Andy Rourke and Mike Joyce of The Smiths threw some flowers out of a dressing-room window and twenty fans dented the roof of a parked car scrambling for them.

Coincidentally, the vehicle belonged to one of the catering staff who would be working backstage at the forthcoming Glastonbury Festival, which gave the Smiths' tour manager a headache, as the Smiths were playing it. So was Billy Bragg. The three-day, open-air Glastonbury, as an annual event, was very much a 70s throwback that had revitalised itself in the Thatcher years by farmer Michael Eavis's affiliation with CND (it quickly became the campaign's biggest single fundraiser, netting £100,000 by 1984). The line-ups were getting stronger by the year, from Hawkwind and Aswad in 1981, and Van Morrison and Jackson Browne in 1982, to a veritable cornucopia in 1984: jazz-funk (Weather Report), reggae (Black Uhuru), folk (Fairport Convention, Joan Baez), blues (Dr John), ska (General Public) and pop (Elvis Costello & The Attractions).

Up on the emblematic Pyramid Stage, underneath the country's biggest CND badge, Billy provided the campers' wake-up call on the Friday. He and Kershaw kipped in the Volvo. It was turning into quite a summer.

In his time, Billy had played garden parties, street parties, birthday parties, Christmas parties, anything. On 6 July 1984, he did his first wedding. Andy Macdonald was marrying Juliet de Valero Wills. It was a happy occasion for Billy, as they asked him to be their best man, and it afforded the first Riff Raff reunion (he, Wiggy and Robert did a nuptially-biased set of covers including 'Going To The Chapel', 'Shotgun Wedding' and 'Jump The Broomstick'). The Boothill Foot Tappers also played, as if to underline the fact that Go! Discs was Macdonald's life. In effect, it *was* a Go! Discs bash, its 250 guests made up of staff, bands, producers, hacks, lawyers, agents, Chrysalis people and only a smattering of relatives. Juliet was marrying the company.

Juliet's role in the Billy Bragg story cannot be underestimated. She became one of those women in his life who give him so much strength – and, although this is not a romantic allusion as far as the Go! Discs years are concerned, the fact that, after 1992, she turned out to be exactly the life-partner he'd been looking for lends a retrospective crackle and significance to her and Billy's professional relationship.

Quite unlike her romance with Macdonald, which was the textbook whirlwind kind (met in October, proposed in January, wed in July), her eventual union with Billy was based on years of friendship. It wasn't until later that they realised quite how much they had in common.

Born two years after Billy, Juliet comes from a Spanish-Catholic background, as opposed to Billy's Italian-Catholic, and both saw their fathers die young. But unlike Billy's fairly steady, traditional childhood, Juliet's upbringing was a mass of contradictions. Her father, Michael de Valero Wills, was born against a backdrop of impoverished Spanish aristocracy, right-wing, pro-Franco land-owners who lost everything in the Spanish Civil War and had an attitude best described as *hidalgo*. They were cash-poor, but carried themselves like noblemen. Michael and his Spanish mother moved to England to escape the Civil War, where, thanks to a bursary, he enrolled at King's College and then St George's in Hyde Park (two of the 'Big Five' London medical schools), and eventually qualified as a doctor. Here, he met and married Juliet's mother, Margaret Pountain, an English nurse from 'an impossibly complicated social background' in Derbyshire.

Michael had started with nothing but an attitude and his degree in medicine (surrounded by doctors' sons and public school stock) was no mean achievement. An outsider by dint of being foreign *and* on a grant, Michael had to work twice as hard to be accepted.

He and Margaret had six children (two boys, four girls), and, according to Juliet, 'a turbulent marriage'. The family moved around a lot, and Juliet was born in 1959 in the Shell hospital, Trinidad, where Dad was working. They moved back to Bristol in 1963, which is where Juliet did most of her growing up. The trappings were middle class – convent school for the girls, Christian Brothers for the boys – but, she insists, 'it was all front' (four cars parked out front, no housekeeping money in the tin).

Juliet won a place at grammar school, and seemed to be on-track for a decent education. Then, one year later, her dad returned from a two-year contract in Saudi Arabia, and the family moved to Whitburn, a small ex-mining village between Edinburgh and Glasgow. Here she and her sisters got nothing but grief at the local school for being English and 'posh', and Margaret was dubbed a witch because she wore kaftans and a vast, purple, hooded cloak (she'd become more of a rebellious, liberal soul during the rise of women's lib in the 60s). 'To survive in Whitburn you had to deny huge chunks of yourself,' Juliet says. 'Your background, your aspirations, in fact any awareness of life and values beyond the village boundaries.' You also needed a big sister who could fight (luckily, Juliet had one of those) – and the 'happening' fashion accessory for girls was a metal comb with the end filed down to a lethal point. From bohemian Bristol to a cultural black hole, the contradictions kept on piling up.

Needless to say, Juliet's education effectively ground to a halt. When her parents finally split for good, her mum moved to London – well, Penge anyway, which is virtually in Kent – where Juliet briefly joined her after her O Levels (taken at fifteen in Scotland, but, swot that she was, she took them a year early). She never quite managed to re-enrol at school down South. Following her creative instincts at sixteen she got a place on an art course at Kingsway College in King's Cross. It was 1975, and she fell in with a music crowd, in particular a former Swedish porn star who was now booking bands on the London pub circuit. Helping her out, and staying up late, Juliet began missing college (she dropped out after a year when 'an urgent need to support myself prevailed').

Punk rock was Juliet's University of Life, from a Saturday job at Rock On, *the* record shop in Camden, onwards. While Billy was up in Oundle living in authentic squalor and sneering at public schoolboys, Juliet was living even rougher and developing her own loathing of students. She was squatting through sheer necessity in Hornsey, 'scared, broke, and not happy', with nowhere else to go, surrounded by middle-class, art-stude poseurs living the same way for a laugh and taking their washing home to Mummy at weekends. Although a clean and tidy individual (she always had a spider plant in whichever hell-hole she was squatting), Juliet discovered what it was like to be regarded as scum, seeing her belongings thrown out of the window into the road by council heavies on more than one occasion.

The people she'd met within the music industry became her support system. She even shared her sister's council flat (although not biblically) with numero uno punk photographer Ray Stevenson, who, incidentally, ruined the toilet by pouring developing fluid down it. Still, Juliet found herself in all the right places at all the right times.

Miles Copeland, son of a CIA boss and manager of then-unknown new-wavers The Police, had started his own label Step Forward Records, and Juliet drifted into a full-time job there assisting the press officer. This was at the deep end of the punk underground: the roster included Squeeze plus such punk almostrans as The Cortinas, The Models and Chelsea, and Copeland also subsidised Mark Perry's seminal fanzine *Sniffin' Glue* from the same office. She did early press for The Police, when they were struggling against the dual stigma of a jazz/prog-rock past and a 35-year-old guitarist – not ideal punk credentials. Thus began what Juliet calls her 'lost years' – staying up all night, and tracing the never-ending gig-crawl (Vortex, Roxy, 100 Club, Marquee) – 'You just couldn't go home, there was too much to see.'

Juliet's accidental career in record company promotion and whatever-else-needed-doing took her to Chiswick Records (she was working there when Riff Raff's *Cosmonaut* EP came out, but against all odds, she and Billy never crossed paths – happily, their names are mentioned on the same page of the booklet that later accompanied the Chiswick Story box set). She managed to get outrageous New York transsexual Wayne/Jayne County on the cover of *Sounds* in a negligee. Then, as part of a small independent press company, Trigger, Juliet pushed Toyah when she was on the tiny label Safari. These were not easy acts to peddle, and the experience drew out the natural hustler in Juliet. Then in 1979 it all went off. A seven-piece ska band from Coventry, The Special AKA, borrowed £700 to cut a single called 'Gangsters', a wired little number that they'd put out on their own label 2-Tone through pre-eminent London indie Rough Trade. The black-and-white graphic of the artwork, and the multiracial nature of band and musical lineage proved irresistible in the post-punk malaise, and Chrysalis picked up single, band and label (plus The Selecter, who were on the B-side), sending 'Gangsters' to a deserved Number Six in the national charts. Seemingly overnight, 2-Tone fever gripped the nation, and Juliet – having dabbled in rock journalism as 'Holly Golightly' in *Superpop* magazine – found herself right in the middle of a mediaquake. Her partner in Trigger, Rick Rogers, was managing The Specials (as they were soon known) and by October, the two of them were booking the 2-Tone Revue tour, with ska revivalist labelmates Madness and The Selecter.

Madness entered the Top Twenty with their first single 'The Prince' (and were duly poached by Stiff, never to peak outside the Top Twenty until 1985), The Selecter went Top Ten with their debut, 'On My Radio', and The Specials had a Number One in January 1980 ('Too Much Too Young'). Britain's youth donned tight suits, loafers, pork pie hats and tonic dresses, and a previously obscure musical form from Jamaica was everywhere. The monochrome madness lasted two years. Juliet and Rick Rogers booked six-week US tours for both The Specials and The Selecter by what tailors are calling the seat of their pants ('We were running on pure adrenaline,' she says). They had no time to enjoy the fact that they were a crucial part of history in the making.

Juliet, a former junior 'rude girl' herself from Saturday afternoons spent at the Bristol Locarno, managed The Selecter (she and Rogers had managed The Damned in late 1978 from the time when they were called The Doomed for legal reasons), and sharpened up another side of her act. These hectic, pick-it-up-as-you-go-along years would later serve her well at Go! Discs, which was a well-oiled operation by comparison.

Sadly, 2-Tone was doomed to fail. For all of its apparent racial har-mo-nee, the audience attracted by the ska/bluebeat revival was fraught with contradictions – as it had been the first time around in the 1960s. Madness, especially (the only all-white group among the crop) drew a lot of skinhead fans who, again, missed the multi-cultural point, moonstomping to the black-influenced sounds and sieg-heiling in between. There is no getting inside the minds of such people, and they were never courted by Madness themselves, but this constituency, Juliet reckons, probably presented a 'truer picture of 2-Tone', or at least the paradox the label was trying to shake off. (By the summer of 1981, when The Specials topped the charts with urban hymn 'Ghost Town', the inner cities were torn apart by riots.)

Before it all fell apart, at Christmas 1980, The Selecter afforded Juliet her first contact with Pete Jenner, a minor managerial summit that would imbue their later professional dealings with an in-built mutual respect. He was managing Ian Dury & The Blockheads, whose Soft As A Baby's Bottom tour ended with two nights at the Michael Sobell Sports Centre in North London. The Selecter, who had just returned from a hellish Scandinavian tour, were booked to support. In the finest tradition of Support Band Paranoia, they complained about the space they'd been granted for their merchandising stall, and Juliet was forced to argue the toss in the foyer with Pete Jenner. 'To his credit he was very accommodating, he bent over backwards,' she remembers.

However, the band's conspiracy theory spread to the lights and the PA, and they were so peeved, they refused to do the second night – even after Jenner had coerced Ian Dury into phoning them personally with assurances that no acts of sabotage were afoot. This was what management was all about: The Selecter were actually on the slide (their last single 'The Whisper' hadn't even made the Top 30), and yet they were acting the prima donna. Juliet had met a lot of prima donnas – which is probably why Billy Bragg came as such a pleasant surprise when they started working together in 1984. After The Selecter, Juliet continued managing their singer Pauline Black – with whom she is still good friends – and endured record company grief when Chrysalis insisted they should market her as a black diva. This did not suit. No wonder the anti-marketing marketing of Go! Discs appealed . . .

Juliet had met Andy Macdonald at Radio 1 in October 1983 – they were both chaperoning artists appearing on Mike Read's *Pop Quiz*: he, Stiff artist Kirsty MacColl (also his girlfriend at the time) and she, Pauline Black. Before romance blossomed, Macdonald gave Juliet a copy of *Life's A Riot* ('I put it on every morning,' she recalls – it really was that sort of record). As she was working with Black, who was still signed to Chrysalis, and had contacts there, she actually tried to stoke the Go! Discs label deal from within. After a full two months of being knocked back for one reason or another, a besotted Macdonald finally talked Juliet into going out with him. He drove her up to a Billy Bragg gig at Manchester Poly on 28 January 1984 (the first time she and Billy met). He apparently pledged to Billy at the end of the night, 'I'm going to marry her.' He proposed three days later at Billy's Kingston Poly date. She said yes.

The most important player in Billy Bragg's life was now well and truly in the story.

In July, Billy started recording his second album *Brewing Up With Billy Bragg* at Berry Street Studio in Clerkenwell with Peel Session engineer Ted De Bono in the producer's chair. Billy would later work with John Porter, also a Maida Vale man, who produced the first Smiths' album. Billy's theory is that bands on smaller labels (The Smiths were on Rough Trade) don't get the pick of all the expensive 'name' producers, and so instead go for the first ones they meet – invariably BBC stalwarts.

Brewing Up, technically, was not so far away from the utilitarian approach of *Life's A Riot* (give or take a toot on the trumpet by Dave Woodhead and a touch of organ by Kenny Craddock) and was soon finished, earmarked for an October release. There would, Billy insisted, be no single. Why? 'Because I was a fucking punk rocker, that's why,' Billy explains carefully. 'Singles were for Spandau Ballet.' This decision led to the first proper row of his professional career, with his label boss *and* his manager. But Billy was adamant, and Jenner let it drop. 'He's very good at not bearing grudges or allowing arguments to spill over into the next day,' says Billy. Macdonald was simply outnumbered.

It's too easy to take for granted Billy's initial hostility towards singles, and indeed, the willingness of those around him to honour his integrity. Pop law tells us that it's commercial suicide not to release singles, as they are a quick, if pricey, route to radio play and act as convenient flyers for bedrock album sales. Led Zeppelin's refusal to release singles in the 70s – interestingly enough, a manager-led stance – denied them a good deal of TV and radio exposure. As it happens, it didn't matter: it increased the potency of their legend, made gigs all the more exciting, and caused buyers of their albums to feel intellectually superior to the hit-parade herd. (Anyway, they put out singles in the States, which is a far more lucrative market, so maybe they weren't so principled after all.) With Billy's first album doing so well on the back of minimal advertising, it would be a dishonest record-label boss who didn't wonder to himself just how many *more* albums he could sell with a hit single upfront. It was not to be.

In August, with *Brewing Up* in the can (or in the pot), Billy was invited on his very first American tour.

Echo & The Bunnymen were a Liverpudlian raincoat band whose morose, Doors-influenced psychedelia had notched up three hit albums (*Crocodiles, Heaven Up Here* and *Porcupine*) and, more surprisingly to die-hard fans, a Top Ten hit single in February 1983, 'The Cutter'. The alternative pin-up status of luscious-lipped singer Ian McCulloch didn't harm their mainstream pop progress. In April 1984, their fourth album *Ocean Rain*, their gentlest affair yet, was a predictable Number Four hit in the UK, but reached a tantalising 84 in the American *Billboard* charts. A full US tour to consolidate was essential. Along with main support act The Fleshtones, the Bunnymen invited Billy Bragg to join them across America. It was his third and final rock'n'roll ambition.

In a letter to Billy, Andy Macdonald wrote, 'Looking forward to the American jaunt where we should GO! and liven the bastards up a bit.'

Due to *Whistle Test* preparations, Kershaw didn't go, but it was a blessing in disguise: Billy did what seemed to be the natural thing and rang Wiggy (whose audio-visual venture had by then folded). 'This is it!' Billy enthused to his oldest friend. 'The American tour! This is what we always dreamt about. I might never do this again, and it will mean so much to me if you'll come with me.' Wiggy *was* planning a conventional holiday after the demise of AVM, but this sounded better. 'I've never had a proper holiday,' he moans. 'What should've been a holiday in Butlin's ended up being Bearshanks, and what should've been a holiday after my video thing ended up being a tour of America.'

'It wouldn't have been the same without Wiggy,' says Billy. 'I'd have felt dreadful writing him postcards telling him all about it, it would've been really, really sad.'

Billy and Wiggy would hook up with Echo & The Bunnymen in Washington DC on 16 August, but before that, Jenner organised a week of self-promotion in New York. The second week in August happened to be the week of the annual New Music Seminar, an industry talking shop where every bigwig and smallwig from every record company in America would descend, a great place for getting noticed, and yet a bloody difficult one. 'We didn't have anything but a good record,' Jenner recalls. 'No corporate clout. And the only point of going there is to be noticed. How do you get noticed? Make a noise. Someone playing music is bound to cause a stir.'

Between them, Billy and Jenner cooked up the idea of the Portastack. They simply took the mobile-musician angle to its logical conclusion, and asked Kenny Jones, engineer on *Brewing Up*, to assemble a PA system that a man could literally wear on his back and carry around – if he were foolhardy enough.

It cost £500, was seven-feet-six-inches high, weighed about 35 pounds and it worked. The image of Billy Bragg strapped into this space-age harness with two speakers above him like deelyboppers and a microphone snaking round to his mouth is now an archetypal one: the world's first electric one-man band, built by madmen, driven by lust for glory. ('He looks like a busker from outer space,' noted *NME* writer Paul Du Noyer.)

'It was a blatant rip-off of Elvis!' Jenner confesses. (Costello had busked outside the London Hilton in July 1977 during a CBS sales conference in order to scare up a US deal. He was arrested and fined £5 for obstruction. Hats off to Stiff records, then.)

Billy was not arrested, but then, at biz schmooze-ins like the NMS, selling your own wares is par for the course, and Billy's Portastack made quite an impact. (Actually, he was at one stage escorted *outside* the New York Hilton by security and he continued to play on Sixth Avenue, but, as Du Noyer pointed out, he couldn't get arrested there!) It took some bottle to do it, but Billy had played the Tunnel and breathed in CS gas. He played four consecutive nights on the roof of the Danceteria club, which faced the Empire State Building and afforded a stunning view at night, and his support act was, poetically enough, Seething Wells, whose memory of the run involves 'screaming abuse at the yanks and generally being booed off stage before Billy came on and won them over'.

Between gigs and biz-busking, Billy and Wiggy behaved, understandably, like 'classic tourists', wandering about, looking up (a dead giveaway in New York) and pointing like idiots at fire hydrants, pretzel vendors and the steam coming out of the manholes. It's just like *Kojak*, you know.

After eight days in New York, suitably acclimatised to being in the mythical big country, the Barking boys joined the Bunnymen for four weeks that shook their world. 'If you want to see the whole of the United States,' Billy enthuses, 'this is the route: Washington, Boston, New York, Montreal, Toronto, Detroit, Chicago, New Orleans, Houston, Austin, Salt Lake City, California. Playing 30 minutes a night, for $50 dollars in your hand.'

Wiggy concurs: 'It was wow after wow after wow.'

Echo & The Bunnymen were good to the support act – which is by no means a given on rock tours – Wiggy and Billy instantly clicked with guitarist Will Sergeant, 'who always knew where the shops were'. Every time they reached a new hotel in a new town, Sergeant would go into his room and empty his entire bag out on the floor like Roy Neary in *Close Encounters*, then, when they left, scoop it up and put it all back in again.

'Mac [McCulloch] was just . . . Mac,' Wiggy remembers. In other words, absolutely icebox cool, sunglasses after dark, and oozing Scouse sarcasm. Mac's favourite joke was asking, 'Can I have a ciggy, Wiggy?'

When offered their first Budweiser from the tour bus fridge, Wiggy and Billy politely refused, then later politely gave in. Wiggy admits he developed his taste for the old rock'n'roll mouthwash on that tour, namely Jack Daniel's whiskey ('Not a letdown').

There were many highlights, not least the gig at Utah University in Salt Lake City, where Billy had $46's worth of coins thrown at him (the Bunnymen's roadies went around afterwards filling pint glasses with change, which, the next day in Reno, they promptly put into slot machines). Another unforgettable occasion came on the long drive from Chicago to New Orleans in the crew bus (the Bunnymen flew the rest of the tour, but Billy and Wiggy opted to stop on the ground, where the view is better). At Billy's behest, the driver made a stop-off at Graceland in Memphis, Elvis Presley's ancestral home. The roadies were all about ten years older than Billy and Wiggy, and excellent, if hard-living, company and they were well into Elv, playing 1950s rock'n'roll tapes all the way there.

Billy remembers running from the car park to Graceland, eager to get his fill of tack: 'It is *the* Great White American Trash Experience. It's like going into Tutankhamun's tomb, the King buried with all his gold, or in this case, his Harley Davidsons.' Entering into the spirit of it (and failure to do this would be like visiting Disneyland and complaining that Mickey was a man in a suit), Billy purchased some fluorescent socks with a *Jailhouse Rock* Elvis image on the ankle. He saved them, and took them home in mint condition, only to discover that they'd been made in Leicester.

While the Bunnymen cruised above the anonymous clouds, Billy and Wiggy squeezed every last drop of first-hand experience out of their maiden US jaunt, usually sitting up front with the bus driver and playing cultural I-spy. (Needless to say, they were forever phoning Ricey from significant points and saying 'Wish you were here.') They were constantly amazed by the stamina of the crew – as the coach pulled into New Orleans, they emerged from their coffin-like bunks, disembarked and, instead of making for the hotel, made a bee-line for the famous Bourbon Street and started championship drinkin' and carousin'. Billy and Wiggy followed, like new kids at rock school. Billy remembers with awe the American guy whose job it was to organise and sell the tour merchandising, estimating that he'd put the equivalent of 'a sizeable townhouse' up his nose over the years. 'It's the one thing I've never been interested in,' Billy says of cocaine. 'And Wiggy neither. Drinking's OK, we'll stay up all day drinking, but never the really stupid, expensive stuff. I'm not as judgmental about marijuana as I was, but cocaine is the most boring drug in the world.'

The comic Robin Williams said that cocaine is God's way of telling you you're earning too much money. It's equally God's way of telling you you're signed to a record company, where the hours are upside down and, as such, consumption is rife. Whatever anybody says, it's virtually institutionalised, even in the health-conscious 90s. It probably never appealed to Billy because it's an aspirational, middle-class drug, a plaything of the not-actually-rich, and a waste of money. And anyway, here was one man who didn't need any help in talking bollocks really fast.

He was certainly utilising this natural skill on stage, bamboozling the Americans with his accelerated patter. 'Sometimes,' Wiggy recalls, 'he'd get into a rap and forget to play a tune.' There was an increased rate of string-breaking in America too, usually one per song, occasionally two, which left Wiggy 'ferociously restringing, or else borrowing guitars from the Bunnymen' in the wings. In New York, Wiggy recalls, a guitar was passed back through the gap in the curtains, and in his haste, he tuned the B-string to an E and confidently handed it back to Billy. Recognising that it was out, Billy subsequently tuned the rest of the strings to match the mistuned B. Ker-lang! It all added to the fun.

At the end of the tour in Los Angeles, Billy and Wiggy stayed on for two extra days – just in case this was their one-and-only trip to America. They checked out of the expensive, paid-for hotel, where they each had a room with mirrors on the ceiling (very off-putting if you wanted to clear the custard), and checked into the legendary Tropicana, where the air-conditioning didn't work but they didn't care. They rented a car and drove to the end of Route 66, which is basically where Sunset Boulevard hits the sea. It was an emotional, you're-my-best-mate sort of moment. 'I can't explain the achievement of seeing the Pacific Ocean,' Billy says. 'It was the conclusion of our childhood dream, the moment where all the things we'd ever wanted to do we could now say we'd done. Me and Wiggs.'

'By the end of the tour we were old hands,' says Wiggy.

Peter Jenner remembers Billy coming home and being 'remarkably relaxed'. He'd had a record out, made the cover of the *NME* and now he'd even gotten his kicks on Route 66.

Anything else would be a bonus. Rudyard Kipling had it right:

If you can fill the unforgiving minute
With sixty seconds' worth of distance run,
Yours is the Earth and everything that's in it,
And – which is more – you'll be a Man, my son!

9. THE WORLD TURNED UPSIDE DOWN

A bit of politics, 1984–1985

From South Wales across to Yorkshire
From Scotland down to Kent
The miners showed the NCB
That what they said, they meant

Dick Gaughan, 'The Ballad of '84'

I thought that if you had an acoustic guitar
It meant that you were a protest singer

The Smiths, 'Shakespeare's Sister'

'If someone says to me, What did you do during Thatcherism? My conscience is clear.'

This is Billy Bragg talking today, at a safe distance from that particular struggle, over 20 years on from the Labour landslide of 1997 and nearly 30 since the tyrannical Margaret Thatcher was ousted from her perch after a leadership challenge from her former Defence Secretary Michael Heseltine. (Hezza was pipped in the second ballot by Chancellor John Major, but the overthrow of Thatcher was a glorious day for the left either way.)

Thatcherism's effects did not magically evaporate when the woman after whom the term had been coined tearfully departed Downing Street on 28 November 1990. The Tories even secured a fourth term of office in 1992, despite the personality bypass of their new leader, and in many ways this was an even more demoralising defeat for Labour. Thatcher's political legacy in this country lives on. As Eric J. Evans notes: 'One of her major objectives was to destroy socialism. In the short term, at least, she succeeded.'

In 1984, at the height of the fighting, for Billy Bragg and many like him, Margaret Thatcher looked as if she was going to dismember Britain with her bare hands, if not, through her 'special relationship' with the gung-ho Ronald Reagan, and actually lay it to rest. And somebody had to stop her.

It would be fanciful to say that you *had* to be political in 1980s Britain. The majority in fact weren't. The Tories' battle for the nation's hearts and minds had been won not on ideological ground but at home. They offered council houses for sale, thereby pulling off the biggest confidence trick of their reign after the meaningless privatisation of utilities (you too can be a homeowner and buy a bit of British Gas – result: you will be deeper in debt, and the well-off will still own the lion's share of the shares). Even though New Labour were often criticised for putting pre-sentation before policy, it was the Conservatives who ran the country using smoke and mirrors, apparently raising the standard of living for all and creating what Major later called 'a classless society' while actually widening the gap between the haves and the have-nots. The average real income of families may have gone up by 37 per cent between 1979 and 1992 (a great Tory statistic to quote), but the real income of the poorest 10 per cent of the country plummeted by 18 per cent and that of the wealthiest 10 per cent shot up by a criminal 61 per cent. This was Thatcher's Britain.

At the 1983 election, the Tories won a 144 majority, the largest since Labour's victory after the Second World War – so *somebody* was voting for them. As a rule, it was people who lived in the South of England, a demographic confirmation that Thatcherite rule was utterly divisive. (In the 87 election, the Tories won 87 per cent of all seats in the South and the Midlands, while Wales, Scotland and the North showed up almost entirely red.) In a report published a year later called *The Nationwide Competition For Votes – The 1983 British Election*, Ian McAllister and Richard Rose concluded: '[Labour] is no longer the party of most working-class voters.'

'By 1983, the scales had fallen from my eyes,' says Billy. He vividly remembers seeing a Tory minister on TV who, when asked, 'Wouldn't it be better if the money spent on Cruise missiles was used to provide free school dinners?', replied, 'What good are free school dinners if they are being fed to our children by Russian paratroopers?' It was, for Billy, a moment of realisation: 'Reagan, Thatcher, Cold War . . . it's going to happen.'

Aside from that, he admits he has no clear memories of the 1983 election, except that Labour got in in Barking. Peter Jenner, more tuned-in politically by dint of age and experience, could see Billy smartening up his act: 'Initially he was a social commentator. He sees what's around him and puts it into a song. Having been involved with Ian Dury just before Billy, I could see that parallel. Within a year of getting out that first album, he'd become much more political.'

Andy Macdonald concurs: 'Intensely political. He became more confident, too. His presence on stage took on more of the avenging angel.'

In March, 1984, the first vital signs of a divided Britain began to show. In opposition to the offer of a 5.2 per cent pay rise, and as a protest against proposed pit closures, 153 out of 174 coal mines went on strike. Industrial action was nothing new, nor was it exclusively reflective of a Conservative government – the Labour government of 1974–79 was characterised by strikes, especially during its winter of discontent: lorry drivers, railwaymen, local-government workers, teachers, even bakers and gravediggers – but the miners' strike ran deeper than mere unrest among the workforce.

In his book *The Miners' Strike*, former *Daily Mirror* industrial editor Geoffrey Goodman writes: 'Primary responsibility for the conflict has to be attributed to the government. It wanted a showdown because it had become convinced that this was the only way to destroy [NUM President] Arthur Scargill . . . and through that route to administer a severe blow to active trade unionism.'

It doesn't take a conspiracy theorist to leap to this conclusion. Thatcher hated the unions, and she regarded the NUM as the Enemy Within, which is why the miners' strike was a gift. The government had even been preparing for it (Thatcher ally Nicholas Ridley had drawn up a plan to defeat the miners as long ago as 1978), and it was the large-scale mobilisation of riot police to prevent flying pickets that most sinisterly summed up the mother of all battles. On 29 May, 8,000 officers mounted charges on picketing miners and their supporters at the Orgreave coking plant in South Yorkshire. It painted an unpretty picture.

While Billy was touring America with the Bunnymen in August of that year, he'd assumed the strike would be over by the time he returned. Far from it. On 21 September, violence flared on the picket line at Maltby Colliery near Rotherham, some of the worst in the strike's seven-month duration. On 26 September, just back from another European jaunt, Billy Bragg went out to the frontline.

He'd been asked to play by various miners' support groups – he'd made quite a few trade union contacts while doing gigs for the GLC, whose festivals and benefits were always overtly political in nature, with pamphlets everywhere and the exchange of ideas in the foyer (the GLC style was very much the inspiration behind Red Wedge). Billy was keen to throw his weight behind the miners' struggle, as fund-raising was essential if the action was to continue: 'And what I could do that the others *couldn't* do was go and play outside London cheaply and effectively.'

He played at the Docks United Social Club in Newport (raising £233.20 for the Gwent and Rhymney NUM food fund), and Corby Civic Centre, but it was the third miners' gig at The Bunker in Sunderland on 28 September that truly galvanised his feelings. Before embarking on this short hop for the miners, his head was full of questions: 'Why am I doing this? Am I just doing it for publicity because I've got a record coming out? What are my motives? Am I really political? Do I really walk it like I talk it?' He knew the answers by the time he got to Sunderland, because he had to explain himself in a more ideological way to the miners and their supporters than he ever had to a music journalist – 'where I was *vis-à-vis* the class struggle, where I was *vis-à-vis* Marx, the Labour Party. They wanted to know.'

The other aspect that struck him in Sunderland was the sheer strength of feeling in those who got up on stage to speak between the music, all of them women, many of them with husbands in jail. Billy recalls the secretary of the Women's Support Group – her husband and two sons had all been put away or were on remand chatting to him in the dressing room while the *other* support group were on stage. Before the strike she'd never made a speech in her life, but now she made one every night. 'This was something you couldn't get doing gigs in London,' he remarks.

The miners' gigs weren't just a political watershed for Billy, they also opened his ears and broadened his musical palette. Here, as with so many get-up-and-play protest gigs, he came into contact with the more politically motivated folk musicians – Roy Bailey, Dick Gaughan, Leon Rosselson – activists in a field from which he'd taken so much indirect inspiration, and yet names he'd never come across.

The folk element in Billy's music had always been there to those in the know, but it played second fiddle to the punk thrash. Despite having been schooled in Simon & Garfunkel and Bob Dylan, and having dabbled with folk sampler LPs from Barking Library, the cleansing fires of punk had burnt Billy's folk sympathies off the map. But he was a big boy now, and rubbing shoulders with Gaughan and Rosselson during 1984's miners' benefits had an effect. The seed had been sown back at the Labour Euro-elections gig at the Free Trade Hall, when Rosselson and Roy Bailey sang 'The World Turned Upside Down'. Here were folk musicians at work, and, as Billy was forced to admit to himself at the time, 'they had a much more radical canon of songs than I did.' It inspired him to play 'Between The Wars', a song that would soon *define* Billy Bragg.

Because of the threat of flying pickets, the black Volvo and its occupants (Billy, Kershaw, Ian Richards) were routinely stopped, searched and questioned by police as they attempted to drive to gigs in sensitive areas: 'The country was turning into a police state in front of our eyes.'

By the end of this short tour, Billy Bragg considered himself totally politicised: 'It had gone beyond being a punk rocker and playing lip service to a set of ideals. It was happening. And it was pretty heavy.'

It took Billy Bragg 27 years to reach this state of finely tuned political activist, and it was anything but an overnight conversion. It is probably wise not to overanalyse this early political poem found in one of his school exercise books circa 1971, but his passion is commendable:

'Let's have a revolution/Kill the government/Kill the monarchy/ Death to Socialism, Capitalism, Communism/Get a gun/Kill the army, navy and flyboys/Destroy religion/Kill the autocrats, bureaucrats, workers/Kill the people on the streets/ We're gonna save the world.'

Billy's first ever true political act was attending the Rock Against Racism march up to Victoria Park in Hackney, on 30 April 1978, ostensibly to see The Clash. He'd had what he now identifies as 'political feelings' at school, such as listening to Bob Dylan's 'The Times They Are A-Changin'' and being inspired by it in a soppy sort of way. He realised that the National Front were not there to be tolerated, or treated as a joke ('they were something to be opposed, physically if necessary'), and that racism was not just a black person's problem. *The Bulldog*, newspaper of the NF's youth wing, was sold outside Billy's school gates by Barking branch organiser Joe Pearce, who, Billy recalls, would also try to set up football teams. South of the A13, east of the sewage works, lies the Thames View housing estate, built in the 1960s. In the 1970s, the fact that there is one road in and one road out enabled the NF to close off the entire estate and allow only white people in, as was their wont.

The local Sikhs in Barking would get gyp for wearing turbans. Not from Billy, but he admits, 'It didn't occur to me that it was anything but spiteful – and there was that terrible feeling: rather them than me.'

Rock Against Racism was, for Billy, 'an eye-opener'.

It is not an oversimplification of events to say that RAR was formed because of Eric Clapton. In August 1976, on stage in Birmingham, he informed his audience, quite out of the blue, that he agreed with Enoch Powell and stated, unequivocally, that he thought black immigrants in Britain should be sent home. (This, from the man who'd made his name playing the blues, and scored a Top Ten hit with Bob Marley's 'I Shot The Sheriff' in 1974.) A wave of embarrassment swept through the rock community. A letter of protest from various media folk appeared in the *Socialist Worker* newspaper and the music weeklies. Support grew, and Rock Against Racism went from being a statement to a movement. In his book *When The Music's Over*, Robin Denselow describes RAR's five-year lifetime as 'embroiled in controversy and chaos. In retrospect, it is remarkable that it survived at all and achieved so much, for it was attempting the near-impossible.'

Nevertheless, it was British pop music's first organised political front, as hamstrung by its affiliation with the Socialist Worker Party as was, for some, Red Wedge with Labour years later. Its heart, though, was in the right place, and it provided just the show of strength needed to counter the rise of the NF, 80 of whose candidates in the 1976 local elections polled over ten per cent of the vote. Rock Against Racism, like the GLC, put on some splendid gigs, mixing white and black artists and helping to promote British reggae to the white punks.

At Victoria Park, Billy felt part of a mass movement: 'Wow! I'm not the only person who's into The Clash and into reggae, there's a lot of us, and we're very, very powerful.' This was a common reaction. The march from Trafalgar Square to Hackney had been organised by the Anti-Nazi League, and the left-wing swell that day was tangible. All pro-liberation life was here. Billy remembers the shock of seeing men kissing (something he and Wiggy had, understandably, never seen in Barking). They felt entirely unthreatened. Billy thought to himself: 'They're part of this, it's all connected, although fuck knows how. I'm not a queer, I'm still heterosexual, but it's OK, it's cool, don't run away, they're not kissing *you*, they're kissing each other.'

It was an education. 'All my politics I've had to learn,' Billy says. From race in Barking, through class in the army, to sexism in later life – which he identifies as 'the hardest lesson to learn for a working-class boy. Nobody's born politically correct. When do you pick it up? When you leave school? No. I was anti-racist when I left school but at the same time I was quite nationalistic. I had yet to learn the politics and language of multiculturalism – and I learnt it listening to music.'

Billy didn't vote in the May 1979 general election because, even though he'd never liked the Heath government (all those power cuts), he found himself enamoured with neither party when it came to putting his first cross in the box. In mitigation, he was also living in Oundle at the time, about as far away from the barricades as you could get, but nonetheless he couldn't see any difference between Labour leader Jim Callaghan and Margaret Thatcher: 'I believed that any party that supported or didn't dismantle the welfare state must be by definition socialist, or give tacit approval to socialism. Quite visionary, I suppose. In 1979 I thought of myself as an anarchist with a small "a".'

By the time of the miners' strike, Billy detected 'a drift back to the Dark Ages', and in an instant was passive no more. 'I was in the right place at the right time.'

Britain's trade unions did not have a good 1980s, their membership falling from thirteen million in 1980 to nine million by 1987. But the miners' strike was not just about union rights, it was about civil liberties, peaceful protest and the dignity of labour. After RAR, the ANL and CND, the NUM became a worthy cause for the *NME*, which, as Billy puts it, 'was trying to be a bit more than a music journal under Spencer'.

Neil Spencer says, of the miners' strike, 'It didn't just energise the *NME*, it energised the entire music industry. And I don't think for a moment you could've had Live Aid if you hadn't first had the more hardcore political battles.'

With its fistful of SWP-influenced journalists, the *NME* came into its own in 1984, truly coming out of its 'head-up-its-own-arsehole period' (Billy's allusion to the florid, situationist prose sculpted by writers like Ian Penman, Paul Morley and Barney Hoskyns who characterised the arty new romantic years). Suddenly, it was all Billy Bragg, The Redskins, Easterhouse and Paul Weller. 'It was up to us to turn out and do stuff,' Billy says. 'And the *NME* really helped to promote and create an atmosphere in which to talk about politics.'

On 9 October, Billy played a miners' benefit approximately 10,000 light years away from the coal-face, at the trendy

Wag Club in London's Wardour Street. It was an ad hoc affair, with Billy performing on a stage made from a row of plastic seats, his amp on the seat beside, wobbling throughout. Rather than bring it all back home, it took the strike far away from home, but every penny counts. The struggle continued, but so did the unstoppable march of commerce. Billy had a second album coming out. In October, he embarked upon his first ever headlining tour with The Hank Wangford Band and crazed Japanese cabaret-pop troupe The Frank Chickens. On 12 October 1984, *Brewing Up With Billy Bragg* was released.

Incidentally, Steven Wells believes he gave Billy the album title: 'He's never thanked me for it. It was my idea. Brewing up is not only a familiar-sounding British teamaking thing, it's also a reference to tanks. When a tank is hit by an anti-tank missile, blows up, and cooks the crew alive, the tank is said to be "brewing up".'

Recorded in just ten days, it featured all the songs that didn't make it on to *Life's A Riot*, which is why it forms such a neat companion to the first album, and why it bears no reflection of the miners' strike. 'Between The Wars', Billy's definitive paean to union rights, had already been written when *Brewing Up* was recorded, but he didn't have the confidence to put it on. His recent experience at the pits vindicated the song's sentiment and style, where, played live, it had very strong resonance.

The most politically charged tracks on *Brewing Up* are 'Island Of No Return' and 'Like Soldiers Do', his response to the Falklands War and his time in the army, while 'It Says Here' attacks the Tory press ('where politics mix with bingo and tits in a money and numbers game'). The rest are love songs, typically forlorn and gloomy in sentiment, like 'Love Gets Dangerous' ('Lust is a cancer, love is a vice') and 'St Swithin's Day' ('And the times that we all hoped would last/Like a train they have gone by so fast'), but sung over sweet, melancholy tunes. 'The Myth Of Trust' contains the disturbing image of 'dancing disgusting and flushing our babies down the drain', showing that Billy Bragg was not afraid to talk about sex either.

In the *NME*'s review, an erudite Danny Kelly astutely picked up on Billy's 'ability as a chronicler of the heart's troubled voyage', noting that *Brewing Up* was split equally between 'overtly political outbursts and excruciatingly personal (and no less political) love songs'. He compared Billy favourably to Elvis Costello and The Jam ('circa "David Watts"'), and correctly identified 'The Saturday Boy' as his best song to date ('Sheer genius,' concurred Bill Black in his four-and-a-half star review in *Sounds*).

'The Saturday Boy' abides today as one of Billy Bragg's most popular tunes. It is autobiographical, simple, heart tugging, funny and, on record, expertly embellished with a medieval-sounding trumpet part by Dave Woodhead that takes it to a new place. With double the conventional number of instruments, it's virtually a production number in the context of *Brewing Up*, but it's the poetic sentiment that fixes it in people's hearts:

> *I'll never forget the first day I met her*
> *That September morning was clear and fresh*
> *The way she spoke and laughed at my jokes*
> *And the way she rubbed herself against the edge of*
> *my desk*

It is the story of Kim, who helped Billy fail his O Levels, and the very act of writing a song about a schoolboy romance once again separated Billy from the mid-80s pop crowd, who were, at that time, singing about wild boys sticking together, careless whispers, smooth operators and war being stupid. There is nothing morally superior in singing the line 'And we'd sit together in double History twice a week' as opposed to 'We'll always be together, together in electric dreams' – indeed, the Giorgio Moroder & Phil Oakey song from which the second line is taken is a cracking electro-pop singalong – but Billy's honesty was certainly refreshing. His best lyrics could happily be read as poems, and the occasional line could have been uttered by Oscar Wilde: 'Some people say love is blind, but I think that's just a bit short-sighted.' References to Kipling, 'Elizabethan girls' and the Battle of Agincourt add to the sophistication. The line in 'The Saturday Boy', 'And la la la la la la means I love you' is a reference to The Delfonics song 'La La Means I Love You'. All this from a performer best known, critics of his singing might say, for going round barking.

Melody Maker's Colin Irwin was more critical of *Brewing Up*, mentioning 'the odd makeweight track' and 'forgettable nonsense', suggesting that the government should make it illegal for Billy to fall in love ('Slush doesn't become him'). It entered the chart at Number Sixteen and stuck around for a total of 21 weeks. Not bad for a record unfanfared by singles and unlubricated by a big showbiz launch party (Go! Discs sent out a 15p Luncheon Voucher with press copies of the album as a Launch The LP In The Privacy Of Your Own Home Kit: 'Simply take the voucher to your local cafe, trade it in for a cup of tea, take the cuppa home and put the album on the deck!').

Meanwhile, out there in the world of retail, trouble was brewing. In line with Billy and PJ's commando raid on capitalism, and appropriate to Go! Discs' cheap'n'cheerful family image, *Brewing Up* had 'Pay no more than £3.99' printed on its sleeve. This did not make record shops very happy, a gripe personified by a letter to Chrysalis, who distributed the album, from a director of Our Price plc in London:

'The industry decided some time ago to abolish recommended retail prices and to let the marketplace decide on pricing albums. It is not possible to have your cake and eat it. There either *is* a recommended retail price or there is not, and it is a dangerous game for an artist to insist along the lines that Billy Bragg is trying to do. I have to inform you that it is likely that as soon as the album drops out of the Our Price chart we will delete it from our shops and will not stock it until the offending price printed on the sleeve is removed.

'I think progress has been made in educating customers that £4.49–£4.99 is good value for chart albums. It is doing nobody any favours for customers to start seeing £3.99 chart albums being displayed.'

An enlightening plea, and one that strengthened Billy and PJ's resolve. It is evident from the letter that Billy's built-in price-cut ploy is only a problem because it is a *chart* album (i.e. one that Our Price would be mad not to stock), and that made his position even more precious. Here was a *chart* act kicking up dust in the world of record retail, not some obscure anarchist selling singles off a trestle table in a church hall. The Our Price letter claims that £3.99-an-album is 'doing nobody any favours' – what about the record buyer who has been so successfully 'educated' to pay a fiver for a chart album?

To his great satisfaction, Billy was playing 'a dangerous game'.

Bête noire of Britain's vinyl emporia he may have been, but the so-called 'Hanks'n'Franks' tour whipped up a lot of praise from the press. In the *Guardian*, William Leith spoke of Billy's 'economy of movement and precision timing. He knows exactly how to tell a story or deliver a one-liner, neither gauchely self-important nor embarrassed.' One Jimmy Mack in *Sounds* joked, 'Gone are the days when Billy Bragg used to outnumber his audience!' Although the evening's entertainment involved the Wangford Band accompanying Billy for a hoedown of 'A13', and all three acts congregating on stage for a ropey dance routine to the Franks' rendition of 'Fujiama Mama', most reviewers saw this as proof that, as *Melody Maker*'s Ted Mico stated, 'Billy Bragg is better off solo.' So there.

In December, he was back out on his own, a month-long campaign through Europe with Kershaw/PJ in the driving seat, talking politics and singing out loud: Frankfurt, Hamburg, Berlin, Bremen, and on into Scandinavia. A classic example of the Billy Bragg work-work-work ethic came in France between Metz and Paris, where, on a supposed day off, Billy and Kershaw travelled back to Berlin for a radio appearance.

There's no airport in Metz, so a geezer they'd met from a puppet theatre gave them a lift over the border into Germany to the nearest airport for an 8 a.m. flight (the puppeteer had never been to Germany before, but there's a first time for everything and being around Billy Bragg usually makes it happen – it was the first time they'd been driven by a puppeteer). Billy and Kershaw boarded a worryingly tiny plane on what turned out to be the fortieth anniversary of Glenn Miller's death ('That cheered me up no end,' recalls the frequent flyer). They were scheduled to change planes at Frankfurt, but it was fogbound, which meant flying round and round in circles for a bit, making them late for their connection. They ran between terminals and made the flight, only to discover that their bags and the guitars hadn't arrived in Berlin. Kershaw agreed to stay at the airport and wait, while Billy flew ahead to Berlin, where he did the gig at the radio station on borrowed equipment ('One song! One take! That's it. I don't even know if it was ever broadcast').

Reunited with Kershaw in Berlin, they bumped into the Leeds band Serious Drinking, accompanied by fanzine writer James Brown (years later he became the editor of *Loaded* and then *GQ*). They were on the guest list at the Serious Drinking gig, and, aptly enough, drowned their sorrows – not an act conducive with getting up the next morning at the crack of dawn in order to get back to Paris. They flew back to Frankfurt, circled around it a few times because it was still fogbound, and when they finally got back to Paris, the gear was missing again. This is a pretty standard slice of on-the-road madness that illustrates the relentless nature of the Billy Bragg touring-promotion treadmill and, when it came to the crunch, just how adaptable and patient he was. (It would've been perfectly acceptable to cancel the Berlin radio slot due to unforeseen circumstances, but that was neither the Bragg nor the Jenner ethos.) In the frustrating event, Billy *almost* threw a tantrum and he certainly stomped back to the hotel to sulk, and describes he and Kershaw being 'at each other's throats' by the end of it ('He accused me of being a pop star, which hurt me the most'). Jenner, with the advantage of having only just arrived from London, kept his cool, mediated, and went off to find the equipment.

The money was coming in. (Billy later happily admitted to *Smash Hits* that he was now earning the same in one night as he was *per annum* at Overseas Containers Ltd, 'an achievement to be proud of'.) Among all the other worthy causes, there had to be, as he put it, 'a few Billy Bragg benefits'. At the end of 1983, Billy describes his position as 'scraping by. By the end of 1984, I was laughing. I had a career, I had a job.'

Money, money everywhere, but nothing much to spend it on. Touring costs barely registered on a calculator. They weren't buying food or drink, and accommodation, however spartan, was laid on. And as we have seen, Billy's rock'n'roll appetite was modest, to say the least. 'Money, to me, is

secondary to health and well-being,' he explains, in reference to his dad's death. 'That is the thing to focus on and
worry about. As such, I've never been inspired to do things
for money. I'm happy to see it in the bank. I wouldn't give
it all away, but I'm happy with the bit I've got. If we do
really well on a tour, everybody should get a little squirt. I
never have to look at the bottom line, Pete does that – even
when I was first going out. I've been very, very privileged
in that sense.'

Back at Go! Mansions, affairs were being put in order, thanks
to new director Juliet Macdonald. To Andy's irrepressible
enthusiasm, Juliet brought a wealth of hard-bitten experience from the shitty end of the music-biz stick. Chiswick,
Step Forward, Wayne County, Toyah, 2-Tone, she'd done
her time, and became what Billy and PJ saw as a stabilising
influence. She earned the nickname Mrs Money-Trousers,
which stuck.

'Finally, there was somebody at Go! Discs who knew how
to run a record company,' says Billy. 'Andy was making it
up as he went along. Juliet was a realist, she knew you had
to pay VAT bills, and she had some great connections. She'd
toured America while I was still farting about with Riff Raff!
Andy's a hirer, but not much of a firer. She cut away the
dead wood. He had the energy and vision, she had the tools.

'For instance, we'd sold a lot of copies of *Spy Vs Spy*, but
fuck knows how or why. Juliet knew how or why.'

At the end of 1984, *Brewing Up* came sixth in *NME*'s
Vinyl Finals (a chart that actually did justice to the overused
description 'eclectic': Bobby Womack's *Poet II* came first,
followed by Bruce Springsteen, Special AKA, Womack &
Womack and Scott Walker). It was picked as one of the year's
best albums by the *Sunday Telegraph* and the *Sunday Times*.

Including weddings, but not Portastack work, Billy had
logged a staggering 156 gigs that year, some of which had
amassed money for people less fortunate than himself.

The country spent New Year singing along to Band
Aid's 'Do They Know It's Christmas?', raising cash for the
Ethiopian famine victims. The charity record was born. It
seemed that, in pop music, everybody was waiving royalties
and putting money in collection tins in a huge wave of guilt

for spending all that cash on making videos on yachts. (Even the record shops donated their profits from Band Aid – in a year when Billy Bragg had robbed them of so much!) Billy looks back on 1984 as His Year, and sees 1985 as one long 'knock-on effect'.

In January, Kirsty MacColl took Billy's 'A New England' into the Top Ten. Produced by her husband Steve Lilywhite with full band backing, it showed just how versatile and populist a song it was. It was the first time he'd been covered by another artist. And, as he was fond of pointing out, very few of the 200,000-odd people who bought 'A New England' knew or cared that it was a Billy Bragg original – they just dug Kirtsy's pleasing, folksy lilt. It was a good moment for Billy, as he saw Kirsty as a like-minded soul (she'd been on Chiswick when Riff Raff were), and the two would collaborate properly later. One misguided ingrate going by the pseudonym of Tippex from Cardiff, wrote to the *NME* to vent his/her spleen: 'Ironic isn't it? That to get played on daytime Radio Uno you have to write a brilliant song and get it absolutely ruined by some pregnant, middle-aged, middle of the road pop singer.' That week's letters editor, David Swift, sent Tippex away with a flea in his/her ear: 'Go away clothears, we rate it, as Billy does, a great version.' There will always be purists, and they will always try to ruin the party.

In February, Billy went back to the States and did his first headline dates at various collegiate venues, racking up quite a bit of local press along the way, and bringing home about 60 vinyl albums (mostly folk, blues and gospel) to add to the 50 or so he'd purchased on the Bunnymen trip. Travel was broadening his record collection.

On 3 March 1985, the miners' strike finally ended. Delegates of the NUM voted 98 to 91 to call it off, having watched thousands of miners drift back into work. By February, only 51 per cent remained on the picket lines. Mrs Thatcher called it 'a famous victory'. A year later, 36 collieries had been closed, as if to catch up on the lost year. It was a depressing outcome, but, as Seumas Milne concludes in his book *The Enemy Within*: 'For those who actually took part, along with millions of their supporters in Britain and abroad, it was a principled – even heroic – stand, which directly confronted the Thatcher administration and its battery of anti-democratic trade union legislation in a way that no other force in the country was prepared or able to do.'

The strike may have been lost, but those who made that heroic stand had proved that there was plenty of fight in them yet. After the 1984–5 strike, Scottish folk singer Dick Gaughan recorded an album called *True And Bold: Songs Of The Scottish Miners* as an expression of 'solidarity and gratitude to the finest people I have ever known', containing many stirring tunes like 'Ballad Of '84', 'Miner's Life Is Like A Sailor's' and 'Which Side Are You On?', a traditional tune with new words by Gaughan about the NUM and Thatcher. The latter would feature on Billy Bragg's next release.

'Between The Wars', left off *Brewing Up* but elevated to anthem status since the first miners' gigs, was Billy's first seven-inch single. Actually, it was a four-track EP, but it sold for 'no more than £1.25', and was resolutely *not* advertising a forthcoming or existing LP. For Billy, 'Between The Wars' itself was an important enough song to relax his principles for, and would be his public statement on the working-class experience as focused by the miners' strike:

I kept the faith and I kept voting
Not for the iron fist but for the helping hand
For theirs is a land with a wall around it
And mine is a faith in my fellow man
Theirs is a land of hope and glory
Mine is the green field and the factory floor
Theirs are the skies all dark with bombers
Mine is the peace we knew
Between the wars

It was a magnificent show of strength, both collective and musical, as folky as anything Billy had recorded and yet shot through with punk dissidence. There were no jokes in it.

The EP was structured conceptually. Alongside the no-messing-about 'Which Side Are You On?' (lyrics adapted by Billy) was an interpretation of 'The World Turned Upside Down', formerly a gently rousing piano-led salute by Leon Rosselson, now a driving, guitar-led Bo Diddley thing. 'It Says Here' was untimely ripped from *Brewing Up*. The complete set formed a supercharged one-man folk festival. The cover image, featuring two happy children, came courtesy of a tin plate advertising Flemish marmalade, that Kershaw had picked up in an Amsterdam flea market. The whole package was, as Billy modestly puts it, 'flying in the face of everything that was going on at the time'.

It charted at Number Fifteen and landed Billy Bragg on *Top Of The Pops*. To quote Virginia Woolf's Mrs Dalloway: 'What a lark! What a plunge!'

Most bands dream of their debut on *Top Of The Pops*. Even when the beleaguered show was set adrift on Friday evenings, when it was *always* a Thursday night fixture, it reamined a landmark for artist and record company promotions department alike. It was never Billy's dream, partly because he didn't watch it as a teenager, and when he did as a young man he kept seeing Spandau Ballet on it, but mostly because he never dreamt he'd be asked on. (Plus, of course, The Clash had famously refused to appear on it, which impressed Billy at the time.)

The first fly in the *Pops* ointment would be Billy's insistence on playing his hit song(!) live. This was not encouraged, as miming gave the show a technical consistency – however, since Billy's recording was so primitive, they let him make his stand. The second niggle was the audience, who were told by the director to wave their arms in the air during Billy's run-through. This was a vast improvement on the awkward dancing and balloon volleyball that characterised the show's 'party' atmosphere, but before the actual performance, Billy leant down from the stage and asked the kids not to. Mercifully, they complied, and Billy was granted the dignity of crowd attentiveness, even if some of them were wearing plastic Union Jack hats and waved the odd flag.

He was introduced by hey-wow, moustachioed Radio 1 DJ Steve Wright (still at it in the afternoon on Radio 2), who'd approached Billy beforehand and asked him to explain the whole song, which he duly did. He then came up afterwards and asked him again. 'I didn't fit in,' Billy recalls. 'And that was the idea.' Marie Bragg tuned in and approved of the 'nice shirt' he had on.

The single didn't even plummet out of the charts the following week, which is the accepted deal – it hung in there for six weeks. Billy still considers 'Between The Wars' 'a high watermark of Billy Bragg singles, and a high point of 1985. It stamped me in people's minds.'

In the solemn and apparently sincere words of Steve Wright that Thursday night: 'This really is an *evocadive* song . . . would you welcome, Billy Bragg.'

Hooray!

10. HOW LONG CAN A BAD THING LAST?

Another bit of politics, 1985–1987

When the world falls apart, some things stay in place
Billy Bragg, 'Levi Stubbs' Tears'

Like many men of below-average height, he wished he were taller
Andy McSmith of the Observer on Neil Kinnock

'Hang on to your ideals!' was Billy Bragg's message to young people on 28 February 1985, when he joined a delegation of disgruntled YTS trainees on the doorstep of 10, Downing Street. An estimated 5,000 had turned out at a rally in Jubilee Gardens to protest at the government's proposed supplementary benefit cut for school-leavers not signed to YTS schemes: it was seen as 'industrial conscription' (a bit like Labour's New Deal in 1998, but dressed in different trousers). The demo was organised by the Youth Trade Union Rights Campaign and the Labour Party Young Socialists, and a petition was signed by such diversely sympathetic pop stars as Big Country, Madness, The Flying Pickets and Frankie Goes To Hollywood, whose message of support was an adaptation of one of their own popular T-shirt slogans: FRANKIE SAY, DON'T RELAX – ORGANISE.

1985 was the year of getting organised. That summer the twin Live Aid concerts raised over £50 million for famine relief, the logical, if staggering, conclusion to pop music's overwhelming bout of selflessness. Billy called it Egos For Ethiopia. Back at grass roots level, the causes being fought were less black and white – after all, it's easy to decide how you feel about a dying Ethiopian child, but more difficult to take sides on a debate about, say, welfare cuts or unilateral disarmament or local council funding. Pop stars, in Billy Bragg's experience, live in fear of being wrong and, as a defence, back only cut-and-dried issues like famine or homelessness. Billy was more interested in getting at the cause than sticking an Elastoplast over the effect ('I applaud the efforts of Band Aid,' he told *Record Mirror*, 'but that song should have been "Smash capitalism *and* feed the world"').

In March, Billy set out on an eight-date Jobs For Youth tour (his *Top Of The Pops* appearance coincided with the date in Southend). Sponsored by the Labour Party as part of their Jobs And Industry Campaign, a couple of MPs were present at each venue to answer questions. Since there is no clear answer to 'What about unemployment?', the sessions provided a lively debating floor and a vital bridge between Young People and the Labour Party. 'This tour is a manifestation of the fact that I can personally, physically do nothing apart from gigs,' Billy told Colin Irwin in the *Melody Maker* cover story (headline: 'WARNING! THIS MAN TELLS THE TRUTH'). 'I don't want to ram it down people's throats. If you don't come for politics, I don't mind. Enjoy, enjoy. I'd like to think you don't have to be a Labour supporter to listen to Billy Bragg.'

Before the tour, Billy had visited the House of Commons to meet some of the MPs who would be attending the gigs (including MP for Livingston, Robin Cook) and put their minds at rest about trouser width. It wasn't his first time in the House. On 26 February, he'd been invited to an informal discussion about youth issues by Neil Kinnock, along with Peter Jenner, Andy Kershaw and others. By all accounts a slightly awkward occasion with bowls of crisps, bottles of claret and Jenner playing the old hippy by quizzing Kinnock on the legalisation of cannabis. 'It was all a bit sad and bizarre,' recalled Kershaw. 'And I felt sorry for Kinnock.' If nothing else it proved the Labour Party – sorry state that they were in – were keen to expose themselves to new voices, and some kind of bond was forged.

The image of Billy Bragg and the Labour leader became ubiquitous in the years running up to the 1987 general election: usually the shot of the pair of them sipping tea and laughing. It was, at least, an improvement on Harold Wilson buddying up with The Beatles at the Dorchester Hotel in 1965. Kinnock was a dynamic figurehead for the embattled opposition party, a sprightly 43 years old, he'd won the 1983 leadership election by 72 per cent of the vote, thanks to almost total support from the unions. He and deputy Roy Hattersley represented the dream ticket for Labour, the dawning of a new, electable era after the scrag-end Michael Foot years. Kinnock's background in CND, the ANL and the Gene Vincent Fan Club made him a relatively hip choice for the two and half million first-time voters coming through at the next election (although he'd lost credibility points for appearing in a Tracey Ullman pop video, and hard-line lefties would never forgive him for equivocating over the miners' strike).

Neil Kinnock remembers his first meeting with Billy Bragg well. 'I'd checked Billy out with my own children, who were then about fifteen and thirteen,' he says. 'They said he was fine. Steve, the eldest, particularly rated him. Billy was open, energetic, articulate. He obviously had a strong sense of mission – but without any pretensions of self-righteousness. He also liked Jerry Lee Lewis and sent me some tapes. That was good enough for me!'

On Labour's apparently deliberate courtship of youth culture, Kinnock today is unbowed:

'For me it was natural rather than deliberate. Democratic politics must speak a language that people understand and it was also essential to identify the Labour Party with freshness, fun, modern ideas and attitudes when it had been seen as stale, outdated and out of touch.

'My action carried risks – the Tories sneered, the press treated it as a "lightweight" gimmick – but it was the right thing to do. The attitude of people like Billy certainly helped.'

So it was that Billy Bragg became inextricably wed in people's minds to the Labour Party, for better or for worse. At the Sheffield University Jobs For Youth date, before a packed 1,500-strong crowd, Billy joked from the stage that

Kinnock would be joining him on trumpet, at which cries of 'Scab!' went out from some militant faction. Billy defused the moment: 'He can't because he's broken his leg – he fell off the fence.'

On 10 March, ITV's flagship arts slot *The South Bank Show* devoted an edition to Billy Bragg (actually, he had to share it with a half-hour film about Michael Crawford learning to tightrope walk for *Barnum*, but you have to take what you can get on Sunday nights). The introduction by his namesake Melvyn was succinctly put – 'At a time when pop music is dominated by lavish production values, glossy videos and massive hype, Billy Bragg has made a virtue of simplicity' – followed by a suitably low-key portrait of an idealistic, self-effacing Essex boy telling us his life story and being driven down the A13. There was also some specially shot live footage from a miners' show at London's Bull & Gate pub. It was a modest film, and one made unnaturally early in an artist's career, but at least it told no lies.

On 5 April, Billy played at the Labour Party Young Socialists conference at Blackpool, a natural enough invite after his solidarity in February. While there, he was, as he puts it, 'summoned to have beer with the Militant Tendency – in the guise of the Young Socialists'. In a crowded room, they explained their programme, 'and I explained that if I believed in everything *they* believed in I would join the Socialist Workers Party, and that was it. We left it at that, and I never really had anything to do with them again.' Although Billy was a believer in direct action and the constant inter-rogation of Labour's policies and motives, he felt that they were the only realistic, democratic alternative to the Tories. As a result, his commitment to Labour was very public, if always questioning. Splinter groups are fine for stirring up debate and doubling the numbers in a mob, but, as far as Billy was concerned, their actions were counter-productive to the Big Push.

Having been in the army, Billy was certain that armed pro-letariat revolution was not a practical option (all those bored squaddies itching for a punch-up, and Northern Ireland-trained), and he drew the line at blowing up Thatcher – as the IRA had tried to do in October '84 in Brighton

('They'll just get someone else in, another figurehead'). To the more strait-laced elements of the Labour Party, Billy was a rabble-rouser; to the hard left, he was a party-line sop, a Kinnockite poodle. In pop music, such distinctions were rarely even contemplated, which is what makes his position from the mid-80s onwards so fascinating.

When Red Wedge was up and running, he believes that the 'Millies' (Militant Tendency) deliberately undermined many of their day events. The Young Socialists would promote the event, advertise that Paul Weller was going to play when he wasn't, and thereby create a bad atmosphere, which discredited the Wedge and soured pro-Kinnock feeling. Some of the local Labour parties made it difficult too, wrongly imagining that anyone under 30 in the party must be tied to Militant – Billy remembers the Derby branch saying, 'Don't bother coming here, we haven't got any young people.' This was the sort of mentality they were up against. Neil Spencer, who'd left the *NME* when Red Wedge started up, refers to 'an *ambivalent* relationship with the Young Socialists. They were a Trotskyist front for the Militant Tendency with impossiblist ideals. You couldn't live up to their expectations.' Spencer goes further than Billy, saying, 'They systematically tried to sabotage everything we did right from the beginning. On another level they were simply a fucking pain – they were damaging the Labour Party's chances of ever being elected again.'

Red Wedge was still a collective twinkle in the eye at the time of the LPYS conference, and it would take a few months before people like Bragg, Weller and Spencer – agitated, educated – got organised. In the meantime, there were gigs to play, countries to visit, records to promote.

A week after Blackpool, Billy played his first hometown gig at Barking Assembly Hall – the one to which O-Level Kim turned up with her mum and the book of teenage Bragg poetry. She wasn't the only ghost: 'Never do a gig in your own town,' he states. 'People who used to shit on you at school turn up and say what great friends they were with you.'

He was back in the USA in May for what turned into a heavy-going six-week tour, consolidating all the university-newspaper interest and the fact that both his albums were now available through a tiny label called CD Presents (CD standing for Civil Defence – not Compact Disc, a two-year-old invention that had yet to take off). Run by a guy Billy had met at the New Music Seminar, CD Presents never actually paid him any royalties, but at least they put his records in the shops. (By the time of his third album, he'd signed a deal with major player Elektra.) Along the route, Billy met R.E.M. for the first time in Buffalo, NY. The jangly garage-rock four-piece from Athens, Georgia, were really taking off in 1985, having breached the US Top 30 with their second album *Reckoning* and become a college-circuit sensation. Billy and R.E.M. hit it off, and their stories would intermingle again later.

Wiggy, who'd 'road-managed' January's US jaunt, couldn't make this one, so Billy was accompanied by a Scottish 'guitar nut' called Geoff Davidson, whose only drawback was a refusal ever to break America's 50 mph speed limit. This became a real problem only once, between Milwaukee, Wisconsin and Cedar Rapids, Iowa. To drive from one to the other involves crossing time-zones – subsequently, they were late for what *was* an afternoon gig in Cedar Rapids. Worse, it was the biggest-paying date on the entire tour, the fee was literally going to see Billy and Geoff from the West coast to the East. They arrived at the college just in time to see the place being swept up – all the kids were off home at the end of semester, which is why Billy was booked in the first place: all the money in the kitty was traditionally blown on whoever the ents officer fancied (he was a massive Bragg fan). 'We'd really stewed the rhubarb,' Billy says.

Determined to do *a* gig (and earn his keep) Billy plugged in and, as they stacked tables around him, took requests off the ents officer for 45 minutes, like a human juke-box. Show over, they joined this grateful student executive for a beer, and discovered, to their dismay, that he didn't actually *have* the money on him – it was in the bank, and he couldn't get it until the next morning. 'We had to be nice to this horrible geezer all night!' Billy laughs. 'Next morning, we were up first thing. We *drove* him to the bank, and walked in there with him.'

The notion of a cross-America tour seems a romantic one, but you have to imagine two men in a rented car, 'let loose in a foreign country with a list of places, times and names of whoever was going to pay us. Off we went.' Billy supported Screamin' Jay Hawkins in Cleveland, Ohio; he played a cowboy festival in Edmonton, Alberta; and then, half-way through the Bragg dates, he got a telephone call from Pete Jenner, saying, 'Join The Smiths!'

It was The Smiths' first US tour, taken somewhat reluctantly (it had almost been cancelled a fortnight earlier in a fit of band pique). Billy met them in Royal Oak, Detroit, for his first gig, where, despite what Smiths chronicler Johnny Rogan calls 'a more restrained welcome', Billy had the time of his life: 'I remember watching The Smiths on that first night, beer in hand, thinking, I'm getting paid for doing this! It can't be right! There must be a catch.'

There wasn't. Good money, travelling on the Smiths' bus, getting on famously, having a long conversation with Morrissey about The Shirelles, whom Billy had always mistakenly called The Shirlettes (he'd misread a sleeve) – the union even lent symmetry to Billy's current inclusion of the Smiths' B-side 'Jeane' in his set ('after the first three nights, they put it back in *their* set').

On his return, Billy did an English festival crawl: The Longest Day, Glastonbury and WOMAD. The Longest Day on 22 June took place at Milton Keynes Bowl and starred U2, R.E.M., The Ramones, Spear Of Destiny and The Faith Brothers (Billy came between SOD and The Ramones). Thanks to torrential rain, and the impatient, blinkered loyalty of U2 fans, it was a grim day, closer in ambience to the film *The Longest Day* about the 1944 D-Day landings. As it poured down, and the Bowl literally filled up with rain and mud, the U2 fans ensured that the impressive bill of support acts felt anything *but* welcome. 'The logic behind the audience's actions was, the sooner we get these bastards off, the sooner U2 will come on, and we can get home and get dry,' says Billy, who, like the others, was pelted with plastic bottles, some filled with urine (what a delightful old English tradition that is, and how we miss it). One struck Billy right on the front of his guitar, prompting the riposte, 'I'd like to thank the man who invented the plastic bottle because I think he just saved my life.'

Later, a bottle knocked over a row of Ramones guitars like skittles. Even R.E.M. got it, at a reduced intensity. 'It wasn't nice,' Billy remembers. 'But I was getting paid a lot of money to do this gig, and I thought I should stand my ground for 25 minutes and play. So I did.'

Bruce Springsteen was rumoured to be flying in for the final encore. Squeeze and The Alarm were apparently surprise guests. None of them turned up, and they were better off out of it.

Glastonbury the next day was a mud-bath. The Style Council were on, and Paul Weller made the memorable error of wearing white jeans. No one threw anything at Billy (it was supposed to be a peace festival, after all), except right at the end of 'A13', his last number, when a soggy, mud-caked rag hit his guitar right where the neck joins the body. It killed the strings dead. Seizing the moment, Billy said, 'Thank you very much!' and walked off.

The festival fest continued in Denmark at the end of June, namely with British band favourite Roskilde in Copenhagen. Billy took the weather with him: it lashed down there too. The Pogues were playing after him, so he loitered at the side of the stage and watched them do their pickled Irish folk-punk thing. Unfortunately, he was standing right next to the band's rider, 'so every time a Pogue came over and cracked a beer, they cracked one for me.' The band encored with 'Honky Tonk Women', and invited Billy to join them. 'It's just G all the way through,' he thought, and mucked in. 'I was well out of it.' At the end of the drunken thrash, Billy fell off the front of the drum riser, and was, to his enormous retrospective pride, carried off by The Pogues!

'Suffice to say, that was one of the few times I've been out there drunk.'

On 1 July, Billy showed his Labour Party solidarity by doing a short-notice gig for the Brecon by-election in Wales, among an all-star MP line-up of Clare Short, Michael Foot and Dennis Healey. Billy remembers Healey sitting at a piano in the dressing room, shouting to the former leader, 'Come on, Michael, give us a tune on the spoons!' These moments stick in the mind. 'Heaven knows what kind of leader of the party Healey would've made, but he's a very funny guy.'

Back in Greater London, at Battersea Park, Billy played the GLC's glorious Jobs For A Change Festival, and the sun shone for socialism. An estimated 100,000 punters enjoyed what was, says Billy, 'the ultimate great free day out on the GLC. It was like a free Glastonbury. The vibe was great, there was a reggae band on before me, and everybody sang "Between The Wars". I thought to myself, This must be what socialism is: free gig, everyone singing, sun shining, this is it.'

The *Daily Mirror* called it 'the first rock'n'roll party political broadcast'. It was shown on BBC1 at 8.50 p.m. and ITV at 10 p.m., 17 July, and the Labour Party's message was delivered not by men in ties behind oak desks, but by musicians. Billy Bragg sang new tune 'Days Like These' and spoke about youth issues between performances by Aswad, Jimmy Somerville and Julie Roberts from jazz-soul outfit Working Week. It set the tone for what was about to happen.

Before that, Billy played his first folk festival at Trowbridge. Any trepidation he might've had about being a square peg in a round hole was washed away when he walked into the tent and witnessed Blowzabella, trad hurdy-gurdy folksters, playing 'Between The Wars'. Back in March, Billy had placed a toe in the waters of hard-core folk acceptance by being interviewed for the specialist *Southern Rag* magazine, and confessing to Colin Irwin his folk affinities, from The Watersons through June Tabor to The Men They Couldn't Hang. Irwin wrote an impassioned sign-off to the mag's readers: 'Don't fret yourself now about the man's right to be in these pages (if you're worried about that, then you've got *big* problems).'

Next day, while the other Trowbridge performers reeled back to the folk circuit, Billy did a gig at Feltham Young Offenders, a borstal in Middlesex. It was a tough one: the body language of the inmates was exactly that of those who'd bullied Billy in school, which cut him to the quick. Through subsequent experience, Billy says he's learnt how to 'do the institution circuit. They are not there to see you, they are there to be with each other. Even if they talk among themselves, they may still be into it.' He later did Barlinnie Prison in Glasgow, accompanied by the evidently unflappable keyboardist Cara Tivey, which he describes as 'a bit heavy', but not for *them* – Billy was embarrassed at the contemptuous way the screws talked to the inmates. He's also played Broadmoor, where they have their own folk club.

And to think, some bands won't play a venue that hasn't got a wind machine . . .

On 23 July, just prior to Billy's first Japanese tour, he found himself in a committee room at Labour Party HQ in Walworth Road with a motley collection of musicians, managers and media types. The job in hand was to formalise the creative community's anti-government sympathies into some kind of organisation-cum-pressure-group. It didn't have a name.

Among those present at this momentous first meeting were Paul Weller, Neil Spencer, Pete Jenner and Annajoy David from Youth CND. A general notion was agreed upon: this creative collective should actively encourage young people to vote by bombarding them with information about Labour's policies and showing them a good time in the process. It was radical, in that no one had ever attempted it before in this country, but it was also disarmingly simple. The new group would not be a pop wing of the Labour Party, indeed it would lobby them on pertinent issues – but if Labour needed help to unseat the Tories, then they could act as a consultant body in matters of youth and the arts.

Looking back, Paul Bower, the group's first coordinator, summed up, 'We were saying that the Labour Party was not talking to young people in *their* language and that it had to use the mass media effectively.' Annajoy David banged the metaphorical table, 'We need to inject people with a new enthusiasm for socialism.'

Billy Bragg came up with the name Red Wedge (from a poster by Russian constructivist artist El Lissitzky, *Beat The Whites With The Red Wedge*) and debate raged – not just on into the next meeting in August, but throughout the Wedge's life. The problem was the word 'Red', which, for some, was too tied in with communism and the Red Army and the Red Brigade and other such difficult associations. Already, the organisation seemed to have a hard left and a soft left (things *were* going well). PR Lynne Franks said, 'We don't want anything with red in it.' The Labour Party themselves were even dubious, worried that Fleet Street would turn it against them. Even Neil Spencer was doubtful: 'I always thought it was the wrong name. I never liked the idea of Red or being Reds. It's a bit fucking clichéd isn't it?'

Cliché or not, Red Wedge they became, leading to many a journalistic swipe about haircuts (thankfully, by then Weller had moved on from his wedge to a fetching feather-cut). Some of the alternatives were Red Steady Go, More To The Point and Moving Hearts And Minds. Quite.

Nonetheless, some artists used their aversion to the R-word as an excuse not to join up, including Elvis Costello – a crushing disappointment to Billy. He remembers one Sunday afternoon, sitting on the stairs of his flat on the phone to Costello trying to persuade him to relent. He failed. Even though Costello had played for the miners, he thought Red Wedge 'a terrible name, particularly if you're going around saying you're just trying to make people politically aware.' (Reassuring for Billy, Costello did turn out once for the Wedge, although indirectly: a Newcastle day event at the Riverside had been stymied by Militant, who'd falsely advertised Weller, and there was a 'near-riot', so Elvis, who was in town for *The Tube*, went over and played to calm the audience down. He may not have supported Red Wedge, but he was not above helping out in a crisis – Billy doffs his cap: 'It was good going, he deserves a lot of respect for that.')

With the ball rolling and the flag flying, Billy sent apologies to the next Red Wedge meeting at Walworth Road on 7 August: he was somewhere between Nagasaki and Kyoto. In his absence, the well-attended meeting agreed upon Red Wedge as a name, set about drafting a credo 'outlining the general beliefs and aims of this group' (*not* a manifesto), and looked into a date and site for the launch: the Tory Party conference in Blackpool? The SDP conference? (The SDP were planning their own artist-led youth campaign, and they mustn't steal Wedge thunder.) Or at the Billy Bragg gig on 1 October at the Labour conference in Bournemouth? A logo was also looked into. The minutes read: 'Pete Jenner and Billy Bragg have a Russian illustration in mind and will bring it to the next meeting.'

Japan is the country where Billy Bragg is famous for knowing Paul Weller. His first tour there – eight shows in August – was low key but no less enjoyable. Billy sums up: 'No one came to the gigs but I loved it.'

Pete Jenner's wife Sumi, though born in Canada, came from a Japanese family and had never been to Japan. As she speaks some Japanese, it was logically agreed that Sumi should tour-manage. The promoter, Masahiro Hadaka (a 'lovely fella' according to Billy, who still works with him), really went beyond the call of duty: he tracked down Sumi's relatives, organised a reunion and helped translate.

Japan has a habit of blowing Westerners' minds, with its bright lights, dried squid and frightening population density (imagine the population of the USA living in an area the size of Wyoming). In fact, the Japanese trip has become something of a cliché in the music press: any two-bit British band can tour there, and journalists are invariably invited along 'for the story'. Billy was asked by *Zig Zag* magazine to write his own account which turned out to be erudite, informative and yet no less gobsmacked. Less an indulgent rock star tour diary, 'Nagasaki Nightmare' as they called it, was an intelligent look at the 'small and fragmented' Japanese peace protest movement (while he was there, he took part in an anti-nuclear demo in Tokyo attended by 200 people). In short, the old O Level was paying dividends.

At Kyoto, which is near where Sumi's people lived, Billy eschewed the Western-style hotels and opted to stay in a traditional Japanese inn, with straw mats, futons and paper walls. You had to inform reception when you wanted to have a bath, which Billy found odd, until he realised that baths were a communal affair. The form was shower down first and then go and sit in this huge bath where everyone perches round the edge with their underpants folded up on their head. It's boiling hot and it opens up your pores. Billy remembers that there were three Japanese men already in there, 'about as communicative as London tube travellers'. He shattered the contemplative calm somewhat as he noisily eased himself into the scalding tub, his pale skin getting redder and redder. There's nothing like immersing yourself in someone else's culture.

Every morning without fail, Billy cracked his head on the low door frame of his room, and the paper walls would shake. He describes the whole experience as 'incredible', not least the day spent wandering round the Sho'gun palaces.

Gigs took place at 6 p.m. sharp (that's stopwatch-sharp) and were over by 8 p.m., which meant pleasant evenings spent in restaurants. In Nagoya, at a venue called The Faithful Yukka, Billy was impressed by a Japanese guy in a robe and turban who sounded exactly like Mississippi bluesman Howling Wolf. During the soundcheck, Billy asked him what tuning he was using on his guitar and discovered that he didn't speak a word of English – he'd learnt these Western songs phonetically. During Billy's set, a fan leapt up, snatched the mic off him and ran around the stage singing, 'I don't want to change the world, I just wanna go to England.' Security slapped him across the chops and took him away. Afterwards, this fan came into the dressing room and prostrated himself before Billy to apologise – on the way to the gig he'd been involved in a train crash and was consequently a little emotional. He gave Billy his sunglasses (in Japan, exchanging gifts is like shaking hands). Billy gave him the sweaty white T-shirt off his back, at which the fan fell to the ground and started sobbing. It was all too much for him.

In Fukuoka (cue: hilarity from Western visitors), Billy espied Steve White in the street, drummer from The Style Council, who were also on tour (another key apology at the 7 August Red Wedge meeting, then). Unlike Billy, the rest of The Style Council were holed up in their nice hotel demanding English beer and eggs and bacon (Weller had toured the country more than once with The Jam and The Council had hit big the last time they were here, so the novelty of the place, for him, had evaporated). There was a subsequent visit to a transvestite club wearing shorts, and the Englishmen abroad parted company ('We left them complaining about the sushi,' says Billy).

Billy was nearly sucked into oblivion by the famous bullet train. While Sumi was off looking for the promoter, he sat at the far end of the elevated train platform with his gear. A terse announcement in Japanese followed, then a bell and flashing lights, to the significance of which he remained oblivious. Out of nowhere, the bullet train came round the bend and passed through the station at 180 mph. Billy describes his near-death experience: 'First, the air pressure hits you, then, in the slipstream, the air is literally sucked out of your mouth. It was the fact that I was anchored there by sitting on the equipment that saved my life.'

Having been wooed by the land of the rising sun, it was back to the land of rising unemployment.

Red Wedge was launched on 21 November 1985. 'Robin Cook MP requests the pleasure of your company,' ran the plain invitation, 'at the marquee on the terrace, House of Commons, London SW1, from 11.30 a.m. Sorry, no parking facilities.'

By now, a simple red-and-white logo had been designed by Neville Brody, groundbreaking designer at *The Face* magazine: a red cheese of socialism driven between two black blocks of capitalism. The marquee on the terrace was, disappointingly, blue and white, but it was soon packed with pop stars drinking hot punch: Billy Bragg, Weller, Jerry Dammers of The Specials, Tom Robinson, The Communards (Jimmy Somerville's new group), Hank Wangford, Heaven 17, Roland Gift of Fine Young Cannibals, Rat Scabies of The Damned, Kirsty MacColl and actor Robbie Coltrane. Big-trousered Latin poseurs Blue Rondo A La Turk even turned up, perhaps the antithesis of Billy's rock'n'roll ideal, but this was not to be an exclusive club. And when Gary Kemp later pledged his support, Billy was forced to soften his view on Spandau Ballet, the very band who'd inspired his crusade back in 1981.

Kinnock made a speech, and a joke: 'Can I first disabuse anyone of the idea that Red Wedge refers to my haircut.'

This was the public's first glimpse of style-conscious pop stars chumming it with self-conscious MPs. It was a slightly uneasy mix. Billy told the *NME* news desk, 'At the moment we're doing the party a mega fucking favour.' Peter Jenner said, 'We're not saying "Vote Labour", we're saying you should become politically involved.' And *then* vote Labour.

Neil Spencer, looking back on Red Wedge, says, 'It was a great idea, but a confused idea, that was the problem. No one could quite decide what it was about. I saw it in much clearer terms than most people because I was politically less naive.' (His father was a Labour councillor in Northampton, and he'd grown up surrounded by Labour Party politics, which gave him 'a perspective. My father was disillusioned, and seeing his disillusionment made me realise you shouldn't have any illusions. Lots of people involved in Red Wedge did become disillusioned, but I never had any illusions to lose. I know what politicians are like, and I knew how much we could and couldn't do.')

Red Wedge campaigned on an assortment of issues – housing, education, employment, the environment – but homed in on the arts, calling for a government Ministry of Arts & Media (there was no Minister for Culture in those days), the reform of arts administration, zero VAT on live performance, opposition to museum charges, reform of the Press Council and so on. It produced attractive-looking literature full of information about the government's poor record on training, allowances and gay rights.

While Billy and Weller provided the public face of Red Wedge, countless others beavered away behind the scenes, from within and without the party. Neil Spencer reserves honourable mention for Geoff Mulgan who drove the minibus on the subsequent Red Wedge tour, went on to found think-tank Demos, advise at 10 Downing Street and now runs the Young Foundation. Ken Walpole ('Mulgan's sidekick – both very influential thinkers'); Pete Jenner ('he brought to Red Wedge some very sussed politics that had been hammered out during the 60s'); Annajoy David ('she brought a lot of energy to it'); Ken Livingstone (during the GLC's arts boom, he'd recognised its great job-creation power, because people will work in the arts for less – a key point in the ongoing Labour carnival); and Peter Mandelson (then a director of communications whose office was next door to the first Wedge HQ in Room 104 at Walworth Road). 'There was a lot of serious thinking going on,' says Spencer. 'We tried very hard to change the party's agenda. Personally, I believed that there was a New Left already there, a rainbow coalition. I believed in the GLC, nuclear-free zones, cheap public transport, free gigs – that showed a bold way forward into the future.'

If Billy Bragg had crystallised the working-class struggle in 'Between The Wars', it was The Style Council who provided the soundbites for the optimism of Red Wedge with their hits of the day, 'Shout To The Top' and 'Walls Come Tumbling

Down' ('You don't have to take this crap/You don't have to sit back and relax/You can actually try changing it').

Back in September, Billy had widened his political net and played two gigs in support of Nicaraguan Solidarity at Dublin's SFX club. But it wasn't the issue of Central America and the Sandinistas that threw up the trip's one sticky moment for Billy. Someone in the appreciative audience called out 'Play an Irish song!' This threw him completely ('It really weirded me out'), because at that point, he'd filled many a waste paper basket with songs about the situation in Northern Ireland that didn't make the grade ('sixth-form shit', is how their author describes them). It turned out afterwards that the heckler was journalist Eamonn McCann, and maybe he had a point.

Billy had a firm handle on British politics, but further afield, even as close to home as Ireland, there was still work to be done and debates to be had. Intervention by one country into another's affairs was the common ground between the question over British rule in Northern Ireland and US government support for Nicaragua's anti-Communist Contra rebels. 'When I used to lecture the Americans about Nicaragua, they would say, well what about Northern Ireland?' Billy recounts. 'All I could say was, it's not a clear-cut issue, we're not trying to destabilise the country, and, with all due respect, they're not bombing your hometown.' Billy realised that the more he travelled the world, the more informed he had to be about domestic issues. (It actually took him another ten years before he nailed the Northern Irish question in song – 'Northern Industrial Town' on the *William Bloke* album – although he had covered Eric Bogle's 'My Youngest Son Came Home Today' in 1990 'which said what I felt: until the killing stops, nothing's going to happen.')

Back at base, October had seen Go! Discs sign The Housemartins, quickly promoted as 'the fourth best band in Hull'. There is a myth that without Billy Bragg, The Housemartins would never have signed to Go!; one that is hotly disputed by biographer Nick 'Swift Nick' Taylor in his book *Now That's What I Call Quite Good!* What is certain is that Andy and Juliet Macdonald went to see the band's self-styled 'left-wing gospel' at the Hammersmith Clarendon pub in May 1985. 'I would have had to be blind not to see their potential,' Macdonald raved, having been pestered for weeks by the band's guitarist Stan Cullimore on the phone. 'It was dripping from their fingertips!' The eventual three-year contract with Go! Discs involved Macdonald providing The Housemartins with two sets of boys' football strips which they presented to a young team on a local council estate (who became Housemartins A.F.C.).

The Housemartins had supported Billy at the Tunnel in London, in Brighton, and back up at Hull Tiffany's in April. The band's Paul Heaton remembers being struck by his busker's zeal, and by his onstage humour, a skill The Housemartins were only in the process of developing. 'He was just funny, and I know he gets really nervous, but he came over really confident,' Heaton recalls. 'What also struck me was what a good guitar player he was. I was pretty mesmerised. And the same way we picked up on Billy's enthusiasm, he picked up on ours. I think Billy had a word in Andy's ear for us.'

Billy liked the cut of their cardigan, and nudged Macdonald in their direction – both had heard the band's first demo tape and were unmoved, but the second one, with what would be their first single 'Flag Day' on it, did the trick. Though Taylor attempts to paint a picture of Billy having *nothing* to do with The Housemartin's Go! signing ('On the contrary, Billy Bragg never championed them'), it is fairer to say that he lubricated the wheels of industry in their favour.

Either way, their addition to the Go! roster was critical: it gave the label a second hit act (they were Top Ten by June 86) and sealed what later became Go!'s irksome reputation as a stable of left-wing boys-next-door. (Macdonald encouraged this initially, saying, 'None of our acts have to get changed to go up and perform on stage.') There was a colour-coded year planner on the wall at Go! Discs, on which the move-ments of The Housemartins were represented by green and Billy's by red. 'Ours started off very occasional and then got a bit thicker,' Heaton says. 'But Billy Bragg's was just a big red wall. Quite often we'd cross off bits of his, and I'm sure he'd cross off bits of ours. We'd only find out that Andy had signed a new band by looking at the wall chart.

Who's this band in brown? It's the Boothill Foot Tappers. It was a very exciting time, but as we got more and more famous we went into Go! Discs less and less, and crossed paths with Billy less. There's only ever been good words said to each other.'

When Billy next toured the States, he took 50 Housemartins records out with him and plugged them at college radio stations.

Around the same time, Billy moved out of Wiggy's and bought a top-floor flat in Acton Green. It was very civilised. Outside the South African Embassy in Trafalgar, things were not so civilised. After a peaceful 3,000-strong picket was barred by the Metropolitan police, preventing those taking part from decorating the building with flowers and tokens as an anti-apartheid action, they opted for a sit-in. Billy was there. He was also among the 322 who were arrested and carted away in vans (he ended up in a cell in Highbury, unable to phone his mum for fear of upsetting her, and missing a Hank Wangford gig he planned to attend). He wasn't charged. Over in Texas, 16 October's edition of the *Dallas Morning News* named Billy 'Britain's Bruce Springsteen'.

'Days Like These', which had been Billy's Party Political Broadcast song, came out as a Christmas single. It only got to Number 43, but he was satisfied (it contained the pertinent line, 'Wearing badges is not enough in days like these'). Macdonald hadn't wanted it out as a single at all, but Billy did and he struck a deal with him: in return, Go! could put out Macdonald's own choice of single (a new song, 'Levi Stubbs' Tears') in the new year. In the personnel department Go! Discs expanded by a third before Christmas, taking on Phill Jupitus, then better known as Porky The Poet (he was quite porky and he performed poetry). He met Billy on 8 March 1984, opening for him at Sussex University. Attila The Stockbroker and Seething Wells were also on, and Porky had a mate at the university who blagged him on to the bottom of the bill. He earned £20, but, more importantly, he found he had a lot in common with Billy – though four years apart, they'd both been to Northbury Juniors, both fallen in Barking Park lake and Porky's granddad had owned the Brewery Tap pub in Barking, where Riff Raff once played.

Porky even shared mutual friends with Wiggy. Naturally, an alliance was formed (long-term, as it happened).

Billy invited Porky along to support him at the Key Theatre in Peterborough ('A ranting poet is a very easy support act,' Porky explains. 'They occupy about as much space as an amp in the back of a car – or slightly more in my case. And Billy just seemed to take to me'.) Among other subsequent supports (including the entire Jobs For Youth tour), Porky did the *South Bank Show* Bull & Gate, which is where he met the Macdonalds. In December, they offered him a job 'answering phones' at Wendell Road, at which time he was unemployed and earning £30 a week learning to be a paste-up artist, so he couldn't resist. 'My job at Go! was making tea and arsing about,' he recalls. 'Which you *could* do at indie record companies. It was very, very matey.'

Billy's final gig of 1985 was on 29 December at the Hammersmith Odeon, then a landmark London rock venue and the biggest Billy had headlined. On paper, he'd done 135 shows that year, but taking into account impromptu performances and double-ups, it was undoubtedly higher.

At that gig was Catherine Fennimore, better known as Tiny, who was then working as a writer for *Jamming!*, the politically conscious music magazine founded in 1983 by Jam fan Tony Fletcher (he'd left school to run Paul Weller's ill-fated Jamming! record label, which had the plug pulled after just over a year). The thrust of the magazine was writing about issues and getting political ideas across to a wider audience. Tiny had become actively self-politicised at South Bank Polytechnic – hailing from Amersham in leafy, Tory-dominated Buckinghamshire. She admits that prior to college she 'knew nothing about politics, until I looked up "apartheid" in the dictionary and was shocked that people were that evil'.

A huge Billy Bragg fan (when she'd bought *Life's A Riot*, she didn't take it off her turntable for five and a half hours), Tiny had been active in support of the miners' strike, and first met Billy at the Wag Club benefit. 'There was this bloke who did what I was trying to do,' she recalls. 'I wanted to be involved in what he was doing.' Having soaked up the collective vibe at Red Wedge meetings, Tiny was heartened by the sheer size and enthusiasm of the Hammersmith Odeon audience: 'I hadn't realised that there were this many people in the world who thought like I did. It was like coming home for me. Politically aware people who were into having a good time . . . or aware enough to cheer at the right bits.'

She volunteered to help out with Red Wedge, as, indeed, had Porky before 'the Macdonald call'. (He's up front enough to admit to slightly questionable motives – 'Am I here because I want to change the world, or to meet Paul Weller?' – and that working for the Wedge involved 'a lot of nodding'.) Tiny did some press work and a lot of writing with *NME*'s Paolo Hewitt and Neil Spencer. 'It was so important to counteract Thatcher's ideas,' she says of that heady time.

Tiny remembers watching Billy find his feet in the first months of Wedge: 'At that stage, Billy couldn't string a political sentence together in public, and it's quite incredible when you listen to him now. The desire was there, but it was new to him. He had a go. Weller said nothing.'

Before long, Tiny would also get 'the Macdonald call' and join the matey staff of Go! Discs. In the interim, she did her bit for the cause, and Andy and Juliet took on Teddy, a stray dog, as their Head of A&R. Twee? Go! Discs?

It's all fallen into place! Socialism isn't a dirty word to me any more. The Labour Party really do care and can make a difference!
         man sees the light in a cartoon by Porky the Poet

Billy had been given the OK by none other than his old mate Steve Wright in the *Daily Mirror* at the end of 85 – 'Whether he likes it or not, Billy will become a superstar in 1986' – and it was with this approbation slung around his neck that he ventured back out into Thatcher's Britain at the helm of the first Red Wedge national tour. It kicked off on 25 January, with a bill containing The Communards, soulster Junior Giscombe, reggae MC Lorna Gee, The Style Council and DJ Jerry Dammers. That was what it said in the programme – by the end of it, Madness, Prefab Sprout, Tom Robinson, Lloyd Cole and The Smiths had also appeared.

On the opening night at Manchester Apollo, Billy went on first (there would be no hierarchy in Wedgeworld), and the good times did not cease for the whole evening. The music was paramount, and the politics came in brown paper bags (CND pamphlets, anti-apartheid bumpf). MPs like Peter Pike from Burnley loitered in the foyer, Gary Kemp did a controversial solo version of 'Through The Barricades' (was-it-brave? was-it-shit?) and a finale of Curtis Mayfield's 'Move On Up' captured the jubilant mood. Robin Denselow compared it to a Motown Revue, and that's exactly how it felt in the bus, too. John Gill, from listings mag *Time Out*, noted that 'out of London and away from the brutish consumerism promoted by the likes of *The Face*, the Red Wedge tour developed a momentum that surprised its most cautious supporters.' In the same issue, columnist Julie Burchill, never one to let a party go unpooped, said, 'Red Wedge are in danger of becoming the Saatchi & Saatchi of socialism.'

The day events, as organised by those pesky Young Socialists, were less slick and clear cut than the concerts, but the groundswell of support was continuous. After the first night, Billy was heard to ask Annajoy David, 'Do you think there was enough politics?'

Tiny enthuses about 'a musical as well as a political buzz. But it *was* great to see the MPs in the hall, being prodded and pointed at by kids who were on *their* home turf, telling MPs who were very definitely fish out of water what they thought. It was a good enough reason for doing it.'

At St George's Hall, Bradford, Heaven 17's Glenn Gregory got up and led the cast in the only ever live performance of the band's rousing 1981 near-hit 'We Don't Need This Fascist Groove Thing'. Porky, who sang backing vocals with DJ Wendy May, is just one who will never forget it.

'We really did think we were going to change things,' says Tiny. 'After the first tour, it was not uncommon for 200 people to turn up at Red Wedge meetings. We didn't know what to *do* with everyone.'

Porky, who was by now a published cartoonist (*NME*, the Red Wedge programme, the first Billy Bragg songbook), was sent out by Go! Discs on the first Housemartins tour in February as master-of-ceremonies-cum-tour-manager. Of his tourmanaging duties, he is very honest: 'I did fuck-all work in that direction, Stan [Cullimore, guitarist] did it all. But I did draw the laminates.' A stringer from the *Sunday Mirror* phoned Porky during the tour and asked if he had any funny stories to tell. 'I was Johnny Naive,' he says, happily telling the hack all about the Adopt-A-Housemartin scheme (by which audience members were encouraged to put the band up for the night to save on hotel costs). That Sunday, the story appeared under the headline: 'COME BACK AND SLEEP WITH US.' The Housemartins weren't quite famous enough to be a front page sensation at that time, so it blew over, and 'band spokesman Porky', as he'd become, kept his job – although knickers and toys did start arriving in The Housemartins' post. This was a taster of the unwanted attention fame can bring.

In June, The Housemartins' 'Happy Hour' single reached Number Three in the charts, thanks to a charming Plasticene video, and suddenly the fourth best band in Hull were the third most popular band in Britain. Billy left a poignant message on the Go! Discs ansaphone on the Sunday evening of the chart: 'Tell the Macdonalds that I'm glad the weight of their mortgage has been lifted from my shoulders.'

Tiny was taken on as Go! Discs' press officer, which meant that she could work with her hero. 'What I've always been interested in doing is pushing Billy,' she says. 'I think he's brilliant, and what he does is very important. I always knew where my interest was.' In February, Billy went to the GDR or German Democratic Republic, otherwise known as East Germany, separated from Western Europe since 1946 by what Winston Churchill termed the Iron Curtain. As *NME*'s Danny Kelly, a recent visitor himself, put it, 'In Europe, only medieval Albania so zealously and jealously guards its borders.' With that in mind, it is easy to imagine Billy's surprise when a gentleman sidled up to him in the gents of a folk club in Edinburgh and went, 'Psssst! Ever thought of going to East Berlin, mate?'

This happened back in September 1985. Billy was at the Left Turns folk club to see Dick Gaughan, an old-style communist, whose most famous album was *A Handful Of Earth*, featuring his version of Leon Rosselson's 'The World Turned Upside Down' – the very song that showed Billy how he could adapt folk music for punk rock guitar. Billy's first thought at the urinals was, 'Brilliant! I'm being recruited for the KGB. This'll look brilliant in the *NME*!' In the event, it was an invitation from a mate of Gaughan's who taught at the university there, to play at East Berlin's week-long annual Sixteenth Political Song Festival.

Billy could not resist. He hated the image that had become ubiquitous in pop videos of young, pale Englishmen dressed as the Thin White Duke, of a romantic, dry-iced Berlin by the wall. 'Get back to art school!' he would shout at the TV screen. But what was actually through there, on the other side? He decided to 'have a butcher's' (needless to say, PJ was gung-ho for it, and bagsyed the driving seat).

The festival drew artists from all over the world – the communist world, that is, but with a smattering of left-wing Africans, plus Billy Bragg. The result was a lefty WOMAD with bad weather.

'The thing about the East Germans is that they were very proud of what they'd achieved,' says Billy. 'The best living standards in Eastern Europe bar none, and Berlin was the Paris of the East. Although the majority of it looked like it had been built by the same architect as Basildon.'

He met Pete Seeger, the legendary protest singer and Woody Guthrie acolyte, for the first time at the festival's opening ceremony, singing 'The Internationale', former national anthem of the Soviet Union and communist signature tune. Not dissimilar to Jobs For Youth and Red Wedge, the East German gigs encouraged discussions afterwards in the foyer, where young punks with green Mohicans turned up and expressed their burning desire to get out. Billy enthusiastically addressed them as 'comrade' and tried to fill them in on a little detail ('It's the same prison . . . with different bars,' he told Kelly in the *NME* story).

'Maybe I flatter myself,' he says. 'But the organisers felt that because I was anti-Thatcher I would be on their side in East Germany, but I found that they were doing exactly the same things that annoyed me about Thatcherism. Once I found my feet, I felt duty-bound to speak out a little bit about how I saw the world.'

One gig took place at the Narva Light Bulb Factory, which instantly reminded Billy of Ford's. He played at lunchtime in front of the toilets: 'The people working there just wanted to get their lunch. They didn't want to watch some noisy oik from Barking – Fuck this, I want me dinner!'

An interviewer from East German radio asked him – live – what he thought of the 'glorious people's light bulb factory'. He replied, 'I do this job so I don't have to work in a shithole like this.' The translator, Jorg Wolter, diplomatically omitted to translate.

Wolter became Billy and PJ's ally, a cultural as well as linguistic translator. He, like the rest of the festival organisers, was entrusted by the State to make contact with foreigners – they were implicit with the State machinery in some way, but our two shit-kicking envoys really tested the limits of Wolter's role. They demanded to go and meet people involved in the alternative peace movement, which was led by a Bruce Kent-style pastor. Despite serious pressure not to go from the festival organisers, Billy and PJ went for dinner, with Wolter at their side. Jenner's dad was a vicar, which they threw in as an excuse, but Wolter still had to report back. His mediator's task became a balancing act: translate the drift of what Billy wanted to say without jeopardising his job.

At the closing gig of the Berlin festival, during soundcheck, Billy saw a young man in a tracksuit with a walkie talkie, clearly a secret policeman. He was there to see Wolter, who was obliged by his position to pass on what the Western visitors in jeans had talked about with the pastor. 'Jorg was very straightforward with us,' Billy explains. 'He put his livelihood on the line by making it perfectly clear that he had an *ambiguous* relationship with his employers, the State.'

The atmosphere was wary, tense and polite, and you could cut it with a knife – and that was precisely what Billy and PJ wished to do. Even casual contact was State-corralled into so-called friendship meetings. But Billy desperately wanted to meet these people who were apparently intent on massacring everybody in Britain and Western Europe – he wanted to see the reds of their eyes. At a friendship meeting with some Actual Russians, a woman from their delegation stood up and sang a beautiful gypsy song. Billy replied with a rendition of William Blake's 'Jerusalem' (a Last Night Of The Proms staple that he is ever keen to reclaim as a socialist anthem – don't get him started on it). Formalities over, they were entitled to go and have a beer, which Billy found fascinating. The 27th Congress of The Communist Party Of The Soviet Union had just happened, and Mikhail Gorbachev, a

Kinnock-like whippersnapper (54) in the leader's chair, had mentioned *perestroika* and *glasnost* for the first time. (These buzzwords were not popular with East German leader Erich Honecker, a crooked fellow who came to represent the old communist regime as progress began its unstoppable march through the latter 1980s.)

After the festival, a tour comprising the 'best of the fest' took off around other parts of East Germany. Billy was honoured if bemused to be selected, along with Leytonstone's honorary Irishman John Faulkner, some polite East German middle-aged musos (more Lennon than Lenin: the highlight of their set was 'Imagine') and Amandla, an energetic African National Congress dance troupe. Hoyerswerda, Magdeburg, Potsdam, Neubrandenburg, Rostok, Leipzig . . . at each gig, the Soviet Army would file in at the back, one officer and twenty conscripts who were bored shitless with East Germany (no money, no vodka). These were the very individuals who, if second-hand American propaganda was to be believed, were going to invade our country. Useful contact was near impossible, but Wolter spoke a little Russian, and Billy managed to hand out some pre-recorded tapes to the squaddies (donated by Roy Carr, who coordinated *NME*'s cassette series, and the Rough Trade shop).

It was the strangest trip of Billy's life, but one he felt privileged to have made. He and PJ had made some rum contacts, they'd seen Bertolt Brecht's grave, hung out with punks and been shown back to one university lecturer's flat who hid the works of Leon Trotsky in his 'poison cabinet'.

The GLC, equally poisonous to the Tories, said farewell on 31 March, with a suitably expansive, lively, *free* concert. There were speeches, fireworks and three stages: Billy Bragg, Eddy Grant, Latin Quarter, Bernie Grant and a shower of glitter over a massed chant of 'Maggie out!' Ken Livingstone promised, 'We'll spend the rest of our lives trying to do it again', and, as I write, it's a very real possibility . . .

While Billy was busy recording his difficult third LP at North London's Livingston Studios behind Wood Green shopping centre, April's *Folk Roots* magazine published its annual Readers Poll. If anyone needed proof that 'Between

The Wars' had opened up Billy's appeal, there it was. Number Two Best Songwriter (behind only the godfather, Richard Thompson); Number One Best Single Of 1985; Number One Best New Song; and Number Four Best New Arrangement (for 'The World Turned Upside Down').

If this unprecedented folk acceptance saw Billy move away from *NME* dependence, the album he was recording with Smiths producer John Porter would help establish him as more than just a live phenomenon. 'It was my first properly realised album,' he says. Without throwing the baby out with the bath water, he made concessions to musicality, with additional musicians on some tracks (organ, percussion, bass, slide guitar, mandolin) and a much longer recording time. Plus, the new songs had all been written post-fame, and were affected by the fallout of the miners' strike (witness the blunt message of 'There Is Power In A Union'). The tube ride was lengthy enough for Billy to read John Irving's *The World According To Garp* from cover to cover during the recording.

On 3 June, Billy found himself under the curtain again, this time in the USSR itself. It seemed like such an impossible feat, but it's all about contacts – and not the ones you make through the record company promotions departments. Billy was playing a couple of gigs in Helsinki, and, by talking to the right people in the Finnish Communist Party, found himself on the train to Leningrad's Finland Station (the same route Lenin took when he returned to Russia in 1917). To his disappointment, there was no committee at the other end, just Art Troitsky, the venerable dean of Russian rock critics. If you leave rock'n'roll's beaten track, you mustn't expect too high a degree of organisation.

For Billy, it was like his first day in New York (Jenner was pretty knocked out, too). Troitsky became their guide and interpreter for the day, during which they met Afrika, a punk artist who, out of necessity, used plastic tablecloths for canvasses, and whose studio was behind the secret police headquarters ('It would be better if you don't speak English now,' Troitsky advised them, as they went inside, mindful of attracting the wrong kind of attention).

The gig took place in a lecture theatre, with Billy standing behind a lectern and, inevitably, taking questions from the floor afterwards. One middle-aged man, obviously a plant, asked, 'What do you think of *perestroika*?' Billy expressed his guarded enthusiasm. Troitsky translated. Billy was the centre of attention until, that is, they discovered that Jenner had managed Pink Floyd: 'That was it, no one wanted to talk to *me* any more. I was knocked over in the rush.'

All told, it whetted Billy's appetite for later Russian invasions.

In July, Go! Discs released 'Levi Stubbs' Tears' as a single (in return for 'Days Like These' at Christmas). It went to 29, which, although lower than 'Between The Wars', did wonders for preconceptions about Billy Bragg. It is a wonderfully sad song that Billy remembers playing on the first Red Wedge tour – Weller said to him, 'Is that about Levi Stubbs of the Four Tops? I thought you were a folk musician!' (Billy often elicited reactions like this from Weller, who saw Billy only in black and white – i.e. mostly white.)

No. 1 magazine called Billy 'The Reluctant Pop Star'. *Record Mirror* recognised him as 'just an old soul boy from Barking' and headlined their cover story 'Socialists Cry As Well'. This was the impact of 'Levi Stubbs' Tears', written on a cross-channel ferry to stop Kershaw talking to him ('That's why the second verse is four bars longer than the first, because I didn't have my guitar with me').

On 22 September, Billy consolidated this new image as a sensitive soul with a whole album of the stuff – or so it seemed. *Talking With The Taxman About Poetry*, named after a poem by Vladimir Mayakovsky, went on sale for the astronomical sum of £4.49, and this time, having been trailed like normal albums by a single (and advertised heavily by Go! Discs), it entered the chart in the Top Ten. If convention had crept into the marketing, the record itself still sounded like a fanfare from an uncommon man.

It opens emblematically with a beautiful love song, 'Greetings To The New Brunette', characterised by Johnny Marr's shimmering guitarwash, and definitely improved by guitar overdubs and backing vocals by Kirsty MacColl. At its heart, it is pure Old Billy (troubled relationship, resistance to domestic convention, football joke). Elsewhere, trumpet and flugelhorn from Dave Woodhead double the melancholy of 'The Marriage', cockney piano from Kenny Craddock jangles through 'Honey, I'm A Big Boy Now', and – gasp! – 'assorted percussion' and something fast approaching a full band turn 'The Warmest Room' from a kitchen-sink drama into an everything-but-the-kitchen-sink drama. The overtly political songs, 'There Is Power In A Union' and 'Ideology' are executed in more utilitarian stand-up style. There are people who still consider *Taxman* to be Billy Bragg's greatest work, the author of this book included. It is an 'ideological cuddle', to lift a phrase from 'Greetings'.

Critically, *Taxman* received many happy returns. Lucy O'Brien declared it 'prosaic and compact' in the *NME*, calculating that it only cost 37.4p a song; Paul Du Noyer, in the first issue of adult-oriented *Q* magazine, put him on a pedestal with Elvis Costello, awarding him four out of five *Q* stars ('He was worth building the A13 for'); and the ubiquitous Colin Irwin in *Melody Maker* summed up, 'He can make you laugh. He can make you cry. He can make you choke with rage. Billy Bragg, the complete song and dance man.' Which was nice.

In October, off the back of another tour of West Germany – Cologne, Hamburg, Bochum, now as familiar to Billy as Birmingham, Manchester and Leicester – he nipped back over to the USSR to take part in the snappily titled Festival Of Song In The Struggle For Peace at Kiev. It had been six months since the world's worst peacetime nuclear disaster at nearby Chernobyl, but Glasgow Rangers FC had recently played there and they looked all right. Billy reassured himself that to get irradiated you'd have to get into the food chain. They took their own Marmite.

Getting back from Kiev for a show in West Berlin turned into one of those Days That Go On For Ever: no direct flight to East Berlin; 6 a.m. connecting flight to Moscow on the day of the gig; all passengers and their luggage put on a weighbridge before boarding the world's shakiest aircraft; 'two hours of Aeroflot hell' with Wiggy in a draught next to the emergency exit; the pilot clearing chunks of ice out of the frozen wing-flaps when back on the ground; friendship meeting in Moscow; whirlwind tour of the city; another huge airport; surrendering their rubles and thus being unable to eat at the deserted airport restaurant; finding a coffee bar that takes dollars with a working cappuccino machine but no coffee to put in it; being rounded up by a bloke with a clipboard ('You must come now!') and led through the also deserted terminal to a plane, mysteriously full of people; PJ being aggravatingly moved from his seat by the cabin crew *during* take-off; arriving just outside East Berlin where the West German promoter is supposed to pick them up in a van and take them to the venue, but because the airport is outside East Berlin, he can't get to it; taxi to Checkpoint Charlie with just two hours to showtime, but they are unable to pass through due to a lack of relevant documentation; Jorg Wolter, who met them at the airport, pulls some bureaucratic strings at the Cultural Ministry; one phone call later and the guard stamps their papers . . . the three men then push the amp through Checkpoint Charlie and hail the final taxi. They made the gig. 'It was a day and a half,' recalls Billy, exhausted at the memory. 'And it's still going on somewhere.'

Whenever things went wrong on tour, Wiggy would say that 'it's all gone a bit Soviet'.

Don't sit on the fence. Cut it!
                              Snowball Campaign slogan

Snowball was an East Anglian anti-nuclear organisation that demanded that the British government voted in favour of multilateral disarmament in the UN, regardless of how the USA voted. Optimism was in no short supply among those who believed we were all going to die in a nuclear holocaust. Billy lent his celebrity support to their CND-endorsed 'mass non-violent open civil disobedience' on 2 November in Norwich, where the plan was to cut the fence surrounding a nuclear bunker at Bawburgh.

It got him arrested again. He later pleaded not guilty to criminal damage but was charged anyway. Wasn't this the bloke who now wrote love songs?

At the end of 1986, The Housemartins reached Number One with an a cappella version of the Isley Brothers' 'Caravan Of Love', provoking a tabloid feeding frenzy, mostly from the *Sun* (the band were outspoken in their condemnation of Rupert Murdoch's union-busting News International empire). In January '87, the *Sun* 'revealed' that two of The Housemartins were gay (still very much a tabloid crime in those dark days), and only one of them was working class and born in Hull. The first count was simply untrue (The Housemartins were heterosexual but pro-gay rights, though the story distressed their families), the second irrelevant. But the whole sorry episode, which set the self-destruct timer for The Housemartins, taught Billy some first-hand lessons about the price of fame. He remembers sitting in reception at Harlech Television in Cardiff while the commissionaire read the *Sun*'s gay exposé and said, 'There always *was* something a bit strange about them.' It put Billy off singles even more.

1987 was Election Year, and a big one for Red Wedge. Although the pragmatic Neil Spencer admits today, 'I never ever thought we could win', Labour and its supporters rode high on a wave of hope.

In Wales, on a small Welsh tour – Wrexham, Aberdare, Swansea, Barry, Newport – Billy saw the downside of Labour in power, the 'dead hand of old-style committee-based municipal socialism' making it impossible for the local youth to express themselves via clubs or gigs. It was a frustrating week, with a lot of friction between the young punters and local MPs and councillors.

Like a walking embodiment of his own *Taxman* album, Billy was half-politics, half-romance throughout 1987, having fallen 'stupidly, madly, obsessively in love' with a girl called Mary Bollingbroke from Clapham. Talk to Jenner or Tiny or Porky or the Macdonalds about 1987, and they don't say 'election year', they swallow hard and roll their eyes and say 'Mary'.

As a brief aside, on 1 February, Billy played the brilliantly named Cheese Pavilion at Bath & Wells Showground in Shepton Mallet. Worth noting, as it's referred to in his 1988 anthem 'Waiting For The Great Leap Forwards' ('In the Cheese Pavilion and the only noise I hear/Is the sound of people stacking chairs/And mopping up spilt beer') – and not a lot of people know that it's a real place. Back to the heartache . . .

Dunedin in New Zealand is geographically the furthest gig in the world – there is only really one more town of note, Invercargill, before you find yourself on a boat to the South Pole, and there's no gig in Invercargill. It's so far south, it looks like the North of Scotland. Hence, being in Dunedin when you're head over heels with a girl called Mary is *wrong* – even when your album's Top Five in New Zealand. 'I was feeling a long, long, long, long way from everybody I cared about,' Billy remembers. 'I could feel the whole of Africa and Eurasia between me and my loved ones. That was a tour memorable for the size of its telephone bill.'

Billy met Mary in November '86. They ran away for his court appearance in Norwich after the Snowball arrest. From then on, it was no peace, lots of love, and misunderstanding all the way: shouting matches, depression, Mary joining Billy on tour only to disappear, 'playing dreadful games with each other – love-me-hate-me games'. A whole swathe of songs would come out of the rocky relationship, but Billy sums it up best for those of us who weren't *there* with a line in 'Life With The Lions': 'I hate the arsehole I become every time I'm with you.'

Virtually every song on Billy's next album *Workers Playtime* (recorded later that year) concerned his and Mary's stormy relationship. 'It was like being on a switchback ride,' he says. 'At one point of total madness, we accidentally got engaged. I bought her a ring, and she thought I was asking her to marry me. We went to Norwich to stay with her brother, and by the time we got there, we were engaged. Once word got out to our mums, that was it. We both knew it was mad.'

It would have been a fractious affair anyway, but with Billy away almost all the time, the angles became more acute, the problems less resolved, and every crisis turned into a drama. Billy knows what a pain he must've become to those around him, so used to dealing with Easygoing Bill ('It was a pain in the arse for everybody') – suddenly, he didn't relish being away, he felt sorry for himself.

With the luxury of hindsight, Billy identifies the possible root cause of all the madness: in December 87 he was going to turn 30. Whether Mary really was a symptom of Billy's pre-mid-life paranoia, or a frantic need to find continuity in his rootless lifestyle, she threatened to take his eye off the ball, in much the same way that Kim had innocently wrecked his O Levels. And there was a general election coming. His country needed him!

Red Wedge had mobilised themselves. They'd produced a suitably cool-looking manifesto, *Move On Up!* (all woodcuts and Style Council typography, with a foreword by Kinnock, drawing on Wordsworth's 'Prelude': 'To be young should be very heaven. Too often for too many, it's very hell'), and organised a national tour to climax on election night, 11 June.

Billy dutifully cancelled some Japanese dates and hopped aboard. All the gang were there, plus Lloyd Cole, The The, Captain Sensible and The Blow Monkeys, who'd released an album full of well-dressed, anti-Thatcher funk in April called *She Was Only A Grocer's Daughter*. Their song titles mirrored The Style Council's for sloganising: 'How Long Can A Bad Thing Last', 'Checking Out' and '(Celebrate) The Day After You' – which, as a single, was banned from Radio 1 during the election run-up. It proves just how threatening a group of men in white trousers could be in 1987.

The Red Wedge Comedy Tour crossed the country concurrently, exploiting the left-wing stand-up boom with performers like Ben Elton, Lenny Henry, Harry Enfield and Mark Miwurdz. Billy, naturally enough, joined the bill on some nights. Comedian Jenny Lecoat recalls that Billy seemed much happier hanging out with them than the musicians. Less comparing of loafers, presumably. True Colours, a Red Wedge visual Arts Show, ran at the Citizens Gallery in Woolwich.

In the week of the election, an advert for *Back To Basics* (Billy's first two albums and EP on one £5.99 disc) was 'rejected' by newspapers because it read 'No one with a conscience votes Tory anyway.' That same week, the *NME* showed its colours and put Neil Kinnock on the cover. 'LOVELY, LOVELY, LOVELY!' it yelled, in reference to his *Spitting Image* catch-phrase.

Looking back, does Kinnock believe that Red Wedge got him there?

'Yes. I certainly wasn't there for my looks or my fashion sense.' Everything seemed to fall into place. Despite a comfortable Tory lead in the polls, Labour seemed to have everything going for them. Young voters accounted for sixteen per cent of the electorate, and there could surely only be one choice for them in the middle of all this music and merriment. Even U2 entered the fray on stage at Wembley Arena, Bono singing 'Maggie's Farm' (a Bob Dylan song lent new meaning since The Specials had covered it in 1980) and 'Springhill Mining Disaster'. At Islington Business Design Centre, Neil Kinnock starred in a prematurely triumphant rally, where Billy and Hank Wangford sang the Woody Guthrie song 'Deportees' (after 'Power In A Union' was deemed unsuitable by image-conscious Labour organisers). 'We Shall Overcome', Bob Marley's 'One Love', balloons . . . it was, as Robin Denselow had it, 'Britain's first pop election campaign'. And Labour's first pop election defeat.

Red Wedge gathered in the coffee bar at London's Mean Fiddler that fateful night, with television screens relaying the results as they came in, and instead of attending the party of the year, they saw their hopes dashed, as the Tories won an historic third term (375 seats to Labour's 229). 'A lot of weeping and wailing and gnashing of teeth went on,' describes Tiny, who was there. 'No one could believe it. At least there were some kindred spirits around on the night.'

Neil Spencer compounds the miserable picture: 'People were literally crying into their drinks. The tears were splashing into the lager. I remember having to put my arm round a lot of people and say, "Come on, it's all right." I was disappointed but I wasn't gutted, and I didn't feel thwarted.'

Many did. Tiny says, 'It put a lot of people off politics.'

The Tories' council house sell-off had worked (40 per cent of council-house owners had voted Conservative), and the illusion of a larger middle class had served the blue vote well in the South. Self-interest won the day. In his book *Mrs Thatcher's Revolution*, Peter Jenkins concludes that Labour had become not the party of the working class but of the underclass. There was some consolation in the fact that Red Wedge had apparently increased Labour's vote among 18- to 24-year-olds. And indeed, that there was something deeply flawed about an electoral system that allowed a party to run the country when they'd been effectively voted *out* in Wales and Scotland – but none of this made the early morning of 12 June any easier to stomach.

Billy remembers trudging home in the June sunshine to his flat: 'I took it really personally. For a few days afterwards, I felt that everyone I saw on the tube was not in the same country as me.'

He'd agreed to appear on Channel 4's *After Dark*, the late-night, leather-armchair discussion show, which is all a bit of a blur to him now, except for one pointed exchange. Tory MP Teresa Gorman – who still had her blue rosette on – leant over to Billy when the cameras were on someone else and said to him, 'You and your kind are finished. We are the future now.'

They got knocked down, and they got up again. Eventually.

'We all took it personally,' says Tiny. 'We felt we had much more to lose. I remember thinking, If people are *still* going to vote for "her", knowing what she does, then what's the point?'

To all intents and purposes, Red Wedge ended on election night. Not administratively – they continued to put on the odd benefit gig (for Nicaraguan solidarity in October, sacked Kent miners in December, a short tour of Ireland as late as June 1988), and the Wedge magazine *Well Red* lasted into 1990 – but the fight had been knocked out of them.

'The wind went out of the sails,' Spencer admits. 'It was never going to be possible to maintain that coalition of people when there wasn't the pressure of a scrap.' He hoped it could continue as a youth- or arts-oriented think-tank, but it was not to be. 'That was it until there was another rallying point.' (In effect, Free Nelson Mandela and Artists Against Apartheid saw the natural continuation of Wedge politics and the Wedge vibe.)

'I think we could've made more difference than we did. I thought the vote would be closer than it was. But I saw Red Wedge not just as intervention into the election, but intervention into the party itself, a way to clue them up, a way to make them aware of issues they were not grasping.'

'We upturned a few stones,' says Tiny. 'We did blow a bit of fresh air into the corridors of power. Not much, but a bit. And if we did, that's enough of an achievement.'

Looking back, Billy is disappointed that The Redskins could never work with Red Wedge. Back in January, he'd been involved in a heated *Melody Maker* debate with Weller, Dammers, Clare Short and himself versus X Moore, Stewart Copeland of The Police and Tory MP for Derby North, Greg Knight. X Moore's criticisms of Red Wedge were indirect criticisms of the Labour Party from a very long historical perspective, while Copeland declared himself a capitalist and Knight babbled, 'You may get a round of applause by slagging Mrs Thatcher but where does that lead?' Billy became incensed, yelling at Moore, 'Look who you're sitting with!'

The Redskins' stubborn SWP allegiance still irks Billy: 'If Red Wedge had been as controlled by the Labour Party as the Redskins were by the SWP, I certainly wouldn't have joined. I wouldn't have touched it with a barge-pole. I've been called "scab" by the SWP. I sat on a panel against them once and one writer said they felt "more comfortable with Billy Bragg's doubts than with X Moore's certainties". God save us from the people who have no doubts, be they left, right or wherever.

'I've watched the Redskins, I've seen Chris Dean, when he's on one, brow-beating the audience into submission, without any hint of doubt or self-effacing humour or anything. It's like making people eat dry bread for an hour. Either they are on your side already or they're just going to be put off. You're never gonna get those people who come up to me and say, "I vote Tory, I've voted Tory all my life, but I really like your love songs." I'll say, well that's cool, mate, you don't have to buy it, the very fact that you're in the room when I'm saying it is enough.'

The whole issue of pop and politics, so vividly animated by the events of 1984–87, left Billy even more convinced that the case was not closed. Debate has always been his favoured tool, and one piffling election defeat hadn't blunted it.

Paradise postponed.

11. BROKEN-HEART SURGERY

Great leaps forward, 1987–1989

At any foreign airport you will meet your sophisticated compatriot who will tell you that everything you are about to see is a cliché and that the real life is behind the scenes. But he himself is the cliché. You will learn more from the local man with the bad shave who sells you dark glasses

Clive James, *Flying Visits*

The stars look very different today

David Bowie, 'Space Oddity'

Unwashed and somewhat slightly dazed, Britain woke up on 12 June 1987 with a hangover. Eight years of partying with yourself takes its toll. Paul Weller decided to play Stalin and airbrush himself out of the Red Wedge photos: 'I had reservations about joining in to begin with and I wish I'd just stuck with my instincts from the start. On the Red Wedge tour we were made to feel guilty for talking about each other's shoes. It was like, "How dare you? Clothes are a bourgeois trapping." I love clothes. I'm just not interested in anything political any more.'

Writer Pete Davies had painted a nightmare local future-vision in his cheerless 1986 novel *The Last Election*. With the fictional, senile Nanny at Number 10, employment a thing of the past, the masses numbed by drugs and snooker, and political broadcasts by the Money Party promoting 'the splendour of our guns or the worldwide sales of nancy boy pop groups'. It was a facile bit of 1980s satire but typical at a time when, if the voice of dissent was to be heard anywhere, it was in the arts, in alternative comedy, in *Spitting Image*, on Channel 4, even in sitcoms about unemployment like BBC's *Bread* and ITV's *We'll Think Of Something*. It was in The The's deceptively soulful tune 'Heartland':

> *This is the land where nothing changes*
> *The land of red buses and bloody babies*
> *This is the place where pensioners are raped*
> *And their hearts are being cut from the welfare state*

Britain had turned into a client state, a missile base for America, and a privatised bloody mess. And the Labour Party had lost Paul Weller. The Blow Monkeys asked how long can a bad thing last? Well, at least another five years.

In July 1987, prosperity reached Go! Discs, who moved out of Wendell Road into a smart office in King Street, Hammersmith (Son Of Go! Mansions). Porky and Tiny were offered real salaries and job titles (Porky had been on £100 a week, now he was on £15,000 a year). Further staff were hired, and Andy Macdonald set up his office a floor above the rest of them. The stars looked very different from up there, and Go! Discs had gone legit. The family atmosphere was still there, as were the fey, whimsical press releases, but they had to be worked on. ('Whenever Billy's stuff was on the schedule everything went a bit more Wendell Road,' Porky recalls.)

After what seemed like the Last Election, Billy had a two-month tour coming up, starting in Canada and ending in Rhode Island – if ending is the right word, as it led directly into a week at the Mean Fiddler, Italy, Hungary, Austria, the UK again, and Scandinavia and the USSR before Christmas. Do not pass Go!

He and Mary talked themselves out of getting married, having got as far as looking at the hall in Ilford where they were going to hold the reception. Billy broke it to Jenner on the way to the airport: 'I don't know who was more relieved, me or him. I have absolutely no regrets about the fact that it didn't come to anything. It would definitely not have worked. It would've ended in divorce, suicide, boredom and probably some of the worst decorated houses you can imagine.' (Mary married the boyfriend-before-Billy a year later.)

After Canada, Billy made concrete his support of the Nicaraguan Sandinistas (and indeed, his increasing interest in Central American music and poetry) by playing at the International Book Fair in Managua. He'd been invited by the poet, Catholic priest and Minister of Culture, Ernesto Cardenal. It was his first visit to what used glibly to be called the 'third' world (these days, the developing world), and to a country with a fine tradition of dissent. He stayed at the Hotel Las Mercedes, built by the Sandinista government to compete with the American-owned, CIA-favoured International (where Howard Hughes once lived). The 1972 earthquake had killed 20,000 people, and as good as knocked Managua down, a situation not helped by the fact that former dictator Anastasio Somoza Jnr had been siphoning off foreign aid and increasing his own personal fortune to £1,600 million. Here was a country at war, and yet, as Billy told *Nicaragua Today* magazine, 'it's more free than Britain is'. For a socialist regime, it was energetic and fresh, unlike the 'staid and dour ambience' of the Eastern Bloc.

There were gigs at the Sandinista Cultural Workers Union and a four-hour meet-the-people session where 300 of the festival's delegates questioned government ministers, the Foreign Minister, the Vice President and the President, Daniel Ortega. 'This impressed upon me how far this experiment in social democracy was progressing,' Billy wrote in the *NME*. 'Can you imagine a Labour government laying themselves open like that?'

Billy had a moment of clarity on the flight home as he cruised over the Northern Honduras, 'where the Man From Delmonte reigns supreme over the seemingly infinite pineapple and banana plantations. I realised the score. The US government wants to snuff out the Nicaraguan Revolution because if the people of Honduras, El Salvador and Guatemala follow the Sandinistas' lead, the interests of the American United Fruit Company and their successors will be toppled.

'I learnt a lot, not least that the Nicaraguans don't seem to like my music very much.'

Nonetheless, as with so many relationships Billy forged, he and Nicaragua would meet again.

In August, Billy deputised for Andy Kershaw in his 10 p.m. slot on Radio 1, his first real taste of broadcasting. In the minutes of the following week's departmental meeting, it was noted that 'he needed very little guidance' from producer John Walters, and was commended.

Billy's week-long Mean Fiddler residency ran from 23 to 27 August. For one night only, Riff Raff reformed with Porky on bass, marking ten years since they arrived at Bearshanks. Another notable aspect of that week was keyboard wizardess Cara Tivey's Billy Bragg debut. He'd seen her playing with Everything But The Girl in America, and the two of them would make some sweet music together (not that kind).

If *Talking With The Taxman* had been 'difficult', the fourth album would surely be 'really difficult'. In October Billy started recording *Workers Playtime* at Pavilion Studios with Joe Boyd – a *proper* record producer whose work included Fairport Convention, R.E.M. and 10,000 Maniacs (hence Billy's interest). Jenner had known him since the 60s, and effectively pulled him out of retirement with the threat, 'Either you produce it or I will' (PJ had produced 'Hit Me With Your Rhythm Stick' for Ian Dury and a few Roy Harper albums).

Wiggy earned a co-production credit by, as he tells it, 'putting my oar in'. Expanding on *Taxman*'s dalliances with instrumentation and knob-twiddling, Cara came on board, as did Mickey Waller on drums, Wiggy on guitar and old hand Danny Thompson on double bass. (To illustrate Thompson's heritage, when, in 1991, Billy recorded Fred Neil's 'Dolphins' with him, he explained how he wanted it to sound – like Tim Buckley's version live at the Festival Hall. Thompson nodded, listened patiently and said, 'Yeah, I played bass on that.')

A curio came out at that time, a single called 'Ballad Of A Spycatcher' by Leon Rosselson, which featured Billy and The Oyster Band. It caused a minor stir because its specially written lyrics repeated an allegation from Peter Wright's memoir *Spycatcher*, then banned from sale in Britain due to an apparent national security threat. You could buy the book in America, naturally. These things tickle a man who has been to Nicaragua. In divine retribution for voting Mrs Thatcher back in, the beautiful South of England was devastated by a freak hurricane in October. Winds of 110 mph left the area between Cornwall and East Anglia with a bill of £300 million, and seventeen people were killed. Three days later, just in case those Tory voters thought it a coincidence, the stock market crashed, and 50 billion pounds was wiped off share prices in London in one day. They called it 'financial meltdown', and all those City boys who'd taken Harry Enfield's character Loadsamoney at face value and waved their wads in Docklands wine bars, kissed goodbye to their Christmas bonus. The Lord giveth and the Lord taketh away.

Billy's return trip to the Soviet Union in November, via Sweden and Finland, took in Estonia, Moscow and Leningrad (very much the rock capital of Russia). This trip was superbly documented by Chris Salewicz and photographer Adrian Boot in the book *Midnights In Moscow*: snow, trains, an assortment of funny hats, cross-cultural community singing in an Olympic weight-lifting hall, exquisite buildings, unexquisite buildings, black marketeers who looked like Alexei Sayle in *Gorky Park*, vodka, chocolate and the Kingston Gas Board (KGB).

Six months later, and in marked contrast to that trip's open-armed, inquiring, fact-finding perspective, Billy returned to the USSR to play the Vilnius Rock Festival in Lithuania alongside West Midlands cartoon rap-rock group Pop Will Eat Itself. With Art Troitsky as mediator (what an admirable cultural go-between he was) and with the *NME*'s James Brown in tow, the Poppies' story was the polar opposite to *Midnights In Moscow*. All they seemed to talk about was the lack of beer and decent food (they led audiences in a chant of 'Beer, beer, we want more beer' and made a mockery of the press conference with the same parched theme). 'Really sad,' Billy concludes. 'English people abroad. If you've got any interest in learning anything from these places, you've got to put your own feelers out. Otherwise you'll just meet the boring people from the Ministry. It's like being shown round the Glastonbury Festival by John Selwyn Gummer.'

On the way home from Leningrad, Billy had a Russian soldier's hat confiscated from his luggage by customs officers.

Memo to Generation X: pull your pants up, turn your hat around and get a job
    P. J. O'Rourke, *Fashionable Worries*

The Housemartins split in January 1988 with the self-penned statement, 'In a world of Rick Astley, Shakin' Stevens and the Pet Shop Boys, quite simply they weren't good enough.' They told the *NME* before they told Andy Macdonald. In February 1988, Billy Bragg played no gigs for the entire calendar month, the first time this had happened in six years (they were sculpting away at *Workers Playtime*).

A track from *Taxman* took on new life in April 1988. Called 'Help Save The Youth Of America' ('A nation with their freezers full/Are dancing in their seats/While outside another nation is sleeping in the streets'), it was a warning against complacency in the Land Of The Free aimed specifically at the sons and daughters of the Baby Boomers, whose idealism was in danger of fading away. May 88 saw the primary elections for the next president, a chance perhaps to replace Ronald Reagan, the man who coined the phase 'evil empire' with a younger man (Reagan was 77) and even a Democrat, Michael Dukakis. It wasn't much of a race, and despite the news images of flag-waving, partisan fervour at US election time, only about 40 per cent of voting-age citizens even bothered to turn out at the polls, but Billy was keen to do his bit for consciousness-raising. (His American fans, largely college types, tend to be at the soft-left, T-shirt-slogan end of the spectrum, but there is always work to be done in a country that produced the bumper sticker 'Guns, God and Guts made America great'.)

A US-only live EP was issued on Elektra, named *Help Save The Youth Of America*, and also containing the politically charged tracks 'Think Again', 'Chile Your Waters Run Red Through Soweto', 'Days Like These', 'To Have And To Have Not' and 'There Is Power In A Union'. The personal message on the back implored buyers 'to take part in the democratic process . . . you are electing a President for all of us. Please be more careful this time.'

On the fourteen-state, 22-date tour that went with it, Billy hooked up with the Democratic Socialists of America and various Central American support groups, and made it a

campaign trail. At New York's Roseland Ballroom, as reported in *Rolling Stone* magazine, he apologised for his hoarse
voice: 'It's nearly gone from me leaning out of taxi windows
and shouting "Asshole" at cars with Bush bumper stickers.'
Jane Garcia, reviewing the Los Angeles University show
for the *NME*, noted, 'Billy said everything about American
politics you wished Bruce [Springsteen] would say because
it would have more effect.' In the event, the Republicans
walked it, and Bush became president.

While Billy was out there, he had a Number One hit single
over here. 'She's Leaving Home' was Billy's contribution to
an all-star remake of The Beatles' *Sgt Pepper* album, *Sgt
Pepper Knew My Father*, coordinated by the *NME*'s Roy
Carr and in aid of the charity Childline. He recorded it
during the *Workers Playtime* sessions in late 87, thinking
it no big deal: Cara Tivey played the tune, Billy did three
vocal takes and it was down in a couple of hours. In May, it
became half of a double-A-sided single with Wet Wet Wet's
'With A Little Help From My Friends'. Thanks to support
from BBC's *That's Life* (host Esther Rantzen had founded
Childline), it topped the charts for four weeks and raised
£700,000. Billy might call it his 'honorary Number One' –
in that the Wets' track received most airplay – and try and
offload the credit to Cara, but no amount of humility can
disguise the fact that it's a magnificent achievement, cover
or no cover, charity or no charity.

'WHO THE HELL ARE WET WET WET?' asked Billy's
T-shirt on the cover of the self-congratulatory *NME*.

Top Of The Pops showed the Wet Wet Wet video three
times but on the fourth week Macdonald begged the producer, 'Let Braggy on!' They relented, and Billy repaid their
generosity by making a pig's ear of his appearance. To be
fair, he'd just flown in from a five-week US tour, and he'd
only ever sung the song three times, but making up the
words during the camera rehearsal didn't please the people
upstairs in the control room (needless to say, he was adamant
about playing live), so he taped the lyrics on the floor beside
him. Wiggy and Dave Woodhead played recorder. During
the actual recording, the BBC dry ice started, obscuring
the lyrics, and half-way through Billy watched a Norman
Wisdom figure with a fifteen-foot ladder distractedly lean it

up against nothing – it fell over with a crash that caused the audience to look round. Assuming this would spoil the take, Billy meandered to the end, at which the director said, 'Thank you. Goodbye.'

He was at his mum's on the Thursday of transmission, mortified that an event she was clearly so proud of was, in reality, going to be so naff. 'It was awful,' he says. 'If you know where the ladder gets dropped, you can hear it.'

A packed June and July later, Billy grabbed some 'little bits of holiday' with a string of ladyfriends in August: messing about on the canal with Texan folkstress Michelle Shocked (a barge from Tottenham Hale to Richmond that broke down near Putney Bridge); a romantic trip to the Lakes with 'a woman from Stockholm'; a bunk-up with 'someone else' in Salisbury – quite a tally, but Billy was on the rebound after Year Mary.

In August, things went 'a bit Wendell Road' at Son Of Go! Mansions and 'Waiting For The Great Leap Forwards' came out as a single. Billy was pretty much trapped in the singles loop by now, but it never reaped great dividends. Since 'Between The Wars'' pioneering work in the Top Fifteen (and discounting May's 'honorary' Childline squirt), Billy Bragg singles hadn't troubled the business end of the chart – 'Greetings To The New Brunette', released after the album whence it came in November 86, had reached 58.

Some valuable Billy Bragg compositions and fine covers have appeared as B-sides down the years (Brunette's twelve-inch contained Woody Guthrie's 'Deportees' and The Smiths' 'Jeane'), but it seems that Bragg fans are albums-buyers and gig-goers by nature. 'Great Leap Forwards' threw up an unfortunate incident: Billy caught Andy Macdonald with a car bootfull of seven-inch promo singles marked 'DJ Edit'. On closer inspection, he discovered that the first verse had been edited off. Billy explains his ire: 'I was angry from an artistic point of view – that nobody had asked me about this – and at the naïvety of Andy and Pete, thinking that chopping off the first verse would get it played on Radio 1. It was so ridiculous. The only way we would've got it played was to get Trevor Horn in to produce it at incredible cost, and cut the politics! But the first verse? Really fucking dumb.'

With a sad inevitability, it got to Number 52.

Workers Playtime, the album, was released on 19 September and went Top Twenty. In full, 'Great Leap Forwards' provided it with a fitting, sing-song finale, one of the few songs on the album not about Mary or inspired by the Mary experience.

'The Short Answer', which actually names her ('Between Marx and marzipan in the dictionary there was Mary/ Between the Deep Blue Sea and the Devil that was me') is actually about a number of Billy's obsessive relationships, and, in true Bragg style, uses actual events as a starting point and takes off down fictional tangents. For instance, there is talk of being duffed up by 'her' two brothers; Mary did have two brothers, but they never took him outside, as it were. Billy will readily admit to using real names in song – as far back as 'Richard' from Riff Raff days, whose protagonists are people he knew ('Richard belongs to Jayne/And Jayne belongs to yesterday') – but it is wise not to take every word he writes at face value.

That said, 'Must I Paint You A Picture', 'The Only One', 'The Price I Pay', 'Life With The Lions' and 'Little Time Bomb' are all fundamentally Mary songs ('Sometimes I think that fate has been against us from the start'). Equally, they can be taken as polaroids of Billy's attitude towards women, towards himself and towards relationships as he viewed them in 1988. Opening jangler 'She's Got A New Spell' – the title of which comes from a phrase Alan Wigg used after a female neighbour was banging and wailing next door – is more general, hinting at the witchcraft of female sexuality first explored in 'Strange Things Happen'. 'I'm not saying they're all witches,' he explains. This perceived hormonal alchemy has come a long way since the boyish frustration of 'A New England' and 'The Man In The Iron Mask' and the disappointed sigh of 'A Lover Sings' and 'The Myth Of Trust'. Billy has become more analytical of love, but no happier, frankly.

David Fricke in *Rolling Stone* called it 'broken-heart surgery'. Porky remembers with some distaste a meeting between Andy Macdonald and Pete Jenner after Mary and Billy had split where, albeit jokingly, they rubbed their hands together at the thought of the album they would surely get out of it. They were, however, on the money (apt, really) – *Workers*

Playtime was a fine cycle of injured love songs. With a bit of politics.

'Valentine's Day Is Over' examines violence towards women from a female perspective. 'This is a song by a bloke about how it is unacceptable to beat up women,' Billy explains. 'I'm not writing it for women, I'm writing it for other blokes to hear.'

'Great Leap Forwards', featuring some of Billy's most memorable lines, pulls off the difficult trick of boiling down the whole pop-and-politics-don't-mix argument. Billy elucidates: 'What I'm trying to say is, the role of the artist is not to come up with answers but to ask the right bloody questions. It's the audience's job to change the world. The artist can talk about the world, and evoke the world, and paint a picture of the world, but the answers aren't given to singer-songwriters. For fuck's sake, my first famous song said "I don't want to change the world", *however* . . . and the important thing is the "however" – while I'm here, there are one or two things I'd like to talk about, if you don't mind, other than just my guitar and the length of my hair. Some people take that and run with it and get a lot out of that, other people are opposed to it, but I recognise that it's a contradiction. I am not kidding myself.

'I was trying to communicate to people that I was aware. It was my post-*Taxman* declaration of who I was. My caveat to Red Wedge: I'm really interested in politics, *however*, I don't know what's going to happen if Labour win the election.'

> *It's a mighty long way down rock'n'roll*
> *From Top Of The Pops to drawing the dole*
> *If no one seems to understand*
> *Start your own revolution, cut out the middle man*
> *In a perfect world we'd all sing in tune*
> *But this is reality so give me some room*
> *So join in the struggle while you may*
> *The Revolution is just a T-shirt away*

It is Billy Bragg's 'Song For However'. It builds and builds until, apparently, everybody Billy knows is singing backing vocals (Porky, Cara, Wiggy, Michelle Shocked, a junior Jenner and Jayne Creamer – the very Jayne mentioned in the song 'Richard', then working at Go! Discs). What a way to go. He always did know how to end an album.

Having rehumanised himself through the songwriting process on *Workers Playtime*, Billy put himself back on the rack for what he refers to as The Tour That Went On For Ever, but was no more punishing than any other. The American leg started on 7 September in Halifax, Nova Scotia and ended 1 November in Montreal. (From there it was Scandinavia, West Germany, Holland, Belgium, Christmas.) The Volvo had been outgrown since Billy stopped playing with himself, replaced by a rented van, containing him, Cara, Jenner, Wiggy and Grant Showbiz aka Grant Cunliffe, sound engineer and producer who'd experienced the early days of The Smiths ('the punk Hollies', as he'd described them) and also worked with The Fall.

Halfway through the American trek, between LA and Dallas, the Bragg party detoured via the Grand Canyon and almost ended the tour there and then. With Jenner driving, and Billy sitting in the front, they came round the mountains at one in the morning at European speed and two huge National Park elks darted across the road in front of them. The van missed the stag but hit the doe, which was killed outright. Mercifully, there was no other traffic, and Jenner managed to keep control of the vehicle and stay on the road, but it was nearly a nasty accident – Cara, six months' pregnant with her first son George, was asleep across the back seat. It shook everybody up, and cost them deer.

A week later, Cara gave them a return shock in New Orleans, but a rather more pleasant one. 9 October is Columbus Day, so there was no gig to be had, and it was designated for laundry. But Cara's boyfriend Mick had joined them, and at 11 a.m., without warning, the party were summoned to the courthouse to witness their wedding. Fortunately, they'd all bought cowboy gear in Austin and were able to dress up. Everyone cried, except Cara and Mick, and despite the public holiday, a visiting Tiny managed to rustle up something old, blue and borrowed. It was a happy occasion, but it meant that they never did get their undies spun for the entire tour. (Cara's baby was born in December.

She worked right up to her ninth month, and was back out on tour when George was three months.)

On 31 December, Billy played the first of what became his annual Hackney Empire New Year's Eve specials. He traditionally spent New Year's Eve at Brenda and Joe's in Oundle (their parties were legendary), but 1987 had seen him and Wiggy wandering the streets of London after a Wangfords gig, eventually washing up on Andy and Juliet Macdonald's doorstep – so Pete Jenner stepped in. He'd find something for them to do. Work.

Marginally fewer gigs had been notched up in 1987 and 1988, but many more miles travelled. Billy was hopping an average of twelve countries a year, many of them covered twice, usually a couple visited for the first time – in 86 it was East Germany, Russia and Japan; in 87, it was Australia, New Zealand and Nicaragua. In 1989, although he didn't know it yet, it would be Mexico, Bolivia and China.

'He was working me hard,' says Billy of Jenner. 'But the things he kept coming up with were too fucking interesting to turn down! It wasn't just, Let's go and tour Germany again, it was, Let's go to China, let's go to Mexico, or Nicaragua. The only thing that used to bug me about it was that there was no time in between, no time for me to assimilate the fact that I'd been in China, and think to myself, God, that was really incredible, and let it sink in. I'd get home, and bang, I was in Mexico! Then back in New York again.

'I'd say to people, It's nothing to do with me, I just go where he tells me!'

Jenner defends his merciless slave-driving tactic: 'You've got to ride the tide, you've got to do it all. If you *can* do everything, you *should* do everything. If you don't open up those markets, you're gonna bore them in England: there you are again, another album, another tour. If you've got a career in all these other countries, you don't have to over-work the UK'.

When you're happening, get to Prague, get to Germany, get to America, get to Canada. You're offered the chance to go to Russia, you go to Russia.

'I wanted to get Billy happening all over the world, which was hard for him, I know, because he never liked flying. He had to screw up his courage and go on dodgy airlines on cheap tickets. I could never afford to book with whoever flies direct from Minneapolis to Denver, so we'd have to go via Memphis. That sort of shit.'

'Pete's so intrepid,' says Tiny. 'He always wants to go somewhere else.'

She remembers him in a German airport brandishing a 1970s-looking brochure saying 'Come To Kazakhstan!' containing a photograph of the local delicacy, boiled sheep's head in its own juices (this was intended as enticement). Tiny assumed he was joking, but you can never tell with Peter Jenner.

It was a mighty long way *round* rock'n'roll, especially the way Billy Bragg was doing it, but aside from the lack of feet-ground interface, it was still the life for him: 'I didn't feel it was pointless. I didn't have anything else to do anyway.'

If nothing else, Brenda and Joe's postcard collection was looking healthy. Ever since Billy left Oundle in 1980, he'd sent regular letters, Christmas cards and tapes to his old mates. It became a custom once he started travelling the world, and the couple were in regular receipt of esoteric missives from far-away armpits or beauty spots. Their anthology today is impressive: postcards depicting the three-storey Uniroyal Tyre in Detroit, Dealey Plaza in Dallas, a rainforest in Queensland, moose calves in Alaska, the Pope in Rome and the people's underground station in Moscow (actually, he bought that one in Camden). These bulletins, often brief and written on knees in transit, are exhausting enough simply to look through, so heaven knows what it must have been like on the other end of the biro.

Here, there and everywhere, but forever writing home: that's Billy Bragg all over.

In February, 1989, he was in the GDR again, by which time *perestroika* was in full swing – not as groovy as it sounds, since the conservative East German State were clamping down in response to Gorbachev's revolution in the head. The place was like a pressure cooker, and the ten-day trip was a depressing one.

The optimism they'd experienced in 86 had gone. Billy remembers that nobody in their party spoke a word on the flight back from East Berlin to Amsterdam.

Billy asked about the elusive *glasnost* after gigs, but no one was particularly open about openness. At the House of Russian-German Friendship in East Berlin, he inadvertently started some big trouble by saying that *perestroika* and *glasnost* wouldn't work unless the Berlin Wall came down. The next day, he was called in by the state-run promoters to be taught a lesson: they took him to the museum at the Brandenburg Gate. As their coach drew into no-man's land between East and West, Jorg Wolter's antennae began twitching. There were TV cameras waiting for them, which meant that Billy's little visit would be on that evening's news. 'Whatever you actually say,' Wolter told Billy, 'you'll be saying that the Berlin Wall is a good idea on TV.'

Billy refused to get off the bus. Wolter lost his temper, got off and walked back to East Berlin, straight through the guards without a care. The whole farrago was 'piss-poor PR for the East Germans', as Billy puts it. While they were between the walls, in an area about 200 yards wide, Billy noticed that it was full of rabbits, which struck him as sweet.

Suddenly he was Mr Refusenik: he declined to play the lightbulb factory again, so they offered him an army barracks where the border guards were based. Here, Billy had a fascinating friendship meeting with the border guard officers – an old timer fixed him with his beady eye and revealed that he actually took part in the building of the Berlin Wall in 1961, explaining that it's there to keep the fascists of West Germany out of East Germany (the 'anti-fascist dam' they call it). Billy's response was direct: 'There aren't any. We are not trying to invade your country – I know it and Gorbachev knows it.'

The lesson from all this was that things change. Politics change. That's why Billy admits he can't keep up with the Labour Party today. Things had changed all around this old guard officer and he hadn't even noticed. Billy did the barracks gig and sure enough, a happy, smiling photo with the guards appeared in the newspaper. He said his Berlin Wall piece again, and got in trouble again.

The closing gig at the Sports Hall was televised live. Never mind Radio Free Europe, this was Channel Free Bragg: through his interpreter, Billy suggested that the Wall was built to house a rabbit sanctuary. 'The time will come when the rabbits of East Berlin will be free to roam in West Berlin,' he said.

A smattering of applause. The cameras moved away. Once Billy was offstage, he was told in no uncertain terms, 'You will never play in East Berlin again.' And that was that.

'Although they didn't know it at the time, they were right,' Billy says. 'Because the next time I came back, there wasn't an East Berlin to play.

'But at the time, I felt that I'd failed all those people I'd had contact with. I was yet another thing they weren't allowed to do.'

Australia and New Zealand saw Cara Tivey back in the saddle: 'If I can do that, I can do anything,' she reasoned. George flew to Sydney aged three months. It was good for everybody to have him there, and anyway, as Billy says, 'Having a baby on the road's not that different from having a rhythm section.'

After a couple of dates in Japan, Billy, PJ and Sumi went to Shanghai and on to Beijing in China – but as sightseers not a rock'n'roll touring party. 'It was really groovy,' Billy enthuses. 'Shanghai was like a big Dixons, but without the variety.' History was brewing up the very weekend they were in Beijing: on 15 April, the liberal reformer and former Communist Party head Hu Yaobang died. A week later, on 22 April, his funeral was marked by a 100,000-strong demonstration by students, who unfurled a huge banner saying 'China's soul! Forever remember Comrade Hu Yaobang!' The next two months saw hunger strikes, martial law and the eventual massacre of 2,600 students by the People's Liberation Army in Tiananmen Square.

All Billy, PJ and Sumi knew of it was the difficulty they experienced as they drove to the airport. PJ's brother, a Sinologist living in Canberra, had sorted out some Chinese contacts for them through the Australian cultural attaché. After Tiananmen Square, every single contact they'd made disappeared.

Billy and PJ had found a stall in Beijing selling cool Chairman Mao badges and bought the lot for $110. It was Mao who had initiated the original Great Leap Forward in 1958, and look where it had got them. It's not enough to buy badges in days like these.

12. STOP PLAYING WITH YOURSELF

A bit of business, 1989–1992

*It waved above our infant might
When all ahead seemed dark as night
It witnessed many a deed and vow
We must not change its colour now*

'The Red Flag'

Putting romance to one side, Billy has always been good at friendship. Quite apart from his lifelong pact with Wiggy, he keeps in touch with his cousins and the rest of the family, knows exactly where Ricey and Robert Handley are, and maintains a rewarding, occasionally long-distance relationship with Brenda and Joe. Peter Jenner is still involved as a friend and consultant, with Juliet doing the full-time management, and from the day Tiny Fennimore joined Go! Discs, she became a constant ally (still chuffed to count him as a friend of the family). In 1988, when Andy and Juliet Macdonald had their son, Jamie, they asked Billy to be godfather – not for sentimental reasons, but because he was precisely the sort of bloke who would *be* there for Jamie. They were spot on. It is not putting him on too much of a pedestal to say that Billy Bragg is a constant in an increasingly unpredictable world. An old Volvo looks unreliable in comparison.

Which is precisely why he decided it was time to terminate his relationship with Go! Discs after *Workers Playtime*.

Five years, four albums, five singles, many a deed and vow. It had been a pleasure, but 1988 had been . . . different. At the end of 1987, Go! Discs' hard-fought distribution deal with Chrysalis expired, and a much more momentous contract with PolyGram was signed. PolyGram, 75 per cent owned by the Dutch electronics giant Philips, was in the process of becoming one of the biggest record companies in the world (in 1989, they bought A&M for £300 million and Island for £200 million). PolyGram's deal with Go! was more than just marketing and distribution – they bought 49 per cent of the shares. This provided a welcome influx of cash (hence the staff expansion), and, for Macdonald, more muscle overseas. Looking back, he says it was 'a deal borne of necessity'. Maybe so, but it seriously queered his pitch with Billy and Jenner.

Up to that point, it had all been fun and games, a contract-without-contracts on Billy and Sincere's terms: no extortionate advances, just percentage points on sales and the eventual rights.

They'd never signed for more than one album at a time, and yet remained loyal. Both sides had made concessions – Macdonald got his singles, Billy got his price ceilings – and, looking at the balance sheets and the press-cuttings file, it had worked in everybody's favour. But the PolyGram deal moved the goal posts.

Andy Macdonald had given Billy a ten per cent share in Go! Discs early on when, frankly, it wasn't worth much – it was his well-intentioned way of counting Billy in when there wasn't a lot of spare cash floating about. Billy had resisted ('I'm not into stocks and shares'), but was eventually wooed by Macdonald's commitment to running Go! like a co-operative – everybody gets a piece. At the time, it was no more than a piece of paper to Billy and didn't have any meaning. However, when 49 per cent of the company was sold to PolyGram, Billy's stake became crucial: he had to sell half his shares in order not to stymie the deal. 'I cashed in my chips,' he says, 'and made a tidy sum, the largest amount of money I'd ever got in a single payment, but I didn't feel like it was my money. I hadn't earned it.'

Out of the remaining 51 per cent, Andy Macdonald owned 41 per cent, Juliet five per cent and Billy now had five per cent. This situation furrowed his moral brow – his shares were now the decider in any future dispute: 'The shares became an issue and I thought it was really out of order dragging me into all this. It turned our friendship into a purely business relationship. It was another thing I didn't need. I felt that it was the first time commerce had come before art.'

There is no doubt about it, things were never the same again after the shares issue. It left a sour taste in Billy's mouth; it went against everything he held dear about his relationship with Go! Discs and with Macdonald: 'It made me realise that Go! Discs was a business, and Andy was a businessman rather than a co-conspirator.'

It was prickly for Pete Jenner too, who'd had his fill of big record companies and had no desire to work for PolyGram again. Plus, with Billy's interests at heart, he recognised a can of worms when he saw one. Jenner today is outspoken on the matter: 'We were furious. I told Andy, Don't give Billy shares! Bigger royalties, fine, but shares have a life of their own. It's one of those things people do to tie you in. Billy felt Andy had sold him to PolyGram and, furthermore, had assumed Billy would be happy about it provided he gave him enough money, which really insulted him. There were a lot of bad vibes.'

In the event, an unprecedented redistribution of wealth put Billy's mind at ease. He came up with a plan whereby he donated the rest of his shares to the staff of Go! Discs by way of a trust. That way, he didn't own them any more, and, should Go! Discs ever be sold off or shut down, anyone who'd worked for the company for two years would benefit when the trust shares were sold. 'It allowed me to make decisions about my career that weren't based on my shareholding with the record company I was signed to,' Billy explains. 'I know it sounds ungrateful to Andy and Juliet, but it was a conflict of interests.'

Andy Macdonald defends the PolyGram deal: 'I'd always wanted to set up a record company that would try and operate on honest principles with its artists, pay them the royalty they're due on the day that it's due, not infringe upon their creativity, and work with the most intriguing and excellent variety of artists possible. But I wanted our records to be of more importance to people working them overseas, and to build the roster. I wanted to be like Island, Motown, Stax. For that, we needed funding. It was a hard decision.'

Go! Discs retained their autonomy as an A&R entity, signing who they wanted when they wanted (in 1988, The La's, The Blue Ox Babes, No Man's Land, money pits to a man), and they still marketed their own records in their own quirky way. 'The ethic of the company didn't change,' insists Macdonald. 'Maybe the aspirations were higher . . .'

Asked if he thinks Billy was being naive resisting the shares, his answer is typically diplomatic: 'Or very wise.'

The rot had set in. But some good came of it: on 25 April 1989, Billy and Jenner launched (or relaunched) Utility as an active, independent label, based in Sincere's offices and distributed by the Cartel, an independent network. This was all thanks to the 'few bob' Billy had made out of selling his Go! Discs shares to PolyGram. (His initial plan had been to give it all to the RSPCA, but Jenner, good manager that he is, said, 'Let's be more imaginative.')

Billy describes Utility, which lasted eighteen months and released ten records, as 'a wheeze that proved you can't be on the road *and* run a record company'. Their releases were attractively colour-coded and designed on the strip-colour *Life's A Riot* template, and featured artists like Boston's The Blake Babies (an early sighting of Evan Dando, later of The Lemonheads and slacker heart-throb), Jungr & Parker, Clive Product and Weddings, Parties, Anything. Billy concludes, 'Some of it was great, some of it was average, but they were all good bands. I'm surprised we managed to put out as many records as we did, in the end.'

If pushed, he feels he may have let down some artists, who signed one-off deals but were expected to organise their own promo – all right for some, not for others. Meanwhile, their label boss was off touring the world, and the money was all outgoing.

Paul Weller, Mick Hucknall, Madonna – successful pop stars start their own labels for a variety of reasons, but they're largely vanity projects, a chance to play God and create artists in their own image. Utility was a well-meaning folly, best summed up by the Clive Product album title: *Financial Suicide*.

Billy missed Glastonbury in 1989, but for good reason. More travel, but this time paid for by the BBC. He and Andy Kershaw were asked to make a pilgrimage for the *Great Journeys* travelogue series, to Bolivia and Chile along the ancient Spanish trade route which used to carry silver across the Andes by llama. Billy got the call while in Shanghai – the Beeb's first-choice of presenter, classical guitarist John Williams, got vertigo on a three-week fact-finding mission and cried off, so they asked by-now-established broadcaster Kershaw. Jenner engineered the double-act, and off the pair of them went. 'The BBC has been sending academic intellectuals up the Limpopo for far too long,' said Billy. 'It's about time they let someone else go and have a look.'

The terrain is perilous, the roads are long and winding, the miners chew coca leaves to 'ward off fatigue', the rocks underground weep arsenic and men retire at 35, unsurprisingly buggered. Although slightly off the rock'n'roll track, it wasn't so strange a trip for Billy: new sights, new sounds, new smells and plenty of opportunities for singing at bemused locals.

Coca leaves were the alternative national dish (an appetite-depressant, they helped the mine workers do longer shifts without food), and the women by the roadside who sold them also did a nice line in sticks of dynamite just like you see in Tom & Jerry cartoons. Kershaw bought half a dozen sticks (three for £1, like disposable lighters outside a tube station). The responsible camera crew declined to film them setting the dynamite off like schoolboys and running away from the deafening blast, but Kershaw made Billy take his photo holding one with the fuse lit. Kershaw was determined to get high on the coca leaves: he boiled them, smoked them, ate them in sandwiches, but got nothing more than a numb gum ('My cheeks were like hamster's throughout the entire film if you look closely,' he recalls).

It was an excellent trip, tear-arsing across the Atacama desert in Toyota landcruisers and staying in Potosi, the highest city in the world (13,350 feet above sea level), where the air is so thin, running up the stairs will make you light headed and a pint of beer knocks you flat on your back. Local customs were suitably rum, particularly watching a llama being sacrificed at the fiesta of San Juan, its throat cut while dopey on coca and the blood thrown over the gables of surrounding houses.

At one tiny village, they all sat round fires while the women cooked sweet potatoes, and the elders played an ancient tune that sounded eerily like 'The Banana Splits Theme'. In return the Brits led a chorus of 'Ging Gang Goolie'. (In November, Bolivia would declare a nationwide state of emergency after labour disputes threatened to get out of control. The world continued to turn upside down.)

The Billy Bragg story is punctuated with epiphanies – the musical, personal and spiritual – moments of truth that either put paid to nagging doubts or made sense of the situation in which Billy found himself. The Clash at the Rainbow; the blokes kissing at Rock Against Racism; Spandau Ballet on *Top Of The Pops*; Route 66 with Wiggy; the Women's Support Group in Sunderland – and now, the flight from Rio to El Alto in Peru on the way out for the BBC trip. Peru is 13,000 feet above sea level, so the plane flies up to 36,000 feet and only comes just over half-way down. Billy hadn't been able to sleep since they refuelled in the Brazilian jungle, there was no coffee, everyone was asleep – not a jolly occasion for the nervous flier. Then, surrounded by cloud over the Andes, the plane's wheels stuck and they had to turn back. Great, Billy thought, putting on his headphones and drowning out the world with a compilation tape. The song was 'Willing' by California blues-rockers Little Feat ('Been stung by the rain, been driven by the snow/I'm drunk, I'm dirty, but don't you know/I'm willing'). It raised Billy's spirits.

'I heard this line and it made me realise that I was there on that plane because this was what I'd always wanted to do. I was scared, I was hungry, but *this was what I'd always wanted to do*. I wasn't some poor bastard in a shack with the rain coming in, I wasn't some poor grunt sitting in a trench. I'd volunteered for this and it's the best thing to do and I'm getting paid for it.'

On cue, the clouds parted and there below him was Lake Titicaca. 'This,' Billy remembered, 'is the best fucking job in the world!'

Bolivia with Kershaw had virtually been a holiday, and it was immediately followed by more touring with the old gang. By October, ten countries later, it was the *worst* fucking job in the world again. 'Mexico is where it really started to get to me,' he says, of the seven-day trip between Pachuca and Toluca. 'I'm going to all these places I've never been to before and then I'm going to other places before I've really had time to assimilate the fact.'

In the second Billy Bragg songbook, poignantly titled *Victim Of Geography* from the compilation album of the same name, there is an amusing 'A To Z Of Life On The Road', explaining colloquialisms such as Gig Spanner (bottle opener), PMT (Pre-minstrel tension), Shitters (foreign currency) and Normans (punters, from 'Norman Hunters'). Here we find the entry 'Xalapa, a bit of a', meaning a totally pointless gig.

On 19 October, Billy and crew were booked to play a show at the university at Xalapa Enríquez (sometimes spelt Jalapa). This involved a long drive through the mountains with dead dogs on the road and, when they got to the venue, no equipment, no PA and no audience. 'They didn't know we were coming,' says Billy. 'It was the last straw for me, a low point. It was all too much, I thought, I should be really getting off on this.' But he wasn't. Not connecting at all. Unfortunately, there were another six weeks of USA and Canada between Xalapa University and home.

Cara hadn't made it to Mexico, which was a pity, as the saving grace of 1989's back-breaking schedule was Cara's baby George, who'd been touring with them since the Antipodes across Japan, France, Canada, the USA and much of Europe (for his first birthday that December, they bought him a world map). George completely changed Billy's attitude to kids and babies, and brought home to him how little time he'd been able to spend with his godson Jamie. The men, be it Billy, Wiggy, Showbiz or Jenner, would find themselves literally holding the baby while Cara ate her meals, and the experience was a great leveller: 'However shit *your* day was, you'd get on the bus and George was either having a really good day and would cheer you up, or he was having a much, much worse day and you wouldn't feel so bad. It made us all think a bit less about being rock'n'rollers.

'Except maybe Wiggy.'

History continued to unfold around their ears that year. After two days messing about in Athens with R.E.M., the party was late for a supper club gig in Nashville. As they finally bundled in backstage, a steward from the venue sorted them out: 'There's your dressing room, there's your rider, I want you onstage at nine o'clock . . . and by the way, the Berlin Wall's come down.'

Just like that. Thousands of Germans from both sides poured through the check-points that night, and many climbed the wall and danced on top of it. It was the collapse of communism as acid house rave, an event few thought they'd see in their lifetime, and a notion so radical only nine months before it had got Billy banned from East Germany. The mayor of West Berlin, Walter Momper, said, 'The Germans are the happiest people in the world today', but Billy and party gave them a good run for their hard currency. Having confirmed the frankly unbelievable truth via the BBC World Service, they led the audience in an evening of celebration – the Americans because they thought they'd won the Cold War, and the Brits toasting the friends they'd made in East Berlin. Après-gig, they all got out of their trolleys watching CNN. The tsars look very different today.

Billy lost his voice in Red Creek, Rochester – hereafter known as Red Croak – and the audience got off on the irony of it, not to mention the sexy upper-register huskiness, passing him honeylaced drinks from the side of the stage (he vividly remembers his fingers sticking to the neck of his guitar). This led, unavoidably, to a rare cancelled gig – apologies to Binghampton in upstate New York.

'It was a long year.'

Billy saw off the 1980s on stage at the Hackney Empire under a rain of balloons, playing covers of The Skatelites' 'Guns Of Navarone' and The Kinks' 'Victoria'. 'Easing off' is not a common phrase in the Bragg story, but that's how he describes his activities of January and February, 1990. There was some recording for his next album, some writing for the *Weekend Guardian* and a bit of 'trying to get my life back'.

It gave him the time to reflect on the passing 1980s – a decade in which reflection, for him, had been at a premium. Ten years of Thatcher, eight years of gigging, the two not entirely unconnected. Billy had watched the world fall apart, but some things stayed in place: his friends, his commitment to socialism, the *NME* crossword. Ten years ago, there was no Billy Bragg, no Go! Discs, no Utility, no Red Wedge and no Portastack. The dictionary contained no compact disc, no Thatcherism, no AIDS, no yuppie, no global warming and no Reaganomics, and *Star Wars* was a film. It was a long decade, a white-hot crucible in which ideas and hopes and fears had been forged, and, spiritually, it wasn't over yet, oh no.

Go! Discs came out of the 80s smiling, having seen a mighty phoenix rise from the ashes of The Housemartins – namely, The Beautiful South, whose debut album *Welcome To The Beautiful South* hit Number Two in November. In February, Housemartins' bassist Norman Cook's new outfit Beats International scored a Number One single with *Dub Be Good To Me*. While PolyGram sat back and smiled benignly at its new investment, Porky decided he'd had enough of the stifling, junior-corporatism of the new Go! and resigned his post. Within five days of handing in his notice, his girlfriend announced she was pregnant. To their eternal credit, the Macdonalds offered him his job back, but he stuck to his plan and struck out into the big, wide yonder, concentrating full-time on being a big, wide stand-up (good decision, as it transpired). Tiny Fennimore had also left Go! – having concentrated her energies so unashamedly behind Billy, it seemed wise to go and work for him. She joined Sincere.

Billy's own relationship with Go! Discs was also up in the air at this point: unbeknown to Andy Macdonald, Pete Jenner was talking to other record companies.

In February, to get away from all this back-stabbing and subterfuge, Billy went somewhere more democratic: the Nicaraguan elections. As one of a staggering 3,000 international observers, Billy watched in disbelief as the Sandinista government were ousted by Violeta Chamorro's National Opposition Union (which, as the *NME*'s Michelle Kirsch noted, is 'a shit name for a new Clash album'). Billy's optimism after the release of Nelson Mandela and the defeat of Mike Tyson by Buster Douglas on the same day less than a week previously was misplaced. He wrote an incisive report for *New Socialist* magazine about his visit, dubbing the election results 'a different kind of earthquake'. The Nicaraguan people simply wanted an end to the war, and a reversal of the US trade embargo that was crippling their country's economy – it was, on the day, deciding which of the two parties could best haggle with the Yankees. These chose Chamorro's fourteen-party coalition. It was Peter Jenner who, in a moment of either inspired irony or foot-in-mouth disease told the *NME*, 'If you have a good, right-on cause, don't ask Billy to play a benefit, because you'll lose.'

At least Billy got to meet another of his heroes in Managua, Jackson Browne – 'After Bob Dylan, the singer-songwriter that really *got* me' – they shared a house, and played each other's songs ('If only Wiggy could've seen me!').

The self-styled 'champion of lost causes' was unbowed. He appeared onstage for the finale of Easter Monday's International Tribute To Nelson Mandela concert at Wembley Stadium – albeit by accident. Billy had been asked by *Melody Maker* to write a report for the paper, which he duly did ('When Nelson Mandela walked out on to the stage and smiled like he had just seen 72,000 of his grandchildren, Wembley erupted. It cannot have echoed to such a tumult since 1966 and there were people on the pitch then too'), but was roped in by Peter Gabriel to join the closing sing-song of 'Sun City' and 'Biko' alongside Chrissie Hynde, Jerry Dammers, Simple Minds, Daniel Lanois, Little Steven and others.

He had but one thought among all the pop unity and political triumphalism: 'I hope Wiggy's videoing this.'

Billy's next Big Important Gig was Washington DC's Earth Day, where he performed with Michael Stipe and Elektra labelmates 10,000 Maniacs. Backstage, he enthused about his experiences in the former East Germany. 'How does that work?' asked Stipe. 'Well,' Billy replied, 'you get on a plane and get off the other end.' He was booked to do a short tour of Germany, Czechoslovakia, Finland and the USSR in June and invited Stipe and Maniacs singer Natalie Merchant along. They happily accepted.

May saw the release of Billy Bragg's most important album since *Life's A Riot*, his seven-track collection of political songs *The Internationale*. It was important for two distinct reasons: it was released on Utility and not Go! Discs, to prove to Andy Macdonald that he could do it, and, self-evidently, it was political at a time when – apparently – all of Billy's causes were either evaporating or being crushed underfoot.

'It was Not The Next Billy Bragg Album,' he explains. 'It confused the fuck out of Elektra in America, and pissed the fuck out of Andy at home. It was a reassertion of my rights as an individual . . . and a childish two-fingers.'

From the album-defining rewrite of 'The Internationale' itself with brass band and Welsh choir ('The Internationale unites the world in song') to the heart-rending anti-war lament 'My Youngest Son Came Home Today' ('While in his polished box of pine/Like dead meat in a butcher's tray'), this all-too-brief album baits those who would seek to stereotype Billy as one-dimensional and over-earnest. On closer inspection however, its broad sweep of anthems and ballads actually presents an artist who's hungry for more. These songs are, for the most part, steeped in history, yet Billy manages to contemporarise them and point them at the future. A far harder album for him to tackle than another one of bruised love songs.

'The Marching Song Of The Covert Battalions' is far and away the album's biggest coup with its near-comedic chorus of 'Tra-la-la-la/We're making the world safe for capitalism' linking decades of local US military intervention from Mexico through Haiti, Cuba and – implicitly – Nicaragua ('We're here to lend a helping hand/In case they don't elect us'). By tackling 'Jerusalem' and 'The Red Flag', Billy exposes himself as punk's first dedicated historian, not just some lyric-mouthing tub-thumper, and his a cappella go at 'Nicaragua Nicaraguita' brings new meaning to the term 'brave'. *The Internationale* may be the least-played of Billy Bragg's back catalogue in many fans' collections, but it is difficult not to like.

For a low-key, non-populist, side-salad release, it was afforded plenty of space in the music papers, met in some quarters by a furrowed brow, others with a raised fist. 'He continues to expand his musical horizons and his un-compromising stance . . . Bragg reflects the hopes and fears of a people,' wrote Dave Jennings in *Melody Maker*. 'A post-revolutionary utopia should be *fun*,' complained

NME's Stephen Dalton, who also decided that Billy's literal interpretation of 'The Internationale' was unadventurous. *Folk Roots*' Colin Irwin saw it as a nice idea that lacked authority. Its 34 placing in the chart was not bad in the circumstances.

The release of an album, however modest, meant another full tour from here to Kalamazoo (no, really). The UK leg in May included a show for 90 inmates of D-wing at Glasgow's Barlinnie Prison. (Respect, as they say, is due to Cara Tivey, who braved the all-male environment just a month after the riot at Strangeways Prison and the others it sparked off.)

On the road from Barcelona to Valencia in May, with no guitar to hand, Billy wrote his English football hooligans song 'The Few' using the tune of Bob Dylan's 'Desolation Row', which is why, if you so wish, you can play one to the tune of the other.

On 3 June, he debuted 'The Few' to great effect at the Big Day shindig, a free festival marking Glasgow's status as European City of Culture. At Custom House Quay on the banks of the Clyde, before 2,000 non-paying punters, Billy was joined by Stipe and Merchant for some choice covers, and then the three of them took off for Berlin, accompanied by affable country-rockers The Coal Porters.

Although on familiar turf for Billy, Stipe was freaked out by Eastern Europe, not least for the fact that no one looked at him twice in restaurants. At Cottbus, which is a pretty heavy fascist town, they played Jugend Greizert Zentrum, a youth club with a tiny stage, where one punter said to Stipe, 'Are you American?' He nodded. 'Say hello to Michael Jackson.' Billy explained that the East German kid hadn't assumed Stipe knew Jacko because he was *Stipe*, simply because he was American – he'd never met one before.

Billy made the tactical error of singing 'The Internationale' at early gigs. The audiences took it badly in Prague, where – just six months after the Velvet Revolution and on the verge of their first free elections – the old Russian National Anthem still stung. Czech singer-songwriter Vladimir Merta tried in vain to translate Billy's explanation of the song's pro-democratic significance, but a strategic re-jig of the set seemed a more sympathetic solution. In the next town, Olumouc, he dropped it.

The sights and sounds were captivating in this stunning country that was more like picturesque Austria than hard-faced Germany: eating fondue in a Gypsy restaurant to violin accompaniment; Billy and Stipe wandering around Olumouc's empty town square and taking pictures of each other; the empty plinth with balloons tied to it, where Stalin or Lenin had once been. Two days away from the election, it became clear that they were witnessing history (one of Billy's hobbies, of course, but humbling for Stipe and Merchant, who stayed on in Czechoslovakia after the shows were over).

22 and 23 June saw a remarkable, cross-border joint festival hosted by Joensuu in Finland and Sortavala in Karelia, USSR. The newly opened border was so new the tarmac was still wet. The border post comprised one sentry box, and a guard saying 'Come in, come in!' Since it didn't actually get dark at all, Billy and Wiggy were unable to sleep, and they recall sitting in another empty square and seeing former Talking Heads singer David Byrne cycle past in a white suit. Somehow, it wasn't even that weird. The World Cup was being played over in Italy, but it couldn't have seemed further away.

In July, Billy managed to squeeze in a week's holiday in St Johns, Newfoundland. Some students found him and made him do a gig.

Life goes on as it did before
As the country drifts slowly to war

Billy Bragg, 'Rumours Of War'

The world was arming for peace once again in August 1990, when Iraqi tanks and planes entered Kuwait, and President Saddam Hussein was roundly condemned by the UN, who quickly proposed mandatory economic sanctions. Within a few days, Jordanian demonstrators were burning the Stars and Stripes, President Bush was ominously warning the American people about 'personal sacrifice', troops from twelve of the Allied nations were building up outside the Iraqi border, and on TV Saddam was asking British hostage six-year-old Stuart Lockwood if he was getting enough cornflakes.

Meanwhile, hoping like the rest of us that it was all a big show of strength and 'the new Hitler' would back off, Billy toured Canada and the USA. While he was in Boston, he ran in some valuable studio time at Fort Apache, the very first work he'd done on his next album, *Don't Try This At Home*. The situation in the Gulf hit stalemate. Germany announced reunification. Billy joined Johnny Marr at his studio Clear in Manchester to work on the album's first track, 'Sexuality'. War clouds loom, life goes on.

On 8 November, the *Guardian* printed an angry response from Billy Bragg in their letters page to an allusion they'd made to Essex Man typifying thuggish, right-wing Britain. He wrote 'We have had to endure the snobbery of the Home Counties often enough without being misused in the media's search for a caricature of the xenophobic national chauvinist.'

Three more nights at Hackney saw the New Year in once again, Billy's people celebrating the recent Tory revolt against Thatcher and getting off on his Essex Suite (covers of Dr Feelgood, Depeche Mode and Eddie & The Hot Rods) – but mindful throughout of George Bush's line in the sand. He debuted 'Rumours Of War', prompting *Q*'s John Aizlewood to note, 'Bragg's black-and-white certainties have been leavened by an edgy paranoia, revealing doubt, puzzlement and shafts of grey.'

The entry for 17 January 1991 in Billy's appointments book says it all: 'Accountants 4 p.m. WAR.'

Over the weekend of 18, 19 and 20 January, while 'our boys' were out in the desert getting Gulf War Syndrome, at Wembley Arena, self-styled music-biz mogul, the since disgraced Jonathan King was hosting The Great British Music Weekend: all the indie news that was fit to print. Wall-to-wall baggy tops captured the *zeitgeist* at an event dominated by fashionable bands from Manchester (Happy Mondays, Northside, 808 State, James), but a welcome blast of realism was provided by South London agit-popsters Carter The Unstoppable Sex Machine, whose anti-war single 'Bloodsport For All' was making the BBC nervous, and of course Billy Bragg, whose speech went: 'We have to struggle against the destruction of all human beings. It's not a fucking video game – it's the Third World War!' (Radio 1 axed his words from the 'live' broadcast.)

A new image of Billy Bragg circulated round the music press: the one 'bothering' other groups backstage. In truth, he did buttonhole Carter and also Blur in their dressing rooms to support the anti-war movement – to *do something* – but at a time of taking Ecstasy and pretending to be Mancunian, you can understand his urgency. As The Fall's Mark E Smith had famously said when faced with the shower of up-and-coming new indie groups: 'God help us if there's a war.' Well, there was, and God help us. Fortunately, the so-called mother of all battles was over by 28 February, when Saddam acquiesced to a cease-fire. Final score: Allied forces 120,000 – Iraq 343. The Kuwaitis lost an estimated 5,000, the price of freedom.

Meanwhile, amid rumours of peace, *Don't Try This At Home* was taking shape at Cathouse Studios, Pavilion and Sonet. It was another giant's step for Billy Bragg: 'It was the culmination of me trying my hardest to stay true to what I do but make an album that was commercially acceptable to a wider audience. I was trying to deal with that artistic compromise for a number of reasons, most important of which was that those were the sort of songs I was writing: big, sexy pop songs.'

In Manchester, Johnny Marr had co-produced and collaborated on 'Sexuality', transforming Billy's 'Louie Louie' guitar riff by sprinkling his own magic fairy dust on it (half-chords, apparently) and in doing so, creating not only an instant Bragg classic but a benchmark for the whole record. Billy knew they had struck gold. '"Sexuality" threw the gauntlet down,' he says. 'We couldn't make a conventional Billy Bragg-style record with "Sexuality" on it.'

Back in London, Billy and the record's main producer Grant Showbiz raised the game, 'aided and abetted by' Wiggy, as it eventually said in the album's credits – carefully phrased so as to acknowledge Wiggy's input without undermining Showbiz's role.

Don't Try This At Home was going to be big. That was the idea anyway.

Pete Jenner liked the idea of a full-on pop album, because he worked out that it would make a fantastic calling card with which to broker the next record deal. He and Billy firmly believed that they'd taken the Go! Discs relationship as far

as they could: now that Billy was established and no longer
a novelty act, his albums hit a steady sales peak of around
70,000 in the UK. He wasn't going out of fashion – he'd
never been *in* fashion – but a plateau appeared to have been
hit. 'There is a frustration in that,' Jenner admits. 'Which is
why, before *Don't Try This At Home*, we were getting ready
to leave. We didn't know where we were going, but it had
become fairly difficult to deal with Andy Macdonald, he'd
become convinced he was God Almighty.'

If this sounds like one-way traffic, Jenner is quick to
own up to his part in the problem: 'I know all the answers
too – so you've got *two* people who know all the fucking
answers. Catastrophic!'

Jenner and Macdonald had always enjoyed a spirited
professional relationship characterised by a free and frank
exchange of views and some swearing. 'Both of them were
a bit volatile,' Billy ventures.

Diplomat to the end, Macdonald calls Jenner 'a fair-minded
person'.

'Billy would be quite good at knowing all the answers
too,' adds Jenner. 'So there'd be three of us! Quite a lot in
one room.' Porky confirms the volatility of the situation,
one he'd experienced from close quarters: 'When he was
in a good mood, Macdonald was one of the loveliest, most
beguiling people you ever met – but "when he was in a good
mood" was the limited proviso on that. When he was in a
steaming rage, you'd be in fear of your life.'

'The problem was,' reasons Billy, 'could anyone bear a continuation of the Macdonald/Jenner ding-dongs? No amount
of money was going to get over the fact that those two had
a bit of difficulty. It was getting on everybody's nerves, particularly Pete's wife Sumi.' Regardless of personality clashes,
Jenner felt that 'Andy had got Billy as far as he could get
him. All the albums did much the same. We spent more on
Workers Playtime, it had more instrumentation but it didn't
make much difference.'

'I was ready to call it quits in order to remain friends
with Andy and Juliet,' Billy says. 'The relationship had run
its course – let's go and find pastures new.'

On 27 April 1991, Billy announced to them that he was
going to sign to Chrysalis. Understandably Andy and Juliet

weren't going to let it lie. In order to dissuade them from pursuing the matter any further, Jenner deliberately raised the stakes to an unrealistic amount of money – £1 million over four albums – this way, Go! would be forced to retire gracefully, Billy could sign to another label, and everyone would remain friends. That was the idea, at any rate.

But Andy came up with the money: £1 million over four albums and PolyGram approved. Billy and Jenner didn't know what to do: the money didn't overcome the deterioration of the relationship. 'Is it worth the aggro?' they asked themselves, as they mulled it over in a hotel room in Georgia. Crucially, Juliet had intervened.

She and Andy had been in the process of separating since January, but she'd agreed to stay on at Go! to help conclude Billy's renewal. (Jenner and Billy knew she was leaving, but no one at PolyGram did yet.) As part of the revised, £1 million deal, Juliet offered to remain at Go! and be their main point of contact, thus removing what Jenner called 'the grief factor'. After all, her role had often amounted to mediator between the two fiery fellows. This 'third way' did the trick – though it meant that Juliet now had to stay on at Go! for the duration of the album. (This was fine until June, when her and Andy's separation turned to divorce. He moved out in July, but they agreed to be 'civilised' and continue to work together.)

At any rate, as of 13 May, the impasse was solved: *Don't Try This At Home* would come out on Go! Discs. In keeping with its Big Pop theme, they would extract *three* singles from it, and make pricey promo videos for each of them – just like everybody else does.

The deal – a compromise of the what-have-we-got-to-lose? kind was signed. In the event, Billy could've got a matching offer from front-runner Chrysalis, but Billy felt they owed it to Go! Discs, and Jenner respected his wishes. 'I felt we'd fucked Andy about so many times with these wacky singles and no videos,' says Billy. 'We agreed to go straight down the middle. This was certainly the record to do it with.'

Of coming up with the large wad of money, Juliet says, 'We'd always made it very, very clear to PolyGram that Billy was the heart and soul of the company. They always understood that. To their credit, they never argued with why we placed such value in Billy, and why it was important for us to spend that amount of money. Plus, the staff that were there would've been devastated if Billy had left.'

It was like taking one more cream cake when you're full. Oh, I shouldn't. Oh, go on then, you've twisted my arm . . .

In the last week of June 1991, Billy was back on the front cover of the *NME*, headlined 'ESSEX SYMBOL' – a decision not without some debate in the *NME* office, as someone who was there will tell you (this was, after all, the time of 'Madchester' and flares, not Acton and big turn-ups). The ultimate decider in Billy going on the cover was twofold: 'Sexuality', the single, and 'Sexuality', the video.

It may have represented an ideological compromise to Billy, but the 'Sexuality' video was made without any grudges, and entirely in keeping with the matey, DIY Bragg ethic. Porky, now trading as Phill Jupitus, had been invited over to listen to some mixes of the album – not exactly textbook still to be mixing the album the week its first single is released, but it had been a prolific session. During 'Sexuality', he suggested some video ideas to Billy – basically visual gags based on the notably humorous lyrics ('I look like Robert De Niro/ I drive a Mitsubishi Zero . . . I feel a total jerk/Before your naked body of work . . . I've made passes/At women of all classes' and so on). At Billy's behest, Porky went home and drafted his ideas as a cartoon strip. The result – as relaxed and likeable a display as anyone in the promophobic Bragg camp could have hoped for – is virtually as per the Porky cartoon, gag for gag. The amateur storyboard artist and conceptualist received what he describes as 'a lot of money' for his efforts.

'Totally inspired,' says Juliet, who produced the video. 'No pressure, shitloads of ideas, and it worked.' Perhaps inappropriately, the CD and twelve-inch B-side was a 'consummate Mary song', 'Bad Penny' ('It's hard to love a girl so near yet so far out of reach . . . She steals more than she buys, you can see it in her eyes').

All in all, 'Sexuality' was the perfect pop package. It even came complete with two two de rigueur dance-style remixes – this from a man who'd been 'ne rigueur' all his life. The *NME* cover; the eyebrow-raising subject matter; the dance angle; the irresistible video – 'Sexuality' could not fail. But sales didn't match the amount of money spent: it charted at Number 27. Disappointment #1.

'He doesn't look like a pop star,' is Andy Macdonald's view. 'It put him into a difficult space.'

It did well on the radio, despite initial misgivings about the G-word ('Just because you're gay/I won't turn you away'), and, in truth, it *felt* like a bigger hit than it was. A slow week meant Billy was invited back on to *Top Of The Pops*, which all concerned thoroughly enjoyed (Cara, Wiggy, Grant), as Billy even conceded to miming: 'I've done it my way all this time, I'll do it their way.' And to think they said Kinnock sold out when he moved away from unilateralism!

The lowly chart placing for such a tailor-made Top Ten smash did not dent Billy: 'It wasn't disappointing to me. Nor was it a surprise.'

At the time, *No. 1* magazine ran a short interview with Billy headlined 'I Hate Being In The Charts!' To an extent, it was true. In the same way that he'd learnt lessons from the way absolute adherence to a single political line had crushed The Redskins, he made a mental note of the fate of The Housemartins (rent asunder by a Number One hit) and The Smiths (weakened by an endless stream of singles). 'I'd also seen pop stardom make it impossible for Weller to get on a bus from Marble Arch to Shepherd's Bush,' he says. 'And I didn't really want any of that. When fame has lifted up its skirt to me, I have made as much accommodation as I can, but I've resisted . . . whatever metaphorical phrase you want to stick in.'

On 16 September, the lavishly tooled, sixteen-track *Don't Try This At Home* was released, advertised full-page, full-colour, everywhere from the *NME* to the *New Statesman*. 'Including the HIT singles "Sexuality" and "You Woke Up My Neighbourhood",' it screamed. Except 'You Woke Up My Neighbourhood' had only reached Number 54 – despite its guest stars Michael Stipe and co-writer Peter Buck from R.E.M. – Disappointment #2 (but that's advertising). The album went Top Ten, which was a tonic in the circumstances, but only sold the usual Bragg 70,000 copies. Disappointment #3.

This was no reflection on the reviews, which were uni-
formly positive about Billy's new direction. 'Bragg has done
the inconceivable,' raved David Quantick in the *NME*.
'Shrugged off the demons of despond and made his best
album.' Mat Snow in *Q* played the football analogy: 'Surely
there can be no doubt now that Billy Bragg, love man,
football fan and worried working-class hero, will be there
or thereabouts among the honours come the end of the
season.' Michelle Kirsch, now writing in new glossy *Select*,
awarded the record five out of five boxes: 'It's been a long
time coming, but he's made that leap.' Even *Folk Roots*,
whose target audience it seemed least likely to appease,
jumped for joy, top man Ian Anderson concluding with
'Stimulating, pleasurable, thought-provoking, entertaining
and inspiring; a perfect combina- tion. Are we good enough
for it?'

There is plenty in *Don't Try This At Home* to make a song
and dance about. There is plenty in it, period – 57 minutes to
Workers Playtime's 42 and *Taxman*'s 38. But filler is nowhere
to be heard. The album's benchmark, 'Sexuality', comes half-
way through – a wise move, since it lifts the record rather
than precipitates a downward curve. Razzamatazz abounds,
on the noisy 'Accident Waiting To Happen', the pan-rattling
'You Woke Up My Neighbourhood', surrogate Smiths song
'Sexuality' and the Riff Raff-and-ready 'North Sea Bubble',
but it's not just the fast ones that are loaded up on production value: slowies like 'Cindy Of A Thousand Lives',
'Dolphins' and 'Moving The Goalposts' ooze multi-layered
atmosphere, and benefit from the attention. At times, it's
as if Billy Bragg has accidentally wandered into somebody
else's album. Even his voice is improved.

The lyrics become the listener's comfort blanket as they
travel through this new and challenging theme ride: they are
instant Bragg, if not always his most truly inspired. 'Moving
The Goalposts' is a lucky bag of various choice couplets
thrown together in the name of a cracking tune: 'I put on my
raincoat to make it rain/And sure enough the skies opened
up again . . . Heavens above/Can this sticky stuff really be
love? . . . Robin Hood and his Merry Men/Are never, never,
never coming back again' – these are nice lines but they are
not necessarily related. ('It was a really nice tune, and you

have to write *some* words to it,' Billy says. 'And they were the words. I'm really sorry. I was throwing lines at it to see what stuck. I don't often do that.')

The aforementioned 'Sexuality' and 'The Few' are solid gold Bragg lyrics – insightful, crafty and wry – and the achingly simple 'Trust' explores the dread of AIDS in a sensitive and original way, relating fear of lethal infection with the age-old fear of pregnancy ('He's already been inside me/And I know it can't be good'). Quite apart from these gems, one song on *Don't Try This At Home* ranks among the most important Billy has ever written – indeed, listening to it, with its music-box accompaniment and the eerie echo on the voice, the inkling that it is *the* most important is hard to shake off. 'Tank Park Salute' is, after fourteen years, Billy's tribute to his father: intensely personal (only the two of them will ever know what the title means), exquisitely moving ('Daddy, is it true that we all have to die?') and universal. Hearing it live can be more difficult for audiences than it is for Billy to play, but that's the power of the song.

On an album that was like a fireworks display of invention, variety and special effects, it was easy to miss 'Tank Park Salute', but more than any political statement, it rescued *Don't Try This At Home* from the abyss of sell-out. Under all the pomp, circumstance and overdub, Billy's heart was still beating.

Andy Macdonald has no qualms about the aggressive marketing behind *Don't Try This At Home*: 'We wanted to reach more people with those songs without making it an undignified exercise.'

Billy was compliant ('I'm happy to jump through hoops if it makes a difference'), and his more approachable 1991–92 hairstyle certainly seemed to signal a softer product, but, after telling *The Face* he once spent £70 on a jumper, miming on *Top Of The Pops* and playing the fool in the 'Sexuality' video, the charm offensive had made not one iota of difference to either his record sales or his public image. Billy looks back on it with no bitterness as 'a very long-range attempt to convert the ball between the posts. It went in the general direction and at the last moment, it sort of spun off into the crowd. But it looked really great. The crowd were going,

"Oh great! Braggy's going to score!" It was up in the air for a long time before it veered off.'

But, come the round-ups at the end of 1991, when the papers said Billy had 'reinvented' himself as a pop star, he was frustrated. 'I was just enjoying myself! But it had become a bit of a cul-de-sac for me. I realised I should be concentrating on connecting with my audience and not trying to draw people in.'

Macdonald is reluctant to call the whole Final Push a failure, even though, on paper, it undoubtedly had been: 'You have to look at what you're competing against. There's a certain category of artists that you don't judge by sales reached over a three-month period. It's like a big old ship sailing out there, it could keep sailing on for ever. I genuinely believe that Billy's songs will have decades and decades of relevance.'

It hadn't been a wholly happy experience. 'You Woke Up My Neighbourhood', perhaps the biggest commercial blow of the lot with its 54 placing, had been an unpopular choice with Wiggy and Showbiz ('Picking singles was not our strong point, which is why we don't do it very often'). It was actually chosen by Macdonald and Garry Blackburn of radio pluggers Anglo as a compromise because Billy wouldn't let them put 'Cindy Of A Thousand Lives' out. Why? 'Because "Cindy" represents the upper end of the album's weirdness. If that had been a huge hit, there would've been nowhere else for me to go.' Even the video for 'Neighbourhood' crackled with negativity. Porky was happy to storyboard it, but didn't want a time-consuming, hands-on directorial role at the shoot as he had with 'Sexuality', due to his new-born baby. 'It's the only time I've ever been cross with Bill,' he reveals. 'He made me do it.'

This unexpected bad blood, borne entirely of pressure and panic, meant that the two friends didn't speak much for a couple of years, but for Porky this was a welcome natural break: 'Everything in my life from 1984 to 1991 was in some way connected with Billy, the jobs I did, the gigs I did, the fun I had, it was all related to Billy.'

And then there was the tour. Boy, was there the tour.

Providing I don't become a parody or hugely successful, I think I can keep on at this level
    Billy Bragg, talking to The Face, September 1991

'It went on and on and on,' says Billy of the Don't Try This At Home tour. He means the length, but he might equally be referring to himself on stage. For this was the biggest show he'd ever taken on the road – in order to reproduce the new album live, a full band was unavoidable – and the awkward combination of one man spinning off into lengthy monologues while the rest of the cast sat on stage and twiddled their thumbs was perhaps the tour's defining image. That or the ping pong table they demanded at every venue – 'which gave us something to do other than drugs'.

It was by no means all bad. For Wiggy, so long sidelined or left in the wings with his tuner in his hand, *Don't Try This At Home* was his big moment, payback for all those years of indispensability. Promoted from Billy's Mate to musical director, he set about recruiting a full touring band, The Red Stars. Wiggy's time had come. 'I thought, This is it!' he recalls. 'Sort the band out and play guitar – instead of *carry* the guitar. I loved it.'

The Red Stars line-up was Wiggy, Cara Tivey, Rob Allum on drums and Nigel Frydman on bass. Hardly an orchestra, but, what with the attendant guitar techs and drum tech and the five-hander soundchecks, it was all a long, long way from Billy Bragg on Shepherd's Bush tube platform with the Roland Cube.

Wiggy may have been happy as a sandboy, but he was under no illusions about how Billy felt: 'He didn't really enjoy it that much.'

Pete Jenner concurs: 'It was a tough tour. Longer sound-checks, more hanging around, more people with claims on Billy's time, more agendas on the road. He was becoming more distant from the audience, there was more security around, more bubbles, less contact with the world. In the old days, it would be four people round a restaurant table, suddenly it's a palaver, it's more social.' The Red Stars' first gig was in Berlin on 1 October. Their last was in August 1992. In between, Billy's worst nightmare gradually became flesh: 'Nobody articulated this to me, nobody inferred it to me, no one gave me the slightest hint of it – but I definitely felt that towards the end of that tour I was becoming a parody of Billy Bragg. This is something I personally felt, because I was bored. It wasn't in the music, it was in the gigs – but you have to remember, I'm a live creature. If the records make sense it's because I've concentrated what I do live.

'On stage, my monologues were getting longer. I am completely capable of going off on a tangent for twenty minutes. The Red Stars used to get bored shitless with me, it was so annoying for them. It was only because they were there that I realised how much of their time in the gig was spent hanging around. I became aware that some of what I was doing on stage was to entertain myself, not to entertain the audience. I was the only one who wanted to pursue these monologues beyond a couple of funny asides. It was for my benefit.

'Not only that, I was fucking around with the lyrics. The punters were losing songs that they really loved. I was breaking their little hearts.'

Ben Thompson hit the nail on the head in his review of 1991's Hackney Empire New Year's show in the *Independent On Sunday*: 'A speech about the Europe-wide advance of racism makes some good points, but then goes on a bit. There probably aren't too many people in a Billy Bragg audience who think racism is a good thing anyway.' In the *NME*, Gina Morris went one step further: 'Racism blah blah fascism, communism blah blah ism ism ism. SHUT UP! Shut up, SHUT UP! We *know*, Billy.'

As if to accentuate the endless nature of the tour, in March 1992, they hit Germany for the second time ('I thought, This is it! We're gonna go round again! We're not going to stop!'). In May, Billy's spirits were lifted by some good old-fashioned Braggmania in Australia. Booked to play a Brisbane boxing arena, they were worried it wouldn't sell but, in the event, it was packed with punters, some of them actually screaming. The Red Stars *were* The Beatles. There were even fans hiding in the bushes back at the hotel, who were invited to an amusement arcade that had been booked all night for an after-show and a half. As Billy played air hockey with his people, life seemed sweeter. They wound up doing a total of six shows in Sydney.

Japan, USA, Canada . . . after nine years of touring, what used to be a pleasure and never a chore had turned upside down.

'It got to be a real strain,' Jenner remembers. 'He wasn't enjoying it. Apart from the odd day, it was the only time I got to thinking, Fucking hell, I've got to go out with Billy on tour. He felt the same way: here's Jenner again, what's he gonna have me doing? It became a situation where he'd dread me phoning up and I'd dread phoning him up.'

Something had to give, and it was Billy's appendix.

13. TRY THIS AT HOME

Rethink, 1992–1995

To kindness, to knowledge, we make promises only; pain we obey
Marcel Proust, *Cities Of The Plain*

'He hadn't told me he was in pain, he was just grumpy,' says Peter Jenner of Billy's escalating appendix trouble.

After nine solid years of getting on with it, of turning up and doing the gig, Billy's refusal to admit there was something wrong with him was consistent with his Catholic work ethic. It was a case of heads down, mustn't grumble, when's the soundcheck?

But his appendix had different ideas.

'If I believed in those things,' says Billy, 'I'd say it was my body telling me to have a break, do something else.'

It doesn't take a gargantuan leap of faith to believe in 'those things'. Give or take the odd barge holiday and the odd album, Billy had been touring constantly since he broke out of the London pub circuit in 1982. Many bands build up a following and a reputation through constant gigging, and a lot of albums are written on the road, but there were two important factors that made Billy's schedule more punishing: his play-anywhere, all-weather versatility, and his political convictions.

What on paper looked like a tough enough tour itinerary would, in reality, take on a life of its own: impromptu gigs, two-shows-in-a-night, shoehorning an extra date into what Jenner refers to as 'that day off after Plymouth', benefits, debates, day events, friendship meetings – all these add-ons put extra demands on Billy's time. Thanks to his pathological approachability, meet'n'greets would invariably seep into what ought to have been his quality time (especially in all those exotic new countries, where chatting to punters takes on the mantle of cultural ambassadorship). Billy often jokes that he had no life between 1982 and 1992, but there is a grain of truth in this: he'd purchased his own flat but could he really call London home? It's little wonder that his body eventually ordered him to stop working. In 'Sexuality', he sang 'I'm sure that everybody knows how much my body hates me', but he had no idea.

He was also 34. A certain age. His diplomatic immunity from the levels of self-abuse that are the rock musician's stock-in-trade afforded him an unusually hearty bill of health; however, unlike the road, Billy Bragg just couldn't go on for ever. The grumbly appendix took a while to get itself heard. Doctors assumed his stomach pains were a case of Irritable Bowel Syndrome (diet- but also stress-related, which was a clue), and prescribed him plenty of All Bran. But in August, during a break in touring, while Billy was up in Manchester working on some new tracks with Johnny Marr, the pain became more than just irritable.

He saw a homeopath and had some X-rays. He was put on a course of antibiotics and ordered to take three months' rest, the first two weeks without solids. 'He finally got a doctor's note,' says Wiggy. The rest of the tour was cancelled.

Juliet, who came to his aid while he was bed-bound, says, 'He looked bloody awful, really gaunt, with deep, dark circles underneath his eyes.'

'My piss had turned to syrup,' Billy adds.

Juliet helped Billy hump his mattress into the front room, where he set up permanent base camp. From his sick bed, he watched the entire Barcelona Olympics. Sally Gunnell, Carl Lewis, Linford Christie, first South African team for 32 years, Bosnia under their own flag . . . Billy can probably tell you who won gold, silver and bronze in the Women's Fencing.

In effect, he'd won a holiday.

This period of enforced exile happily coincided with a new dawn for Juliet, too. In May 1992, her divorce from Andy had come through, and she was in the process of untying the knot with Go! Discs. Having first decided to leave in early 1991, she'd relented and stayed on, solely to work on *Don't Try This At Home*. Then there was Madstock, the live Madness reunion, which she helped get off the drawing board, into Finsbury Park, on to Channel 4 and on to a Go! Discs contract (the group's Chas Smash aka Cathal Smyth was working for Go! in A&R, and he effectively signed himself to the label). Madness actually asked Billy to play one of August's two all-dayers after Morrissey had pulled out – his onstage dalliance with the Union Jack had not gone down too well with the indie kids, and his gold lame shirt had upset the fat skinheads. Billy was unable to step in at the last minute, on doctor's orders.

Having also helped sign Paul Weller to the label, Juliet finally left Go! Discs in September to pursue a solo career in film and video production.

After a spell of playing Florence Nightingale and wounded soldier, she and Billy began to spend more time together: although they'd known each other for nine years, they'd never been in a position where they could really talk – in fact, they realised that they'd never really been alone together in all that time. Billy was concerned that Jamie, now four years old, had grown up without his godfather really knowing him. There was catching up to do, and Billy became very attentive in that department.

Not really up to anything too strenuous, Billy discovered the perfect day out. By 1992, the crop circle phenomenon had really taken off. It was estimated that over 2,000 of these mystifying alien wheat-etchings had been discovered at that stage, and experts were still divided as to their origin (scientists claimed wind vortices, psychics looked to the significance of the ancient sites where the circles cropped up, ufologists watched the skies, hoaxers said 'It was us!' and farmers just got cross). Billy, a self-taught student of ancient history *and* a lover of the English countryside since Auntie Pat's farm, wanted to have a gander, and August's unscheduled lay-off gave him ample opportunity.

Having been up Silbury Hill near Avebury, along with many other circle-watchers, where he'd seen an amazing half dozen crop formations, Billy talked Juliet into regular drives up the M4 to seek them out. It got him out of the house, and out of town, filled his lungs with fresh air, recharged his battered batteries and gave him the chance to talk to Juliet for the first time. 'We'd always had a good rapport,' she says. 'But we started talking in a way we never really had before – about life stuff rather than work stuff.'

First, some work stuff. Summer 1992 saw Billy's final break with Go! Discs, which was an inevitability, but it still took a masterful display of wheeling and dealing to tie up. Billy says his *Don't Try This At Home* deal was 'bleeding the company dry'. Miraculously, minus recording costs, he still had the remainder of the £250,000 in a savings account ('I hate spending money'). Billy could see that the next instalment of his £1 million advance would be crippling for Go! Discs – and the threat of laying off staff was unacceptable – so he came up with a cunning plan that would see *everybody* all right, including himself. He paid *back* the rest of the first advance, and regained ownership of his back catalogue in return. Result: Go! Discs were in pocket; Billy was a free man who now owned the entire Bragg canon. In order not to put the company in a tailspin, Billy agreed not to tell anyone he'd left (he didn't plan on making an album for a while, so had no need to make any announcements).

One final, post-modern wheeze: Billy went into Go! Discs for an 'un-signing session', and asked Juliet to take a photograph of him handing over a cheque for £100,000. They'd tried, they'd done their best, it hadn't worked, Billy had been right.

Andy Macdonald, if the truth were told, was relieved. He was free of a distortedly expensive contract, and conceded that Go! Discs had taken Billy Bragg to the perimeter fence of commercial possibility. Go! had changed, the offices had changed, the staff had changed, and, most importantly, Macdonald himself had changed: his role model had apparently evolved from Stiff boss Dave Robinson (cheap, cheerful) to Island's Chris Blackwell (cool, glamorous) to Richard Branson (rich, powerful). Or that's how Billy saw it. Although Go! were in fact having a very tough year.

Back to the life stuff. Billy and Juliet's friendship blossomed, bloomed and busted out all over. Because they'd known each other for so long, the *lurve* curve was gradual and organically grown. 'When we realised we had the basis of a relationship, rather than just friendship, it was a shock to us,' says Billy. It took the pair of them a long time to admit it to themselves, a longer time to admit it to each other, and the longest time of all to admit it to the rest of the world. But neither of them had any intention of going into this with their eyes closed.

'We also thought, "Why bring this grief to Jamie if it's just a fling? Why put him through it?" '

The umming and ahing went on for a long time. Juliet in particular was concerned about what people would think – even though there had been no cross-over with her marriage, it was still a 'good story' (record company director steps out with pop star). In October, they finally felt ready to go public, and the first person they told was Andy Macdonald, for Jamie's benefit, and also to stem any salacious rumours getting back to him. 'I'm sure a lot of our friends thought, "Aaahh, how long have they been playing this?"' says Billy, 'But it was *because* Juliet was divorced and *because* I was off Go! Discs and out of my career that we found ourselves sitting around, socially, in the same space with nothing to do and no one to see. We saw each other for company.'

'It wasn't quite as sad as that,' Juliet adds.

After months of administrative foreplay, and what they both admit was a period of straightforward denial, Billy and Juliet tested out just how 'Billy and Juliet' sounded. At the back end of 1992, with Billy back on his feet but still taking it easy (Career plan? What career plan?), they came out. In other words, they went out – to the cinema, to gigs, up the football – as A Couple. They gradually let the important people know, and the fallout was minimal. Porky remembers the night Billy and Juliet ventured out to The Comedy Store in London's busy West End where he was doing a stand-up gig. He still has a photograph of them in the bar afterwards 'looking a bit guilty'. They broke the news to him, and like a good mate he acted surprised (he already knew). Unsurprisingly, Porky was delighted for the two of them – after all, what's not to be delighted about? 'Very often in life,' says Porky, 'two people are brought together to form a loving relationship when they've been in the presence of a disaster.' He pauses, and adds, 'I'm not saying Andy Macdonald *is* that disaster.'

On 5 December 1992, a gloomy announcement went out to the trade papers and the music press: due to 'the continuing recession', the workforce at Go! Discs was to be cut by 25 per cent. In shop floor terms, this meant that the staff of twenty would be streamlined to fifteen, the first time in the company's nine-year history that they looked to be slipping down the table. Rumours abounded that PolyGram were moving in to take over, denied by Andy Macdonald as 'idle industry gossip'.

The early 1990s were pretty lean for Britain, with the economy experiencing a cyclical bust after the 1980s boom. We were, as Billy had sung, living in a 'North Sea Bubble', 'trying to spend our way out of trouble'. Job losses characterised the early Major Years, unemployment crept back up towards three million and Britain's recession turned into the longest since the war. So Go! weren't the only company in town forced to tighten their belts, but the entertainment industry traditionally thrives even in times of depression (look at music hall during the war), so it's always a bad sign when record companies lay off staff.

The Conservatives had managed to defy the opinion polls and hobble back into office at the general election on 9 April – their ticket amounted to little more than a pledge not to raise income tax (this was, without doubt, a time of patting your wallet).

Although the Tories' majority had shrivelled from 102 in 1987 to just 21 in 1992, it still spelt five more years of trouble, and Billy admits that the election result 'knocked the stuffing' out of him. Even America seemed to be softening, politically, with the election of their first Democrat president for twelve years – on saxophone, Mr Bill Clinton. But still Britain clung to Tory self-service and what had become the status quo.

In October, Billy had turned out for the miners once again, as 150,000 demonstrated outside Parliament against pit closures (John Peel and Joe Strummer were also there, and the new indie elite – by and large, worryingly apolitical – at least threw up support from Carter The Unstoppable Sex Machine and The Wonder Stuff). Billy spoke out: 'The anger aroused by the government's attempts to destroy the mining community shows the willingness of ordinary people from all walks of life to recognise injustice and take a stand against it remains undimmed.' You've got to take your rays of hope wherever you can get them. The Hackney Empire got its annual dose of Bragg at New Year.

It was a chance for him to reunite with the unemployed Red Stars and 'give them a bit of Christmas money, having pulled the rug out from under them'. In Caroline Sullivan's review in the *Guardian* she noted, rather cruelly, that his 'annual Empire residency is the perfect place to divest yourself of any lingering Christmas cheer. There can't be many less festive sights than that of Bill, miners' collection bucket in hand, orating about the events of April 9.'

But even the Queen was miserable in 1992, the year she called her *'annus horribilis'*. Sarajevo ablaze, Michael Heseltine closing down mines, floods in Pakistan, hole in the ozone layer, civil war in Somalia, General Motors and Ford announcing their first losses in over 80 years, and Canary Wharf, tallest building in Europe and symbol of Mrs Thatcher's Docklands, standing nearly bankrupt and half-empty.

As 1992 faded away, Billy bid goodbye to what had been *his 'annus appendicitis'*. In January 1993, although five years away from becoming a Labour anthem, D:Ream released 'Things Can Only Get Better'.

In April, as if to prove the song right, Juliet got pregnant. They'd timed it impeccably. No tour on the horizon; no duff album to make in order to fulfil some binding contract; a father who'd previously spent so little time at home it was a big commitment to buy a pot plant, suddenly sitting around with days, weeks, even months on his hands. This truly was turning into a unique chapter in Billy's life – all the platitudes that usually come with birth but tied in with the sort of solid-bond relationship that neither he nor Juliet had expected or had been actively looking for. And no gig in Bochum.

Juliet made a deal with Billy: she'd do the hard part if he agreed to do three things in return during the next nine months:

1. Learn to drive
2. Learn to type
3. Learn to cook

Although the third 'might as well have been tightrope walking' as far as Billy was concerned, he agreed. At 35, after ten years on the road, it was high time he joined the motoring classes (whether it was Katy, Tiny, Brenda, his mum or Juliet, he'd been reliant on women with cars all his life). Subjecting the good people of West London to the hazard that is a great big BMW (Juliet's) with L-plates, Billy put the hours in, and duly passed his test in Isleworth on 6 September at 8.45 a.m. His driving examiner had passed pop rapper Betty Boo a week earlier. Confident that Billy's steely determination would see him through, Juliet had already had a cake made with a confectionery effigy of Billy on top beside an old jalopy and a baby's cot, with nappies everywhere. The L-plates were on the cot.

Juliet bought him a word processor, and Billy was soon Grade A at the two-fingers-quite-fast technique, essential now that he was being asked to do so much writing for publications like *New Routes*, the *New Statesman* and *New Socialist*.

Cooking was less successful. Following the scriptures of Delia religiously, Billy mastered the quiche. Sadly, it would take him all day to make, while Juliet could rustle something Mediterranean up in minutes. A registered meat-and-two-veg man, Billy was never going to be able to do Sunday lunch unless he started on Thursday night. Still, two out of three ain't bad. 'I didn't want to feel I was just sitting around waiting for Jack to be born,' Billy claims, 'I was *doing* stuff.'

Radio 4 invited him to make three programmes about anything he wanted: he did one on the history of Barking, one on the mystic power of Avebury and one on the cultural role of the British Museum, further exploring his potential fallback trade, broadcasting, and exploiting his keen interest in history. Juliet summarises: 'He wallowed in being an anorak.'

He appeared on *Newsnight*. He presented an edition of BBC's *One Foot In The Past* on the Cerne Abbas Giant:

a giant chalk figure carved into a Dorset hillside with a prominent erection (it was while on location for this film that Billy became intoxicated with the area, and it eventually led him and Juliet to buying a bungalow called Sea Change, on the coast). There was also Billy's first ever commissioned soundtrack work, for a TV film *Safe* by Antonia Bird (who went on to direct *Priest* and *Face*), and the odd gig.

The inaugural Phoenix Festival, held on an airstrip at Long Marston near Stratford-upon-Avon, saw the last ever performance by the Red Stars, in a tent sponsored by Durex. By now, Juliet was visibly with child, which raised a smile. 'Don't bring Juliet out,' joked Billy. 'We'll lose the sponsorship!'

In December, the specialist indie radio station XFM enjoyed a limited, one-week trial in London (it would take them another three years finally to land a licence), and Billy hosted his own show for four nights. It would have been five, but the last was on Christmas Eve, and the baby's due date was 25 December.

Billy and Juliet had a quiet Christmas Day at her house, waiting for the three wise men to turn up. Jamie was staying with his dad just in case they had to dash off to Queen Charlotte's Hospital in the middle of the night. It was the first TV showing of the film *Ghost*, and Juliet was determined to see it to the end before the baby came. They ate Christmas dinner in stages, so as not to waste any, but the day passed without antenatal incident.

Juliet's waters finally broke early on Boxing Day morning. Billy was concerned, because one of his mum's other grandchildren was born on 26 December, and if *his* was, it would leave her in an eternal quandary over whose house to go to on their birthdays. He didn't trouble Juliet with this niggle at the time.

Jack, as he would be christened, was eventually born 33 minutes after midnight on 27 December. Phew. (Incidentally, he was christened at home by CND boss Monsignor Bruce Kent, as Jamie had been.) Billy was present at the birth. 'I would recommend it to anyone,' he says, defining the father's job as chiefly one of communication. 'It's about listening to what the midwife is saying and what the mother is saying and translating. I likened my role in the previous nine months to Juliet swimming the Channel with me in the rowing boat saying, "Go on, girl!" Men are used to being the one who gets in there and sorts a problem out, but you can't do anything in those nine months except make cups of tea.

'At the birth, you finally get to take part!'

Billy was a dad. And in a very real sense Jack woke up his neighbourhood.

Billy and Juliet had been up all night, moving the goal posts. From this day forward, everything changes.

Family becomes Billy, and not just the writer of love songs, but the political animal too. The ideologies he holds dear can all be boiled down to compassion, and what better manifestation of community than the family? As Billy states, 'Family is a microcosm of the community, the community is a microcosm of the state.' The Conservative government spoke of family values and back to basics, while the effects of their policies undermined communities from one end of the country to another: unemployment, benefit cuts, poll tax, pit closures, union bashing, the North–South divide and shop-a-sneak benefit fraud phonelines. 'Family' need not mean stifling Victorian values or sexual inequality, it can be a simple support system extended out of the house and into the street. That's where Billy's compassionate, humanist politics come alive: looking after your own *without* ignoring everyone else. Socialism begins at home.

Billy's own memories of childhood are precious to him – all the more so for his father's presence – and having Jack around has made life priceless since 1993. After a lifetime of relations with girls from many nations, Billy had come home – to Jack, Juliet and Jamie.

That other important J, namely Peter Jenner, was happy for Billy, but nonetheless feeling a little insecure about his role in the new set-up. 'I think Billy toyed with firing me,' he says, at the time busy managing Robyn Hitchcock and Gallon Drunk. 'I was quite expecting to be fired, and quite happy about the notion of it. It was perfectly natural. I'd done my bit. I couldn't do any more. Billy felt that I didn't respect his judgement and that I was always bullying him, and never listened to what he had to say. I said when he started – Give me five years. And it wasn't until we got to nine years that he screamed, "Halt!"'

Jenner assumed that Billy would want Juliet to manage him, Ozzy and Sharon Osbourne style, but, according to Billy, 'that was never on the cards. Pete's too plugged into my life as a friend.

I obviously didn't make it clear to him that the last thing Juliet and I wanted to do was work together.'

In fact, Billy and Jenner's professional relationship would be strengthened by the enforced break: Billy reclaimed his life; Jenner realised that it was time to ease off the work rate.

'Something had to change,' reasons Tiny. 'It was important that Billy became a bit more of his own man, and did things the way he wanted to, with less Pete influence on it. His appendix gave him room to change the rules.'

In fact, the appendix break and the pregnant pause gave everyone around Billy occasion to reflect.

'I'm more open now,' Jenner says. 'I'm easier about Billy saying no. Over the last couple of years we've built our relationship up. I give him more space. I always used to assume that I could get him to do anything. Now I don't assume. Once he *says* he'll do it, he'll always do it. But equally, if he says he won't do it, it's really hard to get him to change his mind. The art is to try and prevent him saying no! We won't ask him until the right moment.

'He was *too* easy to manage for a long time: he would do anything. The only big crisis we'd had in our relationship was this feeling that I would send him anywhere. He didn't know how to shut me up and tell me no – because I'm a lot older, because he relates to me as his dad. I've been doing everything for ever and I've got a loud mouth and I can talk for an hour and a half about anything. It got too much.'

'My entire life did a loop-the-loop in that period,' says Billy, 'I'm surprised so many people still talk to me.'

Wiggy and Billy temporarily drifted apart after the demise of the Red Stars, the sudden evolution of two good friends into A Couple, and the birth of Jack. The tour had put undue strain on Billy and Wiggy's friendship – after years of playing employee-employer (in both directions), the Red Stars finally put them on a more even keel, and then, without warning, it was all over.

'Wiggy felt that the Red Stars was *his* band,' says Billy. 'And it was to an extent. But he was outside the focus of it

TRY THIS AT HOME

all. He was just enjoying himself. He put up with the stupid hours and the stupid places we went to, but the bottom line was he just wanted to play, and he lived for that, he didn't care where it was, he just loved it.'

Fun, fun, fun, till Braggy took his tour pass away.

'It wasn't the first time that Wiggy had been in this situation,' says Billy in his own defence. 'I'd done the same thing to him when I skipped off to France and when I joined the Army. But it is unfortunate that we fell out over it.'

Wiggy examined his lifelong friendship with Billy and realised that they were not actually as close as they seemed, and the financial returns didn't make up for all the years: 'It's a strange relationship. He's always been there, we know each other inside out, but he's much more like family than a mate you go round the pub with. When we've got something to do, and we've got a mission, we do it really well. We're both professional about it, we get on with it, without whinging. On the road, we didn't tend to be in each other's pockets. I don't think I've ever been in a pub with him and had a pint.'

In the fallout period of 1994 and 1995, when Billy rebuilt his life, Wiggy claims they 'got as far apart as we ever have been. It was a bit annoying really. There was a lot of water under the bridge, none of which we ever sat down and dealt with.'

Wiggy eventually wrote Billy what he classes a 'horrible letter'. Billy wrote back, saying why he thought Wiggy was wrong to feel the way he did. It helped clear the air. Billy said to himself, 'I can't keep doing what I do for the sake of Pete Jenner or Wiggy. I have to ask myself, What's happening in *my* life?'

It wasn't a very jolly episode but ultimately it brought Billy and Wiggy closer together and forced them to address the prickly issue of money between pals. It taught Wiggy that his lifelong friend was 'good at speaking his mind about issues, but not about how he feels. As far as I'm concerned he's very bad at that. He's not very forthcoming on that front – he channels it into his writing. 'Billy's an entertainer. He's quite often the centre of attention. Put him in a room and he'll do the gig. But he's very difficult to get close to deep down.'

At the end of 1993, Billy's quietest year, Jenner struck a licensing deal with Cooking Vinyl, a small but respected folk-tinged indie label who'd released Michelle Shocked's records in the UK and boasted such Bragg favourites as June Tabor and the Oyster Band. Ownership of copyright still rested with Billy, but it meant that his back catalogue could be repackaged and remarketed (re-packaged in the sense of a Cooking Vinyl logo where the Go! Discs logo used to be).

It was a smart deal for Billy, in that his records were in what he and Jenner knew to be sympathetic hands, and it was rewarding for Cooking Vinyl as they gained a prestige artist. 'It helped put Cooking Vinyl on the map,' says Jenner. 'And Billy likes that folky tradition they're involved in. There aren't very many good indies left. He would've felt uneasy being on a relentlessly trendy label. He's not relentlessly trendy, he never has been.'

In December, to mint the new relationship, the whole Bragg catalogue (except *The Internationale*) was reissued on CD, and sent out to the press for review. Or, more to the point, revaluation.

While at one end of the critical spectrum, *Mojo*, the newly launched beard-stroking music monthly, gave Billy's ten-year career a reasoned hearing (a sympathetic Richard Lowe concluded, 'He's part of the furniture, an occasional table in the back parlour that comes in ever so handy every now and then'), over at the inkies, it seemed as if his time was up.

In *Melody Maker*, a self-styled new-breed upstart Taylor Parkes tore into not just the records, but the man: 'The clutter of the unspectacular rings these records like an electric fence, nothing passing in either direction, a tiny, sealed cell full of weak tea and jumpers, a lone voice drifting out like a factory hooter.' The *NME*'s Paul Moody called Billy 'a relic of somehow less exciting times. A pre-boom post-style magazine era when a singer with a horrible woolly shirt and a crap haircut was practically revolutionary . . . Undecided to the end, these albums serve as further proof that we'll only really love Billy Bragg once he stops wringing his hands and lets us know what he *really wants*.'

Although fleetingly hurtful to Billy – this was a life's work, after all – these reviews did not keep him awake at nights

(Jack was doing that), they merely signalled the end of another relationship. In his ten years of playing, the staff at the music weeklies had changed thrice over. The angry early-80s punk writers had been replaced by optimistic late-80s acid house writers and again by early-90s cynics. Somewhere along the line, Billy Bragg had become a symbol of the Old Days, someone your big brother used to like (the one who now gets *Q* and *Mojo* or doesn't buy a music magazine at all).

It was clear to him that his constituency had moved on, and so must he. There's nothing more embarrassing than your dad on the dancefloor at a wedding.

All remained quiet in 1994. Billy refers to it as his 'wilderness period', but in fact he never stopped gathering words and ideas. This was a key stretch for him as a songwriter, just like starting over. 'What do songs written by Billy Bragg, someone's dad, sound like?' he asked himself. 'I don't know, I haven't written any.'

It took a while to formulate entire songs. The first one he completed that would make it on to his next album was 'King James Version', with the telling first line, 'He was trapped in a haircut he no longer believed in', and the mini-manifesto, 'Compassion has to be the greatest family value'. It was an admirable start. 'Rather than not writing, I just wasn't *finishing* songs,' Billy explains. 'I was making a lot of notes. But I was wallowing in parenthood, and not being afraid of it taking up all my free time. Little by little, you get it back, and you're so happy to get it back, you utilise it better. That's the effect it had on me.'

In June, Billy enjoyed a completely unexpected comeback, as, it seems, did politics in pop. The Anti-Nazi League had returned, and this time they were *really* pissed off. The Anti-Nazi League Carnival, backed as before by the SWP, was a show of unity against a new tide of fascism in Britain (in the Isle of Dogs, Derek Beackon of the British National Party had become the country's first fascist councillor in November 1992, leading to a resurgence of interest in the ANL). On the day, 130,000 turned out for a gig at Brockwell Park in Brixton – site of many a musical protest in the 70s and 80s – fiercely supported by the *NME*, who seemed to have found their political feet after five years of dancing or gazing at them. For the over-30s, it was just like the old days, for the *NME*'s younger readers, it must have seemed like a revolution.

The *NME* organised a float to make the journey from Kennington to Brixton, and invited Billy to play on it. He was flattered, and leapt at the chance. ANL? SWP? *NME*? It was like coming home. He was joined on the truck by S*M*A*S*H, a young punk group of questionable ability but inarguable appeal from Welwyn Garden City. If this was Old meeting New, then Old certainly had all the songs and the stagecraft, even if New had all the front covers: either way, it was a shot in the arm for Billy (both the politicised zeal of the new kids on the block, and the renewed relevance of his own position).

The *NME*'s on-the-spot reporter for the day was Stuart Bailie, a man old enough to have a bit of perspective: 'You suddenly realise that in your mind, you always had Billy down as a kid – the upstart who pulled brazen strokes through the 80s, who made folk music and protest funny and accessible. Now you watch him and you notice that his hair has turned fag-ash grey, that he's a doting father, and that he's viewed as a senior figure in today's celebrations.'

The Manic Street Preachers and the Levellers also turned out for the ANL, and the sun reflected off a thousand bright yellow placards and stickers proclaiming 'Shut down the BNP' and 'Stop racist attacks'. Billy injected some humour into what might, in more naive hands, have been a rather po-faced day, singing 'Just because you're gay, Mr Policeman, I won't turn you away' at the edgy constabulary, and announcing, 'I've always wanted to be the carnival queen'. The *NME* coverage majored on S*M*A*S*H, awestruck political toddlers to a man, but it would, wouldn't it? Billy wasn't complaining. He'd done his bit, just when he was thinking his bit was no longer wanted on pop's voyage.

Come Glastonbury, June 1995, Billy was ready to take on the world, with almost a new album's worth of songs, and a son old enough to take to his first rock festival. It was a modest, mid-afternoon slot in the acoustic tent, but he was still nervous. He'd planned to give the Glasto crowd a gentle set on his 335 semi-acoustic, including a rewrite of Woody Guthrie's 'This Land Is Your Land' with British place names, tailored to fit the growing road protest movement. Much to Billy's surprise, prior to going on stage, the crowd were chanting 'Bill-ee! Bill-ee!' In the pre-gig confusion, his guitar fell forward off its stand and the neck snapped off. He would have to use the more conventional Burns electric. Tiny handed him a cup of festival tea that she'd accidentally put salt in, and a mixture of discomfort and despair took hold of Billy as he walked through the curtain to the baying audience: 'I was wound up. The audience were wound up. They went spare, and so I hit the ground running and did a full-on Bragg punk set. It went down a storm.'

The tent was so packed, Juliet and Jack couldn't get in to see Daddy play. A reassuring return.

In July, he chanced a short US flit, but not headlining. He and Cara Tivey opened for Canada's Barenaked Ladies, a quirky bunch of busker types who'd played at Billy's last Hackney Empire. He tried out the new songs on the Americans and they went down well. In November, he was back in the States, 'playing places where I've always been traditionally strong', in other words the big college towns. While he was out there, he recorded some new instrumentals for a forthcoming independent film, *Walking And Talking*, a romantic comedy starring Anne Heche (five old Bragg songs would also appear on the soundtrack).

Back in London, and it was into Cathouse Studio in South London with Grant Showbiz to start work on the *really* difficult seventh album, *William Bloke*. Looking back on it, Billy concludes that '1995 was the first year of me trying to build it back up in a way that was more conducive to my new lifestyle.'

To preview a line from that album's opening track, 'From Red To Blue': *We must all bend a little if we are not to break.*

14. NEW BILLY

Back in office, 1996–1997

To see a World in a Grain of Sand
And a Heaven in a Wild Flower
Hold Infinity in the palm of your hand
And Eternity in an hour

William Blake, *Auguries Of Innocence, c. 1803*

The only thing they hate more than each other is the Tories
Proposed Labour Party poster featuring
Oasis and Blur, 1996

If Billy's life took a new course in 1994, so did that of Britain's Shadow Secretary of State for Home Affairs Tony Blair, but not as the result of a birth.

On 13 May 1994, of all papers, the *Sun* wrote, 'Britain's next Prime Minister died yesterday.' The obituary was for Labour leader John Smith, who'd had a sudden heart attack at his flat in the Barbican. While a tragedy that blurred party-political divides across Britain, the death of Smith paved the way for Tony Blair to lead the Labour Party to a landslide victory in May 1997.

It is a truth universally acknowledged that without Blair at the helm, the rebranded New Labour would never have got in. This, however, is to undermine John Smith's steady hand. A natural successor to Kinnock, and no less a believer in the modernisation of the party, Smith is described by Andy McSmith in *Faces Of Labour* as 'not only a decent man but a potential Prime Minister'. It is fanciful to speculate whether or not Smith could have translated decency into electability; certainly Blair's conspicuously youthful dynamism was a big factor in Labour's turnaround in the public's confidence.

By 1996, Blair had overseen the removal of Clause IV from Labour's constitution (a thorn in the reformer's side, it basically pledged to nationalise everything), which was symbolic of his eagerness to please, and alienated many an Old Labourite. Arthur Scargill quit the Party and set up his own, The Socialist Labour Party, which stood 63 candidates in the 1997 election – none of whom got in – a story repeated in 2001, when Scargill failed to oust Peter Mandelson in Hartlepool). Still critical of Labour, he's something of a recluse in his early eighties, but his party stood as recently as the 2009 European Parliament election.

In return for a few Old Labour defections, the party doubled its membership between 1994 and 1996 to 400,000. On stage at the Brit Awards in January 1996, Noel Gallagher proclaimed, 'There's only seven people doing anything for young people in this country: the five members of Oasis, Alan McGee and Tony Blair.' Any more solid-gold support like that, and Labour's spin doctors would be out of business.

Billy let his Labour Party membership lapse a lot earlier than Scargill did. In 1991, at the time of the Gulf War, he became disillusioned with Kinnock's refusal to oppose military action, and that was that. ('I was so disappointed that Labour weren't able to come up with a different analysis of the Gulf that condemned the war but supported our troops. They were so scared to say anything other than the government line – which was the American line.') He didn't stop voting Labour, although tactical voting would subsequently alter the course of his electoral thinking, as we shall see. He has little time for breakaway parties, but it's interesting to see how far apart the man and the party had drifted by the time of their rise to credibility.

I asked Neil Kinnock in 1997 if he was disappointed by Billy's lapsed membership, and he was very clear: 'I've spent most of my life recruiting people to the Labour Party, so, unless people have broken the rules of the party, I always regret any departures. No matter what the political circumstances, I've always believed that ideals must be organised if they are to have any real effect in a democracy, and I hope Billy will reflect further on that since I know that he understands it.'

In the autumn of 1996, the Labour Party magazine *New Labour New Britain* emblazoned the face of Noel Gallagher across its cover, officially fanfaring Blair's courtship with Britpop. It would all end in tears, but for the time being, in the run-up to the 1997 election, rock musicians were back on Labour's top table. Billy Bragg was not among them – a New Deal that suited both parties.

Kinnock had disappeared to Brussels, but Billy had been much more visible in 1996. By circumstance rather than design, he was New Billy. Whichever clause it was in the Bragg constitution that said he must play 'the day off after Plymouth' had been scrapped. This was a leaner, fitter, more focused troubadour, free of some of the outdated baggage that characterised Old Billy (an anachronistic beast more suited to the struggle of the 1980s). New Billy had a new family and new responsibilities, and was led by realism not ideology. The change had done him untold good.

'I think I would've had to have that time off anyway, with or without Juliet and Jack,' Billy concludes. 'It was coming. People have that in their careers – they work ten years and run out of steam, or run out of ideas, or get bored or get stale or take drugs or fall off a motorbike. Everybody does it, it's just whether you can use it in a positive way.'

After intensive recording from February through April, Billy played a clutch of gigs intended to test the water of his old electorate. On May Day, he ventured out to Clapham Common to play at a festival organised by the unions. 'This was a London audience, not a Glastonbury audience,' he says, and the difference is not hard to surmise (London: hardened, seen-it-all-before; Glastonbury: whacked out of their gourds on scrumpy and blowbacks). There were a number of tents set up, and a smorgasbord of entertainment laid on, so Billy was understandably nervous once again. Before his slot, the tent was practically empty (every performer's cold-sweat nightmare). Then, out of nowhere, thousands poured in through the flaps. They were soon spilling out on to the common, just like Glastonbury.

Billy had been away, but the fans were still here. He played key new songs like 'Upfield' and 'From Red To Blue' with conviction, defining his new outlook on the world ('Upfield' contains the soundbite 'socialism of the heart', and 'Red To Blue' looks at the changing political landscape and bravely asks, 'Should I vote red for my class or green for our children?'). 'There was an electric atmosphere right to the back,' says Juliet. 'No one was talking, which is always a good sign. And they must've shouted out for "The Saturday Boy" fifty times.'

Next, although less revealing in exit-poll terms, Billy agreed to 'fill' for half an hour at the Roskilde festival. But this was no ordinary half an hour. At midnight, after a set by Björk, the organisers had a necessary, scene-changing interval before that summer's number one draw, a re-formed Sex Pistols. 'I got the call,' says Billy, who found the chance to support the Pistols irresistible, regardless of any ideological controversy surrounding their money-motivated reunion. A teacher from Jamie's primary school asked Billy if he'd get her the Pistols' autographs, so, armed with a T-shirt, he sought them out backstage and paid his respects ('It had to be done'). Predictably, they drew ladies' breasts and a rudimentary penis on the T-shirt. Once a bunch of foul-mouthed yobs, always a bunch of foul-mouthed yobs (if the money's right).

Mindful of his own extended absence from the crazy world of pop, Billy went for the traditional single-and-video gambit as a taster for the forthcoming album. 'Upfield', a suitably upbeat, brassy hello, was unleashed in August, Billy's first new release for Cooking Vinyl. The video was summery and relaxed, and the fanfare provided by old pal Dave Woodhead on trumpet and Terry Edwards on sax seemed a fitting wake-up call. 'Upfield' got to Number 46.

After Glastonbury and Clapham Common came the crucial third stage in Billy's confidence-building live experiment: the Reading Festival, a former piss-bottle rock weekender transformed into a cosy (and lucrative) indie T-shirt parade by London–Irish promoter Vince Power. 'Not a Billy Bragg festival,' notes Billy. 'And not a Billy Bragg audience.

I thought, "This'll be a test. It's not easy, let's do it and see if we can get a reaction."'

It was raining, and the crowds disappeared to the safety of the other tents for ethnic food while Billy was setting up, leaving a result wide open. 'There was just a knot of people at the front of the stage. I walked out there, and I knew I had a job on my hands: does anybody give a shit about Billy Bragg any more? I was gonna find out.'

Sure enough, after three or four songs, the crowd had filled out again, right back to the mixing desk (a crucial plimsoll line), and Billy was treated as a minor homecoming hero, even by this conspicuously young mob. After four years away, the enthusiastic response at Reading allayed Billy's worst fears for good.

'Those three gigs gave me a lot of confidence,' he says, all too aware that a warm hand on his entrance was no foregone conclusion. 'I'd become unfashionable. Politics wasn't even fashionable. Weller had started to recant. Nobody really wanted to know. And also a generation had turned.'

But they hadn't turned away. On 9 September, *William Bloke* was released – for no more than £9.99. As Billy sees it, the album said, 'I'm still here. I hope you're still interested in what I'm doing.' He played a gig on the eve of release at London's most famous train shed The Roundhouse. He was still nervous, and remembers going for a solitary post-soundcheck walk along the canal up to Primrose Hill where he got his head together. The gig went well, the punters comprised a heartwarmingly wide age range (defusing fears that Billy might not connect with a new generation) and the *William Bloke* songs sounded tip-top.

After the stylistic cul-de-sac that was *Don't Try This At Home*, Billy surrendered himself to whatever came naturally on *William Bloke*, which is why Jack and Juliet are all over it, and why the music really had gone back to basics.

It had been a very gradual, unforced process. He'd put down the very first, tentative demos back in November with Grant Showbiz, and remembers sitting up late the night before he first went into the studio, with snatches of lyrics spread out on the coffee table and the makings of five tunes in his head. 'King James Version', the difficult first song, came out of that apparent chaos, as did 'Brickbat' – his first song to Juliet, whose lyric contains rare Bragg usage of the phrase

'I love you'. (Billy has constantly shied away from the three little words, always preferring three little euphemisms. This way, he's managed to keep 'I love you' sacred. Saving it for a sunny day, in effect.)

He didn't play 'Brickbat' to its intended that night, he simply went in and recorded it the next day: 'When it came back out of the speakers it really moved me. I realised I *can* write songs about this situation I find myself in, I *can* write songs that are just as powerful as ones I've written about other stages in my life. There was a sense of relief and wonder.

'Me and Juliet have made something really great in our relationship out of something really ordinary: two people being together. It's really hard to say that in a song.'

'The Fourteenth Of February', another no-holds-barred 'Juliet' composition, came about as a tune while Billy was playing his guitar for Jack at bathtime, something he did often (Jack liked the hand movements). A brand new song-writing system had emerged.

William Bloke's politics were trickier to assimilate. Billy's head was in an indistinct place at that time, still dedicated to the notion of international socialism but slightly deflated on the home front ('If we can't beat 'em without Thatcher what can we do?'). Not only that, his pet subjects of old were literally disappearing around him: no Berlin Wall, no Cold War, no Thatcher, no Apartheid, no Soviet Union, no Reagan, even Nicaragua had calmed down since the elections. The direct result of all this was the central thrust of 'Upfield' – positive, determined, direct:

> The angels asked me how I felt about all I'd seen and
>   heard
> That they spoke to me, a pagan, gave me cause to
>   doubt their word
> But they laughed and said,
> 'It doesn't matter if you'll help us in our art
> You've got a socialism of the heart'

He'd written 'Upfield' in September while driving himself down the M4 to a miners' benefit in Rhondda. He had to park at a service station to write the lyrics down, and later sang it all the way home again.

The lyrics throughout *William Bloke* betray a new spirituality in Billy. Mention of angels, souls and the symbolic horizon of a new morning are straight out of William Blake, the eighteenth-century English poet and engraver who lent the album its title and so much more. *William Bloke* – arguably Billy himself – is 'the archetypal Londoner. A spiritual person who goes to football. Someone who can appreciate the beauty of the sunset, or stand on the brow of a hill and be moved by the shadows of the clouds as they roll across the countryside.'

The 'tree full of angels' in 'Upfield' is an image taken from a story about Blake's childhood: as a boy, he claimed he'd had this angelic vision, but when he told his parents they smacked him for telling lies.

Parenthood had definitely unlocked a new emotion in Billy – as an artist he was stimulated by the unconditional, irrepressible feelings he had for Jack. The album begins with 'From Red To Blue' in order to make an opening statement about Billy's political state of mind before the show goes on: 'There's your politics, that's where I'm at. I'm older now. I accept things have changed. I accept that we all make compromises and get on with our lives, if you don't bend you're going to break, all those things. I'll still carry on. The world's changed, but the struggle continues.'

One line, from 'Brickbat', came to sum up New Billy, especially with critics looking for a handle: 'I used to want to plant bombs at the Last Night of the Proms/But now you'll find me with the baby, in the bathroom.' Billy is keen to point out that this line does not connote surrender, merely rearmament at a different armoury.

Musically, *William Bloke* is a continuation of *Workers Playtime*, not *Don't Try This At Home* (which is now viewed by Billy as an anomaly, if a rigorous, thoroughly realised one). It is sparing, considered, and in the case of 'From Red To Blue', 'A Pict Song' and 'Northern Industrial Town', positively nostalgic.

Of all the old running mates involved in the recording – Grant Showbiz, Cara Tivey, Dave Woodhead, Nigel Frydman, even Fionn O'Lochlainn – one is conspicuous by his absence: Wiggy. He wasn't asked.

Wiggy was obviously hurt to be excluded, but, having made it up with Billy since, he is stoic about it today: 'It was probably good for him to do something without me around in any shape or form. It was a bit confusing for me. Pissed off is not the right phrase, but I definitely felt left out. It didn't help our relationship at the time.'

Billy invited Wiggy to be in the 'Upfield' video, but it felt to him a bit like crumbs off the tea-table. Porky, who had become much closer to Wiggy during Billy's fatherly exile, thought it a curious gesture so deliberately to shut him out of the party until most of the balloons had burst, but Billy explains that it was a clear signal to Wiggy that there was no full-time job for him at Camp Bragg any more (no more Red Stars, no more huge tours, slower pace of work). Wiggy had to break out on his own, and, by the time of the 'Upfield' video, he had (he'd set up his own studio and his own band, Click). It was not an easy break for either of them, but there was kindness in the apparent cruelty.

As a record, Pete Jenner believed that *William Bloke* was 'short of a toe-tapper', possibly the song Billy had been working on with Johnny Marr, 'The Boy Done Good' – but Billy was adamant he wasn't going to put this on (at any rate, Marr was too busy making the second album with his side-group Electronic to finish the track in time). Jenner didn't push the matter, which was good for both of them, and indicative of their new, improved, *laissez faire* relationship. 'These are the songs this record's about,' Billy said to him. 'This is the record I want out, end of discussion.'

'It's your record,' said Jenner.

William Bloke charted at sixteen with a respectable 10,000 copies sold in its first week. It went on to sell what was now the statutory 60,000 in the UK and roughly the same again abroad. The way the Billy Bragg business works, he can happily make his money back at this level of sale.

'He makes good money,' says Jenner. 'He does very well on gigs. He doesn't spend much on making his records. We more or less made the money back on *William Bloke* on UK sales alone. Every record sold is money in his pocket. We own everything. Cooking Vinyl make a reasonable amount of money, we pay all the costs and pay them a percentage.'

The *William Bloke* tour was not as other Bragg tours. 'More gaps', is his succinct summary. It was paced so that he didn't have to be away from home for weeks at a time. The tour ended in Ilford.

Back at Billy's *alma mater*, Go! Discs, all was not well. On August, Andy Macdonald announced to the press that he was leaving. The company had finally been bought out by PolyGram after eighteen months of wrangling. Macdonald characterised the acquisition as 'oppressive'. Of the label's future, PolyGram's UK chairman and former rock lawyer John Kennedy admitted, 'It is unrealistic to think everything will be the same without Andy.'

Go! Discs was Gone! Discs.

Billy and Jenner resisted saying 'I told you so.' Macdonald walked away a rich but unhappy man from the label he'd built up from nothing and promptly launched a new one, Independiente, taking some of the Go! staff with him, but none of the bands, who were divvied up among the PolyGram labels (even the Beautiful South – the only act with a 'key man' clause that entitled them to walk away from Go! Discs if Macdonald did – opted to stay).

The trust fund Billy had set up with what used to be his five per cent share was now worth around a cool million pounds. When PolyGram bought out Go! Discs, around 30 employees – some of whom had left, such as Porky and Tiny – received a handsome windfall on top of their severance pay calculated on a sliding scale according to the number of years' service. This came as a shock to many of them, who either had no knowledge of Billy's deal or had simply forgotten about it (some of them had never even *met* Billy). Porky, who received £18,000, went public about the trust fund in *Men's Health* magazine in December 1997, when various notables were asked to nominate their hero. 'I've never heard of anything like that happening before,' he wrote of the payout.

A musician *giving* thousands of pounds to the employees of his record company? Nothing like that *has* happened before.

After today, the Tories must not only rediscover the secret of what it takes to form a government; they must urgently find what it takes to survive as a functioning and truly national party at all.
Peter Kellner, *London Evening Standard*, 2 May 1997

Election Year: the very words filled Labour supporters with icy dread – or at least, they had done for eighteen years. But there was something in the air in 1997 – something in the Blair.

It was a very different election from the last one for Billy, when his old tea-drinking partner Kinnock was still at the rudder. In 1992, he'd turned out to play for Clare Short in her Birmingham Ladywood constituency, and for Bruce Kent, who was standing in Oxford. 'At least in 1992 I had my contacts within the party,' Billy says. 'Now they had a completely new leadership.'

He would have to play this one from the outside if he was going to play it at all. And even though the opinion polls showed a Labour lead, Billy took Blair's own advice and remained cautious.

He feared that potential Labour voters might be antipathetic to Blair's agenda ('a progressive agenda, but not a socialist one') or stay at home because they saw a Labour victory as a foregone conclusion – 'and somehow the Tories would sneak in again, which would destroy the party. So I went out and played around some of the marginal Labour towns in April, some of them safe seats, some not, and basically wound people up. I wanted to steady the Bragg vote – those cynics who say, I really love your music, Bill, but I'm not voting for those bastards again.'

In the approach to 1 May, aside from simply geeing people up to use their vote, Billy was also, in his own words, 'banging away about compassion. I asked myself, What did I believe in before I believed in ideology in the early 80s? What was it that got me to the position where I could define myself as a socialist? It was my fundamental humanitarian ideals. And what are they based on? Compassion. If we have compassion, perhaps that's the place to build the new left ideal, whatever that's going to be.

'I think socialism is an idea that's in a state of flux, if not drained of all meaning. It's a world-changing idea that's been crushed mercilessly between capitalism and Stalinism, one side saying it's *this*, the other side saying it's *that*. It needs to be rebranded!'

The irony of using one of Blair's dreaded buzzwords is not lost on Billy. But you can't be too careful – the smart

BBC2 satire show *Friday Night Armistice* asked Billy to appear on their alternative election night special, singing a pro-Tory song. It was a reasonable gag, but he declined, and the *Armistice* lot became quite shirty with him. 'That sort of thing comes back to haunt you,' he says in his own defence.

Tiny Fennimore – who was now Billy's PA, full time, working from home after the birth of her son, Sam – took a lot of calls, pre-election, from broadsheets like *The Times* and the *Telegraph* angling for a Bragg soundbite and expecting him to rubbish the Labour Party. 'They were very keen for him to be in Arthur Scargill's party,' she says, only too happy to disappoint the Tory press. 'We often declined to comment – after all, we wanted Labour to win!'

On the day, this was not to be a problem. On 1 May, Billy did an election night gig at the Mean Fiddler, Red Wedge heartland and site for so many supporters of that crushing defeat in 87. This one couldn't have been more different. As Billy says, 'It has already gone down in the annals as one of the all-time great Billy Bragg gigs.'

Wiggy was there, as were Jenner, Juliet, Tiny and Norma Waterson – in Billy's eyes 'possibly Britain's finest female folk singer' – on whose miniature television they watched the election in the dressing room. Before Billy went on, he remembers Juliet, Jenner and Norma in a huddle round the TV, posing the hypothetical: what would be the ultimate result on this night? They all agreed it would be Michael Portillo being ousted in Enfield – except Jenner, who plumped for Home Secretary Michael Howard. All fun and games at that stage, of course.

Billy played the first of two sets till midnight, with Jenner relaying information from the wings as he picked it up from his radio – just trickles at this stage, but nonetheless one or two encouraging fourteen per cent swings in Labour's favour. For the second set, the Fiddler patched live TV pictures through to a huge screen at the back of the stage. No sound, just images. The audience cheered every time a result went up in Labour's favour which was often – and Billy would be forced to turn around and have a look. It might not have made for the smoothest of performances, but the backdrop was unbeatable.

A cheer went up when Enoch Powell's old seat in Wolverhampton fell to Labour's Jenny Jones. Another went up when the Basildon result came in, poetically enough, during 'Waiting For The Great Leap Forwards'. 'This is a great moment for Essex!' Billy declared, and he and Wiggy raced through 'A13 Trunk Road To The Sea'.

Billy made a speech when the first Labour victory for 23 years became incontestable, to the effect of 'It's over'. The sense of relief was even greater than the sense of elation. As a final gesture, he sang 'Jerusalem' a cappella, with the whole audience on backing vocals. As divine Blakean intervention would have it, behind Billy as he sang, the count from Sedgefield came in, and there was the new Prime Minister, his head as big as the bloke on stage. He was grinning the grin.

The Bragg entourage and punters alike stayed at the Mean Fiddler almost all night, crying tears of joy into their beer this time as the Tory walls came tumbling down: Ilford, Redbridge, Hornchurch, Romford – even the much-maligned Essex Man had seen sense. 'It was then that it started to dawn on me that we weren't just going to win,' Billy recalls. 'We were gonna blow them out of the fucking water!'

Billy and Juliet made their way home at 5 a.m. Too wired to go to bed, they went out and bought every single newspaper, and watched breakfast news. In this, they were not alone.

At a safe distance from the euphoria, Billy concludes of that glorious night: 'It brought a certain amount of closure.'

As Andy McSmith notes in *Faces Of Labour*, 'Just when the British Labour Party had become really good at being in opposition, it was swept into office.' Not one of the Labour cabinet had been in office before, and many of them had been at primary school when Labour were last in power.

No government could ever match the euphoria of 1 May, and New Labour's first year was fraught with disappointment and controversy as they attempted to do an impossible job with what little the Tories had left in the kitty, and with a promise hanging round their neck not to raise income tax. During the recording of his next album in Dublin in January 1998, Billy reflected on the new government's progress: 'I'm not sure what I think. I feel positive about the fact that a new government will break the log-jam over Northern Ireland.

Gerry Adams has been to Downing Street. They are trying.' (And succeeding, it later turned out.)

On a 'pros' list, Billy includes devolution for Scotland and Wales (referendums for both happened within Labour's first nine months, as pledged) and Britain's improved relationship with Europe (never the Conservatives' strong suit). On the 'cons' list, he cites the cutting of disability and lone parent benefit, trade unions not getting their rights back, and the emblematic Millennium Dome ('a sore on all our backs'). Perhaps more surprisingly, Billy is critical of Labour's new intake of young MPs: 'I don't ask for a revolution from them, just the ability to support Labour when they can and criticise them when they have to, that's all I ask.'

Blair's love affair with Britpop had soured by 1998, the young electorate disenchanted with Labour's policies on student grants, drugs and benefit. The *NME* went political for one week only in March and a motley collection of musicians rose as one in their condemnation of the Blair government. A disarmingly erudite editorial notwithstanding, the thrust of the paper's pull-out anti-Blair supplement seemed to be that rock bands *need* to sit around on the dole smoking legalised cannabis in order to find their genius.

Perhaps they do, but it was difficult not to think back just ten years: to the energetic, multi-coloured, broad-issue activism of Red Wedge, the benign willingness of Neil Kinnock, the cardcarrying conviction of the *NME* and the community spirit whipped up by Billy Bragg.

It was a pity they lost in 1987. If Kinnock had got in, he says that Billy Bragg would have been among the first invited to any post-Election bash at 10, Downing Street – 'Especially if he'd brought his guitar. I must say that I like the idea of a Bragg recital in the drawing room . . . dream on.'

15. LIFE BEGINS AT WOODY

Another bit of history, 1998

Baby don't you marry no farming man,
He'll put a rake and shovel right in your hand
Oh, don't you marry a railroad man,
When you want him, he won't be on hand
Don't you marry no singer man,
He's the brokest fella in the band

Woody Guthrie, 'Don't You Marry'

For Billy Bragg, his eighth album began on 12 July 1992 in New York's Central Park, although he didn't know it at the time. He was asked to play at legendary Oklahoma protest singer Woody Guthrie's posthumous eightieth birthday. Also appearing were Pete Seeger, Jesse Jackson, the Disposable Heroes Of Hiphoprisy and Woody's son Arlo Guthrie.

At that stage Billy was so unfamiliar with Woody's work that between the soundcheck and the gig he nipped into Tower Records on 72nd Street and Broadway to buy a compilation cassette with which to check the words. (He'd first flirted with Woody at Barking Record Library after reading about him in Anthony Scaduto's Dylan biography, but the scratchy recordings didn't do much for him, which proves you should never trust first impressions.)

At the gig, Billy met Woody's then-43-year-old daughter Nora, curator of her father's archive, who was taken with the fact that Billy's song 'You Woke Up My Neighbourhood' had been named after a Woody drawing he'd seen at Washington's Smithsonian Institute in 1990. She subsequently sent Billy a Xerox of that very picture in a frame and broached the subject of a unique project she was hatching.

Woody Guthrie is said to have written a thousand songs in his lifetime – cut short in 1954 when he was hospitalised with Huntington's chorea, an incurable wasting disease. After years of articulating the struggle of working people through his songs (the most famous of which was 'This Land Is Your Land', adopted as America's unofficial second National Anthem), Woody Guthrie was soon unable to hold a guitar and, later, even a pen. He eventually died in 1967, ironically, just as a folk revival had launched Bob Dylan to superstardom (without Woody, there may never have been a Dylan, a debt he has never been shy about).

Before it became impossible for him – around 1957 – Woody continued to write, sometimes dictating to his devoted wife Marjorie. Nora had unearthed whole piles of these lyrics – in their own way little pieces of history – and her dream was to have them brought alive by setting them to music. Having decided that the usual suspects (Dylan, Bruce Springsteen, Neil Young, Arlo himself) were too close to give the words an original interpretation, she asked Billy to take the job. 'Honoured' doesn't do justice to the way he felt.

It wasn't until 1996, when *William Bloke* was in the can, that Billy finally got the project off the ground. He met Nora again in Cleveland on 29 September at the Rock And Roll Hall Of Fame during a week-long celebration marking the opening of the archive, where Woody's songs were played by Springsteen, Seeger, Arlo and Ani DiFranco. The proposed album, later christened *Mermaid Avenue* after Woody's address in Coney Island, was a done deal. Billy had even found his band.

That summer, he saw Chicago country-rockers Wilco play in London. He'd been a huge fan of their second album, the magnificent *Being There*, and, in a bid to sidestep the mire of recruiting a 'supergroup', he asked Wilco if they were interested in collaborating on the Woody songs (he'd been impressed with the group's songwriter Jeff Tweedy since his days in cult twangsters Uncle Tupelo, and wanted someone 'who was going to take it and run with it'). It was all a matter of schedules.

Wilco met Nora at the New York Fleadh concert in the summer of 97, and they all shook hands on it.

Woody Guthrie – in Billy's eyes 'the *first* singer-songwriter' – would soon be alive and well.

If *William Bloke* had been precisely where Billy Bragg was *at* in 1996, how would an album of ancient Woody Guthrie songs fit in to the story? Well, never mind the honour of being asked to carry the torch, *Mermaid Avenue* would arguably be Billy's most important record since *Life's A Riot*.

First of all, it tested his collaborative mettle. The Wilco boys – songwriter Tweedy, guitar-pianist Jay Bennett, bassist John Stirratt and drummer Ken Coomer – were easygoing enough to work with, but the experience during sessions in Chicago and recording in Dublin gave Billy a new perspective on the craft he knew so well. He also picked up some slide guitar tips. In the end, he and Tweedy split the songwriting duties 50-50, and the agreement was, they'd mix their own tracks. Grant Showbiz oversaw the project, and acted as Billy's confidant.

'Making records is usually a very solitary experience for me,' Billy explained at Dublin's Windmill Lane studios during the mix. 'I'm usually leading from the front, and also pushing from the back. This record has been more fun: watching Jeff work, seeing where he's going, then it's my turn, I've got the Wilco guys and I can bring them *my* way.'

The creative buzz over the road at Totally Wired studios, where the new tracks were recorded, was sometimes overwhelming (Billy spoke of 'the ease with which we've been able to do it, the power of the music, it's very, very generous'). The process was epitomised one night when Nora flew in with some new lyrics: at 3 a.m. during some guitar overdubs, a couple of little chords came to Billy; he 'fucked around for half an hour' and formed a tune. Having played it to Nora, Jay Bennett found the chord between E minor and A seventh on the piano, at which point Tweedy woke up from behind a curtain, and sang the words to 'Another Man's Done Gone' into the piano mic. They recorded five versions in fifteen minutes, and it was done.

To add to the cocktail, a Chicago blues prodigy called Corey Harris, aged 28, joined them for a couple of numbers, and, at a later date in America, Natalie Merchant added her voice. The result would be a rich gumbo indeed (they ended up recording *two* albums' worth of Woody songs, although just the one was pencilled in for a summer 1998 release on Elektra, to whom Billy was still signed in the States).

'He needed to come up with something a bit special for this next album,' said Pete Jenner on the eve of release, and with one eye on the marketplace. 'Hopefully it will put him into the mainstream of America. He's seen as being very English and very political over there. This ought to make us part of American culture.'

Woody Guthrie occupies a near-mythical status in American culture (indeed, some assume he never really existed). Because he left scant recorded material behind him, and most of that was primitively captured in the 1940s, his legacy is romantic rather than institutionalised. In folk circles, his name is revered and his songs are widely sung, and, through modern missionaries like Dylan and Springsteen, his work had attained a certain currency – but *Mermaid Avenue* provided a significant stepping stone between forelock-tugging respect and toe-tapping enjoyment.

As such, it was far more than just Billy Bragg's next album. For him, it was a personal connection with a great tradition. In researching Woody Guthrie (and he took care not to read Joe Klein's definitive biography until he'd written the songs), Billy entered a new sphere of Anglo-American understanding. In the same way that he'll always have a job as a local tour guide in Barking, Billy could now make a living on the lecture circuit speaking on The Importance Of Woody Guthrie In Twentieth-Century Culture.

'He's a very underestimated figure in twentieth-century American literature,' Billy raves. (Woody's semi-autobiographical novel *Bound For Glory*, manuscript handwritten *à la* James Joyce, is much-overlooked, best known for the slightly ropey 1977 movie adaptation.) 'He's a very powerful, evocative writer. As a songwriter, he's more of a lyrical poet, he's not got a great ear for a tune. He's quite capable of writing twenty verses, because he came from the ballad tradition that goes back to Elizabethan England.

'If you want to find an American lyrical poet as powerful as Woody Guthrie, someone to compare him to, you've got to start looking at Walt Whitman. Allen Ginsberg doesn't come near it. Bob Dylan? Forget it, he didn't write *Bound For Glory*. He just made some great records. If you're looking for someone who can evoke a certain kind of American childhood, you've got to go back to Mark Twain. You can't compare him to Hemingway, goofing off in Spain with his rolled-up money. He's not Scott Fitzgerald, he's nothing like that. Woody Guthrie is a literary giant, as far as I'm concerned.

'He lit the imagination of that whole generation of postwar Americans who finally had the ability to buy a cheap car and drive across America. Woody Guthrie wrote the manual for that. He didn't go out to find America, he *was* America.'

Billy's evangelistic zeal for the subject is infectious, the album itself likewise. The Tweedy songs may be instantly recognisable to Wilco fans, Billy's less so, even to long-term aficionados. He occasionally sings in an American accent for a start, out of respect for the source material, and the effect is oddly moving. While there are pointers to Braggiosity, the experience of making *Mermaid Avenue* clearly restrung his bow.

There are more parallels than you might imagine between these two men separated by 50 years, one generation and an ocean. Both are singer-songwriters (and politically motivated ones at that), both sing of love, sex and the struggle in equal measures but are stereotyped by the latter, both have had their prose and opinions published by newspapers, both attempt to convey the dignity of labour in songs you can whistle, and both travelled West – Woody from the Texas dustbowls to the promised land of California, Billy from the Essex wetlands to leafy Chiswick and then the south coast. You might say that Billy was born to do this.

On the political side, Woody Guthrie's songs are incredibly powerful, underpinned by I-was-there authenticity. There's no misreading 'All You Fascists Bound To Lose', or the shaken fist of 'I'm Out To Get' ('I'm out to get your greenback dollar/You kept me down on my knees too long'). The titles alone of his Dustbowl Songs speak for themselves: 'Dust Pneumonia Blues', 'Black Wind Blowing', 'Dust Can't Kill Me'. And, in 'Union Prayer', written in 1949, Woody seems to be challenging God on the working man's behalf:

> *Will prayer change shacks to decent homes?*
> *Will prayer change sickness into health?*
> *Will prayer change hate to words of love?*
> *Will prayer give me my right to vote?*

Like Billy's, his love songs are poetic and unpretentious: 'Ten hundred books could I write you about her now,' he says of his wife Marjorie in one of the new lyrics of 'She Came Along To Me'. Sex frequently rears its ugly head, much to Billy's delight ('I didn't want to make a PC album'), personified by what he calls Woody's 'trouser snake songs', like the merrily metaphorical 'Tea Bag Blues', or the unabashed infidelity episode 'Walt Whitman's Niece' ('And as she read, I lay my head – and I can't tell which head/Down in her lap – and I can mention which lap').

Although a worldlier figure than his hillbilly image suggests (Los Angeles, Coney Island, Queens, Greenwich Village), Woody's rural roots never stopped informing his songwriterly vision. Five years before he was born, Oklahoma wasn't even a state, it was still Indian territory, that's how far away he was from the action. 'Oklahoma's not in the South, it's not in the West, it's not even in the Mid-West,' says Billy, 'it's the equivalent of Lincolnshire or Northamptonshire.'

It is perhaps no surprise that there are no statues of this notorious Commie in his strait-laced, redneck hometown of Okemah, where negative feeling still lingers. Some years ago, a sign was erected by a local shopkeeper that read 'OKEMAH: HOME OF WOODY GUTHRIE'. It was illiterately vandalised with the addendum 'COMMIST [*sic*] DRAFT DODGER AND RED', so they took it down again. Things are turning round gradually, with an official Woody Guthrie Day in the town, designated for 14 July, and a late entry into the Oklahoma Music Hall Of Fame ('Some of it was obligatory and not quite heartfelt,' Nora accepted. 'But it still represented a big change of heart').

With *Mermaid Avenue*, Billy intended to spread the news. All those fascists were bound to lose.

As the first edition of this book went to press, the album was ready for release and a Bragg/Wilco tour was planned for the summer (doomed, as we shall see in Chapter 16). It was, whatever the press releases said, ostensibly a Billy Bragg project, but one that had been immeasurably illuminated by Wilco. The idea of Woody Guthrie walking the earth in Billy's green airtex shirt and fag-ash grey neo-flat-top was certainly an alluring one. *Mermaid Avenue* provided a neat link between the Okie whose guitar bore the legend 'THIS MACHINE KILLS FASCISTS' in the 1940s, and the Essex boy who, in tribute, wrote 'THIS GUITAR SAYS SORRY' on his in the 1970s.

'We've had similar influences,' said Billy of the musical ley line that joins the two singer-songwriters. 'But the political angle really binds me to Woody. I'm writing songs about unions too, and there's not many of us about.

'I feel it's Woody's time right now. People are looking for something real and solid that hasn't been done to death in the media. So much of the culture we're part of doesn't go back any further than Elvis.'

As for the novelty angle, Billy never saw *Mermaid Avenue* as that much of a departure for him: 'It's not like I'm doing a Frank Sinatra album. And it's not exactly *Celine Dion Sings Woody Guthrie*. On paper, those people who put me in a ghetto, will find it easy to continue to do so.'

In January 1998, an article about Labour and the arts in the *Sunday Times* glibly referred to Billy as 'the 1980s protest singer'. The Woody Guthrie project would finally earn him the epithet '1990s protest singer'.

Just in time.

16. THE BARD OF BURTON BRADSTOCK

On the map, 1998–2002

Q: How can you tell when a hard Leftie has sold out?
A: They name a road after him.

Sun, 26 August 1999

Let other vo'k meake money vaster
In the air o' dark-room'd towns

William Barnes, 'My Orch'd In Linden Lea'

Just as film historians may divide Steven Spielberg's career into two distinct acts – pre-*Schindler's List* and post-*Schindler's List* – Billy's now hits a similar pivot at *Mermaid Avenue*, June 1998. The fifteen career years up to that precise point can be classed as pre-Woody, and the years since as post-Woody. It's that much of a watershed.

With the finished product such a richly inventive three-way collaboration and so warmly received, it's a shame that it was tainted by a touch of bad blood between Billy and Wilco.

Relations had been fine in Dublin; it was when they returned to their respective cities of London and Chicago that, as Billy puts it, 'communication broke down completely'. Wilco got home and decided they wanted to remix Billy's songs as well as theirs. 'That was when it started to get a bit "oh dear". I lost my rag with them a bit, they lost their rag with me a bit, and a few rattles were thrown out of prams.'

A compromise was reached: Wilco *could* remix Billy's tracks, but, if he didn't like them, they wouldn't go on the album. He didn't like them. They didn't go on the album.

Anyway, despite this slight crimp in relations, the final cut of *Mermaid Avenue* hangs together well. It had been a new experience for both parties, and it allowed them to bask together in the light of some amazing reviews.

Billy had amassed good notices in America before, but not like these. *Rolling Stone* awarded *Mermaid Avenue* four stars, and übercritic Greil Marcus wrote enthusiastically of its unique, co-operative spirit: 'The record is a thing in itself, standing outside the stories told by the careers of its principals, as if already looking back on all their failures, saying this time you got it right.' In the *Village Voice*, Robert Christgau wrote that in 'projecting the present back on the past in an attempt to make the past signify as future', Billy and Wilco 'create an old-time rock and roll that never could have existed'.

Writing in the *New York Times*, Christgau (again) described the project as 'the best of two worlds'. In *Playboy*, Dave Marsh said, 'Billy Bragg and Wilco make the best music of their careers.' Back home, even Steven Wells professed to like it (seven out of ten) in the *NME*: 'Lovely,' he cooed.

Billy now had no say in the matter: such fulsome praise effectively married him to Woody Guthrie. This would be more than a side project or a dalliance. He was even invited to write a foreword for the new print of Joe Klein's definitive book *Woody Guthrie: A Life*.

The hoped-for live shows, however, didn't happen. Billy and Wilco guested with each other on a few *Mermaid Avenue* numbers at various Fleadhs across the US – and they appeared on *Letterman* and *Conan O'Brien* together – but that was it. 'I was at a completely different point in my career to them,' explains Billy. 'They were just about to make the difficult third album, *Summerteeth*, and they really needed to be Wilco – not Wilco and Billy Bragg.'

Residual umbrage over the mixes? Possibly. But Wilco would be keen enough to record and mix some more tracks for what became *Mermaid Avenue Vol II* in 2000. 'They were still committed to the project. They could've said, "Bill, we've had enough of all this bullshit – you've got plenty of tracks, just make it a Billy Bragg record and give us the session money." I'd have said, "Fine," and accepted that as an honourable way to say enough is enough. But they didn't. They wanted to make the second album as good as the first.'

But it was Vol I that shifted units in the US. 'Last time I looked,' says Billy, '*Mermaid Avenue* had sold more than all the other Billy Bragg records put together in America. Whereas, in this country, it sold the same as the average Billy Bragg record.'

Don't you just hate it when our colonial cousins prove they have better taste than us? It's like *Seinfeld* – 30 million watched the final series in the US; 300,000 watched it here. We should hang our heads in shame.

The Australians got it. *Mermaid Avenue* earned Billy his first-ever gold disc there, with sales of over 50,000. In fact, if you put the two volumes of *Mermaid Avenue* together, as you should, they've now racked up almost a million copies worldwide, with about half of those sold in America. Not bad for a '1940s protest singer'.

In the event, Wilco's reluctance to do a piggyback tour had its own positive spin. The London Fleadh, 6 June 1998, was to have been the first official *Mermaid Avenue* gig. Everyone hoped Wilco would come over, but no. So Billy set about looking for a band.

The search, restricted to 'people in the Sincere Management orbit', threw up poly-instrumentalists Ben Mandelson and Lu Edmonds, who came into the frame via Billy's then-road manager Jim Chapman. (They had been, among others, in the 3 Mustaphas 3, a not entirely serious, pseudonymous world music troupe, shrouded in self-generated mystery, but cult favourites.) They were augmented by Martyn Barker (ex-drummer in Shriekback) and bassist Simon Edwards (a long CV, which includes Fairground Attraction).

An ad hoc bunch, they managed to get a decent *Mermaid Avenue* set together for the Fleadh. The Blokes were born. Sadly, there was no time to sort out work permits for the US, where Billy was booked to play the Fleadh tour.

When he'd been in Austin, Texas, that March, for South By Southwest, the alternative music convention, he'd got a call out of the blue from Ian 'Mac' McLagan, keyboard wizard and founder member of the Small Faces and the Faces, now in his early 50s and living in Austin. They'd actually been introduced by Sid Griffin about ten years previously at McLagan's then-local the John Bull pub in Pasadena (an expat hangout, surprisingly) – 'Billy had to be carried out over Sid's shoulder,' Mac recalls of the piss-up. Also, by chance, Billy used to bump into Mac's son Lee in Sainsbury's, Chiswick, so there was a connection.

Mac wanted to know if Billy would sing on a solo track he'd just written, 'Best Of British', as 'a kind of duet'. He and his wife Kim had seen Billy on US TV one night and it made him think of England and Lee. The song, which Mac says he wrote 'in about ten minutes', duly contains an oblique reference to Billy: 'I saw him on the box last night, tellin' it true.' Mac dropped a demo tape off at Billy's hotel but unfortunately wall-to-wall Woody promo meant that Billy couldn't hook up.

Mac subsequently came to London, so they found a window and went and recorded Billy's vocal at Wiggy's basement studio (Mac even brought Lee along). Beneath the veneer of professionalism, Billy and Wiggy felt like kids again in Mac's presence – how vividly they remembered playing along to *A Nod Is As Good As A Wink* and *Ooh La La* back in Barking in the early 70s. Life gets circular.

'It was bloody magic!' says Mac of the session.

Anyway, as a convivial result, Mac offered Billy the rhythm section of his own Texas-based Bump Band (Don Harvey, Sarah Brown) if he should ever need rockin' personnel when on American soil . . .

So they hooked up for the US Fleadhs (along with 'Mississippi' Bob Egan on slide guitar); a firm friendship was forged with Mac. Due to American interest in *Mermaid Avenue*, Billy spent all of June, July and August toing and froing across the Atlantic – while touring the album, he went to America and back a head-spinning twenty times in eighteen months.

Asked if Billy has ever behaved like a fan, Mac says, 'Only once. When we were rehearsing in New York he took some snaps of my red brogues from underneath the Hammond. I thought it was a little odd.'

On 30 June, the day England got knocked out of the World Cup by Argentina, they were playing the Trocadero in Philadelphia. Having watched the team lose, Billy remembers wandering over the road to the Pink Pastry Shop (he's been back since, to verify that he hadn't dreamt it) where they served tea, and rhubarb crumble and custard. 'It fortified me. I thought to myself, there's more to being English than winning penalty shoot-outs.'

England FC may have been a lost cause, but there were always others to support. Back home, Billy donated a track to Creation Records' *Rock The Dock* album, released to raise money for the Liverpool dockers, specifically for retraining. Their dispute had started in September 1995, when 400 were sacked by the Mersey Docks and Harbour Company after a strike over conditions and casual labour. It ended, on paper, in January 1998, but many were still out of work without redundancy pay and, in any case, their struggle had become a powerful symbol – industrial action had not 'gone away' in the 80s. Billy said it 'warmed his heart' to sit alongside younger bands like Oasis, Primal Scream and Dodgy. All hope was apparently not lost, even if music had become woefully apolitical since Britpop.

In October, Billy was back together with the Blokes: 'four guys I'd not worked with before, committed music-makers, not just session players, who all knew each other and were all coming out of left-field musically'. So he re-cruited Mac McLagan, not just because of his Hammond mastery ('contemporary Hammond players have two settings: Booker T and Ian McLagan'), but also as a kind of medium. This completed the 'dream team'. As if perhaps to stamp their authority on given material, they took some of the *Mermaid Avenue* songs apart and put them back together again – a successful jamming exercise which meant that surprises were in store for UK audiences who already knew some of the set from the album. 'Way Over Yonder In The Minor Key', a delicate thing on record, be-came a hoedown; 'Hoodoo Voodoo' went ska, and Wilco's slow-country 'California Stars' came out as a honky-tonk drinking song.

It was, for Billy, a rebirth. Even an old standard like 'A New England' now sounded as if Eddie Cochran had written it. Collaborating with Wilco had opened his mind, and now the Blokes made that spirit concrete. They toured through November up to Christmas, sponsored by the GMB union, there to raise awareness for ROAR (Rage Over Age Rates). Their beef was that the introduction of a national minimum wage – one of the few tangible Good Things achieved under Tony Blair – had an insidious caveat: for 18–21 year olds, it was £3 an hour (compared to £3.60 for 22 and over). Labour governments – you can't take your eye off them for a minute.

As for Mac, as Billy puts it, 'If he was some old-timer who we had there in an ornamental sense it would be really sad. The fact is, he's not only playing at the top of his game, he's really up for it, he loves gigging, he loves playing with us, and he's making a serious contribution in writing terms.

'The joy on the faces of my punters when they see him!' These were some of the best gigs even old-time Bragg fans had witnessed. And union collection buckets were filled.

The year was rounded off nicely with *Mermaid Avenue* on many a best-of list. It was named as one of the 'albums that mattered in 1998' in *Rolling Stone* (between Lauryn Hill and R.E.M.), and was similarly honoured by *Q*, *Uncut*, *Spin* and amazon.com, among others. The *Sunday Times* Culture supplement included it in 'Albums for Christmas'.

The *Mermaid Avenue* juggernaut thundered on into 1999. It was nominated for a Grammy award ('the American music industry Oscars' – as they must be described by law). The ceremony was on 24 February, but Billy opted not to go (he'd been through US Immigration enough times since June). So, fittingly, Nora Guthrie attended, with her kids (who got to meet 'N Sync) and Wilco. Billy believes that *Mermaid Avenue* is her album anyway and should have 'Nora Guthrie Presents' in the title.

A great night was had by all, even though Lucinda Williams' *Car Wheel On A Gravel Road* beat them to the little golden gramophone in the Best Contemporary Folk Album category. You still get a certificate and a losers' medal (Billy awarded his to Juliet, 'because she deserved it' – not least for all the hours she put into co-producing the fine accompanying feature-length documentary, *Man In The Sand*).

A year later, poetically, Woody Guthrie finally got his post-humous Lifetime Achievement Grammy. 'I'm very proud,' says Billy of all this industry recognition, 'but I can't stress enough how much it's down to Woody not yours truly.'

Such characteristic humility is one thing, but one after-noon, while touring Australia with the Blokes, Billy became all too aware of his own celebrity. First, a Melbourne record shop wouldn't let him pay for his records when he got to the till, then a bookshop wouldn't let him pay for a book, and when he went into a chemist to buy some Strepsils, they wouldn't let him pay for *those* either. 'It made me so self-conscious I wouldn't go out of the hotel! I was Madonna for 24 hours.' (Madonna *never* pays for cough sweets.)

When he got back to the UK, with no new album in the pipeline apart from the second *Mermaid Avenue* in May (which was already in the can), Billy decided to spread his media wings a bit. He 'depped' for veteran Radio 2 DJ Johnnie Walker (who'd been suspended following drug allegations in a tabloid newspaper). He narrated BBC1's new-recruits docusoap *Soldiers To Be* (quite a change from John Nettles and Zoë Wanamaker). He wrote opinion pieces for the broadsheets and appeared on *Question Time* and *Newsnight* with alarming regularity. He also contributed to *The Ingerland Factor*, edited by Mark Perryman – a com-pendium of essays on following England FC. And in July, Barking's own Renaissance Man was all over the papers because of a *photograph* he'd taken.

The saga of the 'Battle of Portaloo' began when Billy spied the following hand-written notice on some toilets at Glastonbury: 'THESE FACILITIES ARE RESERVED EXCLUSIVELY FOR THE MANIC STREET PREACHERS – PLEASE RESPECT THAT. THANK YOU'.

This from a left-leaning, working-class band who'd always ruffled rock establishment feathers and were proud of their 'man of the people' credentials. Billy took a snap of the notice ('as a bit of mischief') and smuggled it to *Select*, who were producing an on-site daily news sheet in their wellies.

People around the Glastonbury site sniggered. Word got out. And then it spiralled out of control. The *NME* picked up on the story, followed by the *Guardian* and other nationals.

The Manic Street Preachers hit back at these aspersions of rock-star grandiosity in the only language bassist Nicky Wire understands. When they played T In The Park, before the song 'Tsunami', Wire said, 'This is for Billy Bragg. I wouldn't let his dick piss in my toilet for all the money in the fucking world. Get back in the army, you fucking dickhead, and stop stealing Woody Guthrie's songs, you big-nosed twat.'

'I underestimated how seriously they take themselves,' says Billy. He called for a serious debate via the *NME* but the Manics weren't playing. Please respect that, thank you.

In *The Times*, Caitlin Moran's piece on the matter was accompanied by Billy's photo of the offending notice, with the headline, 'This is their truth. Pathetic, isn't it?'

Another marker flag was planted in Billy's life in August 1999, the same month the B-sides-and-bonuses compilation *Reaching To The Converted* was released to quiet fanfare and only intermittent dancing in the streets.

But Billy had his own street now: Bragg Close.

Boleyn and Forest Housing Association had built some new houses in Barking, behind the very pub, the Roundhouse, where Billy and Wiggy saw their first gig, Alvin Lee, circa 1974. It's now a carpet warehouse. The association rather cunningly decided to name one of the streets after Barking's most famous musical son. Billy was suitably flattered, and, on 24 August, agreed to cut the ribbon. While preparing his speech, he checked out who else they'd ever named streets after in the area and found, in a cluster inspired by the Labour Movement: Bevan Avenue (after Aneurin, father of the NHS); Lansbury Avenue (after George, radical Labour MP who supported women's suffrage); and Ben Tillet Close (more obscure, the leader of the dockworkers' union during the 1899 strike, which sowed the seeds of the Labour Party). Now, Billy's great granddad was a docker, and Tillet had been *his* union leader, 'so I was able to make a connection between Ben Tillet and me'. At the civic ceremony, he claimed

Bragg Close for his family, many of whom were present: his mum, his nephews and Jack.

The *Sun* had a pop, of course. But Billy's just waiting for the day he can say to some rock luminary, 'You might be in the rock'n'roll hall of fame, mate, but I'm in the *A to Z*!'

Now that Billy was finally on the map in Barking, the Bragg wagon train was about to roll once again. While he'd been in the States over the summer of 99, Juliet and Jack had lived almost permanently at Sea Change in Dorset, now more than just their second home. When Billy returned in September, Juliet informed him that Barton Olivers – a picturesque guesthouse further along the coast near the village of Burton Bradstock – was up for sale. They viewed it and fell in love with the place. The fact that it 'needed a lot of work' was music to the ears of the interior decorator within Juliet. October was spent buying and selling. By December they'd done it: relocated, emigrated, escaped, decamped. 'Mum was a bit put out,' he admits.

So the Braggs saw in the new millennium on the Dorset coast (they used Sea Change as a halfway house while the new place underwent major surgery). 'People ask me, "What did you do for the Millennium?" I moved out of London.'

One regret: Billy was now no longer eligible to vote for Ken Livingstone in the forthcoming London Mayoral elections. Ken did all right without him.

In between all the geography, there was still room for a further bit of politics in 1999. It all started when, on *Newsnight*, historian Amanda Foreman said that all of our traditions are under threat if you take the House of Lords away. 'That's such bullshit,' says Billy. 'There are so many different traditions in this country, not just one.' He filmed a 'reply' for *Newsnight* and this was seen by Pam Giddy, Director of Charter 88, a group dedicated to wide-ranging democratic reform (of which Billy was a signatory).

She invited him along to a public consultation held by Lord Wakeham's Royal Commission for the House of Lords on 12 May. It was at this point that the issue of Lords reform captured Billy's imagination: get the composition of the Upper House right and 'everything flows from that'. His notion – apparently radical – was to take the result of the general election and use all votes cast to proportionally decide who sits in the House. Encouraged by Giddy – and, after a chance meeting on the tube with his Chiswick neighbour, the political commentator Anthony Holden – Billy put his idea down on a sheet of A4 paper and submitted it to the Commission. (Holden wrote in the *Express*, 'I am convinced Bragg's solution is as near as we're likely to get to a truly representative Upper House.')

He then 'gave evidence' (as it's grandly called) at the next public meeting on 27 July. Douglas Hurd, who sat on the Commission, approached him before the hearing: 'Mr Bragg,' he said, 'I'm going to be cross-examining you. I don't want you to take anything I say personally, because our job is to scrutinise your idea.' Taken aback, Billy replied, 'It's not a problem. I've been interviewed by the *New Musical Express*, I'm sure I can deal with you.'

'The Bragg Method' was thus scrutinised by Hurd, Bill Morris, Gerald Kaufman, the Bishop of Oxford and the other grandees. Billy held his own.

At the end of 1999, Wakeham's report came out. They essentially bottled it, by recommending that the majority of a 550-member house should be appointed. But for a proposed 'democratic element' within the house, they acknowledged the workability of Billy's method, which became the basis of Model A, one of three put forward. The government is committed to debating the contents of the report so, for Billy, the campaign continues. In 2001, he produced a nicely tooled pamphlet ('A Genuine Expression of the Will of the People') intended to promote the notion of appointment-free composition. He is gung-ho not because it's *his* idea, but because he believes it works.

'Trying to make it sexy is impossible,' he admits. 'And writing songs about it – forget it!'

Billy's other big concern of the new millennium – and one which is far better suited to songwriting – is what he calls 'the crisis in Englishness': the parlous state of national identity, especially in the face of Welsh and Scottish devolution. Billy believes passionately in, well, a new England: 'The place I want to get to is where you see a St George sticker on the back of a van, and you don't immediately think fascist.'

He'd been filling up notebooks for over two years – all of a sudden, everything fed into his new obsession. The Euro.

Hooligans at Euro 2000. Asylum seekers. Race riots. The BNP. The myopic, right-wing thinking found in books like *Nor Shall My Sword* by Simon Heffer and *England: An Elegy* by Roger Scruton.

Here's Scruton: 'Grammar schools, the old House of Lords, the Prayer Book and the English Bible, English weights and measures, English currency, local regiments, the Royal Tournament – every practice in which the spirit of England can still be discerned seems fated now to arouse contempt.'

Billy appreciates that Englishness is an abstract ('it means different things to different people'), but that's what makes it such an inspiring subject for songs.

Billy Bragg began the twenty-first century as fired up as he had been when Thatcher was re-elected in 1983. The battle lines might not have been so clearly drawn under Labour, but even from down there on the beach at West Bexington, Dorset, Billy could still see the class struggle.

The year 2000 started slowly, career-wise, while renovation work continued in earnest at Barton Olivers. On 29 February, Billy addressed the Oxford Union on national identity ('partly because my old man would be so made up').

In May, *Mermaid Avenue Vol II* was released. Less fuss was made of it, predictably enough – it was second helpings after all but it was no less inventive and various than the first. The track listing almost suggests they'd deliberately held some of the best stuff back: 'All You Fascists Bound To Lose' (already a live favourite), 'My Flying Saucer', 'Secret Of The Sea'. And it had a picture of a cat on the front. It was Grammy-nominated, like its cousin, in 2001.

On 29 May, Billy was grilled by future Tory MP, London Mayor, Foreign Secretary and international nuisance, but then simply editor of the *Spectator,* Boris Johnson, for a Radio 4 programme *Why People Hate . . . Tories*. 'It was not so much an interview as a shouting match.'

Johnson, somewhat akin to a public school-educated Dulux dog, accused Billy of being a Tory and 'a great big zeppelin of hypocrisy', to which Billy replied, 'I sold my house not my principles.'

The two of them actually hit it off. So, when Billy was asked to present part of BBC's Glastonbury coverage, he gave Boris a call and invited him along – a festival virgin, of course. The resulting chalk-and-cheese docusoap, which aired on BBC Choice (the precursor of BBC3), was unmissable television. They had henna tattoos, performed in the Poetry Tent (Johnson did part of *The Iliad* in the original Greek, which must have freaked out the stoners) and were accosted by naked protesters in the field with the stones. Johnson admitted he quite liked it, having concluded that everyone there was also a Tory.

Back in Burton Bradstock, 'the village' made first contact. The Parish Clerk came to visit, on behalf of the Millennium Committee, and asked Billy if he would play a gig on the village green. 'You do know what kind of music I play?' Billy asked. The Clerk said he did. So it was a New Orleans jazz band on the Friday, bingo on the Saturday, and Billy Bragg and the Blokes on Sunday all to raise money for the local scout hut (not quite the Youth Trade Union Rights Campaign or the dockers, but good causes begin at home).

To show that he was serious about connecting with Dorset, Billy sang Ralph Vaughan Williams's 'Linden Lea', based on the poem by Dorset-born William Barnes, born in 1801. Barnes wrote in the local dialect. And Billy still sings in his.

In July, they played at the Tolpuddle Martyrs Festival, commemorating the six Dorset farm labourers who were transported in 1834 for forming a union to defend wages and conditions. Proof that moving out of London hadn't necessarily removed Billy from where the left-wing action was.

In September, another first. A new production of Shakespeare's *Henry V* was performed at the Royal Shakespeare Theatre in Stratford, featuring songs especially written by Billy Bragg for the soldiers as they marched towards Agincourt. This radical move can be credited to 33-year-old director Edward Hall (son of Sir Peter). Billy loved the experience (especially as it fitted into his long-term Englishness project) and says he could easily imagine doing a little bit more of that.

The University of East London (formerly Barking Polytechnic) gave him an honorary degree, which was poetic, as the young Stephen Bragg had been denied this particular route after failing his eleven-plus. 'It was a day out for the kids and Mum,' he shrugs. His mum asked the people from the university, 'Why are you giving him this?'

'Because he's from Barking and he's done well.'

'My other son's from Barking and he's done well – can he have one?'

Fair point.

It's important not to observe politics but to be politics. Generate ideas. It's not just writing about it, you've got to engage.

Billy Bragg, 17 September 2001

Another election year, the fifth since Billy Bragg had been a professional singer-songwriter and *agent provocateur*. And a forgone conclusion, now that New Labour had spread their political picnic blanket out, and the Tories had become so fixated on Save The Pound they appeared to have Lost The Plot. A good time for Billy perhaps to disengage from party politics, retire, sit back and think of England.

By now he was deep into the writing and recording of his tenth album, *England, Half English* (the title taken from a 1961 collection of essays by Colin MacInnes). Tracks were laid down with Grant Showbiz at Monnow Valley Studios in Monmouth, South Wales. In March, the family put a nasty British winter at Sea Change behind them and moved full-time into Barton Olivers again. The national outbreak of foot and mouth disease put the countryside on the front pages and, although the burning cattle pyres and the men from the ministry in protective suits didn't actually reach Dorset, it scared the life out of the farming community there. It also drove a nationwide wedge between town and country. Billy found himself seeing both sides of the argument. He'd seen livelihoods destroyed during the miners' strike, but who'd subsidised *them*?

His links with the local community were strengthening the whole time. In March, he started a songwriters' workshop at the local comprehensive Sir John Colfox. This was a result of his appearance at the Burton Bradstock Millennium Festival in 2000, after which the headmaster of Jack's village school, David Powell, hit upon the idea of Bridport World Music Week, involving 1,500 kids of Jack's age writing songs about their experiences of living here, linked via the Internet to India, Gambia and Chile. Billy got heavily involved, and the workshop idea came out of that.

In May, the *Bridport News* ran a big feature on Billy ('Meet the milkman of human kindness – pages 24–25'), detailing all of his community efforts since moving to Dorset, and picturing him with the John Colfox kids. (There was also one of Buster, the new Bragg family dog, a black 'Labradoodle', which is a cross between a Labrador and a standard Poodle.)

But, by then, Billy was engaged in a new battle, a local campaign that gained national prominence thanks to his previous form and a sixth sense for headline grabbing. On 14 April, Easter weekend, Billy was asked by the *New Statesman* to write a diary. 'What are you going to do about voting?' they asked. He hadn't really given it too much thought; he was getting 'a bit of pressure' from the Dorset Labour Party – maybe it was time to weigh up his options. The general election had been moved, because of foot and mouth, from 3 May to 7 June, so there was plenty of time to get his act together.

Dorset West, his constituency, was held in 1997 by the Tories, with the Liberal Democrats just 1,840 votes behind, and Labour in third. A vote for his traditional party would, Billy reasoned, be a wasted one. 'Voting Liberal Democrat became even more attractive once I realised that the sitting MP was Oliver Letwin, the ardent Eurosceptic and rising Tory star.' (And the man who leaked the Tories' secret spending cut figure of £20 billion.)

In neighbouring Dorset South, Tory MP Ian Bruce was a wafer-like 77 votes ahead of Labour.

Inspired by the website tacticalvoter.net, a nationwide vote-swapping scheme designed to keep the Tories out by pairing up tactical voters around the country, Billy looked into setting up his own for Dorset. He met with two local 'netheads', they designed the page and the search engine, he bought the webspace and votedorset.net was go. Billy announced his intentions in the *Statesman* diary.

'We just put the thing up and there it was. I didn't realise how quickly it would take off. The morning the *Statesman* came out, there was a story in the *Guardian*.

They'd rung up the Lib Dems to ask how they felt about me voting for them, and *they* then put out a press release. The *Dorset Echo* faxed it to me. I thought to myself, Jeeeesus, I can see how this is going to go – I'd better get my brain around it.

'I thought, does any of this matter if Labour are going to win anyway? Yes it does. After the election, the Tories will regard the number of seats they've gained as a measure of how well their "Little Englander" rhetoric has gone down in the country. Tactical voting will punish the Tories for their lurch to the right.'

As the votedorset leaflets and posters said: 'Send a message to William Hague: no to racist campaigning.' You could also register your dissatisfaction with Tony Blair.

Billy's tactical crusade generated acres of press, not just local. In fact, tactical voting and John Prescott punching a farmer were the *only* election stories in 2001. The letters page in the *Bridport News* was full of it. 'Have I missed something? Was there a poll that elected [Billy Bragg] spokesman for Dorset while I was away somewhere?' asked reader Derek Jones.

'I think you should come clean and re-title your publication *The Bridport News And Billy Bragg Newsletter*,' wrote Michael West, spookily echoing those old letters in the *NME* which used to say, 'Why don't you just change your name to the *New Morrissey Express* and be done with it?' Oliver Letwin was even forced to write in to defend his record (he boasted of the 31,000 letters he'd written, the 1,200 constituents he'd seen at 129 surgeries, the 239 questions he'd asked in Parliament etc.).

During the election, Jeremy Vine drove around the country in a clapped-out *Newsnight* van looking for stories. In Dorset, he found one. In the spirit of Dorchester's Roman town status, Dorset County Museum had organised a public debate about the future of Durnovaria (Dorchester) with the three election candidates – Oliver Letwin, Labour's Richard Hyde and the Lib Dems' Simon Green. The museum rang Billy up and asked if he would be in the audience.

Because the candidates would be dressed up in togas, Billy had an idea. Bridport Museum were having a Roman week;

he got in touch with the Living History guy who set this up, and asked if he could hire a centurion's uniform . . .

Thus, with *Newsnight* in tow, Billy turned up at the meeting in full Roman soldier's regalia. 'They were just about to convene the vote, and I had to climb over the fence and march through the audience with this great big, fuck-off, eight-foot spear, a big shield and two swords!'

He announced himself as 'Tacticus Braggus'. He pointed at Letwin and said, 'Render unto Thatcher that which is Thatcher's.' The crowd lapped it up; Letwin hated it, whipping off the toga before he was embarrassed by the cameras. And the Lib Dems won the vote.

'So much of what we did during the campaign was focused on using up pages of the *Dorset Echo*; because it was almost silly season, they were looking for stuff to run, every week I was trying to think of something to keep this issue in people's minds. And it paid off.'

Billy's serious clowning (and the shoe leather of those on the campaign with him) literally put Dorset on the political map.

Labour won the election on 7 June, predictably, although the turnout was embarrassingly low. William Hague resigned as Tory leader on cue, and what Billy calls 'the battle for the soul of the Conservative Party' commenced. Sadly, the Lib Dems didn't win in Dorset West; Letwin actually gained 5.5 per cent of the vote ('You can't just expect these people to roll over,' reflects Billy). But, in Dorset South, Labour overturned the Tories with a 153 majority – the only seat Labour took off the Conservatives in the whole country. 'Depending on which paper you read, it was a complete failure or a complete success.'

Ian Bruce, Dorset South's defeated Tory MP, later wrote in *Parliamentary IT Briefing* magazine: 'The real damage to the Conservative cause was the masses of TV time devoted to the message that tactical voting was about Labour and Liberals ganging up against "evil" Conservatives.'

A sore loser, Bruce also gave an interview to the *Express* that led to a piece on 13 June attempting to hold Billy up as a great big zeppelin of hypocrisy, except with none of Boris Johnson's schoolboy humour. 'ANTI-CAPITALIST SINGER'S LIFE OF LUXURY IN £500,000 MANSION' went the headline, above an aerial shot of Barton Olivers, the 'cliff-top mansion' to which 'he has since added an extension'. The traitor!

Ian Bruce said, 'Conservatives like me are very glad our policies and philosophy were able to provide him and his family with such a wonderful environment in which to live.' Touché!

'Perhaps,' wrote yet another local resident in the *Bridport News*, 'now that the dust has settled after the general election, Billy Bragg would like to leave the good folks of Dorset to their own peaceful ways.'

You'll be lucky.

> *I sold all my vinyl yesterday*
> *At a boot sale out on the highway*
> *And now my room is full of fresh air*

'Tears Of My Tracks'

England, Half English, completed in October 2001 and released in February 2002, is a landmark Billy Bragg album, the sound of fresh air blowing through his attitude to writing, playing and singing. It's the first post-Woody record and the first truly co-written and co-performed with his own band, the Blokes. (The Red Stars had, after all, been strictly a touring outfit, despite their crucial role in Bragg history.)

The album's fifteen tracks flit easily between grown-up pop and sit-down balladry ('Some Days I See The Point' is one the most beautiful slowies he's ever written), shuffling through musical styles as though flicking through an atlas: folksy Americana here; Arabic there; a dash of Jamaican; and some English music hall. Billy sings – except when he doesn't – but there's no shock value in that since Woody.

As for words, the balance between the social and the socialist is as we have come to expect, although the older Billy gets, the more we must applaud his righteous, constructive anger – a sentimental lyric like 'Baby Farouk' ('Join us now in celebration/To each child a generation!') is something any songwriting parent might have penned, but 'NPWA' ('no power without accountability!'), 'Take Down The Union

Jack' and the wry, manifesto title track are a long way from what, say, Phil Collins was writing about at 43.

In 'NPWA' the protagonist laments losing his job, car and house 'when ten thousand miles away some guy clicked on a mouse/He didn't know me, we never spoke/He didn't ask my opinion or canvass for my vote'. How frightfully unfashionable to write about job loss, and yet it was only in May 2000 that Ford laid off 2,000 car workers at Dagenham, ending car production at the plant after 69 years (and all because they can make a Fiesta in 24.4 hours in Cologne while it takes 25.3 hours here).

We lived in heightened political times again. Amid all the sabre-rattling and flag-waving in the aftermath of the New York attacks on 11 September 2001 – when Tony Blair turned into a pocket Winston Churchill – it was a thought crime to voice misgivings about the 'War On Terrorism'. And although written before the balloon went up, Billy's new national anthem, 'Take Down The Union Jack', now seems doubly daring:

> Britain isn't cool you know, it's really not that great
> It's not a proper country, it doesn't even have a pa-
> tron saint
> It's just an economic union that's past its sell-by date

If the tenth album tell us anything it's that Billy was still *engaged*. He doesn't just talk politics, he *is* politics. A song is one thing – and an abidingly useful tool – but he's got a pamphlet too if you're interested.

England, Half English is far and away Billy's most musical album. To think that Dave Woodhead's trumpet used to amount to a concession fifteen years ago! And the Blokes don't just colour in the background, they are now intrinsic to the writing process. Almost half of the tracks carry a Bragg/Blokes credit, and the breadth of musical palette would never have been possible without the co-op nature of the new arrangement.

So, the singular, self-sufficient Billy Bragg was no longer 'just' a solo performer. Who'd have thought it? A one-man Clash – that was bloody yesterday. The community spirit that has always informed his politics and his practices, was now part of the music-making process. The world might habitually fall apart, but, for Billy Bragg, it all seemed to be coming together.

For his next trick? A new England.co.uk. Who knew? Strange things happen.

17. THE FULL ENGLISH

A range of distractions, 2002–2006

Gilbert and George are taking the [censored]
>   'Take Down The Union Jack' – the *official version*,
>   *Top Of The Pops*, 31 May 2002

Suzi Quatro, Lesley Garrett, DJ Spoonie, Shola Ama, Carol Decker from T'Pau . . . and Billy Bragg. No, not a bad dream after overdoing it at the cheese pavilion. This was 1 May 2002, and the broadcast of a special 'music industry' edition of BBC's *The Weakest Link* quiz, which Billy had only agreed to do because it was his mum's favourite programme.

The afternoon they'd recorded it, out at a studio in Slough, Billy was under heavy manners to get 'voted off' by 4 p.m., the hour his agitated plugger had calculated they had to leave in order to make Broadcasting House in time for a live radio interview with Johnnie Walker on Radio 2. 'No worries,' Billy assured him. 'I'm not taking this seriously. As long as I'm not the first person off.'

Oh, but he wasn't. A solid grasp of general knowledge, a cool head and a propensity not to rub the others up the wrong way meant Billy kept getting through, round after round. 'All of a sudden, I realised there was only three of us left! Me, Suzi Quatro and Lesley Garrett. To be perfectly honest, I suddenly thought, fucking hell, I could win this!'

Watching the programme go out, Juliet took great delight in recognising Billy's expression change at this point, confirming for her that the dedicated socialist *did* have a competitive streak after all (a trait hinted at by the enthusiastic way he approaches family mini-golf tournaments). He went head to head with Suzi Quatro and won. He was the Strongest Link – goodbye! (They just made it to Johnnie's show, where, sworn to pre-recorded quiz-show secrecy, Billy couldn't even reveal where he'd been, let alone that he'd won. He'd *won*! Still, Mum was happy and he'd banked £11,000 for the Medical Foundation For The Care Of Victims Of Torture.)

It's amusing to hear that Billy has been invited to participate in all the shows with 'Celebrity' in the title – *Celebrity Mastermind, Celebrity Big Brother, I'm A Celebrity . . . Get Me Out Of Here* and reassuring to know that he turned them all down. ('Can't be contemplated.')

Though clearly a major TV highlight of 2002, we mustn't let *Weakest Link* eclipse Billy's fourth appearance on *Top Of The Pops*, essaying 'Take Down The Union Jack', the number one that might've been. It being – flags out! – Golden Jubilee year, they'd cooked up a wheeze: release the single in a multitude of formats (as per venal industry norm) and promote the backside out of it, thus hiking it to the top of the charts in time for Jubilee week. 'It was a moment of madness,' he concedes.

Released on 20 May, Billy took to the tarmac with Grant Showbiz and road manager Jason Bell, and did three in-stores a day for a week. Monday: breakfast in Dundee, lunchtime in Edinburgh, afternoon in Glasgow, that sort of whistle-stop itinerary. Tuesday, Leeds, Sheffield, Preston; Wednesday, Manchester and Loughborough (stuck in traffic on the M62 trying to get over the Pennines, naturally); Thursday, Leicester, Birmingham, Northampton; Friday, Cheltenham, Cardiff, Bristol. The single entered the chart at an impressive Number 22 – Billy's biggest hit since 'Between The Wars' – on the Sunday. The next day it was Eastbourne, Exeter; Tuesday, Camberley, Tunbridge Wells; Wednesday, Berwick St in London, and Thursday . . . *Top Of The Pops*! The triumphant appearance aired the next day, in the show's heretical new Friday slot. Seventeen years after his square-peg debut, he was back, once more confusing the young punters' with his dangerous Republican rhetoric. Even better, the BBC took it upon themselves to bleep him. Twice. Neither 'bum' nor 'piss' were allowed to corrupt the nation's youth. The single went down the following week.

'Surprisingly, I can't quite understand it, but the Jubilee went ahead anyway.'

With barely enough time to read the lavish spread about Barton Olivers in *Homes & Gardens* (a generous plug for Juliet's Design Dorset operation), Billy was deep into the festival circuit – Left Field at Glastonbury, Guildford, Brampton, Tolpuddle, Cambridge – with a short hop with the Blokes to Japan for Fuji Rocks (including a naked dip at some public baths – good bonding for any band). Then Europe, Canada, the USA and back to the UK, some dates with the full squad, others with just Mac, all the while thinking about the book.

The book, which would eventually become *The Progressive Patriot*, was borne out of Billy's obsession with English identity, which threatened to eat everything in its path. 'Having put out an album that made a point of talking about Englishness, I got invited to all sorts of discussions and TV programmes and seminars about the issues and politics of identity, and it made me realise there was a lot more to be said and done about this.'

Being invited to play at an Anti-Nazi League gig in September was another big marker – 'the first one of those I'd done for 20 years'. (Having wound down in 1981, the ANL had resumed life in 1992, eventually merging with the National Assembly Against Racism, with the support of the TUC and various unions, to form Unite Against Fascism.) Also, having put in another insanely busy year, Billy was keen to find 'something else to do'. A challenge.

'I'm good at making Billy Bragg records, I'm probably the best Billy Bragg there is. But if you do it year in, year out, after 20 years it does become . . . not a chore, but predictable.'

Writing and playing with the Blokes had, crucially, allowed him to articulate his feelings about Englishness using polyrhythms and world music shapes. Instead of approaching the subject in a traditional way – like 'The Home Front', which, with its trumpet reveille, had been all 'jam and Jerusalem' – he was able to use musical multiculturalism to head off misconceptions that he was coming at patriotism from a right-wing position. After all, it had been Morrissey's refusal, or failure, to articulate what he meant by 'Bengali In Platforms', and the skinheads and the Union Jack, that left him open in the early 90s to accusations of racism and fascism. 'You don't have to defend yourself, you just have to explain.'

On first hearing the coda of 'England, Half English' – 'Oh my country, oh my country, what a beautiful country you are' – some friends thought Billy was being ironic. He wasn't. But expressing complex feelings in song was, by definition, limiting. Which is why writing a book suddenly felt like the right thing to do; somewhere to organise the thoughts banging around in his head. Plus, he wanted to sort out his 'work-life balance', determined to be around when Jack made the transition from junior to secondary school ('that was the final nudge'). To the constant advances from various publishers, he finally succumbed.

A more profound balance was disturbed on 22 December, by the sudden death of Joe Strummer. With no prior warning, his heart packed up while out walking the dog near his home in Broomfield, Somerset. He was 50, just five years older than Billy.

Numbed by the news, a generation mourned. A lot of Clash records were played on that horrible day. Strummer's importance to Billy has been stated before, but in losing him, it all swam back into focus: how inspiring The Clash had been, how irreplaceable, how enduring. The last time he'd seen Joe was at a Mescaleros gig at London's Astoria, where they ran through the usual fistful of Clash numbers, including 'White Man In Hammersmith Palais'. He'd received a Christmas card from Joe two days before he died.

'I think Joe's passing was a moment to step back and think about what The Clash had done and how it had made a difference to our lives. My whole approach is based on lessons learned from The Clash, both positive and negative.' There are, as Billy notes, a whole generation of 'middle-aged Clash fans' in positions of influence: Mick Rix, former ASLEF general secretary, heavily involved in keeping the BNP out of Barking, Andy Gilchrist, formerly General Secretary of the Fire Brigades Union, now National Education Officer at the National Union of Rail, Maritime and Transport

Workers, who had been at Victoria Park, and the late Bob Crow, RMT boss and 'awkward squad' denizen. They'd all stepped up when battle came down.

Billy and Joe had even been talking about doing some US shows together in 2003. What might have been. A gloomy end to a year otherwise crammed with hope and activity.

At the start of 2003, Billy bought the laptop. 'When you sign a record deal and they give you an advance, you have to make a record and form the band and pay for the videos. When they give you a publishing advance, you just have to buy a laptop. We're in the wrong business!'

He had a clear vision for the book, but no idea how long it would take, or what form. Time to knuckle down.

But distractions were everywhere, and not just the kettle and the dog.

On 15 February, Billy was 'shuffled to the front' of the biggest public demonstration in British history, the Stop The War march in Central London. Amazed and heartened by the sheer variety of the turnout – young, old, hard left, soft right, seasoned politicos, march virgins – he reached Hyde Park and watched as the multitude streamed in, thinking, 'This is bigger than anything I've ever been part of. As the estimated figure reached a million I thought, Wow, something is going to happen. This is going to be really powerful.'

It got to 4 o'clock, and Billy's thoughts turned to the train home. He bought soup and a roll, and cut back through Piccadilly, 'and the march was still going. That really did my brain in.' (The media recorded the final tally at one million, the organisers said two, while the police helpfully massaged it down to 750,000. Numbers aside, as Madeline Bunting wrote afterwards in the *Guardian*, 'The very best of Britain was on the city's streets.')

Billy Bragg was not alone in thinking that this unprecedented display of pacifism might actually stop Tony Blair taking us to war.

On 20 March, the insultingly named 'Operation Iraqi Freedom' was launched, coalition forces entered Iraq and the second Gulf War began. Mission was accomplished by 1 May, when George Bush, a real 'war president' now, entertained the troops on the aircraft carrier USS *Abraham*

Lincoln with some well-chosen words of victory ('the United States and our allies have prevailed'). This speech, historians now unanimously agree, was somewhat premature.

Workwise, apart from a week of gigs in Belgium, a Strummer tribute gig in Southampton, Maydaze in Glasgow, various talking shops, a *Question Time* and *The Weakest Link Champion of Champions*, for the first half of the year Billy kept his head down and his laptop up.

Then, having helped launch the first roadies' union at Glastonbury in June (Roadcrew Provident Syndicate, a branch of the doughty GMB), he was off touring Canada for the whole of July and Australia in September. In between – a quiet year, indeed – he joined an illustrious gang on stage for two Concerts For A Landmine Free World, on a bandstand in Edinburgh and at Leicester's Summer Sundae festival: Emmylou Harris, Joan Baez, Chrissie Hynde and Steve Earle. It was Earle who'd got in touch with Billy: 'Fancy taking it in turn to sing some songs, and do some together?' It was a speedy yes. He'd never met Harris or Baez before.

Walking with these two formidable women in Edinburgh the night before the first gig, and coming upon the statue of Walter Scott, Baez happened to say how much the *Ivanhoe* author looked like tragic folkie Tim Hardin. Conversation got round to '(Find A) Reason To Believe', the Hardin song made famous by Rod Stewart – Baez said, 'It would be wonderful if we could do it.' She wanted to send out for a CD, but Billy said, 'Don't worry, I used to be a busker.'

Their rendition, with Hynde, turned out, in Billy's words, to be 'really beautiful'. He also sang the Flying Burrito Brothers' 'Sin City' with Harris ('I'm flat as a pancake, she's singing like an angel'), and debuted 'Bush War Blues', based on Leadbelly's 'Bourgeois Blues', which stormed it in Edinburgh, at which point Baez, the queen of folk, leaned over and said, 'Fuckin' A, Bragg!' A nice moment.

In August, Billy took godson Jamie, who'd turned fifteen, to his first Reading Leeds Festival. Having been blooded at Glastonbury, it struck him as 'just a gig in a field', which is hard to argue with. Neil Pengelly, booker for the festival and dyed-in-the-wool Bragg fan with a New England tattoo, had convinced Billy to play the Concrete Jungle new bands stage, tipping him off that many visiting American bands – the likes of Death Cab For Cutie – saw his tattoo and expressed their admiration. So he went for it.

Grant pushed the sound right up to combat the DJ in the tent next door, Billy broke three strings in the first song and they stayed up drinking with the whippersnappers keen to touch the hem of his wellies. Next day it was on to the Christian-run Greenbelt in Cheltenham, where he and Jamie got to sing 'Soldier Girl', in robes, onstage with the massed choral ranks of The Polyphonic Spree – because group leader Tim DeLaughter was another Bragg fan. Jamie loved it. Another victory for the smaller festival.

This was the year in which Billy celebrated twenty years in showbiz with a stout, 40-song salute, *Must I Paint You A Picture?*, released in October to mark this historic milestone and supported with assorted radio appearances and in-stores. If nothing else, he'd made it this far without splitting up.

In November, the Tell The Truth tour ensured that his nose wouldn't stay in the book for too long. It was that pesky Steve Earle again. He'd corralled a bunch of activists in America to oppose corporate ownership of US radio, Clear Channel the sorest thumb in this regard, with over 1,200 radio stations in its portfolio, 30 TV channels, outside advertising space in 25 countries, and tentacles in venues and booking agencies. The tour, very much in the mould of Red Wedge, began at a conference in Madison, Wisconsin, and alongside Billy and Earle featured Tom Morello of Rage Against The Machine trading as The Nightwatchman, political rapper Boots Riley, and Lester Chambers from The Chambers Brothers, who'd been active in the Civil Rights movement. They all travelled around in a bus, visiting places Billy had never been: Asheville, Indianapolis, Tampa.

'The great thing about my job is that I get to go America and meet those kinds of people. Your average Brit has this kneejerk reaction to Americans, but there are good people there trying just as hard to rectify what George Bush and the neocons are doing as we are. We mustn't lose faith in those people – they need all the support they can get.'

He's talking about people like musician and activist Jenny Toomey, director of The Future Of Music Coalition, one of the many organisations with a presence on the tour, Mike Mills of R.E.M., who joined for some dates, and comedian Janeane Garofalo, who compered. Awareness was raised, rousing songs sung, questions asked, answers given.

Undaunted by the Truth being Told, the ravenous Clear Channel's next step was to buy out ITB (International Talent Booking), Billy's agents in the UK – 'just after I'd told them not to book me into any Clear Channel venues!'

The solution was clear: he found a new agent.

A new year, 2004, and Billy's book was still languishing in that limbo between intention and prose. Welcome distraction came with Lords reform, still a hot topic for Billy, especially after the Iraq demonstrations, which caused him to wonder who these people would be voting for come the next election. Surely not Labour? A proportionally elected second chamber was more crucial than ever, to convince the public they still had a stake in democracy. Billy had forged a good working relationship with Paul Stinchcombe, Joint Committee member and Labour MP for Wellingborough (albeit one who would not survive the electoral bloodbath in April 2005). He got Billy in to see people like the influential Lord Chancellor, Charlie Falconer, leader of the Commons (and tamed firebrand) Peter Hain and party chairman Ian McCartney.

In February, a debate and vote in the Commons was side-tracked by the issue of what proportion of the second chamber should be elected or appointed. The honorable members ended up with seven options. Everybody voted for the one they fancied and against the other six, and it was eventually thrown out. When Blair came out in favour of an appointed House, that 'fucking killed it dead'.

So was that it? No. With the help of a filmmaker he'd met at party conference in 2003, Billy made a windswept three-minute non-party-political broadcast, *Apathy Into Action*, and, helped by Stinchcombe, sent a DVD of it to all Labour MPs and a VHS each for their constituencies. If nothing else, hundreds of the party faithful would see how splendid the cliffs and beach at Burton Bradstock were.

Over a well-chosen soundtrack of 'NPWA', leaning against a gatepost and facing a prevailing wind, Billy urges, 'Forget the Tories and the Liberal Democrats – at the next election our biggest enemy is going to be apathy.' Summing up the secondary mandate, he says, 'One tick in the box and you're sorted.'

He put forward his proposal at a debate called 'A Democratic Lords: the Third Stage?' hosted by the Fabian Society at the House of Commons. This was flagged up by a hugely supportive comment piece by the *Guardian*'s Jonathan Freedland ('It is not poetry, but it is a compromise that could work – which is what practical politics is all about'). Hain and Falconer praised the Bragg plan publicly.

Billy thrashed it out with anyone who'd listen – Shirley Williams, Tory peer Lord Strathclyde – but kept being told, 'You've got to convince Prescott on Lords reform; if you don't – forget it.'

So it was that in April, between the soundcheck and gig at the Barbican, he was taken to the Commons canteen by deputy PM John Prescott. They had a long conversation about the Lords, 'but there was something else preying on his mind, and I realised what it was when we came to the end of our plates of egg, bacon and chips. He said, "Did I see you with your eye on that spotted dick pudding?" I said, "Yeah, it did look pretty good. With some custard, I thought." He said, "Yeah, it looks really, really good." I said, "I shouldn't really be having this, I've got a gig in half an hour." He said, "I shouldn't be having it either." I never did convince him about Lords reform, but we achieved unanimity on the spotted dick.'

In June, Billy was asked on to the august bill of a Lonnie Donegan memorial at London's Albert Hall (Van Morrison, Joe Cocker, Mark Knopfler, Roger Daltrey, the subsequently disgraced Rolf Harris, convicted of sex offences in 2014). He was squeezed between the Barron Knights and Rick Wakeman singing with a woman from *Cats*. Donegan's widow, Sharon, had seen Billy play in Newcastle, and invited him to come and do a Woody song. It was good to be part of. England were playing Croatia in Euro 2004 that night and Billy will always remember watching the game backstage with Gerry Marsden and a wizened old guy 'like Albert Steptoe', who turned out to be Chris Farlowe (Number 1 in 1966 with the Stones' 'Out Of Time'). 'I was the youngest person there!' he laughs. 'The audience was prehistoric!' Billy had been lucky enough to meet Donegan, the father of skiffle, a few years before his death in 2002, through John Peel. Billy was summoned to Broadcasting House – another canteen in a government building – for no discernible reason, other than Peel wanted him there. Billy duly went along. He and Donegan talked about Woody, a bit of politics, a lot of skiffle, but Peel said nothing for the entire time. Not a word. On the drive home, Billy asked his plugger, Dylan, who'd set the meeting up, what had been up with Peelie. It turns out he was too in awe of Donegan to speak.

Six months later, Billy was doing the Peel show at the DJ's Suffolk home and, off-air, asked him about the incident: 'How could you not speak to Donegan?' In response, Peel went off and came back with an original 10-inch of *New Orleans Joys*, the 1954 Chris Barber album with Donegan's version of Leadbelly's 'Rock Island Line' on it, and started misting up. 'It said a lot about Peel. That he was such a fan.'

On 26 October 2004, John Peel died after a heart attack, while on a working holiday with his beloved wife Sheila in Cuzco, Peru. Billy received the grim phonecall from Porky, now the breakfast DJ on digital radio station BBC 6 Music, just before the story broke. If anything, the waves of national bereavement went further than Joe Strummer's. Billy, who shared his feelings with the listeners of 6 Music that very afternoon, says, 'People always think of the John Peel who helped bands like me and The Smiths and The Fall, but they don't understand how important he was to Led Zeppelin, the Faces, Tyrannosaurus Rex. The Donegan story proves that he was still able to use music to take him back to the first time he heard it.'

The funeral, held on 12 November in Bury St Edmunds, to which a thousand people turned up, and at which eulogies were read by Paul Gambaccini and Peel's brother Andrew Ravenscroft, was 'very, very, very difficult. In the church, I was behind the Undertones and next to Robert Plant, and I came home on the train with Joe Boyd. You expect these people to be around forever, Peel more than anyone else, because he'd *been* around forever.'

The loss of Peel, whose absence has created an unfillable vacuum, not least at Radio 1, threatened to cast a pall over the rest of the year. But a lift, for Billy, came with the publication of Bob Dylan's memoir, *Chronicles: Volume 1*. 'The phones started ringing as soon as the first books came out,' he says. Billy got a mention in Bob Dylan's back pages.

For the record, it's toward the end of Chapter Two, 'A New Land'. Dylan goes to see the ailing Woody Guthrie in Greystone Hospital, New Jersey ('an asylum with no spiritual hope of any kind'). Woody tells him to go to the house at Coney Island, speak to Margie, his wife, and get his hands on a bunch of songs and poems that had never been set to music. Dylan treks out to the end of the subway line and through a swamp, to Mermaid Avenue, but Margie's not there, just their ten-year-old son Arlo and a babysitter. Dylan stays awhile but never does see those songs. 'Forty years later,' Dylan writes, 'these lyrics would fall into the hands of Billy Bragg and the group Wilco and they would put melodies to them, bring them to full life and record them.'

And that's the mention. 'It's like getting a knighthood!' Billy proclaims.

Billy cleared the decks as 2005 rolled around. He was writing his book. No more gigs.

Actually, there was a General Election on 5 May, and he'd promised a lot of MPs he'd turn out for them, those who'd helped him with Lords reform, or those facing the BNP. He played Leeds and Burnley in one weekend, the NUM in Barnsley, in Dewsbury for Labour candidate Shahid Malik and at a school in Keighley on a Sunday afternoon where Ann Cryer was standing against BNP leader Nick Griffin.

Criticism came Billy's way during the campaign for supporting pro-war Labour MPs. We'll call it the Oona King Problem. King, who'd voted for the invasion of Iraq, was fighting what had become an unsafe seat in Bethnal Green and Bow, East London, against Labour-rebel-turned-independent George Galloway, running for his own Respect Party. Billy made an appearance.

'It put me in a difficult position,' he concedes. 'It would have been simpler to duck out, and it did cross my mind when an agent made a speech before I went on stage comparing Galloway to Oswald Mosley. When you get involved in local politics like that, shit hits the fan. My name was added to the list of people Galloway condemned when he got elected. I can live with that. If anyone wants to know where I stand on the war, I made my feelings explicit and I continue to do so within the Labour Party. You can't work with politicians without getting some shit on you. I've always known that.

'I can't remember being involved in a General Election campaign where I didn't get called a scab by the SWP. It's par for the course for me. There are bigger fish to fry – to keep focused on the BNP and the Tories.'

Thanks in part to an unconvincing performance by creepy Tory leader Michael Howard, Labour squeaked home to history: a third term but with a majority of just 66, losing safe seats to the left, the right and the centre. Labour held Barking and Dagenham, but the BNP's Richard Barnbrook overtook the Lib Dems, a worrying trend after the party's showing at the September 2004 council elections, winning the Barking ward of Goresbrook with 52 per cent of the vote. If nothing else, the shifting of the political plates brought Billy's book into sharp focus. 'Is that where I come from?' he asked himself. 'What happened to me to make me different from those people who voted for the BNP?'

Answer: he'd heard The Clash when he was nineteen.

'I've spent all my adult life fighting those people and the first seat they win in the London area in a generation is in my home town. A real shock.'

Billy, the author, was looking at a virtually clear, commit-ment-and-gig-free three months until Christmas. But Maxine Eddington got in the way, and looking back, Billy's grateful that she did. Back in February, he'd been sought out by Rosetta Life, a fantastic charity that sends artists and mu-sicians into cancer hospices to encourage those living with the disease to express their feelings in song, or art, or film, or poetry, whatever captures their imagination. He ended up visiting the women at Trimar Hospice in Weymouth for six consecutive coffee mornings.

'I wanted to do it because when Dad was diagnosed with terminal cancer in 1975; they sent him home from the hospital and said the best way to deal with it was not to talk about it. So we never talked about it. And I deeply, deeply regret that.'

He played them 'Tank Park Salute', and encouraged them to talk about their experiences, which he would help interpret as songs. After a tentative start, he began to 'get a vibe' in week three. One woman wrote a poem. Another had some ideas about a road and a shining light. Another brought in a photograph of herself and her 15-year-old daughter, taken when she was diagnosed: all done up, smiling, laughing. She said, 'I did this because I want her to remember me when we laughed.' This was Maxine Eddington. Week four, Maxine didn't turn up, she was too ill. But she asked her carer to pass an envelope on to Billy.

It contained 36 handwritten pages – 'Do you remember when we went swimming with a dolphin off Portland Bill? And we laughed. Do you remember winning that medal for belly-dancing? And we laughed.' The song wrote itself.

Rosetta Life had sufficient budget to record three songs, using a band recruited by Billy, led by a vocalist he'd found singing in the pub called Helena. 'We Laughed', 'The Light Within' and 'My Guiding Star' were made into modest videos, using family photos, home movies and studio footage and made available on a website. (Artists involved in parallel projects included Michael Nyman, Roots Manuva, and Jarvis Cocker, who conducted a live 'Cyberjam', linking between Great Ormond Street and a hospice in South Africa.)

It all went off beautifully. They'd done what they set out to do. Then, in August, Maxine, now in remission, started pestering Billy about putting 'We Laughed' out as a single. He told her it wasn't as easy as that. 'There's no point putting it out next year,' she baited him. 'I haven't got that much time.'

In the week before World Hospice And Palliative Care Day in October, marked by 74 countries across five continents, he and Maxine appeared on Jeremy Vine's lunchtime show on Radio 2.

She told her moving story and Vine played the song. The BBC were swamped with calls: people who wanted to share stories with Maxine; a lorry driver forced to pull onto the hard shoulder in tears. Listeners loved the song, which was not available in the shops.

So Cooking Vinyl pressed up a thousand copies for free and put it out. Thanks to Vine, and local support from the likes of the *Dorset Echo*, 'We Laughed', credited to Rosetta Life Featuring Billy Bragg, went to Number 11 in the Official UK Chart in November. Maxine was a star, and well enough to join Billy at some in-stores. One, in Poole, 'was like a religious meeting. They were coming to her and she was literally laying her hands on them. It was incredibly powerful. I've never seen anything like it.' Which just goes to show, you never know how a year is going to pan out.

Maxine had been given a matter of months to live when Billy met her at the beginning of 2005. She kept going, powered by the human spirit, until finally succumbing to cancer in September 2006. 'She was a truly inspirational person.'

By February 2006, Billy had writer's block. He'd produced 40,000 words – out of 80,000 – but couldn't get to 50,000, and it was driving him 'fucking bonkers'. Then he was asked by his publishers to talk up the half-written book at a sales conference in Amsterdam. He went on before Bill Bryson, and 'it suddenly got real'.

The experience unblocked him. He had 70,000 words by the time he went to America in March to promote the first Billy Bragg box set, 'pretentiously titled' *Volume 1*. (Pay no more than £46.99, or nearest offer.)

The box came about because Elektra records ('who'd been very kind to me for 20 years – they got my records out there') was effectively boarded up after 54 years. Parent company Time Warner sold the Warner Music Group to private investors, who weighed and measured Elektra and decided to merge it with the better-performing Atlantic. Such decisions are rarely tainted by sentimentality. Still, due to the 'reversions' in his contract, Billy's catalogue all came back to him.

He struck a deal in the States with Anti, who would put out his new records, and Yep Roc, who'd look after the old stuff – hence *Volume 1* (and, in October, *Volume 2*), whose bonus-disc unreleased rarities were mined by Wiggy and Grant. 'It was nice to be boxed,' Billy says. 'I wanted to do something tactile before music became the clicking of a mouse.'

The handsomely tooled box pulled in some nice retrospective reviews (the *Chicago Tribune* wrote, 'Bare and unvarnished, the records function as messenger pigeons whose emotional fury and empathetic pleas fly in the face of empty-headed love songs, harken back to the urgency of first-wave punk and co-opt the spirit of civil rights-era soul'), including a big-up in the *NME*. It further cemented Billy's standing among the next generation of bands: rising stars Hard-Fi, from Staines, invited him to support them for five nights at Brixton Academy; Sheffield popsters Milburn got in touch, and he joined them in the studio.

At the local elections on 4 May 2006, the BNP won twelve seats out of the thirteen it contested in Barking and Dagenham, after a High Court ruling on the 12th. Nationally, it more than doubled its number of councillors, from 20 to 52: Epping Forest, Sandwell, Stoke-on-Trent, Burnley, Kirklees, Redditch, Redbridge.

'It gives me no pleasure', Billy said, 'to say that I got my retaliation in four years early' – i.e. *England, Half English* – 'but it encourages me that my cultural antennae can pick up stuff as it's happening.'

In June, the cover of trade magazine *The Bookseller* was wrapped in the cross of St George – a powerful teaser ad for *The Progressive Patriot* ('a stunning, timely polemic from a straight-talking icon: hardcover, £17.99, October'). The book itself wasn't actually finished. The author had hoped to sign it off by the World Cup. But the proliferation of England flags flying from cars and vans across the land in a wave of optimistic patriotism merited a new chapter. He handed it in on 31 July. England went out in the quarter finals. Some of those flags, tattered and forlorn, are still flying, two interim World Cups later.

One more act of defiance and principle: Myspace, the on-line social networking platform that seemed to be leading the way in the mid-noughties – and still provides a free, user-friendly marketplace for music – had crossed a critical Rubicon in July 2005, when News Corporation bought it for $580 million. Open to anyone with a hotmail address, it was also now prime advertising real estate for Rupert Murdoch. Still, in essence 'What a great idea!' says Billy, without irony. 'You're sitting in your bedroom in your parents' house. You've written all these songs. Now you've got to find a bunch of guys, form a band, learn to sing, get some gigs, get a manager and maybe one day get a record deal, and then people out there will get to hear your music. With Myspace, you write the songs, click click click, and there they are, everyone's got them.'(Myspace was bought by Time Inc. in 2016.)

Sarah Hyde in Billy's office had set a Myspace up for him in October 2005 (he would always need an initial leg-up into Cyberspace). But it took Fionn O'Lochlainn's manager, Sue Ellen Stroum, to bring to their attention the small print of the terms and conditions, through which Myspace claimed a 'worldwide royalty-free licence', giving them the right to sub-license, use, copy, modify, adapt, translate, store, reproduce, transmit and distribute content on and through the service. In May, smelling a rat, Billy pulled his songs off the site, with a message saying, 'We wouldn't grant these conditions to a record company, we don't see why we should give them to a corporation owned by Rupert Murdoch.'

The press picked up on it. Debate ensued. The official defence was that Madonna puts songs on Myspace and clearly they don't own Madonna's work. 'Yeah, but Madonna has a lawyer and a recording contract and a publishing contract. The majority who put their stuff up there have no legal contracts at all.'

The argument pinpointed a paradigm shift in the music industry. Previously, you'd sign to a record label for life copyright, and they own your records until they can't make money from them any more. Record companies traditionally invested in the physical production and distribution of discs. Now all they do is drag songs onto iTunes, so the necessity to sign isn't there. Billy gives the example of Ian McLagan: 'Whenever we're on the road in the UK and we stop at a service station, there'll be a compilation of 60s hits in the shop with a Small Faces track on, from which he earns no money whatsoever.'

This, he reasoned, could be the fate of some future breadwinner on Myspace. (Billy would never sign for life copyright with Go! Discs. 'Whose pension should this be?' he would ask Andy Macdonald. 'Yours or mine?')

A week later, Myspace changed the 'proprietary rights in content' clause in their terms and conditions: 'Myspace.com does not claim any ownership rights in the text, files, images, photos, video, sounds, musical works, works of authorship, or any other materials, collectively, "Content", that you post to the Myspace Services. After posting your Content to the Myspace Services, you continue to retain all ownership rights in such Content, and you continue to have the right to use your Content in any way you choose etc. etc.'

The dominoes fell. After Myspace came Bebo, a then fashionably like-minded, UK-founded social networking site pitched at the McFly demographic. Billy told the *Guardian*, 'If this new medium is to attain its full potential, it is crucial that artists are able to post content secure in the knowledge that doing so will not hinder their future career and earning potential. I believe that all sites which host member content should follow this lead by modifying their own terms of use.'

At the time, the next stop seemed to be YouTube, followed by the internet channel MTV Flux (which actually closed in 2008). Meanwhile, Facebook, launched on American campuses in 2004, and Twitter, in 2006, would soon reach their own critical mass.

An activist can never sit on his hands, as the frontiers keep on expanding.

When spanking new Tory leader David Cameron was interviewed by the *New Statesman* in June 2006, he was fresh from Radio 4's *Desert Island Discs*, on which he'd chosen records by The Smiths, Bob Dylan and R.E.M., hardly the standard fare for those on the right.

Under the worrying headline, 'Equality, croquet, Billy Bragg and me', he revealed that 'A New England' (the Kirsty MacColl version) had almost made the final cut.

On the matter of whether this would have been an appropriate choice, he said, 'This idea that you can't like the music of people who don't agree with you politically would kind of limit your musical choices a bit.'

A near-miss for Billy that said as much about shifting generations as it did about the vacuity of the next Prime Minister. Only 39 when he was elected leader, Cameron was an undergraduate when Billy and The Smiths and R.E.M. first made their mark. Perhaps his appreciation of their pinko sounds was genuine. In some ways, let's hope it was hollow, opportunistic, please-like-me spin.

The only thing David Cameron and Billy Bragg have in common is Oxford. Cameron attended Brasenose College, and Billy was given an Honorary Doctorate by Oxford Brookes University in September 2005 ('the cap and gown, all that shit'). The *only* thing.

This is Cameron, and it certainly rings true: 'When I grew up in the 1980s, there was a big gulf between left and right. You were either for CND or Nato, privatisation or state ownership of industry, cutting taxes and setting people free or high rates of marginal tax, for the trade unions or for trade union reform. It seemed to me we made a choice on those sorts of grounds.'

The question Billy still asked, after 23 years in showbiz, two box sets, a Number One, a doctorate and a 'knighthood', remains disarmingly simple, 'Which side are you on?'

18. A WRITER NOT A DECORATOR

Keeping faith, going to jail and becoming a Guitar Hero, 2007–2013

My practicality consists of this – knowing that if a man beats his head against the wall, it is his head that breaks and not the wall
  Antonio Gramsci, letter from prison to sister-in-law Tania Schudt, 1930

I know it looks like I'm just reading the paper, but these ideas I'll turn to gold dust later
                                               'Handyman Blues' *Tooth & Nail*, 2013

In May 2012, on the first leg of the *Ain't Nobody Who Can Sing Like Me* tour, booked to mark Woody Guthrie's centenary and to promote *Mermaid Avenue: the Complete Sessions* across Europe, North America and Canada, Billy found himself playing 'Levi Stubbs' Tears' at the Paradiso club in Amsterdam. Not an uncommon occurrence in his three decades on the road. But something surprising happened during the second half that firmly nails this gig to the annals. 'There was no security or anything,' Billy explains. 'A tall, drunk-or-stoned guy got out of the audience, walked across the stage and put his arm around me while I was singing, and his mate took a photo.'

Not the first time a punter had wanted his snap taken with the notoriously accessible troubadour – albeit prior to the smartphone 'selfie' revolution – but the first time it had been forced upon him, without warning, mid-song. 'I was fucking outraged!' Billy lilted on to the end, still taken aback by the pitch invader's cheek, and then it happened: the bloke climbed out of the audience again. 'Something snapped' – not a guitar string, but Billy's fundamentally peaceable restraint – 'I ran across the stage and stabbed him five times in the nuts with the neck of the guitar: "Fucking get off my fucking stage, you bastard!" As he turned round I caught him with the tip of my boot and booted him into the audience.'

The unknown soldier was swallowed up by the night and nobody saw him again. But this somewhat out-of-character lesson in Billy Bragg crowd control is not the point of this story.

'When I walked back to the mic . . . b-*rrrrr*-ing! – the Jim Dyson guitar was still in tune.'

Billy refers to the guitar that had seen him alright for ten years as 'a utility guitar for a utility guitar player', but beyond the self-deprecation there is something pleasingly symbolic about the way both man and machine have survived the knocks and surprises of a lifetime spent mixing pop and politics. You might say that this guitar doesn't need to say sorry.

There is a truism that you get more right-wing as you get older. But as Billy stared down the barrel of 2013 and the milestone 30-year anniversary of his first record, he was living proof of that truism's falsity. For some veterans, old alliances just harden like arteries, but not Billy, who has constantly adapted to survive. In a twenty-first century he considers 'post-ideological', he's not just ranging his moral and political artillery against the cosy old enemies – the resurgent Tories, the constantly rearming fascists, the fleetingly significant Tea Party – in days like these he's as likely to rage against big business, the free market and institutionalised privilege; while compassion still burns beneath his other deeply held beliefs, he's as driven in the modern day by the vexing subject of accountability.

Rather than take his foot off the pedal and ease into a dotage of self-parody in his fifties, Billy Bragg found himself still very much in the Billy Bragg business, honing his craft, playing the benefits, curating his own tent at Glastonbury, supporting new firebrands like Jake Bugg and Grace Petrie, and turning headlines into songs. In his forties, he'd forged a lifelong link with history via Woody Guthrie, surrendered himself to the possibilities of collaboration and begun voting tactically in response to his new, non-metropolitan surroundings. As a result, he appeared to be in a good place when he turned 50 in December 2007, a milestone that would've been unthinkable to the Saturday boy and whose official public celebration he had to be gently cajoled into.

For all his tentative paddling in the shallows of new media, the event cooked up to mark the big five-oh was defiantly analogue. Jude Kelly, artistic director of London's Southbank Centre since 2005 and described by the *Guardian* as 'one of the most powerful people in the arts', led Billy 'in conversation' through an evening with himself, at the brutalist Queen Elizabeth Hall. Before a packed house of 900, this night revolved, literally, around a stack of vinyl records he'd selected to conjure previous milestones: Dylan, The Clash, Linda Ronstadt, the Watersons, Thin Lizzy. He stood up from his armchair to play a few tunes, too, mostly greatest hits, a couple from the upcoming *Mr Love & Justice* album, but also a real rarity, Riff Raff's 'Here Comes The Now', which most of us had never heard him play live before.

At the end, he thanked everybody for continued support, and announced, with lump in throat, that he only keeps going because of the inspiration he gets from his fans. One of the new songs was the reciprocal 'I Keep Faith'. Perfect.

Those fortunate enough to have a Golden Ticket – a laminate bearing Billy's school photo and the legend, 'Honey, I'm a big boy now!' – were stewarded into the Spirit Level bar for an after-show that was part underground club night, part wedding reception. The guest list ambitiously mixed close family with old pals and luminaries: Marie, Jenner, Tiny, Jupitus, Jerry Dammers, Neil Spencer, Chas Smash and, representing the post-Blairite Labour government, Ed Miliband, the 37-year-old former Treasury whizz recently sworn into the Cabinet by new PM Gordon Brown, and 37-year-old Culture Minister James Purnell ('They were standing there chatting with each other, looking like a couple of wonks', says Billy, who convinced them to take off their ties). It had been organised by Juliet with 'military precision', not least 'sneaking Paul Weller in the back' so that when Billy arrived at his own party, the Modfather was already the in-house DJ. ('Weller really enjoyed the cloak and dagger of it,' says Juliet.)

There was even a cake in the shape of Billy's old Orange amp. In March 2008, the Southbank-trailed *Mr Love & Justice* was released on Cooking Vinyl, his ninth solo album. A persuasive suite of songs, soulful and mature, with some terrific contributions from the Blokes – notably Mac on the Hammond and Wurlitzer, and Ben Mandelson on bouzouki and lap steel – it arguably lacked the unifying through-line of previous long-players, having been recorded in two chunks, nine months apart.

Half a dozen tracks were recorded with producer Grant Showbiz at The Butchers Shop in North London in September 2006, another half dozen at Chapel studios in Lincolnshire in March 2007. 'Not only does that make for a less focused record, it makes for a much less focused budget.' (Money was about to become a bigger issue for everybody with the financial crash of 2008, and such relative profligacy would go out the window.)

To make matters less focused, when the band had gone home, Billy and Grant had 'a dozen songs, but only six lyrics'. Billy made up the deficit as he walked in the Lincolnshire wolds.

The modestly anthemic 'I Keep Faith' emerged as the beating heart of *Mr Love & Justice*; Laura Barton of the *Guardian* described it as 'a perfect Venn diagram of the political and the personal'. Its deceptively simple lyric – 'It doesn't matter if/This all falls off the cliff/Together we are going to see it through' – is a combined declaration of solidarity with those closest to him and those furthest away, namely, his fans. Keeping faith when 'what you say is met with anger, contempt and lies' has a clear political aspect, and Billy specifically singles out the Labour backbenchers he worked with during the 2005 election, 'those bright young Red Wedgers who are now ministers'. The last verse ('You have to make great sacrifice/For such little gain and so much pain') goes out to Maxine Eddington and the inspiring women at Trimar Hospice.

Talking of Red Wedge, former compatriot Robert Wyatt provides angelic backing vocals on 'I Keep Faith'. Billy explained to Laura Barton how this came about. The studio caterers in Lincolnshire had agreed to cook up rhubarb crumble and custard ('the pinnacle of desserts') as long as Billy provided the fresh rhubarb. While parking in the square of nearby market town Louth in search of 'the celery of the Gods', he was surprised to see Wyatt sitting with his wife on a bench, smoking a cigar. He greeted Billy 'like a long-lost son', and a studio play-date was fixed.

The album, like *England, Half English*, owes its title to Colin MacInnes, whose novel *Mr Love and Justice* is a sequel of sorts to *Absolute Beginners*, in which the ideals of a pimp and a policeman are tested in late-50s London. Although the album's title track is about 'fathers leaving children and leaving women', people still assume Mr Love & Justice is Billy. 'It was going to be *Mr Love & Social Justice*, but that was a bit unwieldy.'

The album charted higher than the more cunningly promoted *England, Half English*, at a respectable if not revolutionary 33. Billy is circumspect about the record: 'Really, I shouldn't have spent as much money or as much time on it. It would have benefited from being done in the first tranche when I was in that more acoustic-y place, recording tracks like "M For Me" and "If You Ever Leave". I just didn't have a dozen like that at the time. It's me working out how to write records in my fifties that resonate and aren't just me writing songs because I can.'

In many ways, *Mr Love & Justice* was a halfway house on the way to the far more radical tenth solo album in 2013. But a lot would happen in the five years between the two.

Back at the beginning of his 50th birthday year, Billy received a letter from Malcolm Dudley, a drug and alcohol rehabilitation counsellor at Guys Marsh, a Category C prison on the site of a former military hospital near Shaftesbury in North Dorset, which had been criticised in a report by the Board of Visitors in 2002 for failing to curb re-offending and coming up short of the quality of its medical care.

Dudley was teaching prisoners the guitar, with access to only two, one of which he borrowed off the chaplain, the other he'd found in a cupboard. He asked Billy if he had any spare guitars. He genuinely didn't, but paid the prison a visit and talked to his class.

Impressed by the good work being done with limited resources, Billy went to Denmark Street – London's 'Tin Pan Alley', still notable for its congregation of musical instrument shops – and discovered you can get a 'reasonable' Chinese acoustic for £50 in Hank's, and bought six, which Jeff Behan ('Jago'), an old Clash fan who helped set up the Strummerville foundation, stencilled with appropriate slogans: 'Strummer', 'This Machine Kills Time', 'Stay Free', and, most resonantly, 'Jail Guitar Doors', the B-side of 'Clash City Rockers' which lent its name to what had now clarified into an initiative. Billy donated them to Guys Marsh, stirred by the fact that ex-prisoners who have actively participated in sessions like Dudley's have a re-conviction rate of between 10–15 per cent, compared to the national average of 61 per cent. 'Playing a guitar can transport you momentarily from wherever you are', says Billy. 'If you apply that element of emotional transportation to someone in prison, you realise how access to guitars could really help.'

Jail Guitar Doors – 'the loudest charity on earth', as it would later be described – was officially announced at the *NME* Awards in March, marking the fifth anniversary of Strummer's death with something more concrete than 'another gig where a bunch of boring middle-aged Clash fans sat around singing his songs'. The band's Mick Jones was the 'first man in the room' to offer his services.

In July, accompanied by the *Guardian*, the pair went to Wormwood Scrubs in West London to play for 'rows of men dressed in grey tracksuits and pale blue T-shirts . . . slouched in their chairs'. The article 'went around the world', and as a result, commemoration of Strummer's death now often involves money being raised for JGD.

He's been into around 50 prisons in the UK since then, initially using the contacts he'd made with the Home Office and the Ministry of Justice while Labour were still in power. He struck deals with British manufacturer Tanglewood and the international Gibson Guitar Corporation, and found like-minded axefolk everywhere. 'You don't have to explain it to musicians twice – they get it straight away.'

Billy has met some 'incredible musicians' inside, perhaps none more so than Leon Walker in Dartmoor, a recovering heroin addict and repeat offender since the age of 17, and the only person Billy ever met in a prison who had heard of him. Since getting out, Walker has forged a nascent career in music, playing Glastonbury's Left Field (which Billy started curating in 2010) and Greenbelt. He has been the star 'graduate' of the scheme.

In 2009, the US chapter was launched by Wayne Kramer, founder of seminal Detroit agit-rockers MC5 and very much the right man for the job, having been locked up in the 1970s for drug possession and immortalised in the original Clash lyric: 'Let me tell you 'bout Wayne and his deals of cocaine'. A dedicated activist, now in his sixties, and a veteran prison lecturer about narcotic abuse, he had previous links with California's powerful prison service union CCPOA ('representing the men and woman who walk the toughest beat in the state'), so, like Billy, 'he knew exactly who to call'.

On 2 May 2009, Billy accompanied Kramer and 'a bunch of rock'n'roll reprobates' including Perry Farrell, Gilby Clarke of Guns N' Roses, Tom Morello and Jerry Cantrell from Alice In Chains to New York's maximum security facility Sing Sing, and JGD USA was born. 'To say it was memorable would be a massive understatement,' Kramer blogged for the *Huffington Post*. He's been to countless penitentiaries since, delivering what one reviewer called 'weapons of peace' to inmates. Billy looks upon this as 'seeding the system'.

Raising money to rehabilitate convicted criminals is not a clear-cut black and white issue – certainly not one that Phil Collins would have touched with a bargepole in the 1980s. But, to quote 'I Keep Faith': 'If you think you have the answer, don't be surprised if what you say is met with anger.' Billy always gets 'the same shit' about JGD, which is: why give money to the prisoners and not the victims? His response: 'I'm trying to stop there being any more victims. If we lock up these people and throw away the key we're just building a criminal class. 25 per cent of the people in our prisons should never, ever come out again, but 75 per cent are undoubtedly redeemable.'

It's an uphill redemption. A cut of 26 per cent was imposed on the Ministry of Justice after the new Tory chancellor

George Osborne's Spending Review in 2010 – that's £1.9 billion over four years – and with the resulting staff reductions, non-vocational 'luxuries' like music lessons will have been the first to go. 'It's mad, because those people who are in now are going to be out next year, and they're going to be living next door to you. Do you want them to have been fucked over in prison? Angry with society? Or do you want them to think, "Do you know what? I don't want to come back here"?' Although it's unlikely that any of them will be living next door to the future 18th Baronet of Ballentaylor and Ballylemon, George Osborne.

Having been announced as one of Q magazine's new star columnists as part of a 'stylish new look' in September 2008 – as well as host of his own show on the digital Q Radio – Billy also increased his contributions to the *Guardian*. From three columns in 2007 and six in 2008, he upped his total to a dozen in 2009, aiming his keyboard at everything from PRS and illegal filesharing to the twenty-fifth anniversary of the miners' strike. (He also commemorated this watershed moment in British industrial history with a nine-date tour of Wales, from Blaenavon to Blackwood, reminding people who didn't need reminding of the 'naked selfishness at the heart of the Thatcherite experiment'.) Contrary to the *Guardian*'s sometimes comically left-leaning editorial stance, its online readership represents the full spectrum of political opinion, and Billy does not get an easy ride 'below the line', where 'comment is free'. Always up for a free and frank exchange, Billy usually parries after publication, as long as his critics keep it clean. (Unfortunately, the anonymity afforded by the internet leads to a lot of time-wasting, mud-slinging and point-scoring from hungry trolls. Let's call them the 'clifftop mansion' brigade.)

He kicked off 2010 with a particularly striking demonstration of standing up and being bean-counted. Headline: 'Why I'm withholding my tax.'

Having been awakened, politically, by the lack of love and justice shown by the Thatcher government – shockingly, not even a distant, dismal memory to first-time voters in this election year, Billy found he had plenty on his plate with the assorted failures and betrayals of New Labour. He'd been pragmatically pro the bank bailout of 2008 when world financial markets collapsed as a result of America's subprime-mortgage bubble ('If the money had stopped coming out of the cashpoints it would have had a terrible effect on millions of ordinary working people'), but when our government used taxpayers' money to underwrite those institutions considered 'too big to fail', such as the emblematically footloose Royal Bank of Scotland, it failed to follow through and curb bankers' bonuses. Billy had 'a right cob on' about this one.

'I'm not paying my taxes so you can pay for those bastards. The free marketeers base their argument on Adam Smith's "invisible hand", which is basically that if you leave the market be, the good will prosper and the bad will fall by the wayside. But the idea that the free market will solve all our problems is over. To carry on with business as usual and deny that the Thatcherite paradigm of the last 30 years is broken, that made me so angry.'

Angry enough to take to Speaker's Corner in Hyde Park ('a place where dissent can be freely expressed'), where he delivered a rousing oratory on a chilly February morning – filmed, of course – and announced that he was 'breaking the habit of a lifetime' by declining to pay his Income Tax. Quoting unlikely allies like Governor of the Bank of England Mervyn King and super-financier George Soros, Billy presented the bank-bonus situation as untenable, and the paying of tax as an 'expression of social solidarity'. He reminded his audience that RBS was now 84 per cent owned by the people, and that its Chief Executive had justified an estimated £1.5bn bonus bill to a Treasury Select Committee by saying that he was a 'prisoner of the market'.

Having made some much-needed noise, and drawn attention to the problem, Billy filed his tax late and was fined for his troubles. The lesson being: there is no talking with the taxman.

The general election held on 6 May was effectively an overdue vote of no-confidence in the New Labour project; an appetite for change seemed tangible, but it was no foregone conclusion. Billy voted Liberal Democrat, again tactically – the Lib Dems were the only side with a hope of worrying

Oliver Letwin in West Dorset but with a clearer heart. 'I did think there was a lot of good stuff in their manifesto that wasn't in Labour's' – not least scrapping Trident and university tuition fees – 'And nobody ever told me I was a traitor to the cause for voting Liberal Democrat so I did what I always do. I would've thought long and hard before voting Labour anyway; they'd run their course.'

Billy exercised his democratic right by postal vote, because, instead of being in Dorset, he found himself in London for April and May, performing in a musical capacity in the play *Pressure Drop* at the Wellcome Collection gallery on London's Euston Road. Named after the Maytals' 1969 reggae perennial, written by Irishman Mick Gordon and directed by Christopher Haydon for the On Theatre group, it looked at belonging and identity among the white working class as a fictionalised far-right party tries to take over an old industrial town in East London. 'Part play, part gig, part installation', it unfolded across three stages representing pub, living room and chapel; on the fourth stage, Billy Bragg and his band, playing songs old ('All You Fascists') and new ('Home', 'There Will Be A Reckoning'). With the audience encouraged to move around the space during the play, Billy acted as host, MC and crowd marshal.

The space was filled; the reviews were good. The *Telegraph* said it addressed the subject of immigration 'with honesty and clarity', *The Stage* praised the 'power, anger and thoughtfully crafted lyrics' of Billy's songs, and, most pertinently, the London *Evening Standard* wrote, 'Gordon's muscular script . . . is far too sophisticated to descend into a Nick Griffin-bashing rant.'

Musical theatre's least likely new diva may have been treading the boards by night, but by day he was walking the streets of Barking and Dagenham trying to convince people not to vote for the sadly non-fictional BNP, whose *ubergruppenführer* and MEP for North West England, Nick Griffin, had taken it upon himself to stand for election in Billy's old backyard. It was such a shock, he remembers exactly where he was when he heard the news: 'Eating my tea at 7p.m. in a hotel room in St John's, Nova Scotia, via the World Service on the internet. I did this apoplectic gig in St John's. BNP: fucking bastards. I really took it personally.'

After its council victories in 2006, the BNP now considered Barking to be its citadel, so Dorset's loss was Essex's gain as Billy channelled all his energies into helping formidable pro-diversity, anti-extremism civil rights campaign group HOPE Not Hate keep the fascists out – and in particular to kybosh their plans to 'take the council'. He kipped at his mum's.

During an often hot-tempered run-up, Billy had 'a couple of close encounters' with Barking's deputy council leader and London Assembly member Richard Barnbrook. Out leafleting on a HOPE Not Hate day of action, during which 541 volunteers delivered 91,000 copies of the group's newspaper, he found himself up Barnbrook's perhaps symbolic cul-de-sac and came face to face with his nemesis. A finger-pointing clash of the titans took place, surrounded by cameras and a film crew, and a loud cheer went up when Billy said, 'I'll be back, Mr Barnbrook.' (It's all on YouTube, naturally.)

Beyond the jostling for council seats, this was the first general election since 1979 where all three main parties fielded a new leader, two of them seemingly genetically modified from the blandly approachable, centrist Blair helix. But no clear winner emerged. The Tories, under former director of corporate affairs for a media conglomerate David Cameron, failed to achieve a majority; Labour, under Gordon Brown, a man whose campaign had been hijacked by a little old lady in Rochdale, sustained the predicted 'bloody nose', losing 91 seats; and the Lib Dems, under Nick Clegg, endorsed by the *Guardian* and inflated with optimism after 'winning' the first TV debate – out of which Brown's repeated refrain, 'I agree with Nick', became an internet meme, a mug and a T-shirt – limped in third.

The resulting hung parliament meant that, in Billy's words, Brown was wearing 'dead man's shoes'. He resigned on 11 May, uncharacteristically smiling with relief, as it emerged that the Tories had done a deal with the Lib Dems. This unexpected coalition was consummated in the Rose Garden at Number 10 a day later. Edvard Munch had painted the reaction of many of us back in 1893.

Having unwittingly voted in a Tory government by attempting to vote out a Tory MP (Letwin actually increased his share by 1.1 per cent), Billy was put in a very difficult public position, as he no longer agreed with Nick, many of whose manifesto promises would soon be worth less than the paper they were printed on. 'The outcome has laid me open to a great deal of criticism, as if I voted in favour of what the coalition are doing! The very tribal Labour people still don't grasp why nobody wanted to vote for them any more.'

Billy had a certain amount of time for new Labour leader Ed Miliband, endorsed by grandees like Kinnock in the leadership election and victorious over his less cuddly older brother David thanks mostly to the support of six major trade unions: 'He genuinely has a grasp of the problems, but he doesn't seem to be willing to pull the levers that might generate the change people are looking for.'

It wasn't all bad news on election day 2010. The BNP lost every single seat they had. 'The blow that was struck in Barking and Dagenham has proved terminal for the BNP. Even left to their own devices, we can trust our neighbours – they are still capable of recognising an arsehole when they see one. They made me proud to come from there.' Mr Barnbrook has since left the BNP and retired from politics in 2012.

Whether or not Cameron's Tories were worse than Thatcher's is something we could hotly debate if we weren't so busy trying to pay our bills, find an open library and adjust to suddenly commonplace concepts like 'the working poor' and 'food banks'.

Neil Kinnock's premonition from 1983 echoes around a nation eviscerated by cuts: 'I warn you not to be ordinary. I warn you not to be young. I warn you not to fall ill. I warn you not to get old.' Council leaders predicted 'civil unrest' if Osborne's raids on the public sector continued. (He stepped down as an MP in the 2017 general election to run the London *Evening Standard*, replaced at the treasury by the greyest of grey men Philip Hammond.) Meanwhile, over the pond, the 'HOPE' embodied by Barack Obama was dashed time and again by a Republican house. If nothing else, it ought to be a boom time for political singer-songwriters.

The financial crash saw belts tightened all round. Juliet's design business suffered when the market for high-end, boutique refits faltered. This sharpened the resolve at Barton Olivers to turn Bragg Central into a home-run cottage industry, with Juliet bringing not just her years in the music industry to the table but also her design skills. Her and Billy's appropriation of the means of production coincided with the ever-energetic Pete Jenner slipping into a more comfortable 'consultative role', busier as he was with the Music Managers Forum ('going around the world talking to people about copyright'). While Juliet gave operations a facelift, Billy took over his own Facebook page and Twitter feed, cutting out further intermediaries. ('My internet profile has never been higher. *Bloomberg* commissioned me to write something about the Leveson Report because they follow me on Twitter.')

Once Jack left school and started sixth-form college in Yeovil, staying with mates for three days a week, Mum and Dad had more time on their hands, and this was one surefire way of filling it. 'We're independent, we're free, and we've never worked so hard in our fucking lives.'

They work in an industry no longer defined by physical product or the best-laid plans of record companies. When they put out the box sets in 2006, cardboard was still just about recognised as a suitable case for music. By 2011, Billy had enough download-only singles from ten years of cutting out the middle man to fill a pugnacious, self-released compilation, *Fight Songs*. This included 'The Price Of Oil', an acoustic condemnation of the real reasons behind the Allied invasion of Iraq ('the Stock Market holds the answer to "Why him, why here, why now?"'), given away free in December 2002, to 'Never Buy *The Sun*', a rapid reaction to the tabloid phone-hacking scandal of 2011 whose rallying cry, 'Scousers never buy the *Sun*', later chimed with a reversal of fortunes for the Hillsborough Families Support Group after a damning independent report. Such bulletins are now just a click away on the rebooted Billy Bragg website.

Billy's tenth solo album, *Tooth & Nail*, says everything about the leaner, meaner business model he and Juliet have worked so hard to establish. Traditionally, Pete would have been 'signing the cheques' while an album was recorded, putting an arm's length between cost and the creative process. Not any more. *Tooth & Nail* was self-financed, and recorded in five days in a basement without telling anybody. 'The idea of making it over a long time and spending a lot of money was no longer viable. Now we need to make a record and be able to afford to tour it. Otherwise it's just pissing it away down the money-hole.' The net creative gain has been healthy, too.

In September 2010, it had been optimistically announced that Billy's next album would be a collaboration with country queen Roseanne Cash, Johnny's daughter, and the alt-rock singer-songwriter and prolific producer Joe Henry, Detroit-raised but now based in Pasadena, California. Henry had united the pair for a 'song cycle' he curated and produced at the international Ludwigsburger Schlossfestspiele festival in Germany, and they'd vowed to record together.

For prosaic contractual reasons, that album was not to be, but Billy and Joe kept the plate spinning, and *Tooth & Nail* took shape 'under the radar' at Joe's home studio in January 2012. Joe regards five days as the optimum time for making a record. He tells me that, initially, Billy was 'a tad reticent of that timeline', but was quickly seduced by Joe's thesis that 'musicians discovering songs together in real time increases the odds of the songs feeling fresh and alive'.

Ever after Wilco and the Blokes, this was a brand new way of working. Billy sang and used his guitar mainly as a prop-cum-comfort blanket, surrendering himself to the dreamily unobtrusive, always sympathetic accompaniment of Joe's trusted collaborators: idiosyncratic drummer Jay Bellerose, Greg Leisz on guitar, lap and pedal steel and mandolin, David Piltch on upright and electric bass, and Patrick Warren on piano, pump organ, autoharp and additional keyboards. After the Blokes, let's call them the Dudes.

Like *Mermaid Avenue*, for self-evident reasons, the result feels like an American record, although Billy keeps it half-English, especially on the endearingly homespun 'Handyman Blues', a comic lament to his own impracticality ('It takes me half an hour to change a fuse'). His voice has never been better: high and delicate on the opener 'January Song' ('touch me and you'll hear me sing'), raw on 'Goodbye Goodbye', impassioned on *Pressure Drop* refugee 'There Will Be a Reckoning', which harks back to Mr Barnbrook's cul-de-sac.

The lyrics are broader but laser-guided, and peppered with evocative imagery: a burning bush, spinning atoms and a coffee pot gone cold. There's a talismanic Woody cover, too, *I Ain't Got No Home*, which feels in tune with a general case of homesickness.

Though country-tinged, it might be described as his 'soul album', or simply his 'roots album'; certainly, its sad songs say a lot about a world in crisis, but venture a glass-half-full positivity to the 'chorus of complaint', not least on manifesto sign-off 'Tomorrow's Going to Be a Better Day'. The plaintive whistling reminds us that, for all the stylings of Americana, he's still the milkman. Bear that in mind as Billy tours *Tooth & Nail* across the States with a brand new band and the self-written brief of progressing the way he is perceived there.

Joe makes this assessment: 'Billy is a hero to many here in America, and I believe that historically he's heard in a much broader context than perhaps he is in England. I sometimes feel that his work on behalf of truth and justice and his reputation as a political songwriter has allowed some to miss just how deep is his song craft – and just how broad his canvas really is.'

The melancholy mood of *Tooth & Nail* was inevitably informed by the sad and sudden death of Marie Bragg on 18 March 2011, another one of life's markers that Billy admits it took time to fully process.

In 'January Song', he sings, 'Tidy up the place for Monday, when she's buried in her dancing shoes', while 'Goodbye Good-bye' bids a more literal final farewell: 'The time has come for me to go . . . the bells have all been rung, the songs have all been sung'.

'The album isn't *about* what happened, but it comes out of that experience, It's connected to Mum's passing in the sense that it made me think: You know what? I need to get back on and ride the bloody horse.'

He admits to 'a catharsis' at the end of 2011. 'Going away to make the record allowed me to come up for air at the end of it, with something in my hand to go and do.'

In January 2011, Marie, still as active, fleet-footed and indomitable as she'd always been, was admitted to hospital with abdominal pains. 'Completely out of the blue', the doctors discovered that pancreatic cancer had spread into her liver and beyond. If the grim prognosis bore any kind of consolation, it was that Marie was *compos mentis* for most of her last month, able not just to make peace with her family and friends, but to stage-manage her funeral with 'a steely determination'. She would have put the placemats out herself if she could, Billy half-jokes.

Though shocked to be bed-bound – she had been doing four dancing clubs a week with her new partner Reg – her stoic attitude was, 'OK, this is where we are, let's do this.' She wanted the arrival of her coffin accompanied by what Billy describes as 'a really naff line-dancing song called "Hillbilly Rock Hillbilly Roll" by a country and western band from Leicester'. She also requested Billy sing 'that song' – 'Tank Park Salute', inspired by the death of his Dad – a tall emotional order. He said to her, 'It's hard enough singing that anyway, now every time I play it I'm going to think about you and your funeral.' She said, 'Good.'

Thronged with around 140 people, the chapel at the crematorium was so full, Wiggy's Dad couldn't get in. At the wake, there was a queue 'out of the door' for the tea urn. Billy pleaded with the organiser, 'I can't run out of tea at Marie Bragg's funeral.'

In common with the other women in her family, Marie had never told anyone her age, and the plaque in the memorial garden simply bears the year of her death. Billy said a few words, breaking the ice with the in-joke, 'My Mum packed a lot into her 29 years . . .'

Having Tweeted about his Mum's passing ('After a long and active life and a short illness, my mother Marie passed away yesterday, surrounded by her family'), he was nonetheless overwhelmed by the thousand or so condolences posted by fans on his Facebook page. It took him a while to read them all.

Fortuitously, Marie had been present at Billy's last gig of 2010 at the Troxy, a refurbished art deco cinema in Stepney, where she used to go to the pictures as a girl. But it was doubly significant.

Jack, on the cusp of turning seventeen and with his own taste for rock'n'roll, had been out on the road, 'hanging out with the support band' after Billy had gone to bed. So, when Wiggy got up to guest on 'A13' at the Troxy, so did Jack, making his live debut. He got into it, throwing shapes, affecting a solo, even throwing his plectrum into the audience. As the last gig Marie ever attended, it was made magical for seeing her son and grandson playing together.

Jack was becoming a chip off the old Bloke, although Billy stresses that he never taught him to play. It all started at the *NME* Awards in 2008, when Jack was fourteen. Billy was there to perform a pan-generational duet with BRIT School-trained, Myspace-enabled singer-songwriter Kate Nash. A mash-up road-tested in January at the Big Day Out festivals in Australia, they segued her DIY number two smash 'Foundations' into 'New England', complementing each other charmingly. (He made her laugh by adapting a line to reference her still-warm Best Female Artist Brit award.)

As with the other VIPs, Billy was let loose in a room full of freebies, 'shirts and shoes and shit' that didn't appeal. But he spotted *Guitar Hero* for the Xbox and took that home for Jack.

An instrumental karaoke game, players simulate onscreen rhythms and riffs using a guitar-shaped controller for points. He hoped that he and Jack might be able to play it together.

'I don't know shit about videogames – I'm the wrong generation for that – so Jack set it up and showed me what to do, and the first couple of days, I kept beating him on the remedial level. He couldn't get it. He was hating it!'

As might any fourteen-year-old being thrashed by his dad. 'Eventually, instead of sitting behind me, he sat beside the telly and watched me. And then the next day, he beat me.'

Once Junior had pulled ahead of Senior, there was no looking back; Jack completed all the levels while Billy was stuck on the first. 'The next thing I know, some of his mates are coming round and he wants to get my amps out.'

After *Guitar Hero*, a standard-bearer for the educational potential of videogames, Jack quickly graduated to strumming along on a real guitar to 'Baba O'Reilly'. Billy showed him 'where to put his fingers' for 'Blitzkrieg Bop', and that was the last song he helped him with, after which his hand was invisible. 'He just went, like a rocket.'

Jack's first band, a three-piece, were initially called Teenage Wasteland – a nod to rock heritage that would make any modern parent proud, and indicative of Jack's sure grasp of musical history – but changed it to RPM, another heartwarmingly retro allusion from a generation supposedly defined by the iTunes Store and Justin Bieber.

Dad was initially banned from RPM's gigs, only hearing them live through the kitchen wall when they rehearsed in the garage. Some impressive, professionally-recorded demos followed, and although allowably self-conscious about his famous dad – Jack has adopted Juliet's surname Valero for the official bio – music continually provides father-son bonding opportunities, whether it's sitting down to watch house-favourite pub-rock documentary *Oil City Confidential*, or stand- ing in the drizzle at Camp Bestival to see an 82-year-old Chuck Berry duckwalk his way through the hits. Billy worked out that Chuck Berry was about as old as his own father would've been. Cat Stevens had a song for it.

Jack was nineteen at the end of 2012, taking a one-year foundation in filmmaking at Bournemouth, then straight off to the British and Irish Modern Music Institute (BIMM) in Brighton to complete a songwriting diploma while also getting his band, now expanded to The RPMs, off the ground. It was beginning to feel a lot like the Circle of Life. Starting 2018 as a Huw Stephens tip on Radio 1, getting plays on 6 Music and Radio X (formerly XFM, who gave the band their first live radio session) and booked for South by Southwest, Jack ensures that the family business rolls on. Fortuitously or otherwise, Jack today looks the spitting image of the young Billy Bragg – although he may not thank you for pointing that out.

19. A HUG AT THE T-SHIRT STALL

*Recharging the activism of the converted,
2013–2018*

Now is the most political time I've lived in
— Billy Bragg, Oxford, 2017

On Sunday 30 March 2013, just a few days after Liberal Democrat minister Chris Huhne admitted to perverting the course of justice over some speeding points, Billy Bragg's tenth studio album, *Tooth & Nail,* motored up the hard shoulder into the Official UK Albums chart at number 13, that week's third-highest new entry. The second highest was *Bloodsports* by Suede, the Britpop dandies who'd reconvened after a seven-year hiatus. Billy, an artist who'd never split up nor felt the need to re-form, sat between multi-million-selling public-school folkies Mumford & Sons and fellow traveller Jake Bugg. After three weeks in the chart, *Tooth & Nail* was hailed as his most successful solo record since the 1990s, when *Don't Try This at Home* charted at number eight and *William Bloke* at sixteen. The twenty-first century was looking up, even if not for Huhne, who, after two months in prison, ended up with his face on a cracked pot designed by Braintree College-educated Grayson Perry, garlanded by a repeat motif of penises. Huhne was described by the eccentric potter as 'Default Man'. This would be a description the fifty-something Billy Bragg would work hard to avoid in the next stage of his story.

Buoyed by this refreshed profile and wider affirmation, Billy 'pushed the boat out – well, the bus,' and put in more gigs in 2013 than he had since the late 1980s, including an unprecedented thirteen weeks in the USA with the *Tooth & Nail* band: 'Having made an album I wanted people to hear, I needed to reconnect with that audience who had loved *Mermaid Avenue*.' Sufficiently self-aware to know that his more Anglocentric records made life difficult for the marketing department of his American label, Elektra, Billy wanted to nurture what he calls 'a bit of a vibe in that Americana space,' which harks all the way back to the 'Ry Cooder-ish' sound of 'The Tatler', the 1986, 12-inch B-side of 'Greetings to the New Brunette', and an American version of 'Power in a Union', with John Porter on mandolin. Defining Americana as 'Country music for people who like The Smiths,' he was confident people would get it: 'I've always been genre-fluid.'

He clocked up 102 gigs in 2013 (compared to 70 the year before, and 54 the year before that, and has the spreadsheets to prove it). The tour, which followed the time-honoured trajectory of 'all around the houses', ended in May 2014, at what we old soldiers still refer to as London's Hammersmith Odeon, at the time of writing known as the Eventim Apollo, with Devonian fiddler Seth Lakeman in support and a fond, poetic introduction by Phill Jupitus. 'We had a really good time,' Billy recalls. 'The big question was: what do I do next?' To which the big answer turned out to be: write another book. A book that would in turn lead to another record.

In between, there was a song in a film. Released in September 2014, *Pride* conjured a very British comedy-drama out of the miners' strike, with specific focus on London-formed action and fundraising group LGSM (Lesbians and Gays Support the Miners) who 'twinned' with pit villages in Wales. Thanks to a witty, empathic script by actor Stephen Beresford, its *Full Monty/Kinky Boots* exuberance and a cast of reassuring household names (Bill Nighy, Dominic West, Imelda Staunton), it found a mainstream audience. One of its great cultural muster points was the climactic rendition of

'There is Power in a Union' over the closing captions. The main protagonist is a real-life founder of the group, Mark Ashton (played by Ben Schnetzer). 'I actually knew him, he was part of Red Wedge,' says Billy. 'An amazing guy, and the first person I knew who died of HIV/Aids. So, at the end of the film, when they started flashing up what everyone had done, I knew what was coming. It was overwhelming.'

Billy was pleased with the part his collectivist anthem played. 'In some ways, for me, it was a great justification. Both Juliet and Jack take the piss out of me in old photographs where I've got my jumper tucked in my jeans, but in the film a guy gets up on the table to speak and he's got his jumper tucked in his jeans. I was poking Jack's ribs, going, "See? That's what we were doing back then!"'

You had to go further back to find the seeds of what would bloom into *Roots, Rockers and Radicals: How Skiffle Changed the World*, Billy's skiffle book. His fascination with skiffle was long-held – he'd made a Radio 4 documentary about key exponent Ken Colyer, played at the Lonnie Donegan memorial, and written a long piece for the *Guardian* in 2004 on the fiftieth anniversary of the recording of 'Rock Island Line', marking the date in 1954 when Chris Barber's Jazz Band assembled in Studio Two, Broadhurst Gardens in northwest London and ran out of repertoire for a planned jazz LP. It was Donegan's idea to 'do a bit of skiffle' and history was sealed. The postwar recovery's newly christened teenagers made 'Rock Island Line' a hit and, as Billy wrote, 'Donegan's music put a guitar into the hand of every working-class lad in the land.' There was a book here bursting to get out.

Billy had never been happy with the accepted skiffle narrative, which runs as if 'Rock Island Line' arrived 'like a singularity' in the mid-1950s. While he rates musician Chas McDevitt's *Skiffle: The Definitive Inside Story* (1997, revised in 2013) and Mike Dewe's *The Skiffle Craze* (1998), 'none of them get to the heart of the moment it happens'. In Billy's view, even Bob Stanley's appealing history, *Yeah, Yeah, Yeah: The Story of Modern Pop* (2013), glosses over skiffle. 'I'm, like, come on, Bob! Everything that comes later, all the music you love, wouldn't be there if it weren't for skiffle.' So, he set out to square the circle.

Because writing *The Progressive Patriot* had been 'a real struggle', Billy began work without announcing it to anyone, tucking himself away in the afternoons in the study. He began to navigate by using Pete Frame's *The Restless Generation: How Rock Music Changed the Face of 1950s Britain* (2011) as his North Star. During a family holiday in the World Cup summer of 2014, Billy left Juliet and Jack on the beach and stayed indoors, making notes and 'trying to pick up threads'. Then Faber got in touch with the idea of producing a Billy Bragg lyric book: would he choose the songs and write 30,000 words of commentary? He couldn't resist. The result, *A Lover Sings: Selected Lyrics,* was published in hardback in November 2015 and exquisitely presented, as if it were an anthology of poetry by Houseman or Cummings. It acted as an illuminated guide: 'Some of the politics in the songs from the 1980s are not easily recognisable to someone who was born in the 1980s.' A classic example is 'Moving the Goalposts', which casually references Gennadi Gerasimov ('Once in a while, he drops his smile'), who was Mikhail Gorbachev's foreign affairs spokesman, and a truly obscure footnote from history.

During discussions with Faber, Billy eventually piped up, 'Oh, and by the way, I've written 20,000 words about skiffle. Would you like to have a look at that?' They did, and ordered up a further 80,000 words.

Projects in Billy Bragg's experience rarely go uninterrupted, and in August, when he was really getting into writing his archaeological excavation of the tea-chest bass, the august American photography journal *Aperture* asked if he'd be interested in working on a photo-essay to celebrate the ninetieth birthday of venerable Swiss-American photographer Robert Frank, who'd been on the road with Kerouac and produced *The Americans* in 1958. With his 'skiffle hat' on, Billy suggested travelling to Rock Island, Illinois, with Magnum-affiliated Minnesotan photographer Alec Soth, who'd been compared to Walker Evans, legendary documenter of the Great Depression in his 1941 book, *Let Us Now Praise Famous Men*, with text by James Agee.

With Billy serving as the Agee to Soth's Evans, they followed the Rock Island line to Little Rock, Arkansas, where the song was originally written by employees of the Chicago,

Rock Island and Pacific Railroad, and on to the local Tucker prison farm, where folklorist John Lomax made a field recording of it with Huddie 'Lead Belly' Ledbetter as his *de facto* roadie. Our intrepid twenty-first-century folklorists went to the old Rock Island station, these days only open to passengers from midnight to 3a.m., when two trains pass through from Chicago and LA. The rest is freight. Soth took photos at midnight and shot video of Billy performing the folk tune 'Midnight Special', recorded in 1926 by Dave 'Pistol Pete' Cutrell, but popularised by Lead Belly in 1934. Chatting to a porter, Billy discovered that Little Rock's platform is effectively used as a siding for the dominant goods trains. Billy had a lightbulb moment in the beautifully tiled 1920s-built station building with its glorious acoustics and ancient history, and the next record flickered into life.

Billy needed a wingman for this special project. He thought of Joe Henry, not only a musician he knew he could work with, but, by now a 'dear friend'. He's the kind of producer who leaves the windows open in his basement studio in Pasadena and lets the street sounds in, and it was this set-up-and-play immediacy that the wheeze that became *Shine a Light* required. 'I didn't have to explain it to him twice,' Billy reports, with satisfaction.

The skiffle book was temporarily parked, although nothing is wasted in the life of Billy Bragg, and a timely journey into what Greil Marcus called 'the old, weird America' dovetailed into the musical and the literary. Billy presented the idea for *Shine a Light* to Cooking Vinyl and they got it. Not exactly a 'concept album' (they are dread words to an old punk): Billy saw it instead as 'a narrative record', an anthology of great American railroad songs. Now all he had to do was get this latest show on the road, or rather the railroad.

In the event, it was relatively straightforward and not expensive. Billy and Joe flew to Chicago with *Tooth & Nail* engineer Ryan Freeland, bought tickets at Union Station, and boarded the Texas Eagle to Los Angeles. They didn't seek permission: they were just two guys playing guitar at stations into a microphone set-up which was a distant cousin of the old Portastack. Covering 2,278 miles over 65 hours, and banking thirteen songs in their own personal library of congress, they 'tried not to get in people's faces', and if a crowd formed naturally, so be it. Joe described the experience as feeling 'beautifully and anomalously invisible'. There was little trouble, except at the spanking-new terminus in Fort Worth, Texas, where they were moved on for fear of blocking a thoroughfare in front of three beautiful murals depicting African-American culture.

The resulting album – full title: *Shine a Light: Field Recordings from the Great American Railroad* – was a triumph; something completely different, but entirely *simpatico*. Billy's fans didn't need it explaining twice either, and it entered the Top 30 on 6 October 2016, in the same week casually topping the UK Americana chart, which launched in January. While Dave Simpson in the *Guardian* erred on the side of caution with a three-star review, he admitted that 'it sounds like a lot of fun'. He also commented on Billy's yodeling, which became a high point of the subsequent live shows that stretched from September to April 2017, across the States, Canada, UK, Ireland and Australia. This major roll-out saw Billy and Joe grow into an increasingly symbiotic power couple for the future.

A busy 2016 had begun with the broadcast in January of the docudrama *Death or Liberty*. Based on the book by Tony Moore, associate professor of communications and media studies at Monash University, and erstwhile programme-maker for the Australian Broadcast Corporation (ABC), it looked at the way the British government transported its own political dissidents to prison colonies in Van Diemen's Land between 1793 and 1867. 'They weren't all sheep-stealers,' notes Billy, who was asked to write songs for the film alongside old mate Mick Thomas of Weddings, Parties, Anything, and Irish troubadour Lisa O'Neil, performing them at Hobart's Royal Theatre in January 2015. The film showed that Britain also exported Chartists, trade unionist, Fenians and 'some crazy Americans who'd tried to invade Canada'.

Back in the former Empire that had purged them, a new English rebel stirred, one who was, like Billy, bearded and bolshie. After the Tory election victory in May 2015, caused, Billy believes, by 'the absolute collapse of the Liberal Democrat Party – they danced with the devil and pissed on their chips,' Labour leader Ed Miliband (or, to give him his full title, 'Poor old Ed') resigned. The expected struggle for the centre of the left of centre began. Except it didn't follow the script. Come the Labour leadership election in June, an anti-austerity, whip-defying back-bencher, committed socialist and rank outsider with the look of Obi-Wan Kenobi became Labour's 'only hope'.

Billy had been sharing platforms with Jeremy Corbyn, the 67-year-old MP for Islington North, for years. But nobody, even those who knew him (*especially* those who knew him!) foresaw his name on a leadership ballot, never mind being chanted by the youth to the tune of 'Seven Nation Army' by the White Stripes: 'Oh, Jer-e-my Corbyn!' Ed's one great legacy was the introduction of the inclusive '£3 member' scheme, through which supporters could join Labour for the price of a latte and have their say. Due to an unprecedented surge of young millennials, the old man suddenly looked dangerous. 'Corbyn started to come on strong, and I thought, this could actually be quite interesting,' remembers Billy.

The final straw for Blairite candidates Andy Burnham, Yvette Cooper and Liz Kendall was Banquo's ghost, Tony Blair, arriving at the wedding – actually, a meeting held by think tank Progress – to say, 'If your heart is with Corbyn's politics, get a transplant.' This proved a red rag. Though Billy didn't attend any of Corbyn's famously rammed, adoring rallies, he spoke to people who did. Photographer Pete Dunwell saw him in Lincoln and 'came back like he'd had a religious experience'. It was like Red Wedge without a guitar. When Burnham, Cooper and Kendall cynically abstained from voting against what Corbyn had called the 'rotten and indefensible' Welfare Reform and Work Bill in July, they may as well have flown the white flag.

On 12 September, Corbyn won by a 40.5 per cent majority. It was the largest mandate ever for a British party leader. By coincidence, Billy was onstage at a demo in support of asylum seekers in Parliament Square when the result was announced, and the newly anointed leader came down. 'I'm doing my bit,' Billy recalls. 'And he's there, to say a few words.' A community rendition of 'The Red Flag' ensued, not a hit many Labour leaders post-Blair knew by heart. Billy's immediate thought was, 'I really must rejoin the Labour

Party, because this is the politics I've always fought for and it's going to be really tough. They're going to bite his arse.' They did. Corbyn was like a chew-toy for the right-wing media that summer, until they ran out of spurious sticks to beat him with.

Billy believes the Corbyn surge is 'of a piece with the electoral results we've had since the crash in 2008 – all of them have been a vote against the centre, a rejection of the status quo. You can even see Trump in that.'

> *Not every Leave voter is a racist, but every racist will vote Leave*
> — Billy Bragg on the EU Referendum,
> Twitter, 16 June 2017

> *The British people have voted to leave the European Union and their will must be respected*
> — David Cameron on the steps of 10 Downing
> Street, 16 June 2017

Billy feels that Corbyn's crowning was 'a rejection of more of the same.' This could also be said or shouted, while brandishing a burning torch, about Brexit. Nest-feathering PM David Cameron made a manifesto promise to hold an in-out EU referendum, essentially to stop Eurosceptic Tory voters defecting to a tumescent UK Independence Party (UKIP), who'd pushed the Conservatives into third place in the 2014 European Parliament election. The referendum was a zero-sum Nigel Farage fever-dream made real, and while the government's official position was 'Remain', i.e. to stay in the EU, its campaigning was smug and half-hearted, while the ardent 'Leavers' made more noise and more claims with more ideological, xenophobic passion. Meanwhile, Labour was in chaos, with resignations from Corbyn's front bench and attempted coups, never mind bet-hedging over the EU.

'The Labour Party establishment were trying to pin the blame for the failure of "Remain" on him, which I think was unfair,' is Billy's assessment. During the Scottish independence referendum campaign in 2014, then-leader Ed Miliband shared a platform with the Tories. As a result,

Labour were wiped out in Scotland. 'Having been bitten by that dog, you can't expect Corbyn to stand up in a referendum on an issue that doesn't float his boat. He's neither in favour of the EU nor against – he thinks there are more important things to be talking about. And if that comes across like he doesn't care, that's unfortunate. I think he does care, and knows that the route to Downing Street lies in resolving the issue of Brexit.'

Billy Bragg was in his sleeping bag at Glastonbury when it was confirmed that, after a cursory glance at some headlines in the *Daily Mail*, 51.89 per cent of 33.5 million people had voted to take the United Kingdom and Gibraltar out of the European Union. Rarely had the Left Field felt more like a safe space than on that Friday. Why didn't Remainers see it coming? 'Because we have a confirmation bias in favour of the EU,' he reasons. 'We have more of an outward look about the world. And I think a lot of people who don't normally vote in general elections stepped up to have a kick of the arse of the Prime Minister.'

Billy headlined Left Field on what he declared to be 'the most divisive day in our history', after leading a memorial on the Park Stage for the murdered Labour MP Jo Cox, whose life was cut short in the summer of the referendum by a far-right constituent of Batley and Spen with psychiatric problems, a gun and a knife. 'It's going to take a lot to heal this wound,' he warned.

He describes that night's 'strange, fired-up' gig as ' . . . like triage. All these confused young people [were] having the experience we had under Thatcher, where you wake up and feel like this isn't your country any more. The noise the crowd made when I came on was the noise they usually make when I come off.' Corbyn had been booked to appear on the Sunday, but an attempted coup by shadow foreign secretary Hillary Benn had kicked off back in the Westminster bubble, and the likes of deputy leader Tom Watson and then-shadow business secretary Clive Lewis had to pack up their wellies and go back to base. Billy, *Guardian* writer and spirit guide John Harris, and economics tub-thumper Paul Mason were left to hold the fort. It was a muddy Glastonbury that year, but as nothing compared to the murky quagmire of Brexit that awaited in the real world.

Once we ruled over an empire
So it feels like some kind of defeat
To comply with rules drawn up by strangers
And measure in metres not feet

— 'Full English Brexit' *Bridges Not Walls*

'If your life has been made chaotic by austerity and an electoral system where not everybody's vote counts, you had an opportunity in 2016 to make chaotic the lives of those in charge,' Billy reasons, a year after the referendum. 'I can understand why you might want to do that, but I don't agree with it.' The shock of Brexit was compounded in November by the election of the sexist, racist, xenophobic, inarticulate, narcissistic non-politician Donald Trump in the United States.

Billy was in the DoubleTree Hotel in Islington with Joe Henry on the UK leg of the *Shine a Light* tour on the night of the US presidential election. The next night they had a show in Canterbury, and Joe didn't know how he would face the audience, as an American. Billy reassured him: 'Mate, they've just been through Brexit, they'll understand!' And so it transpired; punters gave him a hug at the T-shirt stall.

Having launched the tour at the Americana Music Festival in Nashville in September, where Billy collected the Spirit of Americana/Free Speech award, the duo found their groove on the US leg, honing the harmonies, leaving gaps for the other to speak and forging a serious double act. In the UK, Joe seemed shy initially but gradually allowed his articulacy to shine, reassured by showbiz veteran Billy that it was okay to repeat the same repartee ('I say the same shit every night like it's Shakespeare.') Their harmonious union boils down to fundamentals: Billy is a rhythm guitar player, Joe is more of a picker. The tour rolled on into Australia in 2017. For our man, it was a welcome sabbatical from what he calls, with affection, 'bash-'em-out Bragg'.

That said, he bashed out half a dozen new songs in 2017, dropping them as and when to keep up with the pace of events ('life comes at you real fast these days'), via Amazon, Apple, Spotify, Google and all the other tech giants. The Goya-inspired buzzsaw stomp 'The Sleep of Reason'; languid country-style climate-change warning 'King Tide the Sunny

Day Flood' ('We're gonna feel it far inland'); a powerful cover of Anais Mitchell's 'Why We Build the Wall'; anti-fascist lilt 'Saffiyah Smiles'; neoliberal takedown 'Not Everything That Counts Can be Counted'; and in-character music-hall ditty 'Full English Brexit'. If anyone was worried that Billy was turning into Default Man, here was the case for the defence.

The six emerged as an old-fashioned mini-LP, *Bridges Not Walls,* in November, which Billy likes to think of as a 'twenty-first-century Peel session. If you do the sort of thing I do, you're always accused of preaching to the converted, but that's absolute bollocks. I would argue I'm not doing that – I'm recharging the activism of the converted.' Brexit is no longer the elephant in the room: it is the room. Billy's plan is measured: 'If we're gonna resolve this divisive situation, we need to begin by listening to those people who don't feel this is their country any more. Why do they want things to be how they used to be? What's underneath that? It's got to start from a listening point of view, not from, "Fuck off, you racist!" We tried that for a year and it's got us nowhere.'

'I've never sold millions of records,' Billy reflects needlessly, on a day off in Oxford. 'And I certainly ain't going to make a living as an author!' He's between Cambridge Junction and the O2 Academy on the one-man-and-his-guitar *Bridges Not Walls* tour – plus occasional pedal steel and electric by the youthful C.J. Hillman, Americana Music UK's instrumentalist of the year 2017. It seems that the international live circuit will very likely always be Billy's office. He's still able to enjoy a good review (there was one after the first date in Bexhill-on-Sea that he can quote), and when in May he appeared on *Later . . . with Jools Holland* to plug his skiffle book, he found himself energised by the similarly 59-year-old Paul Weller, who was performing his new LP, *A Kind Revolution,* his thirteenth as a solo artist: 'He was so fired up. I was halfway through writing my new songs and I thought, yeah, I've got to bring some of that fire into what I do.'

As he approached the big six-o, Billy said he'd ' . . . consciously worked to hit 60 on a high and not have 60 hit me. You've got to accept you're in the third act, and you shouldn't try and look how you did 20 or 30 years ago. We're looking forward to a break in the new year, and really trying to work out how to approach the next ten.' Billy seems fit, healthy, and comfortable in his own skin and whiskers. He occasionally has a bit of trouble remembering names now, but hey, join the club.

He offers a gentle anecdote from his postponed dotage. 'After the Bluesfest in Australia up in Byron Bay, me and Joe were at the airport having a coffee and people kept coming up and saying how much they'd enjoyed the show. Thing is, they were all bald and grey, and all blokes. And I said to Joe, "Have you noticed how old my audience are?" He said, "Bill, I just notice that you've still *got* an audience."'

20. DELIVERY MAN OF HUMAN LOVE

Who is Billy Bragg, then?

I was hugely influenced by Bob Dylan but I knew fuck all about him. In the end, he turned out to be a bloke who wrote songs.

— Billy Bragg, Dublin, 1998

'Here he comes again: pop's political conscience in his dilapidated trousers and sensible shoes, worthily correcting the unenlightened and uplifting the downtrodden with his unsubtle songs and unlovely voice . . . '

Thus ran the intro to an intended hatchet job back in the October 1991 issue of *Q* — 'Who the Hell Does Billy Bragg Think He Is?' The magazine's 'Who the Hell?' slot was as old as the publication itself, a much-loved monthly assassination of some media tart, usually from outside of music (Edwina Currie, Jeremy Beadle, Eddie 'The Eagle' Edwards). This month, however, it was Billy Bragg who was in for a lashing from its hitman, the late Tom Hibbert.

Unusually for both section and writer, it was a 0–0 draw. Hibbert managed to rile Billy once or twice, for instance over the suggestion that his lack of image was contrived, but no real points were scored. Hibbert was even forced to admit, 'He's a charmer. Hard to dislike' (this from a writer whose love of the rich and famous knew no beginnings). Furthermore, Billy sussed that he was being 'prepared' for that notorious section of the magazine. 'So, who the hell do I think I am, Tom?' he asked. 'I don't suppose you really know, because you come and see me for two hours and, no offence, Tom, but you're just peeking through the keyhole. Peeking through the keyhole.'

It was a fair point, although not one Hibbert would've conceded from the mouth of, say, a pompous Radio 1 DJ or a humourless Ringo Starr in similar Who the Hell? articles. Billy was a bad commission — not only has he never wallowed in self-publicity, nor put his own celebrity before his art, he's an honest man. If he has a major fault, it's that he's all too aware of his minor faults.

The Q piece did throw up a problem, though, one that has continued to dog him into this century. Is Billy Bragg – a sort of leftwing Santa – too good to be true?

The Teflon troubadour has been in the business of making music for more than 40 years now, during which time he's made countless friends and only a smattering of enemies, and then only ideological ones (Theresa Gorman, the East German authorities, Our Price Records, Oliver Letwin, George Galloway, Richard Barnbrook, various members of the constabulary, certain newspapers). The abiding impression that people who meet Billy take away with them is 'nice bloke'. He prefers 'straightforward bloke'; like a certain equally enduring wood stain, he does exactly what he says on the tin. You might think that a man with such lofty political ideals would snort at a legacy so bland and inauspicious, but for Billy Bragg, straightforwardness and blokeness not only have their place in a cruel, dishonest world, but a uniquely persuasive power, too. During Old Labour's darkest years in the 1980s, young voters would never have ear-bashed local MPs if it weren't for the nod from that affable, humorous, straightforward bloke on stage. If you want to plant a metaphorical bomb at the Last Night of The Proms, get a nice, straightforward bloke to figuratively carry it in. Jeremy Corbyn understands the power of approachability and telling it true, and he's why Billy rejoined the Labour Party in 2015 after 25 years.

In the 1990s, when the sun came up and the last punk rocker had been replaced at the NME, Billy found a niche appearing on television discussion shows, where his straight-forward bloke persona smuggled a resonant voice of dissent onto our screens. He has always known how to use the media to his advantage (or to the advantage of his cause), an extension of his acute ability to set political rhetoric to a tune and make 'gold dust' out of what's in the papers. Remember when Our Price threatened to remove his £3.99 album from their racks – but only once it had dropped out of the chart? That's the dichotomy of revolutionary art: it's either too dangerous to be seen and heard by the masses, or else it's sanitised in order to reach a wider audience. When Billy Bragg gets it right – 'Between the Wars' on *Top of The Pops*; 'Just because you're gay, I won't turn you away' on a Radio One Roadshow; a singalong of 'Never Buy the *Sun*' in Liverpool; even Tacticus Braggus on *Newsnight* – he is worth a thousand hectoring extremists urinating in the wind of social media.

Would he have been on *That's Life* or inside the House of Commons if he was a horrible, unpredictable bloke? Would he have met the Queen, as he did when he was invited in 2007 to write new lyrics for Beethoven's 'Ode to Joy' and the work was premiered at a Royal gala?

Billy Bragg is a child of the revolution. He watched punk rock explode in Britain, and he took note as they picked up the pieces. For a while there, as the 1970s turned into the 1980s, it really was like punk never happened – Billy's revolution, Britain's revolution, had failed. But instead of retreating to a life of subservience and reminiscence ('What did you do in the punk wars, Daddy?'), he continued to wage his own war on want, waste and wankers. By the mid-1980s, we were with him; outside of Parliament, Billy Bragg was the most famous left-winger in the country before Ben Elton relieved him for a bit. What sport it was to parody him and mock him (Armando Iannucci's satirical news show *Friday Night Armistice* still considered him the mascot of the left in 1997, and took the rise thereupon; Bill Bailey later essayed a subtler parody with his Bragg-endorsed spoof-along 'Unisex Chipshop') – but he carried the Big-Nosed Bastard from Barking tag with good humour and even a little pride. After all, in the army, he was just a number, and at school he was just an O-Level.

Yes, his nose is big. Yes, he is from Barking, and always will be, wherever he lays his cap. But he is not a bastard. He sometimes forgets to leave enough hot water in the tank after having a bath. He has been driving a 4x4 ever since he escaped to the country. He supports West Ham (the only fault Andy Macdonald could come up with when I asked him to dish the dirt). He uses the word 'twat' and sometimes 'cunt' in unguarded moments. And his anti-smoking fervour borders on the fascistic.

But I'd like to have seen Albert Goldman get a book out of that.

It would be a swiz if, like Bob Dylan, Billy Bragg had turned out to be just a bloke who wrote songs. But while Dylan has been both mythologised by his followers and subsumed by the music industry, Billy has been spared both fates, through his availability and his independence. Love or hate the songs, at least the bloke behind them is neither grisly curmudgeon nor unchallenged elder statesman. When he's on stage with a bee in his bonnet, between racing through 'A13' or barking out 'Between the Wars', it's like the last 41 years never happened. Almost. And even dedicated swallowers of fashion would have to admit, he suits the white hair and beard.

A friend once translated some of Billy's lyrics back into English from the Japanese (always a hoot). 'The Milkman of Human Kindness' came out as 'The Delivery Man of Human Love', a rather poetic adjustment. It's a pity 'I will give you an extra pint' became 'I will give you an extra portion.' Or perhaps it isn't.

Old rock stars never die, they just float themselves on the stock market, buy a farm and get Buddhism. Then they rediscover their roots and play smaller venues in order to get back in touch with their fans, a group who have naturally become more selective. Billy turned 40 in December 1997, and with that became a middle-aged rock star before the first edition of this book was published. At that time, he lived comfortably in west London (Jack was the first ever Bragg to be born outside of Essex, marking a new, cosmopolitan dawn for the family), with a holiday home on the Dorset coast. After 30-odd years living in glorified student accommodation, on other people's floors or out of a suitcase, few except a *Daily Mail* leader writer would have denied Billy Bragg a proper house with stairs and a garden and one of those nice, fitted, stainless steel kitchens.

Some shuddered when he took the plunge and moved permanently to the south coast – the, ahem, 'clifftop mansion' certainly gave ammunition to those that think socialism is about where you live, rather than how you think. But Billy's been even more engaged in grass-roots politics and community issues since he moved to Burton Bradstock. The 2001 general election saw him doorstep campaigning for the first time in his life, something he's carried forward. The *Sun* may have called him a 'country squire', but Billy still calls himself a Londoner, and when the shit went down in Barking & Dagenham, he was always there for his old manor, where, lest we forget, his nephew now lives in the old family home on Park Avenue. He keeps it in the family, too.

'I've never had the urge to wade in wonga,' he says, as if such a thing would unravel all of his good works — and maybe it would. 'Like most couples, Juliet and I put together all the money we saved and did up a nice townhouse.' Selling that townhouse enabled them to buy one beside the seaside. Both of them still work for a living – in fact, since seizing control of Billy Bragg Central with Sarah, as they've stated, 'we've never worked so hard in our lives'.

'I'm a good example of a small, self-employed businessman. I've earned all my money through my own hard work, and at 60 years old, I own my back catalogue, unlike a lot of people in my trade. I lease it out to Cooking Vinyl and they do a good job of getting it into the shops. Thanks to Pete, I have a smart deal with them so that we all make a few bob out of it.

'I pay my taxes on time' – except once, as we have seen – 'and I keep my nose clean. The big mistake of a lot of musicians, especially session musicians and people in bands who get money in lump sums, is they buy a nice house, they live in the house, and ten years later they get a big tax bill and they have to sell the house and they're not in the band anymore. It's gone.'

Billy admits he doesn't like spending money. It's a working-class thing. Just as he has hoarded cuttings, photographs and tour passes, so he's gathered a fair amount of money in 40 years. As we have seen, he could have gathered a hell of a lot more if he hadn't played so many benefits, supported so many causes, toured so many cost-ineffective Eastern Bloc countries and given £1.1 million away to the staff of Go! Discs, but the man before us would not be half as comfortable in his smart, new surroundings if he hadn't given the rest of the world 'a squirt' of his winnings. When he first came into some money in 1984, he paid for his mum to have central heating put in — a lot less troublesome than spending it on himself and a good deed to boot ('I think that tells you a lot about the background he came from,' suggests Kershaw). Because money was always tight at home, Billy appreciates every penny of it, and is subsequently keen to hang onto it. If he feels he's earned it, he's more than happy to bank it.

Kershaw remembers a gig at Leeds University around the time that Billy started picking up a grand a show. As tour manager, Kershaw planned to bank what was a risky amount of cash to carry around at the branch of Barclays at the end of his sister's road in Headingley. Billy wouldn't let him. He didn't feel confident that the money would actually appear in his own account at the Barking branch. This story doesn't just illustrate Billy's initial distrust of international banking, but an all-round unworldliness, confirmed by another Kershaw story from an early trip to Amsterdam.

The Dutch promoter had booked the pair of them a table at an Indonesian restaurant before the gig, but Billy refused to go in. Kershaw takes up the tale: 'I think it may have had something to do with fear of the unknown – which equally applied to marijuana, to Indonesian food or to the business of going in a restaurant, which was pretty alien to him. I was fuming that night! We ended up walking down the bloody street eating chips and salad cream out of a vending machine. And we had a reservation at a restaurant not far from the venue – all paid for!'

The nature of the job soon put paid to this naiveté. As Kershaw says, 'I think he's acquired a certain polish over the years.'

Tiny Fennimore vouches for Billy's generosity (herself a grateful beneficiary of the Go! Discs payout, remember): 'He says money's like manure, you should spread it around.'

Porky used to join Billy on a mooch around the coin collectors' market under the old arches at Charing Cross in London. He recalls one such trip where Billy was taken with a Commonwealth half crown from Cromwell's time. The stallholder was asking £8 for it, but Billy wouldn't pay it because he'd seen the same coin elsewhere for a fiver. 'I know I can get it for the right money,' he told an incredulous Porky, and they left it. While Billy's not quite in the Sting bracket (whose accountant was famously jailed for creaming £6 million off him without Sting noticing), he can surely spare £3. But this was not Billy Bragg being mean, merely demanding value for money.

Although Juliet, Jamie and Jack coincided with an upturn in the quality of Billy's living arrangements, he is not a material man (and always used to make a point of telling you that the 4x4 was Juliet's). In fact, he's become ever more elemental and spiritual, especially since connecting with the Jurassic coast — the mythology of the British Isles and points of rural interest don't just fuel his love of ancient history. There's something in those stones.

'If God is an all-powerful being, he's quite capable of finding me and my family without me going to church to find him,' Billy said, while pondering the subject of religion in Dublin during the *Mermaid Avenue* sessions. Incidentally, on my way back to Dublin airport after that very studio visit in 1998, my cab driver, a devout Catholic, told me he was becoming less and less enchanted with the church, and spoke of 'going straight to the top' instead. It was clearly a common malaise, even before the paedophile priests scandal broke in 2002.

'Whilst I have my moments of rationalist doubt, I think one of the failures of the Soviet Union was to deny that people have a spiritual need, and must to be able to express that in some way. What you don't want is a society based purely on materialism, or one based purely on spiritual fundamentalism, like Iran. My idea of spirituality is to do with being able to stop and appreciate a sunset. It's like seeing heaven in a wild flower – William Blake kind of stuff, without getting too drippy about it.

'I sometimes fear that my spirituality is more of a focused superstition. But equally, after my father died, my mother went back to her Catholic faith quite strongly, and I was really impressed by that. I've never felt able to completely dismiss it.

'Parenthood focuses all of that. It makes you think, What's it all bleedin' for?'

Neil Spencer, a keen astrologist and fellow Blakean, says of Billy, 'He is a deeply spiritual guy but he's still struggling with a way to talk about it. Billy lives up to what is said about Sagittarians: ruled by Jupiter, fire sign, idealistic, moral, noble, prepared to travel a long way both in physical terms and otherwise. Blake was also Sagittarian.'

Spencer, 'the Arch Druid', once drew up Billy's astrological chart for him. He suspects Billy thinks it's 'all a load of bullshit'.

There is no great revelation in Billy's devotion to his partner, his child and his godson, nor to his immediate family, but this long-term, rock-solid loyalty spreads through the entire network of cousins and aunties and, of course, into all of his relationships, professional and social. What does he think these long-standing relationships say about him?

'I don't know. It's not just me – for instance, Pete could've fired me, but he didn't. We do have times when we can't speak to one another, but we overcome them. When you see people around, you say hello to them.'

It's typically dismissive of one of his greatest character traits, but there is no false humility about Billy. How could there be when he continues to divest so much of his own time assisting with a book about his life? He knows how important he is. Even back in prehistoric 1998, before Facebook and Twitter, a glance at what was then a prototype fans' noticeboard on his website confirmed it, contributed to daily from all corners of the globe. A typical day revealed entries from Philadelphia, Harrogate, Barcelona, Toronto, Stockholm, Stirling, Austin and Nyon (it's in Switzerland). Tiny used to keep a letter up on her noticeboard from an American Merchant Marine written to Billy on March 13 1995, which, she said, helped remind her of where her focus should be in her fantastic job as his assistant. 'Billy will tell you that music cannot change the world but I don't believe that, I agree with the bloke who wrote this letter.'

The letter was typical of a Bragg fan then, and remains so now, albeit less likely to arrive franked through a letterbox. Its writer had recently visited Rwanda, where he was appalled by the 'horror and inhumanity' there, and also the subsequent 'lack of compassion and indifference' among those he told about it. 'I am now an activist,' he wrote, 'From fighting for labor or fighting for the rights of individuals. There are too many things wrong in this world just to sit back and relax. So, I want to take the time to thank you for your inspiration. Your music speaks of what is right and wrong, of what injustices have been done and the power of the people. Keep writing your music and keep the fight going, because what you are doing is important and in the end, will make the world a better place.'

Billy gigs less intensively than in the 1980s – describing frugal trips across America as 'three middle-aged blokes on a fishing trip' – and likes nothing better than to put his feet up at Barton Olivers and coo over actress Romola Garai on the telly, until Juliet playfully digs him in the ribs. But the fight has never left him, as a visit to the Bragg-curated Left Field at Glastonbury will confirm. Quite unlike the apparently apolitical Paul Weller, he's still suitable for miners. His faults are the faults of any bloke. Yes, he put it about a bit during his wild years. Yes, he fell in love too much. But at least he's honest about it, and valiantly blames himself for all the doomed romances.

He's ordinary, but, without a shadow of a doubt, a true one-off.

In a dressing room in Leeds on the *Red Stars* tour, whilst poring over the latest questionnaire for a music magazine, Billy asked Wiggy to think of a word to describe him. Wiggy told him to put down that he was conservative with a small 'c'. Billy conceded the point: 'He was right, I am conservative in my taste, in the way I dress.'

Pushed for a further profile of his lifelong friend, Wiggy declares, 'He's definitely the funniest guitar player I've ever heard.'

'What you see is what you get,' concludes Tiny. 'He's real. He has grumpy mornings, I'm not saying he's a saint, but I feel I am really lucky to know Billy personally. You don't often meet people like that in your life, who have that sort of integrity, and are that kind. He's a big, warm, witty person who doesn't take himself too seriously. I'd better not say any more, he'll kill me.'

Phill Jupitus is no less effusive: 'He is one of the few genuinely nice people in a business awash with weasels on every level. He's very placid. I've got a few friends who lost their dads early and they're very calm, level people. They don't lose their temper or get out of hand.'

Andy Kershaw, long-established as his own man, and no longer thumbnailed as Billy Bragg's valet, has nothing but gratitude for those twelve months in the saddle: 'I couldn't have had a better letter of introduction to working in music, radio and television than having been Billy's right-hand man. At that time, you couldn't have come through with better credentials.'

Andy Macdonald's tribute to Billy concentrates on the music: 'His records will still be out there in 50 years' time. Billy's in the same category as Dylan or Woody Guthrie.'

Joe Henry, Billy's most recent collaborator, describes him as the 'perfect houseguest. My whole family loves Billy. He was a dream to work with.'

Perhaps Neil Kinnock's description says it clearest.

'Ginger, angular, restless, earnest, emotional, independent, forceful, funny.'

It sometimes takes a redhead to spot another redhead.

I asked Billy if he had any regrets. He replied that, in 1990, he never got around to replying when the authors of *The Book of Lists* (a well-thumbed Bragg lavatory volume) requested he compile his Top Ten Favourite Songwriters for their 1990s edition. Blowing his chance to be immortalised between 25 Famous People Who Had Tuberculosis and 7 Researchers Who Used Themselves as Guinea Pigs, the experience taught Billy never to put off 'till tomorrow what you could conceivably do today.

He also regrets putting 'Sean Penn' in the 1991 *Q* questionnaire when asked who he would like to play him in a film: 'It should've been the young Bernard Bresslaw.' Neither is he ecstatic about having voted tactically for the Lib Dems at the 2010 general election, as they went on to prop up a Tory administration for the next five years ('I took a lot of stick for voting for them and I totally accept that').

Billy's not one for regrets, or bitterness, or grudges, or re-writing history. Seeing the funny side, even in dark moments, is more his line. He might shoulder what P.J. O'Rourke once called 'all the trouble in the world', but Billy is not unhap-py – at least, not any more. 'There was a feeling I used to get every Sunday night,' he says. 'And the word melancholy doesn't come near it. It was years and years of this repetitive Sunday-night-Monday-morning feeling going on forever. I still do occasionally feel it, once every five or six years, but it used to be every fucking week until I was about 25. It was a deep, deep, totally irrational feeling of melancholy: oh my God, here we go again, the start of another week, and I know what this fucking week is going to be like. But one of the great things about this job is that now, I don't.

'And I'll know when this is all over, because I'll get that feeling every Sunday again. And I'll stop, and I'll go and do something else.'

And so, with another edition reached, it's time for a closing image. The first edition ended with Billy driving down the M4 to Heathrow in January 1998. 'There's no way you can end the book with Jack in the car again,' he challenges. 'What are you gonna do? It's my favourite bit in the book as well!'

What I'm going to do to end it is to go rogue and rerun precisely that image again. Because it's A Moment, and it stars the two people who remain the enduring loves of his life.

Let us rewind again to '98. He is with Juliet and Jack, and they're playing *William Bloke* in the car, one of the records that made it all possible. 'Brickbat' comes on, and after the 'baby in the bathroom' line, in a sudden flash of recognition, the then-four-year-old Jack calls out, 'That's me! I'm the baby in the bathroom, aren't I?' Indeed, he is. Billy smiles. That'll be another epiphany, then.

As they used to say in Riff Raff before racing through 'A13' . . .

Last one to the end buys the drinks.

BIBLIOGRAPHY AND SOURCES

All The Rage, by Ian 'Mac' McLagan (Pan, 2000)
Back To Basics, by Billy Bragg (IMP, 1985)
British Hit Albums (Guinness, 1997)
British Hit Singles (Guinness, 1997)
British Politics Since The War, by Bill Coxall, Lynton Robins (Macmillan, 1998)
Bygone Barking, by Brian Evans (Phillimore, 1991)
Chronicle Of The 20th Century (Dorling Kindersley, 1997)
Danger Over Dagenham (Barking & Dagenham Libraries Department, 1995)
Downsize This!, by Michael Moore (Boxtree, 1997)
The Enemy Within, by Seumas Milne (Pan, 1994)
England: An Elegy, by Roger Scruton (Pimlico, 2000)
England's Dreaming, by Jon Savage (Faber and Faber, 1991)
Faces Of Labour, by Andy McSmith (Verso, 1997)
40 Years Of NME Charts, compiled by Dafydd Rees, Barry Lazell, Roger Osborne (Boxtree, 1992)
Full Metal Jacket, by Stanley Kubrick, Michael Herr, Gustav Hasford (Secker & Warburg, 1987)
Genesis: A Biography, by Dave Bowler, Bryan Dray (Sidgwick & Jackson, 1992)
'A Genuine Expression of the Will of the People', by Billy Bragg (votedorset.net, 2001)
Hope And Glory: Britain, 1900–90, by Peter Clarke (Penguin, 1996)

The King's England Northamptonshire, by Arthur Mee (Hodder & Stoughton, 1945)

The Last Election, by Pete Davies (Penguin, 1986)

Midnights In Moscow, by Chris Salewicz (Omnibus, 1989)

Morrissey & Marr: The Severed Alliance, by Johnny Rogan (Omnibus, 1992)

Nineteen Eighty-Four, by George Orwell (Penguin, 1987)

Nor Shall My Sword, by Simon Heffer (Phoenix, 1999)

Now That's What I Call Quite Good, by Nick Swift (Tales From Humberside, 1988)

Paul Weller, by Steve Malins (Virgin, 1997)

The Progressive Patriot, by Billy Bragg (Bantam Press, 2006)

Q Encyclopedia Of Rock Stars, by Dafydd Rees, Luke Crampton (Dorling Kindersley, 1996)

Recording The Past, edited by Alan Hill, Susan Curtis (Barking & Dagenham Libraries Department, 1996)

Residents And Visitors, by Tony Clifford, Kathryn Abnett, Mark Watson (Barking & Dagenham Libraries, 1992)

Richard Thompson: Strange Affair, by Patrick Humphries (Virgin, 1996)

The Rolling Stones Chronicle, by Massimo Bonanno (Plexus, 1990)

Rudyard Kipling: Selected Poems, edited by Peter Keating (Penguin, 1993)

The Smiths: The Visual Documentary, by Johnny Rogan (Omnibus, 1994)

Thatcher And Thatcherism, by Eric J Evans (Routledge, 1997)

Victim Of Geography, by Billy Bragg (IMP, 1991)

The Wee Rock Discography, compiled by MC Strong (Canongate, 1996)

When The Music's Over, by Robin Denselow (Faber and Faber, 1989)

William Blake: Selected Poetry, edited by WH Stevenson (Penguin, 1988)

Most of the material comes from interviews with Billy Bragg, Juliet de Valero Wills, Tiny Fennimore, Paul Heaton, Peter Jenner, Phill Jupitus, Andy Kershaw, Neil Kinnock, Andy Macdonald, Ian McLagan, Neil Spencer, Andrew Spurrell, Steven Wells and Philip Wigg, and conversations with Marie

Bragg, Robert Handley, Joe MacColl, Steven Rice, Karen Walter and Brenda Woods.

Research material taken from articles by John Aizlewood, Ian Anderson, Stuart Bailie, Paul Barker, Laura Burton, Billy Bragg, Mick Brown, Julie Burchill, Martin Burr, Garry Bushell, Robert Christgau, Gary Crowley, Robin Denselow, Paul Du Noyer, Hugh Fielder, Tony Fletcher, David Fricke, Sheryl Garratt, Rene Gerryts, John Gill, Paolo Hewitt, Tom Hibbert, Dave Hill, Colin Irwin, Dave Jennings, Danny Kelly, Michelle Kirsch, Steve Lamacq, Eleanor Levy, Richard Lowe, Vici MacDonald, Stuart Maconie, Greil Marcus, Gavin Martin, Quentin McDermott, Mick Mercer, Ted Mico, Sean O'Hagan, Betty Page, Chris Paul, Ian Pye, David Quantick, Joanna Quinn, Jim Reid, Will Smith, Karen Swayne, Adam Sweeting, Adrian Thrills, Steve Turner and Steven Wells.

Publications used for reviews, reference and vibe include (deep breath): *Artforum, Barking & Dagenham Advertiser, Barking & Dagenham Post, Billboard, Boston Globe, Bridport News, City Life, City Limits, Daily Express, Daily Mirror, Daily Telegraph, Dorset Echo, Downtown, Express, The Face, Financial Times, Folk Roots, Gay News, GQ, Guardian, Ham & High, Hot Press, Independent, Independent On Sunday, Issue, Jamming!, Kettering Evening Telegraph, London Evening Standard, Mad, Making Music, Mayfair, Melody Maker, Mojo, The Monkey's Face, More Music, Morning Star, Music And Video, Musicians Only, Music Week, New Musical Express, New Route, New Socialist, New Statesman, New York Times, Nicaragua Today, No. 1, Observer, Parliamentery IT Briefing, Peterborough Advertiser, Peterborough Evening Telegraph, Private Eye, Q, Radio Times, Rage, Rebel Youth, Record Mirror, Rolling Stone, Sanity, Select, Smash Hits, Socialist Youth, Sounds, Southern Rag, Spin, The Spire, Sunday Telegraph, Sunday Times, Sydney Morning Herald, Time Out, The Times, Total Guitar, Uncut, Village Voice, Vox, Wake Up, Well Red* and *Zig Zag.*

INDEX

BIOGRAPHIES

BILLY BRAGG

Billy Bragg has been a fearless recording artist, tireless live performer and peerless political campaigner for more than 30 years. Among the former Saturday boy's albums are his punk-charged debut, *Life's a Riot with Spy Vs Spy*; the more love-infused *Workers Playtime*; pop classic *Don't Try This at Home*; the Queen's Golden Jubilee-timed treatise on national identity, *England, Half-English*; stripped-down tenth album *Tooth & Nail* – his most commercially successful since the early 1990s – and *Shine a Light: Field Recordings from the Great American Railroad* with Joe Henry. The intervening three-and-a-bit decades have been marked by a number one hit single, having a street named after him, being the subject of a *South Bank Show*, appearing onstage at Wembley Stadium, curating Left Field at Glastonbury, sharing spotted dick with a Cabinet minister in the House of Commons cafeteria, being mentioned in Bob Dylan's memoir and meeting the Queen. At their best, Billy's songs present 'the perfect Venn diagram between the political and the personal' (the *Guardian*).

ANDREW COLLINS

As well as being Billy Bragg's Boswell, Andrew Collins is an award-winning scriptwriter, journalist, author, critic and broadcaster, whose hit BBC1 sitcom *Not Going Out* (co-written with its star, Lee Mack), won the Breakthrough Award at the Royal Television Society Awards and the Rose D'Or for Best Sitcom. His journalistic career took him from the *NME* to *Q*. On radio, he won a Sony Gold Award for *Collins & Maconie's Hit Parade* (with Stuart Maconie) and on TV, co-presented *Collins & Maconie's Movie Club* on ITV. The author of three memoirs, he is film editor of *Radio Times* and presents a weekly show on Classic FM.